PRAISE FOR

African American History

"In colleges and universities across the country there is a stunning contradiction. Many people recognize the significance of the election of Barack Obama to the Presidency of the United States, and at the same time they have little knowledge about the history of those whose courage and sacrifice made the event possible. Dr. Turner-Sadler's study will help rectify this deficiency. The new edition is considerably updated, and at the same time it remains immanently readable, thorough, and accessible to students at many different levels. The volume lends itself well to many different disciplines and a wide variety of courses."

—Edwin Clausen, Vice President for Academic Affairs and Dean of the College, Daemen College

"*African American History: An Introduction* offers an inspiring history of Black America, anti-Blackness in very inconspicuous intimate spaces. It highlights the need for a broader study of color in America through the lens of geographical, chronological and conceptual terms. The third edition brings a fresh understanding to historical events as well as ties the past to present concerns and issues in African American communities. The book also provides a contextual nexus between American institutions, African History, and the struggles of people of African descent. This book is suitable for students of various ages, the general public, and anyone who has an interest in African American History."

—Lemuel Berry, Jr., Executive Director, National Association of African American Studies and Affiliates

African American HISTORY

This book is part of the Peter Lang Education list.
Every volume is peer reviewed and meets
the highest quality standards for content and production.

PETER LANG
New York • Bern • Berlin
Brussels • Vienna • Oxford • Warsaw

Joanne Turner-Sadler

African American History

AN INTRODUCTION

THIRD EDITION

PETER LANG
New York • Bern • Berlin
Brussels • Vienna • Oxford • Warsaw

Library of Congress Cataloging-in-Publication Data

Names: Turner-Sadler, Joanne, author.
Title: African American history: an introduction / Joanne Turner-Sadler.
Description: Third edition | New York: Peter Lang Publishing, 2021.
Includes bibliographical references and index.
Identifiers: LCCN 2019058490 | ISBN 978-1-4331-7477-3 (paperback)
ISBN 978-1-4331-5478-2 (ebook pdf) | ISBN 978-1-4331-5477-5 (epub)
ISBN 978-1-4331-5479-9 (mobi)
Subjects: LCSH: African Americans—History.
Classification: LCC E185 .T89 2020 | DDC 973/.0496073--dc23
LC record available at https://lccn.loc.gov/2019058490
DOI 10.3726/b13342

Bibliographic information published by **Die Deutsche Nationalbibliothek**.
Die Deutsche Nationalbibliothek lists this publication in the "Deutsche Nationalbibliografie"; detailed bibliographic data are available on the Internet at http://dnb.d-nb.de/.

Map of Africa courtesy of http://www.cia.gov
Photos of Mary Fields and Nat Love courtesy of the William Loren Katz Collection
All other images not otherwise specified are courtesy of the Library of Congress and the New York Public Library

© 2021 Peter Lang Publishing, Inc., New York
80 Broad Street, 5th floor, New York, NY 10004
www.peterlang.com

All rights reserved.
Reprint or reproduction, even partially, in all forms such as microfilm, xerography, microfiche, microcard, and offset strictly prohibited.

Note to the Reader

The intent of this book is to provide the readers with a chronological survey of African American History, that is easy to read and understand. The book is designed to help readers make important connections between past events, historical milestones in American history and peoples of African descent. To that end, the language was kept plain, and the concepts were drawn from commonly known ideas in American history. It is hoped that readers will better understand how African American history is an evolving discipline, that is relevant to all peoples. Ultimately, it is hoped that students, educators, and inquisitive readers are inspired to learn more about African American history by reading this book.

Dedication

The third edition of *African American History: An Introduction* is dedicated to my children (Elizabeth, Michael, his wife—Ericka Jackson Davis), and all my grandchildren. All of you have been a true source of inspiration, and encouragement.

Knowledge is power. May truth, understanding, and love guide your path and be your passion in your life achievements and triumphs.

All my love,
Joanne Turner-Sadler, Ed.D.
2020

Contents

Prologue: African American History Is Now xxiii

Acknowledgments xxv

Introduction xxvii

    Significant Content Updates xxviii

    New Chapters to Third Edition xxxi

    Continuing Features xxxiii

1. Early African People and Civilizations 1

Africa: Home of the Human Race 1

    Paleoanthropological Evidence 1

    The Genetic Record 2

    The Concept of Race 3

The Civilizations of Kush and Kemet 3

    The Old Kingdom: Dynasties 1 and 2 (c. 3150–2649 B.C.E.) 6

    The New Kingdom: Dynasties 18–20 (c. 1783–1550 B.C.E.) 7

        Influential Women of the New Kingdom 8

        Ancient Kemetic/Egyptian Education 9

The Late Period: Dynasty 25 (c. 750–675 B.C.E.) 11
    The Kushite Female Rulers 12
The Kingdom of Axum (c. 100–940 C.E.) 12
Summary 13
References 14

2. African Empires 17

Exploration and Sphere of Influence Before Enslavement 17
    The Fall of the Roman Empire and Its Geopolitical Consequences 17
    Africans in the Iberian Peninsula (c. 711 C.E.) 19
    Africans in the Americas 20
The Medieval Empires of Africa 24
    Ghana 24
    Mali 25
    Songhay 26
    Kanem-Bornu 27
    Other Kingdoms 27
Summary 28
References 30

3. A Peculiar Institution—with Unintended Consequences 31

Slavery and Three Historical Considerations 34
    The First Consideration: The Origins of European Enslavement
    of Africans 34
    The Second Consideration: The Exclusivity of African Enslavement 35
    The Third Consideration: The Mechanics of Why and How
    African Slavery Was Possible 37
The Challenges, Hardships, and Struggles of Newly Enslaved Africans 39
    The Triangle Trade 39
    The Colonial Plantation System 42
    Two Early Courageous Abolitionists 44
Summary 50
References 51

Contents   xi

Review 53
    I. Checking What You Have Read 53
    II. On Your Own 54

4. Resistance to Enslavement in the Americas 55
Resistance in Latin America and the Caribbean 55
Rebellions Against Enslavement in the English Colonies 57
    Violent Protests Against Enslavement 58
        Gabriel Prosser 58
        Denmark Vesey 58
        Nat Turner 59
        John Brown 59
        The *Amistad* Revolt 60
    Non-Violent Protests Against Enslavement and the Abolitionist Movement 61
        Frederick Douglass 62
        Sojourner Truth 63
        West Coast Abolitionists 64
        Newspapers for Liberation 65
        Prince Hall 65
The Road to Freedom 66
    The Underground Railroad 66
    A Matter of Conscience 67
The Great Compromise 68
Free Africans 69
    The Free African Society 69
    The Quality of Life 71
    Early Repatriation 72
    The Question of Emigration and Seeking a Better Life 72
Summary 73
References 74

5. Choosing Sides in America's Early Wars 75
The Revolutionary War 76
The War of 1812 77
Growing Tensions Between the North and South 78
    The Missouri Compromise 79
    The Compromise of 1850 79
    The Kansas-Nebraska Act 80
    Dred Scott 81
    Secession of the Southern States 81
The Civil War 82
    Africans Volunteer 83
    Africans in the Union Army 84
    Africans in the Union Navy 84
    The Emancipation Proclamation 85
    Discrimination in the Union's Armed Forces 85
    Jubilee at Last 86
The Spanish-American War 86
Summary 87
References 88

Review 91
I.   Checking What You Have Read 91
II. On Your Own... 92

6. Reconstruction 95
The Fate of Newly Freed Africans 95
    Reconstruction's Constitutional Amendments 96
    The Freedmen's Bureau 99
    Forty Acres and a Mule... 101
    The End of Reconstruction 101
    Sharecropping: The New Agricultural Slavery 101
    Freedmen and the Move West 102

Contents

African American Institutions: Building Community ... 103
    The Black Church ... 104
    The Founding of Historically Black Colleges and Universities (HBCUs) ... 106
The Rise of Black Political Power in the "Old South" ... 106
    The Party of Lincoln ... 107
The Fall of Black Political Power and Jim Crow ... 108
    Black Codes ... 108
    Ku Klux Klan and White Supremacists ... 109
    The Repression of Constitutional Rights ... 109
    Freedom and New Achievements in Post-Civil War America ... 109
Summary ... 111
References ... 111

7. Westward Movement ... 113
African American Pioneers ... 113
Explorers ... 113
Fur Trappers ... 114
Cowboys ... 114
African American Women in the West ... 115
Buffalo Soldiers ... 116
African American Californians ... 117
Settlers ... 118
Summary ... 118
References ... 119

Review ... 121
I. Checking What You Have Read ... 121
II. On Your Own ... 122

8. New Century, Old Problems ... 123
The Eye of the Storm ... 125
    Race Riots and Lynching ... 126
    The Red Summer of 1919 ... 127

    Black Wall Street 127
    Rosewood 129
A Red Record 129
The Great Northern Migration 130
    The North and More Problems 131
    The Unions and African American Workers 132
        A. Philip Randolph.. 133
        A New Labor Union 133
World War I 134
    African Americans Distinguish Themselves 135
    The 369th Regiment ("Hellfighters") 135
Summary 136
References 136

9. The Early Struggle for Human Rights 139
The Problem of the 20th Century 139
Political and Social Activists 140
    Marcus Garvey 140
    Monroe Trotter 141
    Mary B. Talbert 141
The "Great Debate" 142
The Normal/Industrial School Model 144
The Niagara Movement 145
The National Association for the Advancement of Colored People (NAACP) 146
The National Urban League 147
The Pan-African Movement 147
Summary 148
References 149

Review 151
  I.   Checking What You Have Read 151
 II.   On Your Own 152

Contents

10. African Americans in American Society 153
Early Literary Achievements 155
The Harlem Renaissance 156
    Writers 157
    Visual and Performing Arts... 158
    Popular Music 159
    Classical Performance.. 160
    Theater 161
Scholars and Scientists 162
    Carter G. Woodson 162
    Ernest Just 163
    Benjamin Quarles 163
    The Schomburg Collection 163
The Negro Baseball Leagues 164
Summary 165
References 165

11. Old Problems, New Deals, and Continued Hard Times 167
The Great Depression.. 167
    Leaving the Party of Lincoln.. 169
    The New Deal 170
    Two Influential Women 171
Unrest and Protests: The New Deal 171
    Adam Clayton Powell, Jr. 172
    A Renewed Focus on Civil Rights 172
World War II 174
    Discrimination in Employment... 174
Service in World War II 175
    An African American Naval Hero 176
    The Tuskegee Airmen... 176
    The Red Ball Express 177
    African Americans in the Midst of Combat.................................. 177

Trouble on the Home Front 178
    Return to the Racist Nation 178
    The Blood Bank 179
    Resistance and Riots at Home 180
Notable Figures of the Period 180
    Jesse Owens 180
    Joe Louis 181
The African American Middle Class 182
    The Multifaceted Issues of Class in African American Society 182
    The Origins and Development of the Black Middle Class 183
Race and Distinctions Within the African American Community 186
Summary 187
References 187

Review 191
I.   Checking What You Have Read 191
II. On Your Own 191

12. The Modern Struggle for Civil Rights 193
The Civil Rights Era 193
    Emmett Till 194
    Martin Luther King, Jr. 194
The Southern Christian Leadership Conference (SCLC) 196
The Desegregation of Schools 197
    The Little Rock Nine 197
    James Meredith and "Ole Miss" 199
The Congress of Racial Equality (CORE) 200
The Student Non-Violent Coordinating Committee (SNCC) 200
The Mississippi Freedom Summer Project 200
Sit-Ins, Freedom Riders, and Marches 201
    Sit-Ins 201
    Freedom Riders 202

Contents xvii

    Marches 203
        The James Meredith March 205
The Civil Rights and Voting Rights Acts 205
Summary 206
References 207

13. The Black Power Movement 209

Other Means of Protest 209
Black Power and Black Pride 210
The Black Panther Party for Self Defense 210
Other Activist Groups 211
    US Movement 211
    Revolutionary Action Movement (RAM) 211
    The Republic of New Africa (RNA) 212
COINTELPRO 212
The Nation of Islam 214
    Elijah Muhammad 214
    Malcolm X 214
    Louis Farrakhan 215
A New Cultural Renaissance 216
    The Black Arts Movement 216
    American Popular Culture 217
    African American History or Black Studies 218
Black Power and Politics 218
    The Congressional Black Caucus 219
    Women in Politics 219
    The Rainbow Coalition 220
Summary 221
References 222

Review 225
  I.   Checking What You Have Read 225
  II. On Your Own 225

14. African Americans and Military Conflicts..227
The Asian and Middle Eastern Conflict.. 227
    The Korean Conflict 227
    The Vietnam War... 229
    Opposition to the War.. 231
        Muhammad Ali and the Conscientious Objection 231
The Persian Gulf Wars 232
    The Persian Gulf War (Desert Storm)... 232
    The Iraq War.. 233
        Who Fights in These Wars? 234
    Global War on Terror... 235
Summary... 236
References 237

15. From a Legal Point of View 239
Civil Rights and Legislative and Judicial Milestones............................. 239
    Laws and Amendments That Hurt 239
        The Three-Fifths Compromise... 239
        Slave Codes to Black Codes and Jim Crow 241
        Plessy v. Ferguson... 241
    Laws and Amendments That Helped... 242
        The Early Civil Rights Acts... 242
        The Early Education Cases 243
        Brown v. Board of Education 244
        Civil Rights Legislation of the 1900s.. 246
        Voting Rights 247
        Affirmative Action: A Tool of Opportunity..................................... 247
        Croson v. Richmond.. 249
        Bakke v. Regents of the University of California........................ 249
        University of Michigan 250
        Fisher v. University of Texas.. 250
Summary... 251
References 252

Contents

Review **255**
I. Checking What You Have Read 255
II. On Your Own 255

16. Achievement Against the Odds **257**
Black Creativity Redefines American Culture 257
Entertainment 257
Sports 258
Law 259
Education and Government 260
The Military 262
Entrepreneurship 264
Science and Invention 265
    African American Inventors 265
    Contemporary African American Scientists 266
    Notable Professional Black Achievers 267
    Significant Contributors to Government/Public Service 267
    Media/Entertainment 268
    Business 269
Summary 269
References 270

17. The Quest for Quality Education: Past and Present **273**
Education: The Mainstay of African Americans 273
    Schooling vs. Education 274
    Early/Global Models of Education 275
    Schooling in America for Blacks 275
School Choice 278
The Policies, Practices, and New Education Initiatives 279
    No Child Left Behind Legislation 279
    Alternative School Choices for African Americans 280
        Independent Schools 280
        Charter Schools 281

School Vouchers 281

The Privatization of Public School Administration and Management 283

Higher Education and African Americans 284

Remembering Their Roots 286

Summary 287

References 289

Review **293**

I. Checking What You Have Read 293

II. On Your Own 293

18. Barack Obama: The 44th President of the United States 295

The President and His Lineage 295

    Higher Education and Career 296

    The Roots of Community Activism 297

Early Political Career 298

Personal Struggles and Search for Identity 299

The Presidential Campaigns 302

    The 2008 Election 302

    2012: The Re-Election of Obama 304

The Politics of Race and Division 306

The Presidency of Barack Obama: Challenges and Successes 309

The Obama Political Legacy 311

Summary 313

References 314

19. 2016 Presidential Election: A Campaign of Polar Opposites ... 319

The 2016 Major U.S. Presidential Candidates 320

    Hillary Clinton: Democratic Insider and Operative 320

    Senator Bernie Sanders: Independent and "Insurgent Progressive" 321

    The Republican Candidates 323

        Donald Trump: Nativist, TV Reality Personality,
        Republican Nominee 324

Contents   xxi

The 2016 Presidential Campaign 325
     Some Major Campaign Issues 326
         Immigration 326
         Affordable Health Care 327
         Gun Violence 328
         BlackLivesMatter 328
         Cyber Security 329
Summary 330
References 331

Review **335**
I.   Checking What You Have Read 335
II.   On Your Own 336

20. The Browning of America and Its Implications **337**
The New Demographics of a Changing Population 337
The New Civil Rights Challenges 339
     Popular Vote vs. Electoral College 344
Post-Obama Neo-Conservative Policies and Practices 344
     The New National Conservatism 344
     Voter Suppression Practices 345
     Post-Obama Political Era: Trump Versus Biden 348
President Joseph Biden: Diversity Without Division 350
Summary 352
References 353

21. The Road Ahead: Issues and Challenges **361**
Understanding the Interplay of Race, Culture, and History 362
     Race and Inequality: Why the Disparities? 364
     The Legacy of White Supremacy 368
BlackLivesMatter: A Community Response to Injustice 370
     BlackLivesMatter Movement Goes Global 373
A Future of Uncertainty Beyond 2020: What's Next? 374

The Color of a Pandemic 374
The 2020 Presidential Election 376
Summary 376
References 377

Review **383**
I. Checking What You Have Read 383
II. On Your Own 384

Epilogue **385**
Index **387**

Prologue: African American History Is Now

There seems to be a tendency to isolate ethnic studies from other academic disciplines that are considered more mainstream. Whether the subject is Native Americans, Latino, or Asian peoples, these groups' role, significance, and importance to the development of American institutions should not be viewed as isolated events. A more holistic perspective is needed that acknowledges a series of events that have collectively impacted all Americans. By adopting an integrated approach to the study of African American history, three things are gained: (1) a more comprehensive awareness of the contributions of Black people to larger national institutions is gained; (2) a more dynamic and contextual connection to broader issues related to America's past and present racial challenges are recognized; and (3) issues surrounding diversity, culture and race are better understood in a cause and effect manner. African American History completes the mosaic of a rich tapestry of struggle and achievement against odds within American History.

Acknowledgments

In the Gospel of Luke (12:48) it reads, "To whom much has been given, much is required." The inspiration for this book is deeply rooted in the fertile soil of my parents' love, faith, traditions, and the countless sacrifices made on my behalf. This book parallels their struggles, those of my parents' generation, and all the generations who sought to realize the fruits of American opportunity. A lifetime debt of gratitude is owed to my parents—Mr. Odell and Elizabeth Turner.

I am indebted to friends and colleagues, who contributed their thoughts and ideas initially to the second edition of this book. Specifically, Adriane Williams and Beverly Weeks whose insightful feedback were reliable "sounding boards." Ed Clausen was a thoughtful benefactor to the book as well. I would also like to thank Marianne Partee and J. Glenn Davis for their suggestions and technical assistance. In this third edition, I would like to recognize the continued support from my colleagues at Daemen College. This includes friends and colleagues who contributed their thoughts and ideas to this edition. Equally, Tiffany Hamilton was a thoughtful commenter towards the direction of this book.

The editorial and production team at Peter Lang Publishing was invaluable with the development of the original book. Many thanks to Phyllis

Korper, who was a guiding force, assisting me through the publication process of the first book. For this third edition, I wish to thank the current editorial and production team at Peter Lang Publishing. Gratitude is owed to Patricia Mulrane Clayton and Jacqueline Pavlovic at Peter Lang Publishing Their stewardship of the third edition brought the book to fruition.

Lastly, I am eternally grateful to my friend and mentor, Mr. Dominic Langston. He provided research assistance for the third edition. Mr. Langston generously gave countless hours to the book's first and third editions with proof-reading and "unfiltered" feedback. He was a wealth of information and with much patience helped me to refine parts of the book to achieve greater clarity that enhanced the contextual meanings of complex historical relationships for younger adult readers. Mr. Langston's contributions to this book were innumerable. Ultimately, the publication of this book will provide a reader friendly, concise, academic platform to share the history of African peoples in the Americas.

Introduction

This book is intended as an introduction to the study of African American history. It serves to guide readers through a series of historical topics about people of African descent. There is a diversity of resources cited in the book that are designed to aid in further topical investigations. The book is meant to be a general guide for those who seek a fact-based introduction to the study of African American history.

Like the two previous editions, the third edition seeks to offer the readers a balanced, fact-based, and meaningful analysis of the role that African Americans have played within American history. The struggles that peoples of African heritage face today is related to the legacy of decisions, polices, practices, and beliefs made generations ago. The impact of historic events still influences Black lives today.

This third edition was developed based on the students' questions, professional insights, and teaching activities. This text provides readers with greater information along with a chronologically based survey of American history. The third edition builds on the two previous texts but it has been updated and now includes topics relevant to current events. An emphasis has been placed on helping readers to draw connections and parallels to current social, political, economic, educational, and legal issues without guided commentary. Ideally, readers will able to easily digest the materials and formulate fact-based opinions about the role that people of African descent played in the development of America—past and present.

Significant Content Updates

Specifically, this book examines the relationships of Africa to Africans in the Americas today. It documents the history of people of African descent who were forced to leave their homes and survive in the United States of America. Who were these people? What made them so strong? How they survived and under what circumstances and the future of African Americans are some of the questions addressed in this book.

New factual data was added throughout the book based on information that appeared in earlier editions. Specifically, updated information has been added to the following chapters:

- **Updated Chapter One** of this book focuses on the fact that race is a false concept and that humankind is one family, not three subgroups of races. It also highlights the research showing that the beginning of the human race is in Africa. Furthermore, this chapter confronts the myth that Africans contributed nothing of worth to civilization. This chapter discusses records that show the first high civilization was created by African people, most specifically, the ancient Egyptians. **New Content** about Egyptian education has been included.

- **Updated Chapter Two** addresses how this pattern of nation building continued right up through the Moors of North Africa and the West African empires. It focuses on the relationships of Africans with Europeans prior to entering the Atlantic slave trade. This chapter outlines the accomplishments of the West African empires and the early connections of Africans not only to Europe but also to the Americas through the Olmecs. **New Content** about education and Timbuktu as related to Medieval Empires of Africa has been added to this chapter.

- **Chapter Three** outlines the events that forced a once-great people into enslavement. It addresses the establishment of chattel slavery and how only Africans were targeted. Indentured servitude is addressed as it was the method used for the first Blacks brought to America as well as for Whites. This chapter, while looking at the hardship and injustice of enslavement, also highlights the accomplishments of people such as Benjamin Banneker, scientist and mathematician, who assisted in the surveying of Washington, D.C.

- **Chapter Four** chronicles the struggle against enslavement that took several forms in the Americas, both violent and non-violent. It discusses resistance in the New World such as in South America and the Quilombos communities of Brazil, the Caribbean, Toussaint L'Ouverture in Haiti, and by slave revolts of Nat Turner and others in the English colonies. This chapter also describes the non-violent efforts of abolitionists and people like Harriett Tubman.

- **Chapter Five** addresses the early wars in which African Americans participated, beginning with the Revolutionary War and the founding of America. African Americans fought in every war, notwithstanding the fact that many Whites opposed it. However, African Americans did so and with great distinction. This chapter also examines the effects of these wars on all Americans including those of African descent.

- **Updated Chapter Six** details the period of Reconstruction in the South and the implications for African Americans. This chapter focuses on the establishment of the Freedmen's Bureau, the rise of Black political power, and also the rise in terrorist groups designed to threaten Blacks. In addition, this chapter covers the advent of sharecropping as well as the establishment of African American institutions such as churches, colleges, and universities. The beginnings of the Black middle class and the movement of Blacks to the West is also covered. **New Content** has been added to include expanded sections about the historical emergence and development of the Black middle during the Reconstruction Era.

- **Chapter Seven** continues with a look at what happened after the Civil War when African Americans moved westward. This chapter focuses on the ways they attempted to escape oppression and better their lives by becoming cowboys, fur traders, and settlers. Others became the Buffalo Soldiers who protected the White settlers.

- **Chapter Eight** covers the Great Northern Migration from the South, which was the attempt by African Americans to escape sharecropping, the new form of enslavement. Unfortunately, Blacks could not escape the race riots of the times. This chapter covers the race riots that Blacks were subjected to as they settled in the North and other parts of the country. It addresses Rosewood, the Chicago race riots as well as Black Wall Street, a prominent and highly successful Black community in Tulsa, Oklahoma. This chapter also covers the Blacks and their role in World War I.

- **Chapter Nine** addresses the early struggle for civil rights with the formation of the National Urban League and the National Association for the Advancement of Colored People (NAACP). The chapter highlights the political and social activists of the time such as Marcus Garvey, W.E.B. Du Bois, Booker T. Washington, and others. This chapter also addresses the debate over the type of higher education that African Americans should receive in America.

- **Chapter Ten** is devoted to the explosion of creativity and talent of the Harlem Renaissance that greatly affected American society. While the chapter highlights the great writers, visual and preforming artists, it also recognizes the scholars. This chapter also delves into the involvement of African Americans in organized sports with their own baseball leagues and later in the major leagues.

- **Updated Chapter Eleven** addresses the Great Depression, its effect on African Americans and the change in party affiliation from the Republican Party to Democratic Party. It also looks at African Americans and their role in World War II, such as the Tuskegee Airmen. While this chapter examines the continuation of race problems in America, it also addresses some proud moments for African Americans. Additionally, this chapter delves deeper into the formation of the African American middle class.

- **Chapter Twelve** speaks to the Civil Rights Movement that defined the 1960s in American history. It focuses on the various non-violent protests and the leaders of the movement such as Martin Luther King, Jr. This chapter also highlights the legislation that desegregated schools and the events that led to the Voting Rights legislation that was signed by President Lyndon B. Johnson.

- **Chapter Thirteen** focuses on the Black power movement. This chapter addresses the activist organizations that were founded due to civil unrest in the nation. Of these groups, one of the best known is the Black Panthers. The chapter also describes the FBI's goal of destabilizing and destroying these groups. In addition, this chapter also describes the rise of Black power and pride.

- **Updated Chapter Fourteen** discusses the wars and military conflicts of the twentieth and twenty-first centuries and African American participation in them. This chapter also considers some of the injustices that continue to plague Blacks in the United States and the Armed Services. **New Content** is included about the desegregation of the Armed Forces and the transition from the "Cold War" to the global war on terror.

- **Chapter Fifteen** highlights some of the laws that have affected African Americans, both positively and negatively. This chapter examines the early elementary and higher education Supreme Court decisions such as *Brown v. Board of Education* and later ones such as the 2003 Supreme Court ruling in the University of Michigan case and *Fisher v. University of Texas* in 2013.

- **Chapter Sixteen** focuses on the accomplishments of African Americans in every field of endeavor. It includes public figures in government, and entrepreneurship such as Colin Powell, Condoleezza Rice, and Reginald Lewis. This chapter also includes scientists and inventors, notably Katherine Johnson who worked on the NASA space mission.

New Chapters to Third Edition

- **Chapter Seventeen** addresses continuing issues involving the fight for quality schooling. It looks at the early forms of schooling for Blacks and the school models of the twenty-first century. This chapter particularly focuses on charter schools, school vouchers, and the privatization of public schools to make them profitable for outside investors.

- **Chapter Eighteen** provides an in-depth look into the background and the presidency of the first Black president of the United States, Barack Obama. It chronicles his rise to the highest political office of the land. This chapter also details his two-terms in office, successes, as well as the backlash against him. The chapter analyzes the attempts to nullify and block President Obama's work on behalf of the American people by Republicans in the Congress.

- **Chapter Nineteen** focuses on the 2016 presidential election and Hillary Clinton's bid to become the first woman president of the United States. It covers the major candidates and the campaign issues. This chapter also addresses the disaffection with Clinton as the Democratic candidate. This chapter also discusses Russian interference in the 2016 election, other issues, and the ultimate election of Donald Trump by the Electoral College.

- **Chapter Twenty** focuses on the "browning of America" and the ramifications of forthcoming population changes. It also looks at the changes in demographics which will ultimately affect voting. Additionally this chapter looks at efforts to suppress minority voting and the new national conservative political philosophy during the Trump era.

- **Chapter Twenty-One** tackles the issue of race, culture, and history in relationship to African Americans and economic security. The chapter describes the role of BlackLivesMatter and the social unrest by diverse groups regarding police brutality. This chapter also seeks to explore the disparities of wealth for African Americans when compared to others. It looks at identity politics, tribalism, and the effect of White supremacy on economic and other issues of concern for African Americans.

Continuing Features

Like the first two editions of this text, each chapter provides the following segments:

- Basic content facts with names, dates, and details.

- Summary of major themes and some narrative remarks help congeal the information in a contextual manner that demonstrates its significance.

- Review sections that are designed to assess the reader's understanding of how the facts and information relates to larger historical themes. Also included are a series of thought-provoking research questions that educators may use for intensive writing assignments.

- References have been moved to the end of each chapter to help students, teachers, and casual readers locate helpful primary sources.

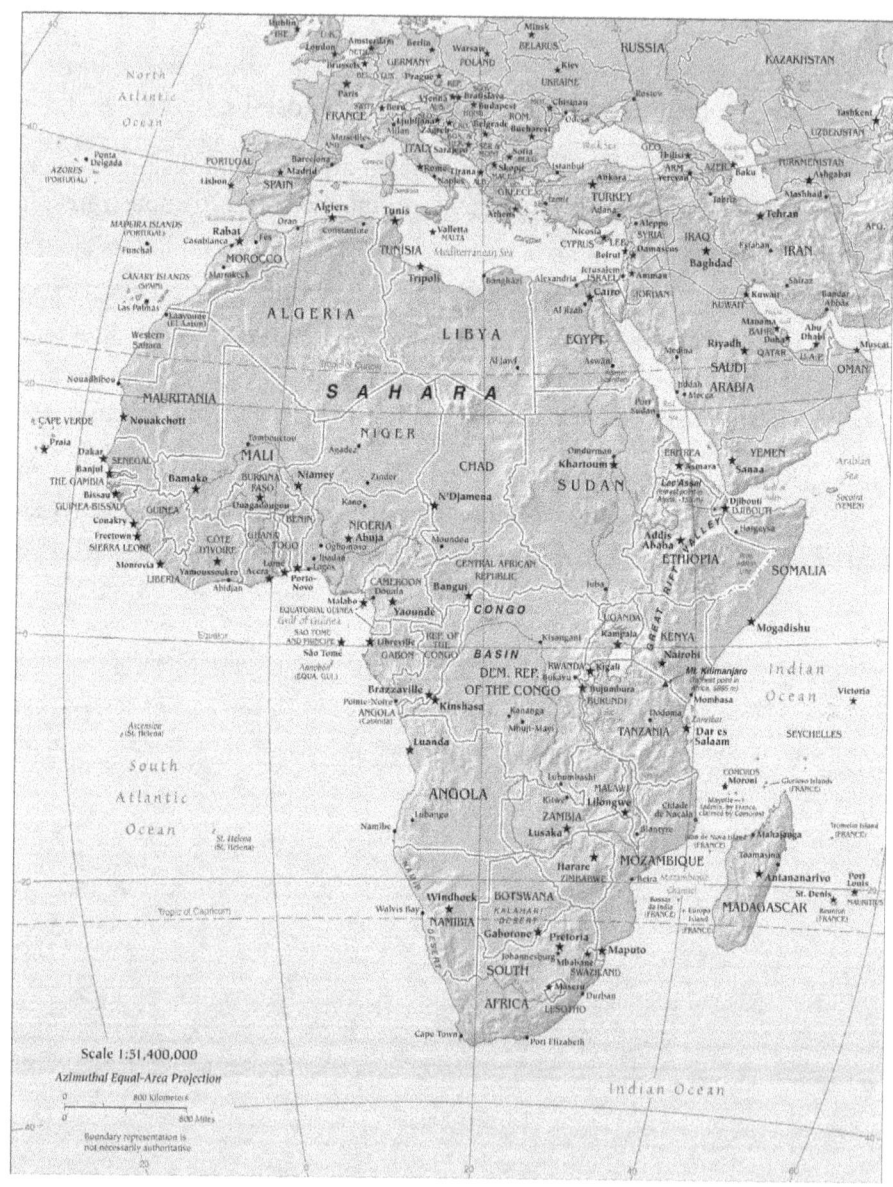

The African Continent

Early African People and Civilizations

Africa: Home of the Human Race

The origins of African people is many thousands of years old. In fact, it starts with the beginning of the human species. Scientific evidence, such as DNA genome typing and the discoveries made by the Leaky family in Africa, confirms the origins of humans about 200,000 years ago. These early humans gradually migrated to other land masses. Scientists and scholars agree that Africa is the birthplace of modern humans.

Paleoanthropological Evidence

Paleoanthropology is the study of bones and bone fragments of humans from the ancient past. The oldest paleo anthropologic finds that trace the history of the development of man have been discovered in Tanzania, Kenya, and Ethiopia. The Louis Leakey family began to find hominid fossils (ancient skeletal remains) in Tanzania in the Olduvai Gorge in the 1950s. In 1972, Richard Leakey found remains of what was then thought to be the oldest bones discovered to date. What was unique about this find was that this hominid made tools.

Then, a few years later, an Ethiopian team led by Donald Johanson discovered a fossilized skeleton, which they named "Lucy." The evidence pointed to her existence about 3.2 million years ago. There were several species of humans in ancient Africa about 2–3 million years ago. One of the most famous of the *Australopithecus afarensis* species was "Lucy," Other types included *Australopithecus robustus*, who lived about 2 million years ago and *Homo erectus*. *Homo Habilis* lived between 2 and 1.5 million years ago. There was also *Homo neanderthalensis*. Eventually, *Homo sapiens* ("modern" humans) appeared about 200,000 years ago.

The Genetic Record

In addition to the fossil remains that have been discovered, mitochondrial DNA (deoxyribonucleic acid) studies also suggest Africa as the origin of the human race. In fact, DNA studies trace the human race to one African woman. It is known that genes carry information about cells, therefore controlling heredity. Mitochondrial DNA is a specific genetic code that is found in the area of a cell outside the nucleus. This area contains the energy needed to keep the cell alive. This cell is important because it is only transmitted from the mother and can be used to trace family descent or history. Scientists who are trained in molecular biology have studied these cells and provide additional evidence.

Research by Rebecca Cann, Allan Wilson, and Mark Stoneking in 1988 has traced the descendants of all humans to one African woman. To do this, they compared the DNA of many different people from around the world. This African woman is thought to have lived somewhere between 200,000 and 100,000 years ago. Cann and her associates do not claim that she was the only woman living at that time, only a common ancestor. They hypothesize that there were a fairly large number of men and women living then, but that only her line, or "gene pool," survived through thousands of years of evolution.

Some scientists calculate that African people eventually migrated to other land masses 80,000 to 50,000 years ago, including Europe. Upon migration to other environments and climates, genetic adaptations began to occur. The physical features, including skin color, changed or adapted to the new environment.

Skin color, for example, was affected in the following way. Melanin is a substance in the skin that provides color. It interacts with the ultraviolet

(UV) rays of the sun. The more exposure to the sun, the more melanin is produced. Melanin protects against high levels of exposure to the sun. The black color, in southern or equatorial countries, protects people from the sun's harmful UV rays. People in colder climates (northern Europe, etc.) do not need as much melanin to protect them from the ionizing radiation from the sun. The white skin color protects people in northern countries from UV rays by absorbing them. Ultraviolet rays help to produce vitamin D for people with lighter skin. People with darker skin, however, are more susceptible to vitamin D deficiency.

Since recent scientific studies indicate that humans originated in Africa, the ancestors of modern man must have had dark skin because of the production of melanin. Through migrations to areas of less intense sunlight, the production of melanin decreased to allow acclimation to other geographic locations. Scientists estimate that it takes a few thousand years for skin color to change.

The Concept of Race

Although some cultural anthropologists have attempted to divide human beings into classifications or "races," the noted cultural anthropologist Ashley Montagu suggests that race is a fallacy. All human beings are a part of one race, the human race, which most anthropologists now accept. Furthermore, the preponderance of evidence points to the birthplace as Africa and one African woman as our common ancestor. Race is merely a "social construction." It is a concept devised by one group of people to provide advantages and privileges to themselves at the expense of others. Race is used to justify oppression and unfair discrimination.

The Civilizations of Kush and Kemet

Among the earliest organized human societies was the civilization of Kush in Ethiopia and the civilization of Kemet in ancient Egypt. The earlier of these civilizations was Kush. It was located along the Nile River in the region of the present-day Republic of the Sudan. The ancient Hebrews called this area Kush. The ancient Greeks called this same area Ethiopia "the land of the dark-skinned people" or land of the burnt-face people. This information is found in the classical writings of Homer and Herodotus. In fact, Herodotus concluded that all the people of the territories that are formerly called the Republic of the Sudan, Egypt, Arabia, Palestine, Persia, and India were known as Ethiopians. Present-day Ethiopia occupies a much smaller area than ancient Ethiopia because of the many boundary changes that have occurred throughout its history. Herodotus was not the only Greek who traveled to Egypt. Other Greeks came to study at the Egyptian schools, some of which taught medicine. These visitors included Pythagoras, the philosophers Thales and Anaximander, and Solon, a statesman.

The area known as Kush was located south of Kemet/Egypt. Its origin is believed to go back to even before the civilization of ancient Egypt, around 5,000 B.C.E. (Before the Common Era). Please note that a number of modern scholars prefer to use the dating system B.C.E. since it is in accord with Christian, Jewish, and Muslim scholarship. Likewise, C.E. is used to refer to the Common Era. Therefore for this book, that tradition is followed.

Two important centers of the Kushite civilization were the cities of Napata and Meroe. The city of Meroe was known for its line of female rulers called Candaces. A high government official of Meroe is mentioned in the New Testament of the bible. As the story goes, this Ethiopian official, an eunuch, was secretary of the treasury in the government of the reigning candace. He was riding in his chariot when he was approached by Philip, who was a follower of Jesus Christ. Philip engaged him in conversation, and the Meroitic official became a Christian because of this encounter. This event occurred around 37 C.E. The kingdom of Kush existed until 350 C.E.

There was considerable interaction between Kush and ancient Egypt during the development of the Egyptian civilization. Kush was the source of many of the ideas of government, culture, and religion for Egyptian civilization. In fact, remains of pyramids and temples recently found in ancient Kush appear to be relics that provided the models for the later Egyptian pyramids and temple structures. These two civilizations were, at times, under the rule of the same monarch. The last time this occurred was in the 8th century B.C.E., when Kush conquered Egypt. The Kushites then formed the 25th dynasty of Egypt.

The original inhabitants of Egypt called their land Kemet (Kamit). The Hebrew people called it Mizraim. The Greeks and the Romans called it Aegyptcus. The current name, "Egypt," which evolved from "Aegyptcus," has lasted through these many centuries. Menes, who was also called Narmer, was the first great ruler of Egypt. He united the southern and northern areas of what are called Upper and Lower Egypt.

Early African People and Civilizations

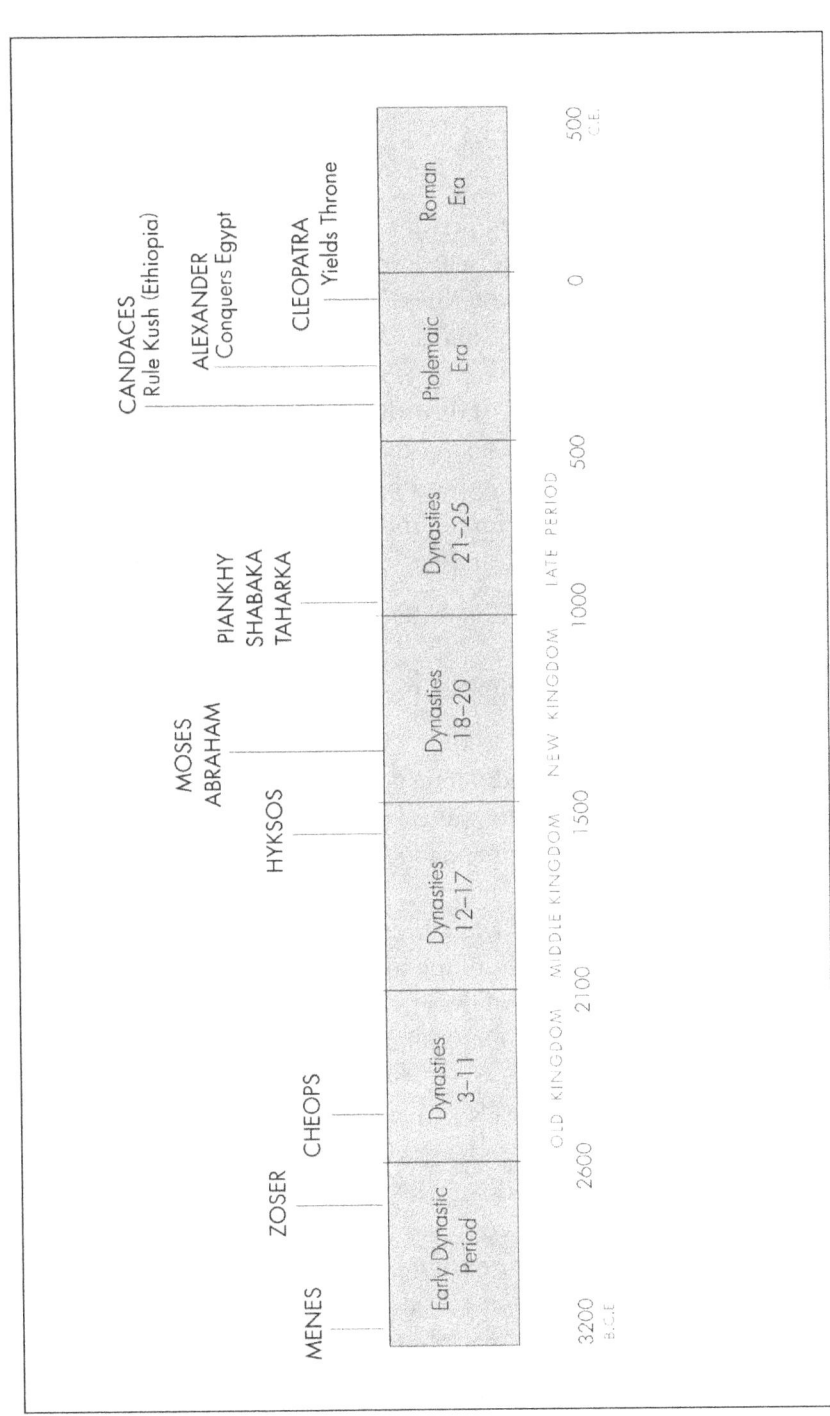

Dynasties of Egypt

Egypt was governed by a succession of dynasties or ruling families, each begun by a king or pharaoh. Egypt flourished under many great pharaohs. It developed commercial and diplomatic relations with other African nations and with countries in Asia and Europe. Egypt was a cultural crossroad for trade and travel and contained a blend of many groups. It was usually from the South, however, that new ideas were introduced and progress was made.

There were four periods in ancient Kemetic or Egyptian history. They were the Old Kingdom, the Middle Kingdom, the New Kingdom, and the Late Period. Since there are many sources of information on the people of these periods, this book mentions only a few of the most notable personalities. The first dynastic period was called the Old Kingdom. Menes, Zoser, and Imhotep were noted figures from this dynastic period. The most colorful and significant pharaohs, such as Akhenaton and Tutankhamen, were from the 18th dynasty of the New Kingdom. There was the decline of the pharaonic dynasties in the Late Period, and one of the last was the 25th dynasty and the Pharaoh Taharka.

The Old Kingdom: Dynasties 1 and 2 (c. 3150–2649 B.C.E.)

There had been many insignificant kings in both Upper Egypt and Lower Egypt. However, it was Menes who united the two kingdoms and became the pharaoh of the first dynasty. He was from Upper Egypt, the region south of present-day Egypt. After his father had conquered Lower Egypt, he combined the two kingdoms. At that point the white crown of Lower Egypt was combined with the red crown of Upper Egypt to make the famous double crown that is depicted on the walls of the tombs and temples.

Zoser (or Djoser), a pharaoh of the 3rd dynasty (c. 2700–2615 B.C.E.), was an important pharaoh of the Old Kingdom. He initiated the age of pyramid building. Imhotep lived during the reign of this monarch. He was not only prime minister to Zoser, but also an astronomer, the chief architect of the first Egyptian step pyramid, and a famous physician. The Greek Hippocrates is usually credited with being the "Father of Medicine." Imhotep, however, preceded him by many centuries and is rightly the bearer of that title. Hippocrates himself recognized Imhotep as the "God of Medicine" and referred to him under the name Asklepios (Aesculapius) in the medical oath (or Hippocratic Oath) that physicians take to this present day. The Hippocratic Oath originally began with the words: "I swear by Apollo, the physician, and Aesculapius, and Health, and All-heal and all the gods and goddesses that according to my ability and judgment, I will keep this oath...." Imhotep was considered a multifaceted genius. Egyptians later elevated him to the stature of a saint or god (Chaney, 2014).

The New Kingdom: Dynasties 18–20 (c. 1783–1550 B.C.E.)

King Akhenaton or Amenhotep IV was a ruler from the 18th dynasty. He was the son of Queen Tiye and King Amenhotep III. He was seen as a rebel against certain traditions. In fact, he is called the "Heretic King" because he forced the people to change their religious practice. Akhenaton stopped the worship of many gods and established the worship of one god in whom all the good qualities of the others were combined. This type of religious view is called monotheism. This action displeased many of the priests and others who remained loyal to the worship of many deities. There is speculation that it also brought about Akhenaton's demise. It is thought that his death was at the hands of the angry priests who represented the old religious beliefs. After Akhenaton's death, his son, Tutankhamen (or "King Tut") became king and allowed a return to the previous form of worship.

According to some records, however, a student at one of the schools that Akhenaton had established, a man called Moses, led a great number of people out of Egypt. These people, many of whom were Hebrew, agreed with Akhenaton's view of religion. There is no record of this in the ancient hieroglyphs or "medu neter" (the writings of the Egyptians), but noted historian, John Jackson, suggests that the historian Manetho, an Egyptian priest who lived during the 30th dynasty, provides the source for this information. Ptolemy II, the ruler at that time, hired Manetho to write the history of Egypt. Manetho had to reconstruct this information as carefully as possible from fragments and other sources since the books in the library at Alexandria, Egypt, were deliberately destroyed by fire by invading armies.

King Tutankhamen, who succeeded Akhenaton, was the grandson of the great pharaoh, Amenhotep II. He was very young when he ascended the throne of Egypt. King Tut and his wife Ankhesenamene attempted to undo what his father, Akhenaton had done and restore the old gods. He moved the religious capital from Amarna back to Thebes, however, his reign was very short. It is believed that he died around the age of seventeen; therefore, he is also known as the "Boy King."

CHAPTER 1

Influential Women of the New Kingdom

Women have always played an important role in African societies, and Egypt was no exception. Women were greatly respected and exerted a great deal of power and influence. One of these women from the New Kingdom was Queen Ahmose Nefertari. She was venerated for both her wisdom and beauty. It is said that she was instrumental in the re-building of the country after the invading Hyksos were driven out. She was the wife of Aahmes I and the co-founder of the 18th dynasty. She was said to have been a capable administrator during the reign of her husband. Queen Nefertari was the first woman to hold the title of "Second Prophet of Amun." In this position, she was responsible for all civil and religious functions.

Another African woman, Queen Tiye (1415–1340 B.C.E.), ruled with her husband, Amenhotep III, during the 18th dynasty of the New Kingdom. She was the mother of Akhenaton (Amenhotep IV), who became known as the "Heretic King." She was a capable and well-educated woman. When her husband Amenhotep III died, she ruled as regent until her son was of age to take the throne. During her co-rule with her son, she exerted a strong national influence in determining Egypt's domestic and foreign policy.

Queen Hatshepsut of the 18th dynasty (1500–1300 B.C.E.) was the only woman who actually took over the leadership of Egypt not only as queen but also as pharaoh. Initially, she co-ruled Egypt with her father, Thothmes I, then later she shared power with her half-brother, Thothmes III. She eventually took over the throne for herself, thus becoming the first female pharaoh of Egypt. As pharaoh, Hatshepsut was even known to wear the ceremonial beard that the pharaohs wore. She ruled for approximately 21 years. Hatshepsut had a magnificent temple built, which still exists today. It is called Deir el-Bahri.

Queen Nefertiti may be the most familiar ancient Egyptian woman in the world today, as her likeness often appears on charms, necklaces, decorations, and so forth. She was the companion and later the wife of Akhenaton, her cousin. They appeared to be very close if the images on the Egyptian tombs and temples are any indication. In these portraits, they are depicted in loving poses. It is said that their relationship was the first true romance.

Ancient Kemetic/Egypt Education

Education and learning were important to African people. Traditional educational systems have existed from ancient times. In fact, all civilizations from early hunter-gatherer groups instructed their young in survival and domestic life skills. This is what may be called traditional education. They also had an oral tradition where information was passed on from one generation to another. Later, the high civilizations that included reading and writing created much more sophisticated educational systems. Take for example, the high civilization of ancient Kemet or Egypt, where one finds various types of programs. One was the elaborate apprenticeship-type training, but another even more sophisticated program involved the Mysteries system. According to Hilliard (1995) the Kamits (Egyptians) developed a higher-level educational system or what was known as the Mysteries School System. Hilliard (1995) described the schools as mysteries in the sense that rigorous program had to be mastered before a person could proceed to advanced learning. Much like today, primary school education is needed before more advanced knowledge can be understood. These schools, no doubt, seemed to be a mystery, especially to the outsider who did not have access to them.

The ancient Kamits created a place of learning which was their university. This university, Ipet Isut which means "the most select of places" was a center for education and religion. It was located in what was known Thebes, after the European invasion. The city was also called Luxor by the Arabs. The Mystery School had six departments or schools. They were the Mystery school of the Heavens (astronomy, astrology); the Mystery school of all Lands (geography); the Mystery school of all Depths (geology, cosmology); the Mystery school of the Secret Word (philosophy, theology); the Mystery school of the Pharaoh; and the Mystery school of the Word (language, law, communications). The faculty, who were called Hersetha or teachers of the mysteries, covered many topics. For example, among the subjects taught were the seven liberal arts of grammar, rhetoric, logic, geometry, arithmetic, harmony/music, and astronomy. No doubt prophetic leaders such as Moses studied in Kemet at a Mystery School. To outsiders, the ancient Kamits (Egyptians) guarded their knowledge. Only a few outsider males eventually gained some of this information. Among them were Pythagoras, Thales, and a few other Greek philosophers.

Ancient Egypt needed educated people to ensure the success of their society. The first step to obtaining formal education was to be trained as a scribe, therefore, boys attended the scribal schools. This was regarded as a highly honored profession. Egypt also needed warriors, so boys could receive military training as a result of joining the army. While schooling for the masses did not consist of such formal education, some may have learned to read, write, and do arithmetic. Boys learned the trade of their father or were apprenticed out to other men to learn a trade. Girls did not attend school unless they were a member of the ruling family.

Egyptians sought to live in harmony with nature and high moral behavior. This is reflected in a number of virtues that were also taught. They used various treatise, or books called the Books of Instruction and the Teachings of Ptahhotep. This latter book is thought to be the oldest book in the world. Ptahhotep lived in the fifth dynasty and was thought to be the vizier of the Pharaoh at that time. He is credited with many sayings that are appropriate even for today. The teachings were so that people could lead a well-ordered life. Truth telling and fair dealing were highly valued. The sayings of Ptahhotep include the following:

- "Take advice from the ignorant as well as from the wise, since there is no single person who embodies perfection nor any craftsman who has reached the limits of excellence."

- "Silence is more profitable unto thee than abundance of speech."

- "Good words are more difficult to find than emeralds."

- "Be a craftsman in speech that thou mayest be strong, for the strength of one is the tongue, and speech is mightier than all fighting." (*Ptah-Hotep > Quotes*)

Some of the oldest medical papyri were from Egypt. These ancient documents contain information about a number of subjects. They include the Rhind papyrus and Moscow papyrus which contain mathematical problems that originated from Egypt. There is also the Edwin Smith papyrus, the Ebers papyrus, the Hearst papyri, and the London Medical papyrus. These were medical books from Egypt. Other books or papyri from Egypt covered biographies, religious subjects, and maps.

Early African People and Civilizations

The Nile River: A Great River of Africa

There are three great rivers in Africa. One of them is the Nile. It is the longest river in the world and stretches for 4,187 miles. The Nile River flows from Uganda in the South to the Mediterranean Sea in the North. The Nile is formed by three major tributaries—the White Nile, the Blue Nile and the Atbara. Egyptians depended on the annual summer flood of the Nile for water to irrigate their crops and deposit fertile topsoil.

The Late Period: Dynasty 25 (c.750–675 B.C.E.)

There were also times when Egypt fell under foreign rule. At these times, little or no progress was made and the civilization even declined. This occurred when weak kings came to power and fighting resulted among ruling families. This pattern continued until the last great dynasty, the 25th. Piankhy, a ruler from the southern kingdom of Kush, grew tired of being controlled by Egypt and rebelled. He continued the fight until he ascended the throne of Egypt in 761 B.C.E. Shabaka, his brother, succeeded him. He brought even more Egyptian territory under Kushite rule.

Taharka succeeded King Shabaka, and his reign marked a period of prosperity and cultural advances. This line of Kushite kings lasted for 60 years before falling to defeat by the Assyrians. It was the last time that Egypt would be ruled exclusively by African people. Ahmose II, who was of Libyan ancestry, ruled the 26th dynasty. The Greeks called him Amasis, and though he was a great statesman, he could not prevent Egypt from becoming dominated by foreign rulers.

In the 7th century B.C.E., the Kushite rulers were forced to withdraw to the south to make their final stand. They concentrated their power first at Napata and later at Meroe. Kush, or Nubia as the Romans called it, existed for nearly a thousand years, during which time Meroe became a famous center for the production of iron. This line of rulers was followed by a succession of female rulers, the Candaces.

The Kushite Female Rulers

A female line of queens, or Candaces, of Meroe actually ruled. As stated earlier, women always played an important role in African society. This was true in Meroe also, and while there were "Queen Mothers" who were prominent in the affairs of the empire, there were some who were actually in power. They did not share power with their husbands. Makeda, the Queen of Sheba, is specifically mentioned in the biblical passages of Acts 8:26–39. It is said that from a meeting with King Solomon of the Israel tribe, a relationship ensued, which culminated in the birth of their son, Menelik. He, however, lived in Ethiopia with his mother, the Queen. Haile Selassie, the former ruler of Ethiopia, is said to have descended from the line of Menelik.

Four other queens were Amanirenas, Amanishakhete, Nawidemak, and Maleqereabar. One of these queens, Amanirenas, is said to have fought the Romans with her army. She negotiated a treaty with the Roman general Petronius. What is known about these queens is found in Roman literature and particularly the writing of Strabo, a Roman historian. Other information has been unearthed in archaeological finds in present day Ethiopia.

The ancient Egyptian/Kemetic civilization was remarkable because it was responsible for the development of the solar calendar and other important areas of knowledge such astronomy, mathematics, science, and the arts. These ancient Egyptians invented paper, ink, and a system of writing. They invented the alphabet and numbers. The ancient Egyptians skillfully practiced medicine that included surgery. They also studied the treatment of various illnesses. They designed and built the great pyramids, and they built irrigation systems and dams for flood control. In other words, ancient Egypt provided the foundation for what is modern civilization.

The Kingdom of Axum (c.100–940 C.E.)

With the end of the 25th and 26th dynasties and the fall of Egypt to foreign invaders, the original Kushite Empire broke up into smaller states. One of the states was Axum. This state took shape in the 1st century C.E. It grew rich from controlling trade from the Red Sea, through the Nile River, especially to Meroe. During the 4th century C.E., the Axumites began to challenge Kush. After a series of wars, Kushite power ended and the Axumites dominated. The Axumite culture was maintained for a while but could not sustain itself as well as did the old Kushite Empire.

The Axumite ruler, Ezana, converted to Christianity in 350 C.E. Christianity soon became the religion of the majority of the Axumite people. In the middle of the 7th century, the religion of Al-Islam arose on the Arabian Peninsula, just across the Red Sea from Axum. It spread throughout Arabia and was taken into the area around Ethiopia through the trade routes. Some of the people around Axum gradually accepted Al-Islam. Axum successfully resisted Al-Islam and maintained its Christian faith. Ethiopia, the name by which Axum is known today, thus has the distinction of being the oldest Christian country in the world.

Summary

Whenever research is conducted, different theories are proposed. Often these theories are in conflict with each other. One of the theories in question was the origin of human beings. Research by paleoanthropologists has determined that human beings originated some 200,000 years ago on the continent of Africa. This has been documented by fossil evidence, which shows that although fossil remains have been found in other parts of the world, such as Asia and Europe, none are older than those found in Africa. The DNA research is newer, but it suggests the origin of the human race can be traced to one African woman. The fossil evidence along with the mitochondrial DNA research both support the "out of Africa" theory.

While it is one thing to acknowledge the origin of humans in Africa, it is another to develop a high civilization. Contrary to the early notions of Africa as a "Dark Continent" with nothing to offer the rest of the world, the records show that not only was Africa the cradle of civilization but of a high civilization. The ancient Egyptian civilization was distinctively African. Much of its progress and prosperity was due to the influence of the strong rulers from the African kingdoms of the South. It was a learning center for Greeks such as Herodotus, Pythagoras, and others who came to study in the "mysteries system" (Egypt's education system). Egypt was also a cultural blend of many groups because of its strategic position for trade and travel. Even so, distinctly African people played a major role in the development of what was to become Egyptian civilization.

Unfortunately, some present-day scholars and Egyptologists continue to contest and debate the identity of the ancient Egyptians. They do not want to consider, much less concede, that Black people could have established such a well-developed civilization as Egypt. The reason goes back to the issue of racism based on color and the need for some Whites to feel that they are better than Blacks. In terms of Egypt specifically, it is a matter of laying claim to the greatness of that civilization. Whichever group can lay claim to Egypt can also claim greatness for its group. These ethnic groups can feel justified in saying that only White people were capable of developing a civilization such as Egypt. These people can deny that African people ever contributed anything to the world. In the past, people used these false notions first to justify enslavement of African people and then to continue discrimination and oppression against people of African descent. The ancient Egyptians, however, left images carved in stone and painted on their tombs and temples, and they left their writings—all of it as evidence of who they were.

This chapter has addressed the origins of all humans to Africa and traced those early beginnings to the first high civilization of ancient Egypt. The next chapter will look at how African civilizations continued to thrive. It will also discuss the accomplishments of African people from about 700 C.E. up until the time of enslavement.

References

African-American baseline essays. Portland Public Schools, 1987.
Ancient Egyptian social life. Accessed May 29, 2004. http://www.bergen.org/AAST/Projects/Egypt/social_report.html
Asante, M. K. (1993). *The Afrocentric idea.* Revised and expanded edition. Temple University Press.
Asante, M. K. (1993) *Historical and cultural atlas of African Americans.* Macmillan Publishing.
Asante, M. K. (2001). *African American history: A journey of liberation.* Peoples Publishing Group, Inc.
Barras, C. (2017). Ancient humans: What we know and still don't know about them. *New Scientist.* https://www.newscientist.com/article/2129775-ancient-humans-what-we-know-and-still-dont-know-about-them/
Ben-Jochannan, Y. (1971). *Africa, mother of western civilization.* Black Classic Press.
Browder, A. T. (1992). *Nile Valley contributions to civilization.* Washington, D.C. The Institute of Karmic Knowledge.
Cann, R. et al. *Mitochondrial DNA and human evolution.* Accessed September 5, 2005, from http://www.artsci.wustl.edu/~landc/html/cann

Chaney, P. (2014). *Modern Hippocratic Oath holds the underlying values of medicine in a digital world*. UCLA David Geffen School of Medicine—Los Angeles, CA. https://medschool.ucla.edu/body.cfm?id=1158&action=detail&ref=1056.

Diop, C. A. (1974). *The African origin of civilization: Myth or reality?* Lawrence Hill and Co.

Gardner, A. (1961). *Egypt of the Pharaohs*. Oxford University Press.

Greek Medicine—the Hippocratic Oath. (2012, February 7). Nih.gov, U.S. National Library of Medicine. https://www.nlm.nih.gov/hmd/greek/greek_oath.html

Hendry, L. (2018). *Australopithecus Afarensis, Lucy's Species*. National History Museum. https://www.nhm.ac.uk/discover/australopithecus-afarensis-lucy-species.html

Hilliard, A. (1995). *The maroon within us: Selected essays on African American community*. Black Classic Press.

Hilliard, A., Williams, L., & Damali, N. (2018). *The teachings of Ptahhotep: The oldest book in the world*.

Jackson, J. G. (1993). *Introduction to African civilizations*. Carol Publishing Group, 1993.

Montagu, A. (1997). *Man's most dangerous myth: The fallacy of race*. Sage Publications.

Ptah-Hotep > Quotes. Goodreads. Accessed 2018. https://www.goodreads.com/author/quotes/4883657.Ptah_Hotep

Shiel, W. *Medical Definition of Hippocratic Oath*. MedicineNet, https://www.medicinenet.com/hippocratic_oath/definition.htm

Species. (2009, December 22). The Smithsonian Institution's Human Origins Program, https://humanorigins.si.edu/evidence/human-fossils/species

Teaching of Ptahhotep. (2003). University College London. 2003. Accessed 2018. https://www.ucl.ac.uk/museums-static/digitalegypt/literature/ptahhotep.html

The Editors of Encyclopedia Britannica. (2017, November 15). *Hippocratic Oath | Ethical code*. Encyclopædia Britannica. https://www.britannica.com/topic/Hippocratic-oath

The Maxims of Ptahhotep. Ganino. Accessed March 24, 2021. http://ganino.com/ante-anus/the_maxims_of_ptahhotep

Trotter, J. W. (2001). *The African American experience*, Volume I and II. Houghton Mifflin.

Wallace, D. (1988, January 11). The search for Adam and Eve. *Newsweek*.

Williams, B. (1982, November). The lost pharaohs of Nubia. *Journal of African Civilizations*.

Williams, C. (1987). *The destruction of Black civilization*. Third World Press.

African Empires

Exploration and Sphere of Influence before Enslavement

The early relationships between Africans and Europeans were quite different before the introduction of the European slave trade around 1400 C.E. The people of North Africa could boast of great accomplishments and the influences of their culture on the various places. These African people were also warriors and conquerors of European countries. Some Africans traveled with the European explorers, and other Africans may have sent people to the Americas before Columbus. One of these groups of conquerors were the Moors of North Africa. This occurred after the fall of the Roman Empire in 476 CE.

The Fall of the Roman Empire and Its Geopolitical Consequences

The invasion of the Moors around 700 C.E. was largely due to the fall of the Roman Empire and the start of the early middle ages, about 500 C.E. The invasion took place during a time that is often referred to as the "Dark

Ages." The Dark Ages, also known as the middle ages, began around 500 C.E. It was a period of decline when there was little or no intellectual or economic growth in most of Europe. The exception was in the Iberian Peninsula which are Spain and Portugal after the Moorish incursion. These two countries benefitted greatly from the cultural, scientist, and intellectual traditions of the Moors of North Africa. As such, while the rest of Europe was in decline, the peninsula flourished.

Some scholars place the blame for the Dark Ages on the fall of the Roman Empire around 476 C.E. The Empire faced a number of challenges. The Roman Empire was under assault by various barbarian groups, such as the Germanic tribes, the Vandals, the Angles, and the Visigoths. Rome also had economic troubles. Its society encouraged slavery and when the flow of slaves from conquered peoples slowed to a stop, Rome no longer had the workers it needed. There was an increase in taxation which caused an even greater divide between the rich and poor. Rome had also become militaristic and the overspending on the constant wars made the situation worse. There was a weakening of the Roman Legions, especially when the government resorted to hiring foreign mercenaries. There was also the loss of traditional values.

All of this, including political instability and government corruption combined with economic mismanagement of the government are also cited as reasons. To further complicate matters, the Roman Empire had two seats of government, one in Rome and the other in Constantinople. Some scholars say that the Dark Ages resulted from invasion by barbarians. However, other scholars blame the early Christian church, which later became the Roman Catholic Church. The Christian church, itself, was fragmented with four different centers of leadership, Rome, Antioch, Constantinople, and Alexandria.

The Church in Rome eventually stepped in to defend what was left of the Roman Empire from the barbarians, which also meant initiating the Crusades to take back the "Holy Land." It apparently worked and the Church began to exert its authority. However, as the Church became more powerful through exerting control over the various tribal kings and leaders, it also became corrupt. In any case, the Dark Ages began around the year 500, and is known as a period when Europe was stagnant and unproductive.

Africans in the Iberian Peninsula (c. 711 C.E.)

An African people called the Moors, of North Africa, had developed a thriving culture in southern Morocco. The Moors eventually became united with another people, the Arabs. Together they made a powerful force. The Moors provided both the manpower and leadership for the conquest of other places. One of these places was Europe. In 711 C.E. the Moors invaded Europe through the Iberian Peninsula. Their general, Gibril Tarik, led the invasion in 711 C.E. They first controlled Portugal and then Spain.

Many of the Moors were Muslim, and Arabic was their language of religious and scholarly communication, just as Christians used Latin. Some of the Arabic words they introduced are still found in the Spanish and Portuguese languages. Arabic words are also found in the English language. They include words such as algebra, alcohol, chemistry, nadir, alkaline, and cipher. The Moors also brought to the Iberian Peninsula distinctive African Muslim styles and techniques in architecture, irrigation, music, and literature as well as everyday manners and customs. There were various religious groups that lived under Moorish rule, including Christians and Jews. While there were some restrictions, according to some reports, the three groups managed to get along. The Moors also allowed religious freedom, for the most part. The "non-believer" was subject to a higher tax than the believers in Islam.

In Moorish society education was very important and schooling was universal. Universities and schools were established, and both women and men of any class could get a basic education. Van Sertima (1992) writes that there were 800 public schools and 70 public libraries. In Moorish Spain, Cordoba was the capital and location of one of the seventeen universities. Other universities were located in Granada, Malaga, Seville, and Toledo. In the universities the Moors taught geography from globes long before Magellan circumnavigated the world, so they knew that the world was not flat. They invented the astrolabe, which was used for navigation, and many were among the explorers to the New World.

In mathematics, the Moors used Hindu Arabic numbers rather than Roman numerals which made algebra possible. Van Sertima, a scholar, explains that Moorish medical practices included "extensive training and a code of conduct" (1992). Physicians were trained in the technical science of healing and knew the healing properties of various drugs. Other subjects taught included the physical sciences and religion, therefore the Koran was a major part of schooling. The subjects became the basis for the European universities. Much of the schooling was based on the Egyptian Mysteries school system which they had preserved.

The Moorish occupation of Spain brought many advances to the people. Beautiful palaces were built for the rich and for the rulers. There were 900 public baths which were important for health reasons. One of the great calamities in medieval Europe during the Dark Ages was the bubonic plague which killed thousands of people. More sanitary conditions might have lessened the devastation there. The people enjoyed the comforts of paved street, raised sidewalks, and street lighting. The silk industry was introduced, as were agricultural products such as rice, sugar cane, dates, ginger, strawberries, and cotton. Other items, such as African ivory, ebony, Indian spices, and leather, were also available.

Although the Portuguese were able to defeat the Moors about 300 years before Spanish rulers could, many African influences remained. In addition, the population of Africans increased dramatically. Africans became an integral part of the Portuguese population. They could be found at every level of Portuguese society, from peasants to royalty. Africans intermarried with the Portuguese, including the royal family. There were also enslaved Africans and indentured servants. The first enslaved Africans were brought to Portugal in 1444 from West Africa. It is interesting to note that race or color was not a factor in these early cultural exchanges and contacts. It was only later, in the context of the Atlantic slave trade and the massive depopulation of African people from the continent of Africa, that race became a factor. For approximately 800 years, the influence of the Moorish presence and rule in Spain was profound. Spain managed to defeat the Moors and expel them in 1492, ironically the same year Christopher Columbus sailed to the Americas.

Africans in the Americas

Scholars are quick to discuss the evidence that supports the travel of the Vikings to North America. There is considerably less discussion about the evidence that suggests that Africans traveled to the Americas before the Vikings or before Christopher Columbus in the 1400s. Some scholars such as, Ivan Van Sertima (1976) have compiled information from various disciplines, including art history, American archaeology, and botany, that indicates that Africans had traveled to the Americas. Van Sertima (1976), a scholar and researcher, asserts that Africans influenced the culture of the people they met long before Christopher Columbus ever arrived.

Other scientists have been studying some extraordinary statues that were found among the ruins of the Olmec civilization in Mexico. These statues are huge stone heads that resemble African people. The first of these statues was uncovered at Tres Zapotes in eastern Mexico in 1939 by anthropologist, Dr. Matthew W. Stirling. Dr. Stirling, who was with the Smithsonian Institute at the time, subsequently went to La Venta, where several more heads were discovered. Even more were uncovered in San Lorenzo in 1946. According to Van Sertima, clay sculptures have been discovered which depict skin coloration and hair texture which provide an even stronger connection to the huge stone heads. In addition, pottery figures similar to the statues have been found as far away as 2,000 miles to the south, in Peru.

A date inscribed in stone near one of the Olmec figures was deciphered as November 4, 291 B.C.E. The carbon-14 process has been used to date material found with the statues to an even earlier time. Carbon-14 is a complicated testing process that measures changes in the natural radioactivity of materials like wood or coal. In addition, materials (ceremonial platforms) found with the statues have been dated to a time between the 7th and 10th centuries B.C.E. Scientists are still studying this question: When, exactly, were the statues made, by whom, and why? Ivan Van Sertima (1987) has suggested that a fleet of ships sent from Egypt to trade for tin in Britain may have been blown off course and ended up in Central America. The currents in the Atlantic Ocean move in a circular direction that could have easily carried boats from the coast of northwest Africa to the Americas. Those same currents, however, would have made it more difficult to return to Africa from the Americas unless one was familiar with the circular patterns. The circular pattern of the currents in the Atlantic Ocean was not understood until later. He has also noted the similarities of the Olmec culture to Egyptian culture as has Indian scholar Rafique Jairazbhoy (1987).

In addition to these stone heads, author Michael Bradley (1992) states there are "black warriors depicted on the walls at the Temple of Warriors at Chichen Itza" in southern Mexico. Other records indicate that Africans were in the Americas as early as the 7th century B.C.E. There are also reports by the first Spanish and Portuguese explorers who traveled to the Americas that they found Black men living in colonies in the eastern areas of South and Central America. Black men were also found in the Yucatan Peninsula and in Nicaragua.

It is also reported that the Mandinka (Mandingo) people of the West African Empire of Mali engaged in expeditions to America. Arab historians and African historians, such as Al Omari, wrote of voyages to the Americas that took place during the reign of Mansa Musa I in the 14th century. One of these voyages involved a ruler of Mali named Abubakari II. It is reported that he gave over the leadership of his country to Mansa Musa and launched a large expedition to cross the Atlantic Ocean. Harold Lawrence provides some additional information on this topic. In the book, *African Presence in Early America,* Lawrence described events as follows. When Mansa Musa traveled through Cairo on his way to Mecca, he told people there the following:

> . . . The ruler who preceded me (Abubakari/Mansa Muhammed) would not believe that it was impossible to discover the limits of the neighboring area: he wanted to find out and persisted in his plan. He had two hundred ships equipped and filled them with men, and others in the same number filled with gold, water, and supplies in sufficient quantity to last for years. He told those who commanded them: return only when you have exhausted your food and water. They went away. Their absence was long before any of them returned. Finally, a sole ship reappeared. We asked the captain about their adventures. "Prince," he replied, "We sailed for a long time, up to the moment when we encountered in mid-ocean something like a river with a violent current. My ship was last. The others sailed on, and gradually as each one entered this place, they disappeared and did not come back. We did not know what had happened to them. As for me, I returned to where I was and did not enter that current." But the emperor did not want to believe him. He equipped two thousand vessels, a thousand for himself and the men who accompanied him, and a thousand for water and supplies. He conferred power on me and left with his companions on the ocean. This was the last time that I saw him and the others, and I remained absolute master of the empire. (p. 203)

The coast of West Africa has few natural harbors, and the winds blow strongly from south to north. Therefore, it is easy to sail from south to north but is more difficult to travel back again. Despite these problems, people who lived along the West Coast of Africa fished some distance from land and traded by boat up and down the coast. For centuries, they had been trading with the inhabitants of the Cape Verde Islands that lay several hundred miles from the African continent. Over the years, the rulers of Mali had organized large expeditions to cross the Sahara desert. The rulers did this in order to trade in North Africa or to make the pilgrimage to Mecca in Arabia. That kind of experience would have prepared them for planning and gathering necessary resources for sending expeditions to sail the Atlantic.

Other indicators that Africans were present in the Americas during the 15th century include the eyewitness accounts and entries from Christopher Columbus's personal journal. It contains references to Africans having previously sailed into the Atlantic with merchandise. The historian John Boyd Thacher described Christopher Columbus's voyage in 1498. He quoted a journal reference that stated, "Certain principal inhabitants of the island of Santiago came to see them and they say that to the southwest of the island of Huego ... which is one of the Cape Verdes distance 12 leagues from this, may be seen an island, and that the King Don Juan ... was greatly inclined to send to make discoveries ... and that canoes had been found which start from the coast of Guinea and navigate to the west with merchandise." In that same journal, it is also stated "that he [Columbus] thought to investigate the report of the Indians of this Espanola, who said that there had come to Espanola from the South and Southeast, a black people who have the tops of their spears made of a metal which they call guanin...." Van Sertima tells us that the word "guanin" is derived from the Mande languages of West Africa.

In addition to these eyewitness and journal accounts, there are other evidence of pre-Columbian contact. At the Olmec sites, terracotta sculptures with African features and masks have been found. Skeletal evidence also has been found at these sites. The skeletons reveal two types of skeletal frame. One is similar to that of the Olmecs, and the other is most similar to that of African people.

Other evidence includes the presence of plants that are not native to the Americas. One of these is the jackbean. Other plants include the yam and the banana, which was found in Peru. The banana was originally introduced into Spain by the Arabs and cultivated there. No such plant was known to have grown in the Americas.

It is more commonly known that Africans participated in some of the earliest Spanish expeditions to the Americas. In 1513, Africans crossed the Isthmus of Panama with Vasco Nuñez de Balboa. Several Africans explored Mexico with Hernando Cortez in 1519. Africans were in Peru with Francisco Pizarro and in Florida with Pedro Menendez de Aviles. Africans were also with Cabeza de Vaca in 1527 when he explored the southeastern part of what is now the United States. The best known of these African explorers was Stephen Dorantes, or Estevanico ("Little Steven"), who was gifted as a linguist. He could learn the language of the Indian tribes in very little time and was very knowledgeable about medicines. Another African, from the Hernando De Soto expedition, chose to remain with the Indians who lived in what is today Alabama. Many of these Africans, and those who came later, either as indentured servants or as slaves, were skilled in leather-working, iron-working, and carpentry (Bennett, 1993).

The Medieval Empires of Africa

It is not possible to adequately describe all of the regions and centers of cultural development in Africa throughout its history in this book. Although some of these city-states and regions have been included here, there are many resources from which one can choose for more detailed information. However, in terms of African American history, it is of major importance that the West African empires be discussed, for it was from this region that millions of Africans were brought against their will to the Americas. Although it is thought that most of the people of African descent came from the West African countries, it has been shown that their culture and that of the Nile Valley people were similar.

There are common cultural traits shared among the people of the Western Sudan and the earlier Nile Valley civilizations of Kush and Egypt. Cheik Anta Diop, among others, has documented information that indicates that fundamental African cultural traditions, ideas, and influences were exchanged between people living in the northern and southern areas of Inner Africa and the Nile Valley of Egypt and Kush. When people migrated from the Nile Valley to the western part of the continent of Africa, they too carried many of the same ideas. This includes similarity in languages. The western Sudanic empires of ancient Ghana, Mali, and Songhay continued the great traditions of their Nile Valley predecessors. These civilizations were notable for prosperity, learning, and magnificence.

Ghana

Ancient Ghana was the earliest of these great civilizations of the western Sudan. The Soninke people founded ancient Ghana. According to their tradition, Ghana began about 300 C.E. It grew rich because of its fertile lands and excellent location for trade. By the 10th and 11th centuries, its people had become very prosperous. The people of the western Sudan, south of the Sahara Desert, had plenty of gold, but they needed salt from north of the Sahara Desert. The people who lived north of the desert wanted gold from the people who lived south of the Sahara. Ghana was located in a strategic geographic location in western Africa between the people who had gold and the people who had salt. Ghana became very rich and powerful by controlling the trade and exchange of goods between the two. It became so wealthy that it was known as the "Land of Gold." During the middle of the 11th century, however, Ghana fell into decline. Neighboring countries, such as Mali, began to attack. These attacks along with the invasion by the Almoravids, a Muslim religious sect, caused Ghana to fall in 1240 C.E.

Mali

A branch of the Soninke people had also founded Mali. They, in turn, made alliances with another group of people called the Malinke who lived in the region south of them. This city-state had been a part of the ancient kingdom of Ghana. In the 13th century, Mali began to challenge the authority and ruler of Ghana. Under the leadership of Sundiata, whose family had been killed by the ruler of Ghana, the Mandinka people of Mali conquered the territory of Ghana. They then established rule over an even greater area. The rulers of Mali became Muslim and led their state into an age of learning, economic development, and territorial expansion. During this time, the great University of Sankore was built. There were studies in mathematics, medicine, government, geography, art, literature, and grammar.

In 1324, one of Mali's greatest rulers, Mansa Musa, took over the leadership from his brother Abubakari, who had abdicated the position. During his reign, he made a spectacular pilgrimage to Mecca, the holy city for Muslims. On this pilgrimage, Mansa Musa displayed the fantastic wealth of the empire. It is said that he gave out so much gold to the people along his route that the gold market in Egypt was devalued. It caused a slump in gold prices, which lasted over ten years. In order to understand how this can happen, one must understand the economic concept of supply and demand. A commodity, which is in short supply, becomes valuable because everyone wants it. But when one has too much of an item, such as this precious metal, its value decreases.

The Congo

The Congo in Central Africa is the second longest river in Africa with a length of 2,720 miles. It is not only one of the longest in the world but also one of the largest in terms of the volume of water discharged. Nearly the entire Congo is readily navigable; and therefore it serves as a main artery for transportation and trade for the entire region.

Songhay

The Songhay people had been under the rule of Mali. Two sons of the Songhay king had been taken to Mali as hostages to ensure the loyalty of the king and his people. The princes managed to escape, and one of them, Ali Kolon, established a new line of rulers. Led by Sunni Ali the Great, as he was called, the Songhay Empire rose to power about 1475. It took control over what had once been Ghana and Mali. Sunni Ali the Great went on to become one of the most famous rulers in the western Sudan. He added much of the previous Mali territory to the Songhay Empire before his death in 1492.

The people of Songhay continued to enjoy great wealth and attained great intellectual achievement under the leadership of Askia Mohammed. He ruled from 1492 to 1538, during which time he established a strong central government and increased commerce. The cities of Timbuktu, Gao, and Jenne had become major educational centers. The universities that were established in these cities attracted scholars and students from Europe and Asia as well as other parts of Africa. Timbuktu alone had three universities: Sankore, Jingaray Ber, and Sici Yahya. The University of Sankore was the largest. It consisted of several independent colleges or schools which were run by a single professor. Subjects such as logic, diction, rhetoric, law, and philosophy were taught. Other subjects included medicine and surgery, astronomy, math, chemistry, geography, music, art, and hygiene. However, the principle subject was Qur'anic and Islamic studies. Unlike modern classrooms, instruction was conducted in open courtyards.

Songhay was a powerful nation in the 15th and early 16th centuries. Timbuktu alone had a population of over 100,000 people. Askia Mohammed was succeeded by his son, Daoud, who ruled from 1549 to 1583. The empire disintegrated when Songhay was invaded by Moroccans, which ended the Golden Age of the western Sudanic empires. By the beginning of the 17th century, this area had fallen into decline. Also by this time, the Portuguese had begun to trade with East African countries. This was swiftly followed by the European slave trade. The invasion from Morocco in 1591 completed the demise of the empire. Europeans were then free to use their weapons to invade and kidnap African people and rob their resources and artifacts.

Kanem-Bornu

Kanem was an empire in Central Africa, near Lake Chad, that arose around 1200 C.E. in the central part of Africa. Another group of people called the Kanuri, who established the empire of Kanem, conquered the various ethnic groups in the area. At one time, the Kanuri controlled the territory from Libya to Hausaland. Internal fighting, however, began to weaken the empire, and power then shifted to another Kanuri state called Bornu. The two empires of Kanem and Bornu became united and lasted until the rise of the Hausa states.

Other Kingdoms

Other empires or states emerged, such as Benin, Ashanti, Hausa, to name a few. There were the Forest Kingdoms south of the Sahara desert in West Africa, the Hausa Kingdom in northwest Africa and the Swahili states in East Africa. The Forest Kingdoms in Africa included Benin, the Oyo Empire of the Yoruba, and the Manikongo (Congo).

 The Niger

The Niger is the third longest river in Africa and takes one of the most unusual routes of any major river. It is the principal river of western Africa. The Niger runs in a long arc from Guinea to Mali, past the fabled trading city of Timbuktu and Gao, right up to the edge of the Sahara. There it turns south to the sea. It was also important in terms of trade.

Benin was the longest lasting and most powerful of these kingdoms. Located in southern Nigeria, Benin developed a craft and art society. As well as being a powerful city-state, it became known for its artwork, particularly its sculpture made of terra cotta, ivory, and brass. The early art works primarily recounted the history of Benin, and its art traditions influenced many cultures in the area near the Niger River. Benin was one of the most difficult conquests for the Europeans when they began to invade Africa.

The Swahili Kingdoms included such city-states as Mombassa, Kilwa, Mogadishu, and Sofala in Zimbabwe. There was a flourishing trade between the Arabs and the Africans there. The Swahili language grew out of the mixture of Arab and Bantu languages. These states were separate from each other and traded in ivory, ebony, gold, and sandalwood. During the early part of the 15th and latter part of the 16th centuries, these states entered into the European trade market. At first, both African and European traders regarded each other with mutual respect. Although these empires and states retained their political identities and established flourishing societies, none of them was able to maintain their societies once the European slave trade took hold.

Wars and conflict within the continent weakened the various nations. The African people were no match for the invaders who were very brutal and used new weapons, especially firearms. These intruders robbed the African people of their natural resources, such as gold and other precious metals, rare woods, and many of the sacred artifacts. This disruption was made by the loss of people through the European slave trade. These people who were sold away from their families possessed skills, knowledge, and ability. They are the ancestors of many African Americans today.

Summary

Although the Moors came to conquer Spain and Portugal, they also introduced many advances and a higher form of culture. The Moors knew that the world was not flat, as did Henry the Navigator of Portugal, who gleaned much of his information from these African people. The Moors knew and taught geography from globes and invented the astrolabe, which was used for navigation.

There is evidence to suggest that it was possible, and probably likely, that Africans traveled to America long before Columbus did. A variety of material evidence, including reports and journal entries, and particularly the stone heads with African features, strongly argues for the presence of an African people. Although this evidence is available, it is still under debate by scientists and others who refuse to recognize the possibility that someone other than Columbus or the Vikings could have traveled to the Americas.

The West African empires from the thirteenth through the sixteenth centuries were thriving productive centers of government, education, and culture. The empires of Ghana, Mali, Songhay and others were organized into city-states. The people could boast of universities, cultural exchanges, and trade. In many ways these empires continued the cultural exchanges and centers of learning that had developed in ancient Egypt.

There was a great amount of interaction between Europe and these empires in terms of trade, diplomatic relations, and Europeans attending the African universities. This was before some European invaders saw their opportunity to take over and control the riches they found in Africa. The decline of the last of the great West African empires began about the time that the Africans first began to trade with the Portuguese. It also coincided with the beginning of the European slave trade, the death of the last strong king of Songhay, Askia Mohammed, in 1538, and finally the invasion from Morocco in 1591.

From Griot to Folktale

In West Africa, the history of the people was told by storytellers or oral historians called griots. The job of griot was usually passed down from one person to the next, usually in the same family line. When ceremonies were held, it was the responsibility of the griot to remember the experiences of the past. This art of storytelling became very important to enslaved Africans. They told stories to help themselves survive. Many of the stories have come down to us as Black folktales. They include such characters as "Brer" Rabbit and Anansi, the spider. The stories were about the smaller and weaker characters outsmarting the bigger, stronger ones. Many of the stories incorporated the difference between right and wrong and taught the principles of good moral behavior.

This chapter addressed the medieval West African empires and their great accomplishments as centers of learning and trade. It also discussed the relationships Africans had with Europeans before the Atlantic slave trade and before the Europeans came to conquer the continent. The next chapter will focus on how all of these interchanges and interactions changed from mutual respect to oppression and unspeakable cruelty. It will address how indentured servitude turned into chattel slavery and why only Africans were targeted to carry its burden.

References

Asante, M. K. (1993). *The Afrocentric idea*. Revised and expanded edition. Temple University Press.

Asante, M. K. (1993). *Historical and cultural atlas of African Americans*. Macmillan Publishing.

Asante, M. K. (2001). *African American history: A journey of liberation*. Peoples Publishing Group, Inc.

Ben-Jochannan, Y., & Clarke, J. H. *New dimensions in African history: The London Lectures of Dr. Yosef Ben-Jochannan and Dr. John Henrik Clarke*. St. John, Brawtley Press.

Bennett, L., Jr. (1993). *Before the Mayflower: A history of Black America*. 6th edition. Penguin Books.

Bradley, M. (2011). *Dawn voyage: The Black African discovery of America*. EWorld.

Jackson, J. G. (1993). *Introduction to African civilizations*. Carol Publishing Group.

Jairazbhoy, R. A. (1987). The Egyptian presence in South America. In *African presence in Early America* (pp. 76–136). Transaction Books.

Lane-Poole, S. (1996). *The story of the Moors in Spain*. Putnam.

Lawrence, H. (2002). Mandinga voyages across the Atlantic. In I. Van Sertima (Ed.), *African presence in Early America*. 3rd print ed. Transaction Publishers.

Trotter, J. W. (2001). *The African American experience*, Volume I and II. Houghton Mifflin.

Van Sertima, I. (1976). *They came before Columbus*. Random House.

——— (Ed). (1983). *Blacks in science: ancient and modern*. Transaction Publishers.

——— (Ed). (1987). *African presence in Early America*. Rutgers University Press.

——— (Ed). (1988). *African presence in Early Europe*. Transaction Publishers.

——— (Ed). (1988). *Black women in Antiquity*, 2nd edition. Transaction Publishers.

——— (Ed.). (1992). *Golden Age of the Moor*. Transaction Publishers.

Williams, C. (1987). *The destruction of Black civilization*. Third World Press.

3

A Peculiar Institution—with Unintended Consequences

America was founded on a contradiction of values, religious ideals, political principles, and economic exploitation. Indentured servitude led to the institution of slavery that forever crystalized the formation and perpetuation of racial disparity in America. The institution of slavery and its vestiges have left a pronounced mark on every component of American history and society. Oppressed and oppressors were tied together in a relationship that neither benefitted from, nor were able to escape the tragic consequences that followed. Slavery and all of the other forms of oppression have tested the nation's resolve towards its ideals of freedom, justice, and equality.

During the early 1600s, the first African people were brought to the English colonies in America. They came to America in the same way that poor Europeans came, as indentured servants. This meant that they worked for a certain length of time, usually three to seven years, to pay off a debt or the price of their passage to America. When their debt was paid, they were free. Most Europeans came because they were poor and had a hard life in Europe. They were looking for a better way of life. Others came to escape prison, which was where the government not only put criminals but also those who could not pay a debt or did not have a home. The first Africans did not come because of those reasons. Among the indentured Africans who arrived in America were artisans and skilled farmers.

Noted historian Lerone Bennett (1993) tells us that the first African immigrants to the Jamestown Colony were referred to as servants, not as slaves, in 1621. There is a reference to "Antonio a Negro" who was listed as a servant in the census of 1625. At that time there were many "servants," as the colonists were seeking to survive and return a profit to their sponsors the English government.

Initially, there was no distinction made between European and African servants. These Africans worked for three to seven years as indentured servants and then were freed. These people, both the Africans and the Europeans, accumulated land and even bought the labor of other servants. Antonio (Anthony) became free. He eventually became a landowner and he and his wife purchased the services of another African servant. The court records of 1641 indicated that he owned such a servant. Other African immigrants consisted of those who came from the West Indies as well as a few who paid their way to America from Africa.

African and European immigrants lived together on an equal basis for approximately forty years after the establishment of Jamestown. Both groups could vote and they shared the same human and civil rights. This was true also in the Massachusetts colony. The colonial officials made no distinction between either the European or African indentured servants. They both performed the same tasks and received the same punishment and contempt. Discrimination was based on class and not color.

There were problems with the use of indentured servants, however. First, it was quite expensive. The colonists found it was very costly to have to replace indentured servants who had gained their freedom. Sometimes the colonists would not honor their contracts. Second, there was fear that Black and White indentured servants, who were often the majority of the population, would unite against their situation. Third, the indentured servants, both European and African, had begun to form bonds.

Eventually, those in power found a way to disrupt and destroy the bonds that had been formed between the African and European indentured servants. Laws were made that prevented former European and African indentured servants from working or living together and from intermarrying. These laws gave the indentured Europeans more privileges than the indentured Africans.

A Peculiar Institution—with Unintended Consequences

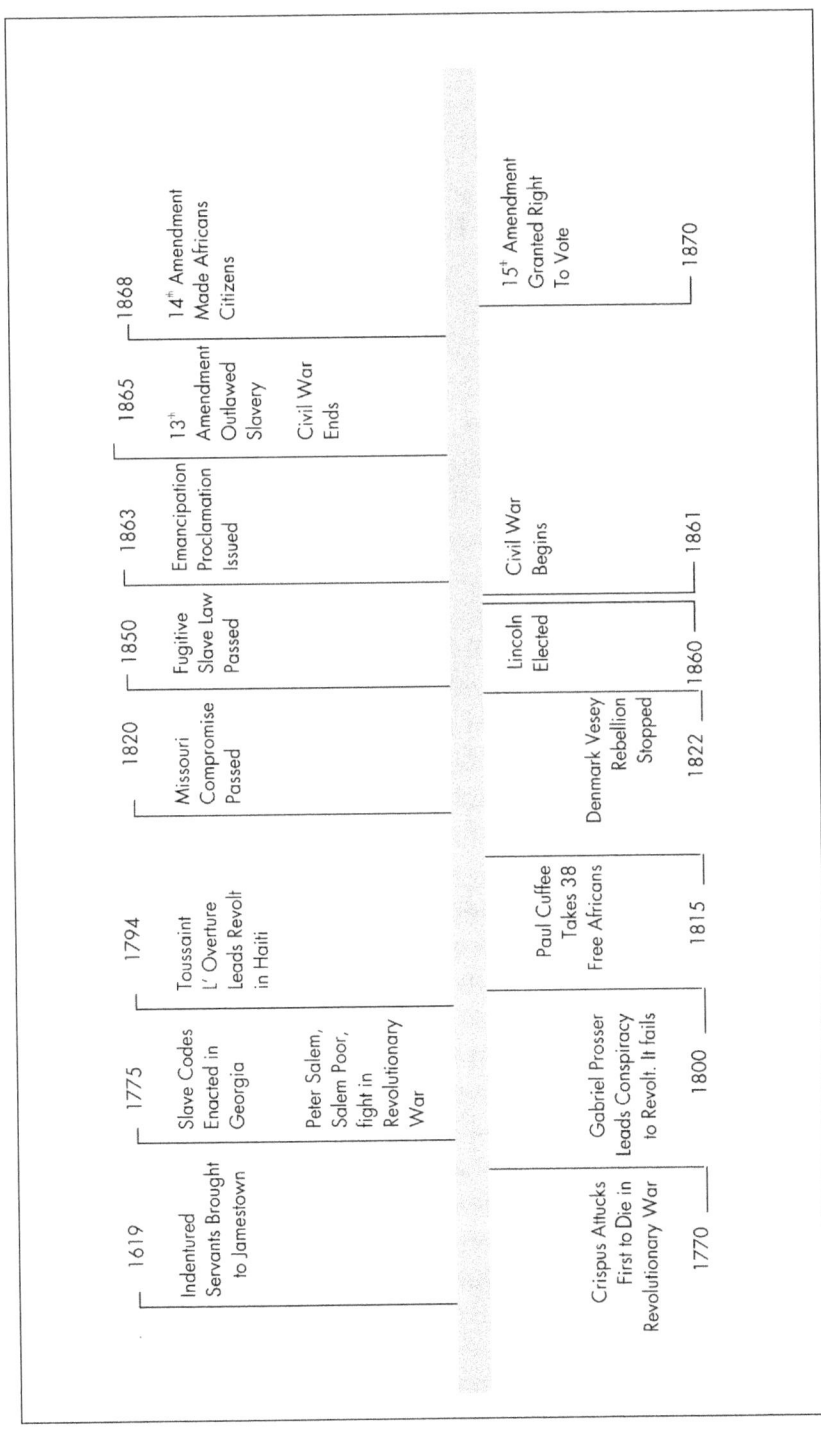

African American History 1619–1870

The English colonists turned to outright enslavement. This solved both their problems of indentured servitude and the fear that all the indentured servants might unite and rebel. At first it had been all right to enslave anyone who was not Christian. However, Africans converted to gain their freedom. Then in 1639, a law was passed in the Maryland colony that stated that a Christian baptism did not make a slave free. In addition there were fewer English people who were willing to be indentured. Finally, in 1641 Massachusetts legally recognized slavery. Connecticut and Virginia followed shortly thereafter and indentured servitude became enslavement.

During the shift from indentured service to slave labor and the laws designed to disrupt amicable relations between Africans and Europeans, the concept of "being White" and "better" was instituted. Bennett (1993), in his book *Before the Mayflower: A History of Black America*, states that the first European colonists apparently did not think of themselves as "White." They were identified as being English and/or Christian. At the same time, Africans in the colonies did not think of themselves as "Black" but were identified according to their country of origin in Africa. These new laws were now based on the color of one's skin. From this point on Africans were enslaved for life, and discrimination was based on black skin color and not class. It became the major factor as to whether a person would be free or not, and it determined how that person would be treated. Unfortunately, to this day, skin color continues to determine how one is treated.

Slavery and Three Historical Considerations

There are three historical considerations must be addressed to fully understand the enslavement of Africans by Europeans. First, how did the European practice of enslavement begin? Second, why were only Africans subjected to enslavement? Third, how could historically powerful and influential people allow themselves to be enslaved? Understanding those three considerations provides the reader with a comprehensive and contextual understanding of the evolution of chattel slavery that was practiced by the Europeans on Africans.

The First Consideration: The Origins of European Enslavement of Africans

First, many people and nations practiced the enslavement of others very early in human history. It was practiced by the ancient Egyptians and

Hebrews, by the ancient Greeks and Romans, and later by other African and European peoples. It was common practice to use criminals and prisoners of war as forced labor (enslavement). Some historians, perhaps in order to justify the European operation of the slave trade, are eager to point out that Africans themselves participated in this activity. Slavery in Africa, however, was very different from the form of slavery practiced by Europeans from the 16th through the 19th centuries in the Americas. African rulers sold prisoners of war or those who had broken the law. In their culture, as in the earlier cultures of Greece and Rome, the captive was reduced to servant status. Such servitude did not necessarily destroy the person's culture or separate family members. Therefore, the practice of enslavement was not new. The Portuguese were among the first Europeans to engage in the enslavement of African people. They did not practice chattel slavery, however. The Spanish initiated that.

The Second Consideration: The Exclusivity of African Enslavement

The second consideration is this: Why were Africans singled out and subjected to enslavement? In the 8th century, the Moors, an African people, invaded Spain and Portugal and dominated that area. The Spanish and the Portuguese tried to re-establish rule over their homeland. The Portuguese finally succeeded in 1143. They were then able to establish trade and other relationships with Africa before other countries did. The Portuguese began to bring Africans from the West African coast to do all sorts of labor. Africans worked in soap and grain factories. Some were paid servants and others worked on the docks. (The modern term for these workers is longshoremen.) Some Africans who were brought were enslaved. In fact, so many Africans were brought that they rivaled the Portuguese population. Bennett (1993) states that this was a relatively unimportant phase of the enslavement of Africans. It was limited to one country and it was not chattel slavery.

Spain, on the other hand, did not overthrow the Moors until 1492, when the last of the Moorish rulers, Boabdil, was removed from power. After the Spanish ended the African domination, they considered it most natural and appropriate to use captives from among their former rulers, the Africans, for forced labor. As in Portugal, Africans became numerous in Spain. This trade in enslaved Africans in Spain was also on a much smaller scale until the conquest of the Americas.

The initial phase of the slave trade began with Portugal and Spain. After the Spanish had conquered lands in the Americas, they extended their sugar plantations into the Americas. The Spanish needed many more laborers but were unsuccessful in persuading Spanish peasants to come to America to work. The Spanish attempted to force the native people (misnamed "Indians") to work. This attempt to enslave Native Americans failed. Frequently the Native Americans, who were not accustomed to forced labor, either became ill and died or simply ran away. Europeans who were enslaved because they had broken the law, or who were debtors, also became ill and died. These people, too, were unaccustomed to the climate, the heat, and the harsh conditions on the plantation or they succumbed to tropical diseases. Those who survived could appeal to a monarch or to public sympathy, or they too could run away and blend into the dominant population.

At first the Spanish brought in Africans who had been baptized or born in Spain. The monarchy was barred from trading in Africa by a decree from the Catholic Church called a papal bull. The papal bull of 1493 gave Spain most of the New World but gave Portugal the sole right to trade with Africa. The Spanish got around this by contracting with Portugal for captive Africans. In the beginning, they bought just a few, but the demand rapidly grew and eventually led to the outright kidnapping of Africans.

Although the Portuguese were given the right to trade in Africa, they could not maintain control of the entire coast of Africa. Eventually, Spain took over the major part of the market. They contracted with the Portuguese through an arrangement called the "asiento," or rights/permission to trade. The asiento allowed Africans to be sold directly from Africa to the New World. Eventually, Spain began to contract with other non-Spanish traders to supply captive Africans to colonies in the Americas. Spain made money by requiring the traders to pay a tax on each African brought to the Americas.

Soon the greed for profits evolved into one of the cruelest forms of servitude ever known, chattel slavery. This form of slavery meant that the enslaved individual was regarded as an item of property, like a house or an ox, and had no rights as a human being. One of the most devastating aspects of chattel slavery was the inability to maintain or develop family and community ties. Entire families were broken up, and extra effort was made to keep those who spoke the same language apart so that they could not communicate with each other.

The Dutch and the French soon took up the institution of slavery. The trade in captured Africans grew to such enormous proportions and was so profitable that the White colonists began to look for ways to justify it. They needed to make the practice seem right and fair. After all, the people who engaged in the enslavement of others were supposed to be Christians. Stories were made up that depicted the Africans as uncivilized. The fact that they were not Christians was also used to justify enslavement. Yet, as Bennett points out, that status could be remedied, because one could easily become a Christian. Many Africans became Christians and some were already Christians, however, so this was a very poor means of justification.

As described earlier, the English relied on indentured servitude in order to provide cheap labor. Many poor English people came to the colonies in America this way. In fact, during the early phases of the English colonization of the Americas, about 75 percent of the labor force arrived as indentured servants. However, it was an expensive way to obtain labor. When the demand for labor in the English colonies became so great, this system was abandoned. The colonies adopted the system of forced labor, which they had seen successfully used by the Spanish in the Caribbean. The Dutch and the English began to challenge the Spanish control. In the end, they came to dominate the European slave trade.

For Europeans, there were distinct advantages in enslaving Africans. They were perceived to be strong physically, and many of them had farming skills. Moreover, their labor was inexpensive compared to the cost of European indentured servants. Africans could be pressed into bondage for life, while Europeans could only be forced to work for three to seven years. Africans were physically distinguishable from Europeans so that they could not run away and conceal themselves among the general European population. Another advantage was that since Africans were from tropical regions, it was assumed they could better resist the heat and sicknesses of tropical America.

The Third Consideration: The Mechanics of Why and How African Slavery Was Possible

The third question is how could Africans have allowed themselves to be enslaved? African people share many similarities in their way of life, but then, as now, they were divided into many different nations. In Africa, as elsewhere in the world, each nation looked out for itself and its own people. Sometimes they did this by allying themselves with other African nations, and sometimes they did this by making war. When the Europeans landed on

African shores, they attempted to ally with African nations but also tried to exploit them. One African nation might fight with one European nation and make treaties with another. However, when the demand for laborers in the Americas grew so rapidly, as did the profits made from selling captives, traders began to encourage and even instigate wars.

The European traders stimulated warfare between African nations by supplying the Africans with guns. In exchange, the traders received African captives. The wars created among these African nations and groups of European slave traders supplied prisoners of war, who were sold as enslaved workers. When even these tactics did not provide enough captives, the Europeans themselves resorted to kidnapping people.

Africans did not practice chattel slavery but a form of domestic slavery; therefore, African rulers did not realize the kind of cruelties that the people they had sold into bondage would endure. Some rulers, like the Fanti king, Kwame Ansa (in present-day Ghana), opposed the intrusion of the Portuguese into his land. Other rulers also resisted the practice of enslavement. One was Queen Nzingha (in present-day Angola). She fought the Portuguese advances into her country for almost 30 years. Another ruler who resisted was King Nzenga Maremba, in the Congo, who tried to resist the Portuguese incursions by establishing diplomatic and trade relations. However, he realized the futility of it all as he saw his country overrun by the Portuguese and his own children held as hostages. The king of Benin restricted the sale of captive Africans and eventually banned it entirely.

In Africa, as in other parts of the world, some nations, such as the Ashanti, were stronger than others. The stronger African nations were able to protect their people from wars and slave trading, at least for a while. They kept the Europeans under control and required them to pay taxes for the privilege of living and trading in their countries. In some African nations, it was required that anyone dealing with royalty had to approach the African kings on bent knee. This was expected of Europeans and Africans alike. One such powerful nation was the Ashanti, which had grown rich from trading with the Europeans. Another was Benin in present-day Nigeria. Its capital city was greatly admired by European travelers who found it cleaner and more beautiful than their cities at home. They, too, were able to protect their people for a while.

The weaker nations, however, could not defend their people against the growing number of wars. They lost not only the people who were captured but all those killed trying to resist capture as well. As more African nations became armed with guns, the wars cost more and more lives. Some regions lost all their people. The villages, towns, and cities that had once been filled with people fell into ruin.

Too little is known about these great African nations because people who wanted to justify slavery created the idea that African people had no culture or history. Over the centuries, many artifacts displaying African arts and sciences have been stolen or destroyed by foreign invaders. Thus, much of the rich cultural heritage that belonged to the Africans was lost and eventually forgotten. African achievements were even credited to non-African people. The remaining evidence of past African accomplishment that could not be explained away was purposely ignored for many years.

The idea of savage Africa became a popular belief in Europe. Even the Christian church justified the slave trade by saying that enslavement of Africans was necessary in order to bring them to Christianity and save their souls. In the end, it became routine to deliberately perpetuate the myth that Africa had no history, culture, or valid religious beliefs. Ultimately, the slave trade cost millions of human lives and fostered many false ideas about African peoples.

The Challenges, Hardships, and Struggles of Newly Enslaved Africans

Except for the earlier visitors or adventurers, explorers, and indentured servants, the vast majority of Africans who came to America were involuntary immigrants. They were uprooted from their homes, families, cultures, and traditions. Thousands of African people were kidnapped, packed into the cramped, dark holds of ships, and brought to the Americas.

The Triangle Trade

The European slave trade was also called the Triangle Trade. It is called that because of the triangular route the slave ships took. The ships sailed from Europe and went to Africa to get captive Africans. Slave traders sold the captive Africans in various places in the Americas for sugar, rum, tobacco, and money. The ships would then return to Europe and the process would start all over again.

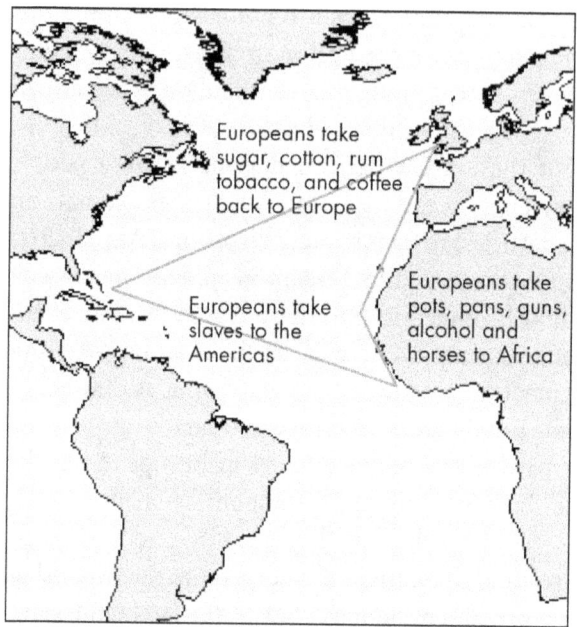

The segment of the trip from Africa to the Americas was called the Middle Passage. During the transatlantic crossings of the Middle Passage, Africans were chained together and lived under filthy conditions. They had little food and water and were often beaten and otherwise abused. Many Africans died before reaching America. They died because of disease resulting from the unhealthy conditions on the ships; others died from starvation, madness, or suffocation. Many captives committed suicide by jumping overboard and drowning.

Who were the Africans who came to America? Since it was impossible to satisfy the need for the vast numbers of Africans with a few lawbreakers or prisoners of war, slave merchants encouraged the ravaging of whole communities. Captives were taken from many different areas and ethnic groups in West Africa. They were taken from the areas known as modern-day Senegal, Ghana, Benin, Guinea, and the Cote d'Ivoire. They were from the ethnic groups of the Hausa, Mandinka, Fulani, Yoruba, Wolof, and Akan. Some of the captives also came from the present-day Congo and Cameroon. These Africans had many different skills and were from all levels of African society. They had established flourishing societies. Some of the captives had held various positions of power and influence within their communities or were warriors or merchants. Others were priests, princes, or other nobles. Yet despite their status, men, women, and children were chained together and forced to march hundreds of miles to locations where they were confined in tight quarters before being put on ships. According to Bennett (1993), sometimes Africans who had engaged in the selling of other Africans were captured themselves and sent away on the slaving ships.

Some historians estimate that at least 10 million captive Africans were brought to the Americas, but other estimates are even higher. It is also estimated that another two million died in the Middle Passage. Most Africans were sent to the Spanish colonies in the West Indies, Central America, and South America. Bennett (1993) states that there were 20,000 Africans in Mexico alone by the mid-1500s. Brazil had several million. Hundreds of thousands of captive Africans were sent to Colombia, Chile, and Venezuela. Many hundreds of thousands were brought to the English colonies.

Some scholars say that the treatment of Africans, once they reached their destination, depended upon the religious affiliation of the European enslavers. All Africans were treated cruelly, but slave masters in some areas were not as thorough in their efforts to erase all memory of culture, traditions, family, or language. For example, in those areas of the Americas dominated by the Portuguese, Spanish, and French, who were Roman Catholic, African customs, religion, music, and ornamentations were not completely banned.

Slave ships brought millions of Africans to the colonies of North and South America. People were packed in chains in the holds of slaving ships with no room to move, inadequate food, and little air to breathe. Many died from disease and others committed suicide by refusing to eat.

Also, enslaved parents in Hispanic America might win freedom for their whole families if they had ten children. Family members were not sold away from one another, and, in many cases, groups of Africans who spoke the same language were kept together. Thus, they were able to continue some of their cultural traditions. Their revolts also became more successful. An example of just such a revolt was one led by Toussaint L'Ouverture in French-ruled Haiti in 1791. It showed Africans were not willing to submit to enslavement by Europeans. Secondly this rebellion made Whites wary of their enslaved captives.

The enslavement of Africans in the English Protestant colonies was often the cruelest. The myth had been created that Africans were less than human. The colonial ruling class and the slave owners actively promoted it. Sometimes biblical scriptures were interpreted in such a way as to promote the idea that Africans were naturally inferior. The slave owners felt that they could treat the African captives as animals. Many forms of physical and mental torture were used to dehumanize the Africans and to break their spirit and pride.

The Colonial Plantation System

By the end of the 1700s, so many African people had been brought to the English colonies in the Americas that there were more enslaved Africans than European colonists in many parts of the South. Upon arrival in the colonies, the enslaved Africans were separated from relatives (if this had not already been done), friends, and those who spoke the same language. This practice of keeping the enslaved African people isolated made it difficult for them to maintain or develop their own sense of community and togetherness. Laws were passed to limit the rights of Africans and to control them. These laws, known as slave codes, prohibited enslaved Africans from meeting in large groups or from being legally married. They were not permitted to testify against European colonists in court as the first indentured Africans could. Enslaved Africans could not learn to read, nor could they own land or animals. Even those indentured Africans who had bought their freedom often had their rights taken away from them. They were compelled to live under conditions that were just as bad as, if not worse than, the conditions of Africans who had been enslaved from the start.

The colonists discovered that certain foreign crops grew very well in the American colonies in the South. Sugar cane, rice, tobacco, and cotton were among the crops that produced the largest profits. Large numbers of Africans were sold to people who owned the plantations that grew these crops. Plantation life differed depending upon size and location. A large plantation was similar to a small town. The enslaved Africans manufactured all the necessities for the plantation. Since many of the enslaved Africans had been farmers and artisans (such as leatherworkers, builders, etc.), they were very successful in carrying out their jobs. Enslaved Africans produced food for all the people in the community. Often, however, they were given only leftovers and food that was not wanted by the families of the plantation owners.

Plantation life was very hard. The old and the sick were forced to work. Women often cut down trees and dug ditches. African men, women, and children were sent to the fields early in the morning, where they worked until night. After dark, their work still was not done because they had to care for their families. The children who were too young to go to the fields were kept in a nursery with one woman to care for them. This meant that most of the mothers could work either in the fields or in the "big house." The working conditions for field laborers were harsher than for those enslaved Africans who worked in the plantation owner's house. Although working conditions might have been better, working in the "big house" also meant that one could be more closely watched.

The treatment of enslaved Africans on the larger plantations, which had overseers or managers, was usually worse than on small plantations. The overseers could punish the enslaved Africans under their control as they saw fit. They had a great deal of authority and were responsible for seeing that the work was done and the laborers remained at their tasks. Those very large plantations that required an overseer were fewer in number than the smaller farms and plantations.

The largest number of Africans worked on the smaller farms throughout the South. The Africans working on these smaller plantations were more isolated from one another, making communication among them extremely difficult. This isolation made it more difficult for enslaved Africans to plan or organize large scale resistance to their situation. Individually, however, they resisted in a variety of subtle ways, such as pretending illness, being careless with property, setting fires, and performing other acts of sabotage.

It is important to note that a number of Africans were not in bondage during this period, even in the South. There were three ways that enslaved Africans could become free. First, those who had valuable knowledge and skills could earn enough money to buy their freedom. Second, slave owners could voluntarily grant freedom. The third option was that one could escape to freedom.

In the North, the practice of enslavement began to die after the Revolutionary War. This added to the number of free Africans. There were probably several reasons for this. One important reason was that the economy of the North was different from that of the South. There was no long growing season to encourage the cultivation of crops, so other industries were pursued. Vermont became the first state to abolish slavery in 1777 and other states followed. The greatest number of free Africans, however, lived in Philadelphia and New York.

The Gullah/Geechee People

The Gullah/Geechee people, are the descendants of enslaved people from West Africa, in particular Angola and Sierra Leone. They possessed the knowledge of rice planting and harvesting so proved invaluable on the rice plantations on the Sea Islands off the coast of South Carolina, Georgia and Florida. They were also skilled in the planting and harvesting of indigo, cotton and tobacco. The first commercial crops of indigo, a plant from which blue dye was extracted, were planted and harvested in Charleston. By the mid-1700s, indigo was a major cash crop in the Low Country. Work on the plantations of South Carolina and Georgia was some of hardest work that an enslaved person had to endure. It often resulted in death because the wet, swampy conditions that were needed also produced malaria.

Two Early Courageous Abolitionists

Contrary to popular belief and racist Hollywood depictions of happy, dumb, and compliant slaves nothing could be further from the truth. Despite the brutality, psychological trauma, and insecurities of enslavement, Africans understood how wrong and unfair their servitude was. Freedom was valued and sought, even at the risk of death. Two examples of early protests and moral grievances against slavery were written by Phillis Wheatley and Benjamin Banneker. Their writings and publications show the intellectual capabilities and understanding of philosophy, politics, history, and science. These two pioneering thinkers are remarkable because of the breadth of their knowledges, scope of their intellect, and the depth to which they articulate their concerns.

During the period from 1777 through 1780, when the northern states were slowly abolishing slavery, early African abolitionist emerged and began to take up the cause of freedom. Phillis Wheatley (1753–1784) was born in

Senegal, West Africa, and was captured and brought to the Americas when she was eight years old. She worked as a domestic companion, but learned English and read many books while living in the Wheatley home in Boston, Massachusetts. Phillis understood the condition of enslavement and the struggle to be free. Armed with life experiences and the gifts of literacy and scholarship she became a noted writer who chronicled life in servitude.

She was given her freedom by the Wheatleys at the age of twenty. Eventually, she wrote the first book by an African American, *Poems on Various Subjects, Religious and Moral*, which was published in London in 1773, three years before the Declaration of Independence. It started the African American women's literary tradition. It was also only the second book ever written by any American woman. Anne Bradstreet's collection of poetry was the first. The following is an excerpt from Wheatley's book.

On Being Brought From Africa to America

'Twas mercy brought me from my Pagan land,
Taught my benighted soul to understand
That there's a God, that there's a Saviour too:
Once I redemption neither sought nor knew.
Some view our sable race with scornful eye,
"Their colour is a diabolic die."
Remember, Christians, Negros, black as Cain,
May be refin'd, and join th' angelic train. (1887)

Wheatley also wrote a poem in honor of George Washington, which she sent to him. He liked it so much that he invited her to visit him. Her writing of this poem was in keeping with the African tradition of composing poems to honor important persons. These poems are called praise songs because they are usually sung. The poem was published in the *Philadelphia Magazine* by Thomas Paine.

Benjamin Banneker (1731–1806) was a free man. His mother had been an indentured servant and his father had been an enslaved African. He attended school near Baltimore, Maryland, and developed a strong interest in mathematics and science at an early age. Banneker became an astronomer and mathematician and wrote one of the first almanacs in 1792. Because of his intellectual abilities, he was appointed by President George Washington to be a member of the commission that surveyed and laid out the nation's capital. Banneker played a major part in the design of Washington, D.C. He also made the first wooden clock in America, although he had never seen one.

Phillis Wheatley was remarkable because of her accomplishment in learning to read and in publishing her book. In her writing, however, she did not address the issues of slavery and the false notion of African inferiority. Banneker did address them, though. In 1791, he wrote a letter to Thomas Jefferson about the hypocrisy of professing the belief that people had rights, as stated in the Declaration of Independence, while allowing the enslavement and cruel oppression of Africans. President Jefferson replied by thanking Banneker for the almanac that he sent but did not comment on the contents of the following letter.

BANNEKER'S LETTER TO JEFFERSON

SIR,

I AM fully sensible of the greatness of that freedom, which I take with you on the present occasion; a liberty which seemed to me scarcely allowable, when I reflected on that distinguished and dignified station in which you stand, and the almost general prejudice and prepossession, which is so prevalent in the world against those of my complexion.

I suppose it is a truth too well attested to you, to need a proof here, that we are a race of beings, who have long labored under the abuse and censure of the world; that we have long been looked upon with an eye of contempt; and that we have long been considered rather as brutish than human, and scarcely capable of mental endowments.

Sir, I hope I may safely admit, in consequence of that report which hath reached me, that you are a man far less inflexible in sentiments of this nature, than many others; that you are measurably friendly, and well disposed towards us; and that you are willing and ready to lend your aid and assistance to our relief, from those many distresses, and numerous calamities, to which we are reduced. Now Sir, if this is founded in truth, I apprehend you will embrace every opportunity, to eradicate that train of absurd and false ideas and opinions, which so generally prevails with respect to us; and that your sentiments are concurrent with mine, which are, that one universal Father hath given being to us all; and that he hath not only made us all of one flesh, but that he hath also, without partiality, afforded us all the same sensations and endowed us all with the same faculties; and that however variable we may be in society or religion, however diversified in situation or color, we are all of the same family, and stand in the same relation to him.

Sir, if these are sentiments of which you are fully persuaded, I hope you cannot but acknowledge, that it is the indispensable duty of those, who maintain for themselves the rights of human nature, and who possess the obligations of Christianity, to extend their power and influence to the relief of every part of the human race, from whatever burden or oppression they may unjustly labor under; and this, I apprehend, a full conviction of the truth and obligation of these principles should lead all to. Sir, I have long been convinced, that if your love for yourselves, and for those inestimable laws, which preserved to you the rights of human nature, was founded on sincerity, you could not but be solicitous, that every individual, of whatever rank or distinction, might with you equally enjoy the blessings thereof; neither could you rest satisfied short of the most active effusion of your exertions, in order to their promotion from any state of degradation, to which the unjustifiable cruelty and barbarism of men may have reduced them.

Sir, I freely and cheerfully acknowledge, that I am of the African race, and in that color which is natural to them of the deepest dye; and it is under a sense of the most profound gratitude to the Supreme Ruler of the Universe, that I now confess to you, that I am not under that state of tyrannical thraldom, and inhuman captivity, to which too many of my brethren are doomed, but that I have abundantly tasted of the fruition of those blessings, which proceed from that free and unequalled liberty with which you are favored; and which, I hope, you will willingly allow you have mercifully received, from the immediate hand of that Being, from whom proceedeth every good and perfect Gift.

Sir, suffer me to recal to your mind that time, in which the arms and tyranny of the British crown were exerted, with every powerful effort, in order to reduce you to a state of servitude: look back, I entreat you, on the variety of dangers to which you were exposed; reflect on that time, in which every human aid appeared unavailable, and in which even hope and fortitude wore the aspect of inability to the conflict, and you cannot but be led to a serious and grateful sense of your miraculous and providential preservation; you cannot but acknowledge, that the present freedom and tranquility which you enjoy you have mercifully received, and that it is the peculiar blessing of Heaven.

This, Sir, was a time when you clearly saw into the injustice of a state of slavery, and in which you had just apprehensions of the horrors of its condition. It was now that your abhorrence thereof was so excited, that you publicly held forth this true and invaluable doctrine, which is worthy to be recorded and remembered in all succeeding ages: "We hold these truths to be self-evident, that all men are created equal; that they are endowed by their Creator with certain unalienable rights, and that among these are, life, liberty, and the pursuit of happiness." Here was a time, in which your tender feelings for yourselves had engaged you thus to declare, you were then impressed with proper ideas of the great violation of liberty, and the free possession of those blessings, to which you were entitled by nature; but, Sir, how pitiable is it to reflect, that although you were so fully convinced of the benevolence of the Father of Mankind, and of his equal and impartial distribution of these rights and privileges, which he hath conferred upon them, that you should at the same time counteract his mercies, in detaining by fraud and violence so numerous a part of my brethren, under groaning captivity and cruel oppression, that you should at the same time be found guilty of that most criminal act, which you professedly detested in others, with respect to yourselves.

I suppose that your knowledge of the situation of my brethren, is too extensive to need a recital here; neither shall I presume to prescribe methods by which they may be relieved, otherwise than by recommending to you and all others, to wean yourselves from those narrow prejudices which you have imbibed with respect to them, and as Job proposed to his friends, "put your soul in their souls' stead;" thus shall your hearts be enlarged with kindness and benevolence towards them; and thus shall you need neither the direction of myself or others, in what manner to proceed herein. And now, Sir, although my sympathy and affection for my brethren hath caused my enlargement thus far, I ardently hope, that your candor and generosity will plead with you in my behalf, when I make known to you, that it was not originally my design; but having taken up my pen in order to direct to you, as a present, a copy of an Almanac, which I have calculated for the succeeding year, I was unexpectedly and unavoidably led thereto.

This calculation is the production of my arduous study, in this my advanced stage of life; for having long had unbounded desires to become acquainted with the secrets of nature, I have had to gratify my curiosity herein, through my own assiduous application to Astronomical Study, in which I need not recount to you the many difficulties and disadvantages, which I have had to encounter.

And although I had almost declined to make my calculation for the ensuing year, in consequence of that time which I had allotted therefor, being taken up at the Federal Territory, by the request of Mr. Andrew Ellicott, yet finding myself under several engagements to Printers of this state, to whom I had communicated my design, on my return to my place of residence, I industriously applied myself thereto, which I hope I have accomplished with correctness and accuracy; a copy of which I have taken the liberty to direct to you, and which I humbly request you will favorably receive; and although you may have the opportunity of perusing it after its publication, yet I choose to send it to you in manuscript previous thereto, that thereby you might not only have an earlier inspection, but that you might also view it in my own hand writing.

And now, Sir, I shall conclude, and subscribe myself, with the most profound respect, Your most obedient humble servant,

BENJAMIN BANNEKER
University of Virginia

THOMAS JEFFERSON TO BENJAMIN BANNEKER

Philadelphia Aug. 30. 1791

Sir,

I thank you sincerely for your letter of the 19th. instant and for the Almanac it contained. no body wishes more than I do to see such proofs as you exhibit, that nature has given to our black brethren, talents equal to those of the other colours of men, & that the appearance of a want of them is owing merely to the degraded condition of their existence both in Africa & America. I can add with truth that no body wishes more ardently to see a good system commenced for raising the condition both of their body & mind to what it ought to be, as fast as the imbecillity of their present existence, and other circumstance which cannot be neglected, will admit. I have taken the liberty of sending your almanac to Monsieur de Condorcet, Secretary of the Academy of Sciences at Paris, and member of the Philanthropic Society because I considered it as a document to which your whole colour had a right for their justification against the doubts which have been entertained of them. I am with great esteem, Sir, Your most obedt. humble servt. Th. Jefferson

Summary

Contrary to the stories that may have been previously taught about the arrival of Africans in America in 1619, one finds that these people were indentured servants and not enslaved captives. One also finds that Africans and Europeans in Virginia and in the Massachusetts colony lived in harmony. Discrimination was based on class and not skin color. However, laws were made to destroy the bonds between the two groups by the ruling elite in order to ensure their continued control.

Unfortunately, most history books used in most public schools continue to omit certain information. Without accurate information, it is difficult for one to understand how the issues of race, color, and enslavement started or how they continue to affect peoples' lives in the United States today. The books do not mention how the first Africans were servants and how they interacted with other indentured Europeans. Neither do the books discuss the fact that these Africans had the right to vote, hold office and had other rights and privileges. This freedom ended with the introduction of slavery into the colonies.

Slave codes were passed, which not only prevented the enslaved Africans from coming together but which also took away the rights of the freed Africans. These codes were considered necessary because in many places Africans outnumbered the colonists. The codes were enacted to restrict their movement and reduce the possibility of mounting rebellions against their enslavers.

Despite these measures, however, Africans resisted enslavement in many ways. Free Africans also assisted them. The next chapter will address the ways in which Africans resisted enslavement in Latin America and the English colonies.

References

Ajayi, O. (August 1996). Phillis Wheatley: A life of triumph over obstacles. *The Brown Quarterly*, 1(1). Special Introductory Edition. http://brownvboard.org/brwn-qurt/01–1/01–1f.htm

Asante, M. K. (1993). *The Afrocentric idea*. Revised and expanded edition. Temple University Press.

Asante, M. K. (1993). *Historical and cultural atlas of African Americans*. Macmillan Publishing.

Asante, M. K. (2001). *African American history: A journey of liberation*. Peoples Publishing Group, Inc.

Asim, J. (2005, December). A Slave Poet's $253,000 Letter. *The Washington Post*. Accessed 2018. https://www.washingtonpost.com/archive/business/technology/2005/12/05/a-slave-poets-253000-letter/0778c48d-d8f8-4466-8e90-4441f6e0df82/

Banneker's Letter to Jefferson. PBS. Accessed August 28, 2004. http://www.pbs.org / wgbh/aia/part2/2h71.html

Bennett, L., Jr. (1993). *Before the Mayflower: A history of Black America*. 6th edition. Penguin Books.

Bradley, M. (1987). *Dawn voyage*. Summerhill Press Ltd.

Franklin, J. H., & Moss, A. A., Jr. (2000). *From slavery to freedom: A history of African Americans*. Knopf.

Loewen, J. W. (1995). *Lies my teacher told me: Everything your history textbook got wrong*. Touchstone.

Louisiana Purchase. http://gatewayno.com/history/LaPurchase.html.

Phillis Wheatley. Poetry Exhibits. Accessed August 28, 2004. http://www.poets.org/poets/poets.cfm?45442B7C000C02010D.

Phillis Wheatley, comments on *Poems on various subjects, religious and moral*, *Poetry Foundation*. Accessed 2018. https://www.poetryfoundation.org/poets/phillis-wheatley

Spacey, A. Analysis of poem "On being brought from Africa to America" by Phillis Wheatley. W. H. Lawrence & Company, 1887. Updated March 2017.

Swartz, E., & Lessie, R. (1985). *The role of Black Americans in the development of the United States: A supplement to our country's history*. Rochester; City School District.

Thacher, J. B. (1903). *Christopher Columbus. His life. His work. His remains*. G. P. Putnam.

Thomas Jefferson to Benjamin Banneker. Library of Congress. Accessed August 28, 2004. http://www.loc.gov/exhibits/jefferson/79.html

Trotter, J. W. (2001). *The African American experience*, Volume I and II. Houghton Mifflin.

Wheatley, P. (1887). *Poems on various subjects, religious and moral*. W. H. Lawrence.

Wheately, P. (1773). *Poems on various subjects, religious and moral*. Printed for Archibald Bell and Sold in Boston by Cox and Berry.

Review

I. Checking What You Have Read

1. Why do many scholars consider Africa to be the birthplace of modern humans?
2. Where was Kush and why was it significant in African history? List at least three ways in which Kush influenced Egypt.
3. By what other names was Egypt called?
4. Give an example from your reading that illustrates the important role of women in ancient African societies.
5. By what other names is Imhotep known? Why is he referred to by these names?
6. How did King Akhenaton change the religion practiced in Egypt?
7. Describe some major accomplishments of the ancient Egyptian civilization.
8. How did the 25th dynasty end? What happened to the original Kushite Empire? What major 9 effects did the Axumite ruler, Ezana, have on his people and country?
9. Where was the city of Timbuktu located? Of what accomplishments could it boast?
10. How did ancient Ghana gain great wealth?
11. What is mitochondrial DNA and why is it important?
12. Name two women from the New Kingdom and tell why they are considered notable.
13. Who were the Candaces?
14. For what reason was the kingdom of Benin famous?
15. What empire arose after the fall of the Songhay Empire?
16. Who were the Moors? Describe several of the advancements they brought to Spain and Portugal.
17. Evidence suggests that Africans sailed the Atlantic Ocean before Columbus did. Cite some of this evidence.
18. List several Spanish expeditions to the Americas in which Africans participated. What particular skills did these people have?
19. Describe how Africans came to have a presence in Portugal.

20. Where can large stone heads that have African features be found in the Americas?
21. Explain the term "indentured servant."
22. How did early forms of enslavement in Greece, Rome, and Egypt, for example, differ from chattel slavery in the Portuguese and Spanish colonies in South America and the English colonies in North America?
23. Who were the people forced to participate in the Middle Passage?
24. Name three restrictions placed on enslaved Africans under the slave codes.
25. How did Africans resist enslavement?
26. Compare and contrast the letters of Banneker and Wheatley.

II. On Your Own

1. Draw a map of the ancient West African empires. Include some of the major cities or centers of importance.
2. Using library sources or the Internet, research two Egyptian rulers. Write a one-page summary of both of the rulers.
3. Imagine you lived in one of the ancient West African empires of Ghana, Mali, or Songhay. Write a brief story about what you have seen, such as various traders in the markets, scholars at the universities, the pilgrimage of Mansa Musa to Mecca, or Sunni Ali preparing for battle.
4. DNA is a chemical substance that carries genes and determines heredity. Explain its importance in the recent studies that have traced human origins to the continent of Africa. (See *Newsweek*, Jan. 11, 1988.) Note that there are some recent studies also available on the Internet.
5. On a map of Africa, see if you can locate the areas of the Forest Kingdom or Great Zimbabwe. Describe what it might have been like in those Kingdoms during the 1600s.

4

Resistance to Enslavement in the Americas

Resistance in Latin America and the Caribbean

Africans never accepted their enslavement in the Americas. There was resistance to slavery in the Americas throughout the 17th, 18th, and 19th centuries. There were two basic ways to resist. The first way enslaved Africans resisted captivity was through acts of violence. Violent actions took the form of revolts against plantation owners. These revolts occurred throughout the Americas. There were uprisings and revolts in Mexico, Peru, and Ecuador. In many parts of Latin America and the Caribbean, enslaved Africans ran away and banded together to form communities. Those acts of defiance were considered passive resistance.

The African fugitives were called "cimarrons," or "maroons." The name maroon came from the Spanish word cimarron, which meant wild or untamed. It eventually came to mean all Africans who lived away from their European enslavers. They built communities or safe havens, which were called different names depending on the country. In Brazil they were called "quilombos," but in Peru, they were called "palenques." It was from these communities that attacks on the former slave owners were carried out. One famous community called Palmares, was in Brazil. It lasted for most of the

18th century until the Brazilian authorities finally destroyed it. The Africans of Palmares not only protected the people in their communities, they also executed raids on their former slave owners. Africans in other communities did the same.

In Jamaica, the fighting was particularly fierce. Spanish slave owners fled the country when the English arrived, leaving behind the enslaved Africans they had brought. These Africans fled to the mountains to escape the new conquerors. The attacks conducted against the English colonists challenged them to the point that the colonists signed a peace agreement with the Africans to stop the raids. Many African heroes emerged from these revolts. Zumbi was one of these in Brazil and Cudjoe was another in Jamaica; however, the one leader who had a great effect on the United States was in Hispaniola, by the name of Toussaint L'Ouverture.

Toussaint L'Ouverture was a key figure in the liberation of the island of Hispaniola in 1791. The island was known as Sante Dominque and was imperialized by the Spanish and the French governments. L'Ouverture worked tirelessly to expel the Spanish from one side of the island, and then turned his attention to expelling the French from the other side of the island. It is important to note that the liberation of Hispaniola was at approximately the same period as the French Revolution in Europe. The themes of equality and justice were garnered by from the French Revolution.

In the part of Sante Dominique that became Haiti, there were many freed persons of mixed African and French parentage who did not have the same rights as the French inhabitants of the island. On the other hand, there were the enslaved Africans who made up the majority of the population. The freed persons saw their opportunity to gain the same rights as the French inhabitants. They mounted a rebellion against the French rulers. The enslaved Africans also recognized their opportunity and joined the revolt. L'Ouverture did not participate in this early phase of the Haitian Revolution. It was not long after the Haitian revolution that Toussaint turned his attention to the French-ruled part of the island.

L'Ouverture was eventually defeated by the French. He was tricked into attending a meeting with one of the generals sent to stop the rebellion. The meeting, however, was just a way of getting L'Ouverture out of his fortress. He was captured and sent to France, where he died in prison. But he was never forgotten. He laid the foundation for the independence of Haiti, which was finally won by Jean Jacques Dessalines, one of his lieutenants.

L'Ouverture's martyrdom inspired others to fight for their freedom. Consequently, Haiti became an independent nation in 1804, ruled by African people.

Thanks to all of the products that could be produced in Haiti, it had proven itself a lucrative acquisition by France. But the French emperor Napoleon Bonaparte was also fighting a war in Europe that was very expensive. It was difficult to fight on two fronts and for all his efforts, he had been unable to recapture Haiti.

It just so happened that President Jefferson had sent two people, James Monroe and Robert Livingston to negotiate with the French to purchase a portion of the area on the Mississippi River or at least to guarantee safe passage on the river. Apparently, Napoleon saw his opportunity. He agreed to sell the holdings of the French in North America. Jefferson was certainly surprised and pleased that the French wanted to sell. This transaction became known as the Louisiana Purchase, and it doubled the size of the United States. The failed campaign to recapture Haiti, together with the ongoing war in Europe, probably led to Napoleon's decision to sell the remainder of the French-owned territory in North America to the United States.

Rebellions Against Enslavement in the English Colonies

In the English colonies, enslaved Africans and European indentured servants planned a rebellion as early as 1663. Enslaved Africans fought in any manner they could. Enslaved Africans attacked slave owners, burned plantation homes and warehouses, and seized guns and ammunition. They were also accused of trying to poison water supplies. Africans knew which plants could cure and which were poisonous. The slave masters knew that they did, and no doubt were fearful that this knowledge might be used against them. In Virginia some enslaved Africans were accused of poisoning Whites and executed in the early 1770s. One South Carolina newspaper printed an enslaved person's antidote for poisoning for over a month. This was apparently done because slaveholders were fearful. Whether the accusations were true or not, it was something that caused them concern.

Violent Protests Against Enslavement

Plantation owners attempted to keep the news about revolts and uprisings a secret, fearing attacks by enslaved Africans. However, the secrecy was unsuccessful because Africans were constantly being bought and sold, and many were brought from the Caribbean countries where there had been uprisings. These rebellions influenced acts of resistance in the United States although they were not as frequent. Unlike the areas in Latin America, Africans were not allowed to gather into groups, and in most places, they were outnumbered by slaveholders and other colonists. Many of the enslaved Africans, however, turned to passive forms of resistance.

Gabriel Prosser

Although plantation owners attempted to prevent opportunities for Africans to get together to plan revolts, they were not always successful. There were many revolts. Gabriel Prosser planned one in August 1800. He was an enslaved African who devised a plan to capture Richmond, Virginia. He managed to enlist the aid of several thousand other Africans in the conspiracy. Before the plan could be executed, however, a rainstorm arose, which disrupted the plans. The storm destroyed the bridges that were to provide access to Richmond. Before the Africans could regroup, two enslaved house workers betrayed the plan to their master. Prosser and 34 of his fellow conspirators were arrested and hanged.

Denmark Vesey

In Charleston, South Carolina, Denmark Vesey planned another revolt. Vesey purchased his freedom in 1822 with some money that he had won in a lottery. He learned to read English as well as several other languages. Vesey was a member of the African Methodist Episcopal (AME) church, where he was very active. He often read to his fellow Africans about what the abolitionists were doing to end slavery.

Vesey soon progressed from talking about freedom to organizing an attack against the colonists. He enlisted the help of Gullah Jack and Peter Poyas, a ship's carpenter and a remarkable organizer. Poyas and Vesey designed an elaborate plot, recruiting whole plantations of enslaved Africans from Charleston and the surrounding area. But an enslaved house worker who had been approached by one of the conspirators exposed the plan.

Vesey and five of his aides were captured, tried, and put to death by hanging.

Nat Turner

One revolutionary who succeeded where Vesey and Prosser did not was Nat Turner. On August 21, 1831, in Virginia, Turner began his insurrection with six men. The number quickly grew to sixty. He killed his owner and the owner's family, then traveled throughout Southampton County, Virginia, killing more than 55 Whites. While attempting to capture the county seat of Jerusalem to get guns and ammunition, the group was met by a posse of angry European Americans. The rebels scattered and fled to the Great Dismal Swamp, where they hid out for six months. Eventually they were captured. Nat Turner and 16 members of the group were hanged. Although Turner's goal of ending slavery was not realized, his actions had a strong effect on European Americans. They now feared for their lives more than ever.

These uprisings took a terrible toll on the enslaved Africans. In the Nat Turner rebellion, over 100 people were killed. In many instances, large numbers of innocent African people were put to death along with those who had participated in the uprisings. So many enslaved people were put to death that the owners themselves began to protest the loss of "their property." Punishment for rebellion was then changed from death to still severe but non-fatal penalties, such as public whippings and jail sentences.

John Brown

There was growing sentiment among many European Americans for the abolition of slavery. Often, sympathetic Whites helped enslaved Africans, and sometimes they were killed for helping them escape. John Brown was one of the first European Americans to die in the fight. Brown was a deeply religious man and felt that slavery was wrong.

On October 16, 1859, Brown led a group of thirteen European Americans and five Africans in a raid on a federal arsenal at Harper's Ferry, West Virginia. They intended to capture weapons and give them to enslaved Africans for a rebellion. The rebellion never happened, however, because of poor communications. Several days later, Brown was captured by a detachment of Marines. He was convicted of treason and hanged.

Up to that point, many Africans had felt that the White abolitionists were only willing to go so far—that they were only willing to talk about the abolition of enslavement but nothing more. John Brown's sacrifice of his life demonstrated that some White people were serious enough to put their lives on the line. The song "John Brown's Body" commemorates his participation in the struggle for freedom for Africans. Because New York and New England abolitionists had backed John Brown's raid, the South viewed the North as willing to use force in the attempt to end enslavement, and hostility between the two sides increased.

The Amistad *Revolt*

Another daring act of rebellion occurred in 1839 on a ship called the *Amistad*. A group of 48 Africans seized the ship, killing all but two of the ship's crew. Sengbe Pieh, a member of the Mende people in West Africa, led the rebellion. Pieh was also known as Joseph Cinque. He had been kidnapped by Portuguese slave traders from the area known as Sierra Leone. From there he was put on the *Tecora*, a Spanish slave ship, and taken to Cuba. While in Cuba, Cinque and 52 others, including four children, were bought by two Spanish men and put aboard the *Amistad* to be taken to Puerto Principe, another part of Cuba. On the ship, he managed to free himself and the other Africans. Cinque ordered the crewmen to sail them back to Africa. He ordered them to set sail to the east because he had observed that the boat traveled west from Africa. The crewmen, however, had tricked them by sailing west at night, and they eventually sailed into the waters of the English colonies. The Africans were discovered off the coast of Long Island, New York. The Africans who had not died from the revolt on board were arrested and taken to New London, Connecticut.

The two crew members, Hosea Ruiz and Pedro Montes, went before Federal District Judge Andrew T. Judson in Connecticut to demand the return of the remaining 39 Africans. They claimed that this was their right because the Africans were their property. Several abolitionists, such as Lewis Tappan and the Rev. Joshua Leavitt, however, raised money to prepare a defense for the Africans. Some of the Africans were from the Mandingo ethnic group and some were from the Mende ethnic group. None of them, however, spoke English. Joshua Gibbs, a Yale professor, found other Africans who spoke both English and the African languages. They were asked to translate in order to understand the situation from the Africans' point of view.

John Brown (1800–1859)

Brown was an abolitionist and the leader of the attack on Harper's Ferry in 1859. He was born in Connecticut but raised in Ohio. During his life he lived in various places including Ohio, Pennsylvania, Massachusetts, and New York.

In 1847 Frederick Douglass met Brown for the first time in Springfield, Massachusetts. Brown outlined his plan to lead a war to free slaves at this meeting.

Brown moved to North Elba, New York, in 1849. However, he soon followed five of his sons to the Kansas Territory to participate in the antislavery fight. After the ill-fated attack at Harper's Ferry and Brown's execution, Brown's wife returned his body to his farm near Lake Placid, New York, for burial. It is now a New York State Historic Site.

The abolitionists argued that the Africans should not have been enslaved in the first place. They claimed that it was illegal to bring Africans into Cuba after 1820. The Federal District Court ruled that the Africans were illegally taken from Africa and that they were not guilty of the murder of the other crewmen. The case was appealed before the Supreme Court. John Quincy Adams, a member of the House of Representatives and former president, argued the case. He also presented information that accused President Van Buren of falsifying documents. The Supreme Court upheld the decision of the lower court and the Africans were freed.

Non-Violent Protests Against Enslavement and the Abolitionist Movement

Non-violent opposition to enslavement involved free African American men and women who worked to emancipate their enslaved brothers and sisters. It took the form of anti-slavery speeches, the use of newspapers to publicize the cruelty and inhumanity of slavery, and the running away of enslaved people. Free African men and women started a huge movement by joining with European Americans to form abolitionist groups. Members of these groups initiated a number of activities in their campaigns against enslavement. They began newspapers in order to publicize the horrors of enslavement. Abolitionists also raised money to support the fight. They sponsored speeches throughout the north and lobbied in Congress against the practice of enslavement. Some of the most important people in American history were part of the abolitionist movement.

Frederick Douglass

During the 1800s, a remarkable speaker named Frederick Douglass emerged. He was born into enslavement but managed to escape to New York in 1838. He began to travel throughout the country speaking about the evils of slavery and advocating its abolition. He was such a gifted speaker that he could arouse many kinds of emotions in his audience, from tears to anger. Before Douglass, many people could just ignore the evils and conditions of enslavement. He, however, put a face on enslavement and caused people to examine their consciences.

Sometimes the audience became so angry at what he said that they threw eggs and other objects at him. In spite of this, Douglass continued his public speeches. His audiences grew larger and larger. More often than not, people came away singing his praises. Most importantly, he convinced them of the inhumanity

Frederick Douglass was born a slave in Maryland. He managed to teach himself to read by the age of 12 and to write by age 15. He escaped enslavement dressed as a sailor. Douglass became a great orator against enslavement. He published the *North Star*, an abolitionist newspaper, in Rochester, NY.

Resistance to Enslavement in the Americas

and injustice of enslaving African people. In 1845, Douglass wrote his autobiography. It was a instant success, but it also put his life in jeopardy because he was still a fugitive slave. He was forced to flee to England for fear of the slave catchers.

Douglass spread his anti-slavery message throughout England, Scotland, and Ireland. The crowds of people he met there were very enthusiastic. English friends who were opposed to slavery raised enough money to purchase his freedom from the Auld family. The reception he received in England almost enticed him to stay, but he didn't. He returned home in 1847 and started a newspaper called the *North Star* in Rochester, New York. The newspaper was the first that gave voice to the abolitionist movement from the perspective of the enslaved African. Douglass remained an essential force in the abolitionist movement until the end of enslavement.

Sojourner Truth was born a slave in Hurley, New York. She became free in 1827 when the State of New York abolished slavery. She changed her name from Isabella Baumfree to Sojourner Truth and went around preaching. She eventually added abolitionism and women's suffrage to her speeches.

Sojourner Truth

Other African men and women also traveled throughout the country speaking for African liberation in America. The first outstanding female African American orator was Sojourner Truth. She had been bought by a Dutch family and spoke only Dutch until she was 14 years old. She was born Isabella Baumfree, in upstate New York. When New York abolished slavery, she became free. She then took the name Sojourner Truth because she felt that she had been sent on a journey to tell the truth.

Truth lectured widely against slavery and became a leader in the women's movement for equality. Because she was such an advocate for women's rights, she was most eloquent in her speeches about the rights of women and African Americans. Truth became a great asset to Susan B. Anthony, with whom she closely worked.

West Coast Abolitionists

Two wealthy women who lived in California were also quite outspoken in the struggle for human rights. They advocated for women's rights also but were very clear that it had to be through the abolition of enslavement. Mary Ellen Pleasant and Biddy Mason organized female anti-slavery groups and even initiated protests. They felt that the abolition of slavery was the only solution.

There were two distinct issues. One was the struggle for basic human rights for Africans. The other was the extension of rights for women. Susan B. Anthony and Elizabeth Cady Stanton advocated extending rights for women. This would have benefited White women but not necessarily enslaved Africans. This caused tension, at times, between the two movements. It eventually alienated some African Americans, such as Frances Ellen Watkins and Frederick Douglass, from the women's movement.

Many White women had opposed slavery and worked for its abolition. They also supported the right to vote for both women and African American men. They had even temporarily put aside their fight for suffrage although many believed that their work in these areas would lead to women suffrage. White women, particularly Susan B. Anthony, were angered when it did not. Anthony split from the American Woman Suffrage Association after the passage of the 14th Amendment and just before the proposed 15th Amendment. She founded the National Women Suffrage Association. This organization refused to work for the passage of the 15th Amendment.

Edmonia Lewis was America's first black woman sculptor. Her father was an African American and her mother a Chippewa Indian. Lewis was raised by her mother's tribe after being orphaned at a young age. She attended Oberlin College but did not graduate. Lewis moved to Boston in 1863 and became a sculptor, specializing in images of abolitionists and Civil War heroes.

Not only did the issue of suffrage split the abolitionist movement, it was also felt among African Americans. There were others who felt the issue of women suffrage was more important than the suffrage of African American men. Sojourner Truth and Harriett Forten Purvis were two people who held this view. Forten Purvis' family established the first biracial organization of women abolitionists. Eventually, the two groups put aside their issues and formed the National American Woman Suffrage Association.

Newspapers for Liberation

Another means used to protest slavery was the printed word. Samuel Cornish and John Russwurm started a newspaper in New York called *Freedom's Journal* in 1827. Samuel Cornish was a minister of an African Presbyterian Church in New York. John Russwurm was a graduate of Bowdoin College in Maine. *Freedom's Journal* was the first African newspaper. The purpose of this publication was to recount the experiences of Africans from their own viewpoints and to advocate for the abolition of slavery. Russwurm believed in returning to Africa as a solution to the problems experienced by Africans in America. This ideology split the two men apart and Russwurm eventually emigrated to Africa. In 1831, a European American, William Lloyd Garrison, founded the *Liberator* in Boston. It was also a newspaper devoted to abolishing slavery. He and Wendell Phillips were both among the founders of the abolitionist movement.

Prince Hall

Some African Americans protested in the form of legal actions. In 1777, Prince Hall, a free man born in Barbados, West Indies, and others petitioned the Massachusetts legislature to free its enslaved Africans. The petition was sent to the Congress of the Confederation, essentially the federal government at that time. However, slavery was eventually abolished in 1783 by a state judicial decision that presumably had nothing to do with Hall's petition. He also petitioned the state to provide education for African Americans in 1787. African Americans were being taxed similarly to Whites, but they did not receive the same services. This petition failed. He, however, established a school in his home for African American children.

The Road to Freedom

Enslaved Africans also fought the system of enslavement by running away from their owners. In many cases, Native Americans assisted them and even formed alliances with them because they viewed the elitist European Americans as their common oppressors. Many enslaved Africans who managed to escape found safety with the Native Americans. One example of this was the Seminole Indians in Florida. Many Africans escaped and went to live with the Seminoles. In fact, so many found asylum with them that the Seminoles were considered to be a Black tribe.

Some groups, such as the Quakers, also took a strong stand against the enslavement of Africans. They issued the first group protest against slavery and began the Pennsylvania Abolition Society in 1775. Later they assisted runaway Africans to reach freedom.

The Underground Railroad

One of the most famous persons who escaped from bondage was Harriet Tubman. After her own escape from Maryland, she risked her life repeatedly by returning to the South to lead other enslaved Africans to freedom. Her role in the liberation of her people has been compared to that of the biblical Moses, and she was and still is often called "the Moses of her people." She returned to the South many times and led over 300 people to freedom. She frequently traveled through the area around Buffalo, New York. Harriet Tubman continued to show her dedication to the defeat of African enslavement by later serving in the Union Army as a nurse, scout, and spy during the Civil War. When African

Harriet Tubman is also known as the "Moses of her People" because once she escaped enslavement, she risked her life more than 19 times to return to the South to bring others to freedom. She is pictured with seven other people, presumably escaped slaves.

people were finally freed, she returned to the North and made her home in Auburn, New York, where she died in 1913.

Harriet Tubman traveled by way of what was called the Underground Railroad. It was not an actual railroad but a system of secret routes and safe houses where Africans could stay. It was made up of free Africans and Whites who were willing to help runaway Africans to freedom. Tubman made her way to New York State and Canada using some of these routes. There were many other underground railroads leading to other free states and Mexico, but the one to the North and Canada is one of the most famous.

The Underground Railroad

The term "Underground Railroad" was first used about 1830. The system helped thousands of enslaved Africans escape. Some of the most heavily traveled routes of the Underground Railroad were through Ohio, Indiana, and western Pennsylvania.

Although they could settle in the North, many were afraid that they would be recaptured and returned to enslavement. After Congress passed the Fugitive Slave Act in 1850, many fled to Canada, especially Ontario. Many fugitives followed these routes to Canada by way of Detroit, Michigan, or Niagara Falls, New York. Others sailed across Lake Erie to Ontario from places such as Erie, Pennsylvania, and Sandusky, Ohio. A large number of fugitive slaves went to Nova Scotia.

Escaping slaves were secretly guided as they made their way along a trail of safe houses from the southern states up through the North and eventually to Canada. Guides were called conductors, and information was passed through stories, songs and covert signals such as quilts hanging on clotheslines.

From 1827, when slavery was abolished in New York, until the end of the Civil War in 1865, many New Yorkers assisted fugitive slaves by providing refuge in churches, barns and elsewhere, passage to freedom, and protection from slave catchers.

A Matter of Conscience

The enslavement of Africans was always a problem of conscience for some European Americans. It was hard for many people to justify being Christian while allowing the enslavement of their fellow human beings. Enslavement was also in direct contradiction to Thomas Jefferson's declaration that "all men are created equal, that they are endowed by their Creator with certain unalienable Rights that among these are Life, Liberty, and the Pursuit of Happiness." Even the people who signed the Declaration of Independence acknowledged that slavery was a moral issue. This is demonstrated by the fact that the original Declaration of Independence contained a clause blaming the king of England for starting slavery. Although the colonists decided to remove that clause from the final version of the Declaration, several important colonial leaders went on record in opposition of the practice. Two of them, Thomas Paine and James Otis, asked that the enslavement of Africans be discontinued under the newly formed government.

William Still (1821–1902)

William Still is sometimes viewed as the father of the Underground Railroad. He was born in New Jersey in 1821 to Levin and Charity Still, who were former slaves. He was one of 18 children. William's father, Levin, moved to New Jersey after he bought his own freedom. William's mother, Charity, managed to escape from her slaveowner to join her husband. Still left home when he was twenty and in 1844 went to Philadelphia. He got a clerk's job at the Pennsylvania Anti-Slavery Society in Philadelphia in 1847.

Still later served as the secretary of the Philadelphia Vigilance Committee. This committee helped fugitive slaves find shelter on their way to safe places in the North or Canada. Still kept careful records of his secret activities. He often hid fugitives in his home. He published a book, in 1872, called *The Underground Railroad*, which detailed all these activities.

The Great Compromise

Many colonial government leaders during the late 1700s owned enslaved Africans. Many of these people were also Southerners who greatly depended on the profits made from the system of enslavement. These Southerners needed to maintain control over the enslaved Africans in order to expand their profitable agricultural way of life. It was necessary to reduce Africans to a less-than human status in order to justify continued control over them. These people actively promoted the idea that Africans were less than human, without a culture or history. Slaveholders also attempted to justify enslavement by saying that Africans had no valid religious beliefs. This was the same as saying that they were not Christian.

In 1787, an agreement called the Great Compromise was reached. It is also known as the Three-Fifths Compromise. The compromise was reached because in the newly independent country, each state was allowed representation in the Congress. Then as now, the number of representatives from each state depended on the number of people who lived in the state. How this number was to be determined was greatly debated, because the South had many more people than the North due to the number of enslaved Africans. This agreement, however, allowed Southern plantation owners to count Africans as three-fifths of its population. What this basically did was to reduce the enslaved African to a partial human being, to be counted as three-fifths of a person for the benefit of determining the number of votes in Congress. It was included in the Constitution. In response, William Lloyd Garrison, the abolitionist, remarked that the Constitution was a "pact with the devil."

Free Africans

The Free African Society

During the late 1700s, the majority of free Africans lived in Philadelphia, Pennsylvania. In 1787, free Africans there began a very important organization. Two preachers, Absalom Jones and Richard Allen, along with six others, founded the Free African Society. It followed on the heels of the Declaration of Independence. The organization was designed to serve the African community. It was a mutual aid society that provided aid to the jobless, the sick, and the widowed. It was the first of its kind to attempt to empower African people and address the economic, political, social, and educational needs of its members. The Free African Society and others like it supported the struggle of abolitionist societies. The Society eventually split into two groups. The larger number of members followed Absalom Jones and the others followed Richard Allen. This set the stage for the next development for free Africans.

Several other religious movements began after the founding of the Society. This was the establishment of the African church. Initially, Absalom Jones joined the White Episcopal Church. Richard Allen, on the other hand, saw much discrimination against the African members of the White church. He began an independent church called the African Methodist Episcopal Church. Absalom Jones, too, found resistance to Africans worshipping with Whites. In 1795, two years after Richard Allen founded his church, Jones founded the African Methodist Episcopal Zion Church.

Following the example set by the Society, other preachers established independent African churches. Initially, these churches were started because free Africans were not allowed to worship with European Americans. Soon, churches began to be a major focal point in the lives of free Africans. Various organizations, including churches, all provided a safe haven for free Africans and became the centers for many social and political activities.

Prince Hall—Portrait of Prince Hall from the Grand Lodge of British Columbia and Yukon, artist and date unknown. (*Image is public domain and available through Wikimedia Commons.* https://www.historyisfun.org/learn/learning-center/prince-hall/)

Another segment of the movement for Africans was the establishment of fraternal organizations. Two of these were the Odd Fellows and the Knights of Pythias. Another organization was the Masonic Lodge, started by Prince Hall. Again, the churches and the fraternal organizations provided a way for Africans to help each other.

The fourth part of the movement was the establishment of schools. As previously stated, Prince Hall established a school for African children in Boston. Richard Allen started a school in Philadelphia. Groups such as the Quakers also supported these activities and established a school in

Philadelphia. A group called the Manumission Society (manumission means freedom from slavery) established schools in New York City.

The Quality of Life

During the various uprisings in the South by Nat Turner and others, free Africans who lived in the North were concerned with the racist caste system in which they lived. During the 18th and 19th centuries, free Africans were forced to live under terrible conditions. Although these Africans were free, living conditions were not much better for them than for those who were enslaved. The caste system was a means of directing unfair discrimination and prejudice against Africans. It prevented free Africans from getting jobs and from living in decent housing, which resulted in a very poor quality of life.

Free Africans were always conscious of conditions around them. They knew they were subject to being enslaved again, especially if they could not produce papers stating they were free. So, the threat of re-enslavement was ever present. A prime example of the threat that free African Americans faced was the case of Solomon Northrup, who was actually born in New York and was free. Northup was on a visit to Washington, D.C. but he was kidnapped, taken to Louisiana and sold into slavery. His story is documented in his autobiography, "Twelve Years a Slave." He was able to get his freedom after he managed to get a letter to friends in the North. It was a very precarious situation if you lived in states close to the South and were free. It was common practice to kidnap free African Americans and sell them into slavery, especially if one was not carrying the proper documentation. In the case of Northup, he writes in his autobiography that he was drugged, and both his money and free papers were stolen from him. So, as can be seen, there was no real assurance of not being sold into slavery even for free Africans.

Hostility against free Africans also increased in the 1800s. Laws were passed that took away the right to vote. These laws also prohibited free Africans from gathering in groups, traveling without permission, or carrying arms. One could compare these laws to those of apartheid, which were dismantled in South Africa in the 20th century.

Early Repatriation

Bennett refers to African people who, despite the adversities of enslavement and cruel treatment, were able to accomplish great things. He calls them Black pioneers. One of these people was Paul Cuffee, who lived in the early 1800s. He was a ship builder in Massachusetts and owned one ship and several smaller vessels. Cuffee made many voyages to Europe and other countries. When some Africans felt that the only solution to the problems, they faced in America was to immigrate to Africa, he was contacted to take them to Sierra Leone. Another was James Forten, a sail maker. He made a device to handle sails. He became one of the major sail makers of that period and became very wealthy.

The Question of Emigration and Seeking a Better Life

Many free Africans felt that the only solution to the situation they were in was to emigrate or go back to Africa. They felt that was the only way to get the quality of life that they wanted. Free Africans in Massachusetts petitioned the state for help in emigrating to Africa in 1773. Prince Hall and 75 others filed a similar petition in Boston in 1787.

In 1815, Paul Cuffee and 38 other free Africans emigrated to Sierra Leone, West Africa. Some European Americans agreed with the idea of the resettlement of Africans to Africa. Some Whites became alarmed at the growing numbers of both free and enslaved Africans. They were also uneasy with the growing racial tensions. These Whites formed the American Colonization Society and wanted to resettle Africans in Liberia, West Africa. However, many of those in the Society were slaveholders who wanted to continue the enslavement of Africans. Many free Africans looked upon the motives of the Society with suspicion. They felt that this group wanted only to deport those free educated Africans, who were outspoken and troublesome to them, and keep only those Africans they could control. Richard Allen and James Forten, who had originally supported Paul Cuffee and his back-to-Africa movement, reversed their opinions and spoke against the American colonization group.

Some free Africans still argued for emigration to other places, such as Haiti and Canada, but on their own terms. Henry Highland Garnet, a preacher, and Dr. Martin Delany, a commissioned officer in the Civil War, were two people who kept the idea of emigration alive. Delany spoke out firmly against racism. He urged the use of force when necessary to defend one's rights. He not only suggested that African Americans move to Africa as a solution to the problem of slavery, but in 1859 he actually went to the continent in search of a suitable place for resettlement. He pressed for the idea of Black Nationalism right up until the beginning of the Civil War, when he entered the Union Army. He visited President Lincoln during the Civil War to offer his plan for an army unit of African American officers and men. Lincoln was so impressed that he appointed Delany as the first African American major in the U.S. Army.

Some free Africans did emigrate to other places, such as Canada and England. Most free Africans never intended to emigrate to Africa or anywhere else. However, the poor treatment of free Africans, who were prevented from earning a decent living and participating fully in American society, kept the discussion alive. Through it all, Africans remained steadfast that their plight would someday end. They participated in the various wars and conflicts fought in America.

Summary

There was the rise of many freedom fighters, both men and women, during the 17th, 18th and 19th centuries. The struggle for freedom took two forms, passive resistance or violence. Africans either participated in rebellions or engaged in other acts of sabotage against the plantation owners. Some resisted by running away. Other enslaved Africans bought their freedom, only to have it taken away in other ways. Sympathetic European Americans assisted Africans in the struggle and were ready to die for their beliefs. The abolitionist movement took hold, as did the efforts of such people as Frederick Douglass and the African women in California who led the liberation struggle.

During the late 1700s, self-help organizations and churches were established to improve the conditions of free Africans, and schools and fraternal organizations were founded. There were even ideas and plans for free Africans to emigrate to other countries because of poor treatment and sanctions that did not allow them to participate fully in American society. Still most Africans were determined to stay. Many even participated in the war for independence from England and in subsequent wars. The next chapter will address African participation in the colonial period of wars of America and the fights for freedom.

References

"American Woman Suffrage Association." *The Reader's Companion to American History.* Accessed August 29, 2004. http://college.hmco.com/history/readerscomp/rcah/html/ah_003700_americanwoma.htm

Appiah, K., & Gates, H. L. (Eds.). (1999). *Africana: The encyclopedia of African and African American experiences.* Basic Civitas.

Asante, M. K. (2001). *African American history: A journey of liberation.* Peoples Publishing Group, Inc.

Bennett, L., Jr. (1993). *Before the Mayflower: A history of Black America.* 6th edition. Penguin Books.

Brenton, F. *African Colonization Society.* BlackPast. Accessed 2018. https://blackpast.org/aah/american-colonization-society-1816-1964

Franklin, J. H., & Moss, A. A., Jr. (2000). *From slavery to freedom: A history of African Americans.* Knopf.

Katz, W. L. (1993). *The Black West.* Open Hand Publishing Inc.

Katz, W. L. (1974). *Eyewitness: The Negro in American history.* Pitman Learning, Inc.

Louisiana Purchase. http://gatewayno.com/history/LaPurchase.html

Maroons of the Blue Mountains. (2001, February 25). *Newsday Historical Digest.* http://www.nalis.gov.tt/Communities/MaroonsofJamaica.htm

PBS. *American Colonization Society.* PBS. Accessed 2018. https://www.pbs.org/wgbh/aia/part3/3p1521.html

Risjord, N. (1986). *History of the American people.* Holt, Rinehart and Winston, 1986.

Trotter, J. W. (2001). *The African American experience*, Volume I and II. Houghton Mifflin.

Choosing Sides in America's Early Wars

From the beginning, Africans played an important role in the armed conflicts in America. The colonial militia called many of them into service, and others defended the frontier settlements against Native American attacks. During the period 1775–1898, Africans fought in every war or battle, from the Revolutionary War of 1775 to the Spanish-American War of 1898. Both free and enslaved Africans fought. Free Africans chose to believe in the Declaration of Independence by fighting. Many also hoped that their situations would improve.

But why would enslaved Africans fight? A very powerful reason was the chance for freedom. During the Revolutionary War, the British promised freedom to enslaved Africans if they joined them. This turned many enslaved Africans against their colonial masters. Other enslaved Africans felt that fighting for the American colonies would also entitle them to freedom.

Many enslaved Africans joined with the British forces in the war against the colonies. At the end of the war, many of these Africans left for England aboard ships as free men. Others went to Canada, the Caribbean, or back to Africa.

Still others joined the Continental Army of the colonies.

CHAPTER 5
The Revolutionary War

Africans were part of the colonial struggle for independence. The major reason for the Revolutionary War was the increasing dissatisfaction of the colonists with the way in which England was governing them. They were especially displeased about the high taxes they had to pay for items imported from England. The colonists were also displeased that they were taxed but had no representation in the British Parliament. A number of conflicts broke out between the colonists and the British authorities that governed the colonies.

One of these conflicts was in 1770 on the docks of Boston, Massachusetts. A confrontation occurred between a group of African and White colonists and some British soldiers. When the group of colonists backed down, Crispus Attucks led the advance. This encouraged colonists to join him. On that fateful night, in the confusion and screaming, a stick was thrown and then a shot was fired. An African man and former slave, Crispus Attucks, was hit. He was the first person to die in what came to be known as the Boston Massacre. Attucks was buried in the Park Street cemetery along with other honored dead, all victims of the massacre.

In 1775, the colonists rebelled and declared themselves free from British rule and the Revolutionary War began. Africans fought against the British in the first battle of the Revolutionary War, at Bunker Hill in June of 1775. Salem Poor, Cuff Hayes, and Peter Salem were among those African patriots who fought in the battle of Bunker Hill. Salem Poor was singled out for special commendation for bravery. Africans served with Ethan Allen at the battle of Fort Ticonderoga in 1775 and with the Green Mountain Boys, a citizens' militia from Vermont.

In spite of their enslaved status and the mistreatment they suffered, many Africans fought on the side of the colonists against the British. Approximately 5,000 Africans fought in the Revolutionary War. Some were free, but most were enslaved. At first the slaveholders attempted to keep the Africans out of the war because slaveholders feared that the Africans would try to escape. Those in authority also argued that White soldiers would not be willing to fight alongside Blacks, or that Blacks were cowards and would not fight. Even so, Lord Dunmore, the governor of Virginia, had begun to recruit Africans. He promised them freedom if they deserted the colonists and joined the British. Some 15,000 to 20,000 Africans fought with the British. Faced with the recruitment of the Africans by the British, the colonists decided to recruit Africans also.

The American colonists, for their part, found it difficult to get enough recruits for the Continental Army. Many of the colonists who were recruited deserted. When George Washington took over the army, he prohibited Africans from enlisting. But some states had begun to recruit free Africans. Then, when Lord Dunmore began to recruit Africans, Washington reversed his earlier policy and allowed free Africans to enlist, especially those who had fought in earlier battles. Finally, after the battle at Valley Forge, where 3,000 White soldiers deserted, he welcomed both enslaved and free Africans.

The Africans, for their part, felt that fighting for the freedom of the American colonies would entitle them to freedom, but it didn't. Those Africans who had fought with the British, however, decided to ensure their freedom by leaving with the British when the British were defeated. Many of these Africans went to Canada, especially Nova Scotia. Others went to England, the West Indies, or Sierra Leone, West Africa.

The new government created after the Revolutionary War did not address the issue of freedom for all the people who fought for it. Most Africans were still considered property. The reason for this was that many of the southern plantation owners still needed the labor of the Africans to produce profits and continue their way of life.

The War of 1812

It was not long before the newly formed American government would again have disagreements with England. These disagreements centered on the trade restrictions placed on the Americans by the British. One problem was that the Americans did not like the fact that the British would take Africans off slave ships and settle them in other countries. Another problem was the failure of England to abide by the Treaty of Paris, which gave the western frontier to America. The War of 1812 was the result of these disagreements.

In the War of 1812, one out of every six members of the American Navy was an African. Many Africans served with Naval Commodore Matthew Perry. Although he originally doubted the ability of his African recruits, Perry was forced to admit their bravery, after his victory at the Battle of Lake Erie. Approximately 10 percent of the naval fleet was made up of Africans. The war ended in 1814 with the Treaty of Ghent. Yet the new republic still had to deal with the issue of enslavement. There was no easy solution—and the bondage of Africans eventually would lead to the Civil War.

Growing Tensions Between the North and South

There were growing disagreements between the North and the South which focused on control, power, and economics. A major source of irritation between the northern states and the southern states centered on the issue of enslavement.

By the end of the Revolutionary War, most of the northern states were in the process of abolishing slavery. For some Whites the ideals of life, liberty, and the pursuit of happiness, which were expressed in the Declaration of Independence, were in direct opposition to the system of enslavement. How could a nation fight for the freedom of some people and condone the enslavement of others? It was a matter of conscience for many Whites. The abolition of enslavement in the North was also shaped by White and African abolitionists. This emancipation, however, did not necessarily mean equal treatment or freedom for the Africans living in the North.

Another and probably the biggest factor for the abolition of slavery in the North was the change in its economy. During the early colonial period, the economies of the North and South were similar. Both were based on agriculture and trade, and both the North and South profited from the labor and sale of enslaved Africans. After the separation from England, however, the South and the North began to develop new economic bases. In the North, economic development focused on expanding industries, such as shipping and manufacturing. Simultaneously, the North was experiencing waves of immigration from other European countries. This supplied cheap labor for the growing number of factories. The South, however, continued to expand its agricultural base and its dependence on labor of enslaved Africans.

The increasing disparity in the economies and the increasing tensions about enslavement led the government to seek compromises to prevent a major conflict. These compromises were for economic reasons only. The government was interested only in profits and power, not humanity, and each compromise only created a greater sense of hopelessness for enslaved Africans. During this time, various laws were passed to appease both the North and the South.

The Missouri Compromise

The South continued to maintain its position based on the need for forced labor. By the middle of the 19th century, slavery was linked with the issue of states' rights. Each state felt it had the right to manage its own affairs apart from the federal government, especially on the issue of enslavement.

Many compromises, such as the Missouri Compromise, also known as The Compromise of 1820, and The Compromise of 1850, were designed to prevent conflict. The intent of these compromises was to keep the number of free states and slave states equal, so that neither one would gain an advantage over the other. However, plantation owners in the South wanted no threats to enslavement. In fact, they wanted to extend it into the new territories wherever they could. The North, on the other hand, did not want that.

In 1819, Missouri applied for admission to statehood. It sparked a debate as to whether it would be admitted as a free or slave state. It just so happened that there was also a consideration of granting statehood to Maine. The Missouri Compromise provided for Missouri and Maine to become states with the proviso that one came into the Union as a free state and the other as a slave state. It also established a line north of which enslavement would not be allowed. Given the location of Missouri, this violated the Northwest Ordinance of 1787, which prohibited slavery northwest of the Ohio River.

The Compromise of 1850

Then in 1850, the state of California asked to join the Union. Another compromise had to be reached, because California wanted to come in as a free state. The compromise was another attempt to appease both the North and the South and to prevent possible armed conflict. The first part of the agreement stated that California could be free, but there were three other parts to it.

The second part of the Compromise of 1850 provided that two other territories would be created from the western land taken from Mexico. The people who lived there could decide whether to allow slavery or not.

The third part was that enslavement would be allowed in the District of Columbia, but no Africans could be sold there. Runaways, however, had to be returned.

 U.S. Senator William H. Seward (1801–1872)

Seward was a leading figure first in the Whig Party and later in the new Republican Party. He served as state senator (1830–1834) and state governor (1838–1842). Seward was an outspoken abolitionist. He claimed in a speech, in 1850, that if slavery was not abolished America would become embroiled in a civil war.

Seward provided a two-story brick home for Harriet Tubman in Auburn, New York. She later bought the house from Seward for a small amount of money. He was governor of New York State at the time.

The fourth part of the compromise was the Fugitive Slave Law. This law stated that Africans who escaped bondage could be tracked down and returned to their former slave masters. It was a serious setback for enslaved Africans. It also presented a serious threat to free Africans who could be taken away and be enslaved if they could not produce papers or other evidence to prove they were free.

This law also mandated federal marshals to arrest those suspected of being runaway slaves under penalty of a $1000 fine. It was also a setback for the abolitionist movement. Many members of the Methodist Episcopal Church were active in the abolitionist movement. The church officials, however, were reluctant to speak out publicly against enslavement for fear of losing their churches. It caused a splinter in the church, which witnessed the founding of the Wesleyan Methodist Church and the Free Methodists.

The Kansas-Nebraska Act

Slavery continued to be a source of tension between the northern and southern states. Under the previously enacted Missouri Compromise, those territories gained as part of the Louisiana Purchase were designated as free. However, there continued to be debate about them. Finally, in 1854, the Kansas-Nebraska Act was enacted. The Act set up two territories, Kansas and Nebraska. It was left to the people who lived in those territories to decide whether they would be free or allow enslavement. This arrangement flatly contradicted the provisions of the Missouri Compromise.

Dred Scott

Other tensions over the issue of slavery continued to further divide the North and South. One such tension was the U.S. Supreme Court's Dred Scott decision in 1857. Dred Scott was enslaved in Missouri, but he was taken to the free state of Illinois. Scott later sued for his liberty, maintaining that he had become a free man by living on free soil for four years. Scott pursued his fight against the fugitive slave laws all the way to the Supreme Court. The court ruled that Africans had "been considered a subordinate and inferior class of beings" and as property, from the founding of the country. They therefore could not rightfully become citizens of the United States. They had no right to sue any court, state, or the federal government.

The Supreme Court actually declared all anti-slavery laws, such as the Missouri Compromise, to be unconstitutional. This decision, making slavery lawful anywhere in the United States, caused more European Americans in the North to join the anti-slavery movement. Many northerners felt that the Supreme Court decision would have the effect of restoring enslavement to northern states where the practice had previously been outlawed. In the end, none of these laws and compromises could prevent the inevitable, the secession of the South and the start of the Civil War.

Secession of the Southern States

In 1860 Abraham Lincoln was elected president of the United States. It was inevitable that the southern states would secede. Southerners viewed Lincoln as being anti-slavery. A last-minute effort to avert the secession or breaking away of the southern states was introduced by Senator John Crittenden of Kentucky. The Crittenden Compromise, was simply a way of protecting the slaveholders of the South and disenfranchising those Africans in the North who could still vote.

The Crittenden proposition introduced a number of constitutional amendments designed to protect enslavement. The bill was defeated, but it did not make any difference, because the South was intent on secession, especially when Lincoln was elected. Southern slaveholders viewed Lincoln and the Republican Party as a threat to their plans to expand enslavement.

Several months before Lincoln was sworn in, South Carolina seceded. Virginia, North Carolina, and Tennessee followed and formed the Confederacy. Other southern states followed in quick succession. When Lincoln sent supplies to Fort Sumter, South Carolina, in 1861, it was considered a threat. The fort was fired upon and the Civil War began.

The country had been bitterly divided on the issue of slavery, and a number of compromises such as the Missouri Compromise, the Compromise of 1850, and others did not stop the South from doing what it intended all along. The southern landowners were determined to keep Africans in bondage even at the cost of splitting the Nation.

The Civil War

Contrary to what many texts and sources would have us believe, the Civil War was not fought to free enslaved Africans. The war was fought to save the Union. To be sure, there was concern over the issue of enslavement by the southern states. Southern states wanted to keep their economic way of life, and they had threatened to secede on several other occasions. They were concerned with states' rights. They wanted to run their affairs unhampered by the federal government.

Lincoln, for his part, viewed slavery as morally wrong but felt also that Africans were inferior to White people. He also held the view that White people would accept abolition of slavery if Africans were removed from the country. But his main concern was in keeping the southern states from leaving the Union. He said that would not interfere with slavery where it existed. Lincoln stated the following in a 1859 speech in Cincinnati, Ohio.

> I think Slavery is wrong, morally, and politically. I desire that it should be no further spread in these United States, and I should not object if it should gradually terminate in the whole Union. I say that we must not interfere with the institution of slavery in the states where it exists, because the constitution forbids it, and the general welfare does not require us to do so. We must prevent the revival of the African slave trade and the enacting by Congress of a territorial slave code.

However, Lincoln also stated in the Lincoln–Douglas Debate in Ottawa, Illinois, on August 21, 1858, the following:

> I will say here, while upon this subject, that I have no purpose, either directly or indirectly, to interfere with the institution of slavery in the States where it exists. I believe I have no lawful right to do so, and I have no inclination to do so. I have no purpose to introduce political and social equality between the white and the black races. There is a physical difference between the two, which, in my

judgment, will probably forever forbid their living together upon the footing of perfect equality; and inasmuch as it becomes a necessity that there must be a difference, I, as well as Judge Douglas, am in favor of the race to which I belong having the superior position.

So, as is indicated, Lincoln had mixed feelings about the question of slavery.

Africans Volunteer

Africans were eager to fight for freedom. Lincoln, however, refused to let even free Africans enlist. This was not supposed to be a war to abolish slavery but to save the Union. In addition, Lincoln was afraid that the border states of Missouri, Kentucky, Delaware, and Maryland that held enslaved Africans would also secede if he allowed Africans to join the army. Many Whites, including northerners, felt that Africans should not be allowed to fight. They felt it might cause White soldiers to desert because many Whites did not want to fight alongside Africans. Some Whites felt that Africans might fight savagely or were too timid to fight. Many Whites seemed to have forgotten about those Africans who had fought valiantly in the Revolutionary War and the War of 1812. Africans from the North volunteered to join the Union Army, but they were rejected.

This did not stop them, however. Many Africans formed training camps and prepared themselves to go to war anyway. One of these was the 54th Massachusetts Volunteers, who were featured in the 1989 movie *Glory*. They fought bravely at the Battle of Fort Wagner in Charleston, South Carolina.

Africans worked as laborers, nurses, scouts, and spies before they were allowed to enlist. One of the most famous spies and military scouts was Harriet Tubman. She was issued a pass that allowed her to travel in the war areas. Tubman organized intelligence networks and led scouting parties for the Union troops. Her way of dressing led Whites to think that she was a "mammy." The mammy image is a stereotype—a false perception of someone or some group. To Whites, a mammy was a docile, enslaved woman who worked in the "big house" and was entrusted with the masters' children and household. Because a mammy was not perceived as a threat, this was the perfect disguise for Tubman, and she was successful as a spy.

Another important figure in the Civil War was Sojourner Truth. She moved from Michigan to Washington, D.C., to help former slaves and served as a nurse to wounded soldiers. Truth also helped form an organization to aid former enslaved Africans who went to the Washington, D.C., area during the war.

Africans in the Union Army

The Civil War did not end as quickly as the Union forces thought it would, and it was not going well for the North. Lincoln had to rethink his policy. In July 1862, Congress passed a law that finally allowed free Africans to enlist. The Union Army recruited 90,000 Africans in the South. In all, about 180,000 Africans joined the Union Army and another 29,000 enlisted in the Union Navy. They were forced to serve in segregated units, but the African soldiers proved to be outstanding. Some members of Congress began to change their minds about excluding them from the army. African soldiers were especially helpful toward the end of the war, when northern troops invaded the South. President Lincoln admitted that the Civil War could not have been won without the help of the Africans.

Fugitive Africans who had escaped from the South also wanted to join. But Lincoln refused to allow them to enlist and even ordered them returned to their masters. In spite of this, some generals recruited Africans from the South.

Africans in the Union Navy

Unlike in the Union Army, Africans were not prevented from joining the Union Navy. They made up the support staff as cooks and dishwashers but also distinguished themselves in battle. Black sailors served on the Union ship *The Monitor* and other Union vessels, where eventually the rank of seaman was opened to them by the Navy. Eventually, many Whites who thought that Africans could not fight or provide valuable service changed their minds. In fact 25 percent of the naval forces were made up of Blacks according to Bennett (1982).

In 1862, an African troop, led by Robert Smalls, captured *The Planter*, a Confederate gunboat. Smalls sailed it to Union lines. Later, during the period called Reconstruction, he became a representative in the South Carolina legislature.

The Monitor was one of the most famous northern ironclad ships of the Civil War. It also had a multiethnic crew. Pictured here is the crew on deck of *The Monitor*. An African American is in the foreground.

The Emancipation Proclamation

In July 1862, Abraham Lincoln drafted the Emancipation Proclamation, but it was not issued until the following year. Members of Congress wanted to wait until a large battle had been won before the document was issued. They did not want to appear weak and in need of help from Africans in order to win the war.

The Union won the Battle of Antietam in Maryland in September 1862. Lincoln warned that he would free all enslaved Africans on January 1, 1863, in all states in rebellion against the government. The proclamation did not free Africans who lived in the border states of Delaware, Kentucky, Maryland, or Missouri but only those in the states that had seceded. One might say that it did not free them, either, because the plantation owners did not recognize Lincoln's authority. Still, it allowed enslaved Africans to enter the Union Army and Navy.

Discrimination in the Union's Armed Forces

African soldiers were paid less than White soldiers were, and many were not paid at all. Finally, after protests by African soldiers, a law was passed in

1864 that gave African soldiers the same pay, equipment, arms, and health care. Still, discrimination persisted. White officers mistreated Africans in the racially segregated units. Promotions were restricted. African soldiers were also responsible for the major part of the work duty. This meant that they spent more time hauling logs, loading ammunition, or digging ditches than White soldiers did.

By the end of the Civil War, more than 600,000 Union soldiers had died. Africans played a major part in the war and 16 received the Congressional Medal of Honor.

Jubilee at Last

The end of the Civil War signaled a new beginning for the newly freed Africans. Word of the outcome of the war and the new status of Africans spread unevenly across the country, though. The news of the Emancipation Proclamation did not reach Texas until June 19, 1865—two and a half years after it had been signed. Still, it was a great day, a day for jubilation. Africans in Texas celebrated the abolition of slavery, the first real celebration of its kind, and coined the term "Juneteenth," a combination of the date and month of the news. This is the origin of the current tradition of Juneteenth, an event that is celebrated all over the country. The largest Juneteenth celebration is held in Houston, Texas. Some other large celebrations are held in Milwaukee, Wisconsin; Minneapolis, Minnesota; and Buffalo, New York.

The Spanish-American War

Just before the turn of the century, the American government found itself at war again. The Spanish-American War of 1898 started because the battleship *Maine* was sunk in the harbor of Havana, Cuba. At the time, Cuban rebels were in armed conflict with Spain, who still ruled them. The ship was there to protect American interests.

To this day, no one can say exactly what happened. The mishandling of explosives aboard the ship could have just as easily been the cause of the explosion. The United States, however, used the loss of American lives as the reason to invade Cuba and participate in the conflict between Cuba and Spain. The U.S. government saw an opportunity to continue its policy of Manifest Destiny, which was intended to extend its power and influence.

Robert Smalls (1839-1916)

Smalls was born enslaved in Beaufort, South Carolina. He made a daring escape at the beginning of the Civil War. He had become the pilot of the Confederate transport steamer, *The Planter*. Smalls managed to smuggle his wife and three children aboard the ship, which he then sailed past the other Confederate ships and out to sea. He, with his crew of 12 enslaved Africans, raised a flag of truce and delivered the ship to the commanding officer of the Union fleet.

Lincoln rewarded Smalls by giving him official command of the ship, *The Planter*. He was also made a captain in the U.S. Navy, a position he held throughout the war. Smalls returned to South Carolina after the Civil War and served in the Carolina Senate from 1868 to 1870. He was elected to the U.S. Congress in 1875 where he served for five terms. Smalls fought for equal travel accommodations for African Americans and for the civil and legal protection of children of mixed parentage.

Many African Americans had mixed feelings about joining the Spanish-American War, particularly when it shifted to the Philippines. Yet African American soldiers once again went into battle. Many of those who served in the war were the Buffalo Soldiers from the 9th and 10th Calvary, African American soldiers who, years before, had protected White settlers in the West. They fought at the battle of San Juan Hill along with Teddy Roosevelt and the Rough Riders. But, the extent to which the soldiers saved the battle and even the lives of White soldiers was not told.

The Congressional Medal of Honor was awarded to four African Americans from the 10th Cavalry of the army after the Spanish-American War. When the honorees returned to civilian life, however, they did not receive the same recognition and respect that was given European American military heroes.

Summary

During the first 100 years, slavery and race relations were central themes in America. The issue of enslavement had always been a dilemma for the founding fathers. James Otis and Thomas Payne denounced slavery during the writing of the Declaration of Independence. The first draft of the

Declaration of Independence even had a clause in it that blamed the king of England for starting the institution of enslavement. Even though the clause was removed from the final document, it showed how uneasy many European Americans felt about the issue. Many of them found it a matter of conscience during the Revolutionary War, when they were fighting for their freedom from England.

The issue of enslavement, however, continued to be a major issue in the affairs of the newly formed United States. The enslavement of Africans caused tensions and conflict. It caused struggles between the North and the South. These conflicts finally erupted into the Civil War.

African people fought in every war and practically every battle of the United States. They chose sides depending on who promised them freedom. Many enslaved Africans chose to fight on the side of the colonists, hoping for freedom in the country whose economic basis was built on their sweat and unpaid labor. Other enslaved Africans, however, were uncertain of what would happen to them and decided to take the freedom that the English offered. These Africans started new lives in places such as Nova Scotia, Canada, and in Sierra Leone and Liberia, West Africa. Others went to England.

In all of the wars, Africans had to continually prove that they were as capable, if not more so, as White colonists. In the end, Africans got their freedom not because of moral reasons but economic ones.

Once, however, enslaved Africans got their freedom there needed to be some way for them to make a living. They had a poor existence while enslaved, but upon receiving their freedom, they needed food, housing and a way to make a living. Little thought was given to this just prior to the Civil War. The next chapter will address the new conditions facing the newly freed Africans.

References

African-American baseline essays. Portland Public Schools, 1987.
Appiah, K., & Gates, H. L. (Eds.). (1999). *Africana: The encyclopedia of African and African American experiences.* Basic Civitas.
Asante, M. K. (1993). *The Afrocentric idea.* Revised and expanded edition. Temple University Press.
Asante, M. K. (1993). *Historical and cultural atlas of African Americans.* Macmillan Publishing.

Asante, M. K. (2001). *African American history: A journey of liberation.* Peoples Publishing Group, Inc.

Bennett, L., Jr. (1993). *Before the Mayflower: A history of Black America.* 6th edition. Penguin Books.

Franklin, J. H., & Moss, A. A., Jr. (2000). *From slavery to freedom: A history of African Americans.* Knopf.

Gates, H. L., Jr., & Higginbotham, E. B. (Eds.). (2004). *African American lives.* Oxford University Press.

Hine, D. C. (Ed.). (2005). *Black women in America.* 2nd edition. Oxford University Press.

Shujaa, M. J., & Shujaa, K. J. (Eds.). (2015). *The Sage encyclopedia of African cultural heritage in North America.* 1st Edition. Sage Publications.

Trotter, J. W. (2001). *The African American experience,* Volume I and II. Houghton Mifflin.

Review

I. Checking What You Have Read

1. What was the Free African Society?
2. Where was resistance to enslavement the greatest in Latin America?
3. What did Joseph Cinque order the two *Amistad* crewmen whose lives he spared to do?
4. What happened to the Africans from the *Amistad*?
5. By what other name is Joseph Cinque known?
6. There was always resistance to slavery in the Americas. Give three examples of people who resisted their enslaved condition and tell if they were successful.
7. Explain the importance of each of the following in the struggle for freedom:

    Frederick Douglass Prince Hall
    Sojourner Truth   Harriet Tubman
    John Brown   Cornish and Russwurm

8. Who was Toussaint L'Ouverture and why is he important in American history?
9. There were two ways to oppose enslavement. What were they? Give examples of each.
10. What is emigration as opposed to immigration and why did some free Africans favor emigration?
11. What was the main reason for Africans fighting in America's early wars? Explain.
12. Match the battle or conflict with the famous person involved.

    (1) Crispus Attucks   (a) Battle of Lake Erie
    (2) Salem Poor   (b) Bunker Hill
    (3) Mathew Perry   (c) Boston Massacre

13. Who was Dred Scott and why was his case important to the eventual Civil War in the United States?

14. What battle was won just before Lincoln issued the Emancipation Proclamation?
15. Lincoln reversed his decision to not let Africans fight. Why?
16. What did Africans do to assist the military in the Civil War before they could enlist?
17. What was the intent of the Crittenden Compromise?
18. Many people believe that the Emancipation Proclamation immediately freed all enslaved Africans. Explain why this view is incorrect.
19. What was Lincoln's position on Africans and enslavement?
20. How did the celebration of Juneteenth start?
21. Why did the northern states begin to abolish the practice of enslavement after the Revolutionary War?

II. On Your Own

1. Do some research on the Underground Railroad and try to plot a course from a city in North Carolina or Virginia to a city in the North that would have been considered a free state. Describe how enslaved Africans moved from place to place, where they would have stayed, and when they would have traveled.
2. Imagine that you lived during the time of the Nat Turner rebellion, and he has approached you to participate. Explain your thoughts on why you would agree to join him or why you would not.
3. Abolitionists used public speaking, newspapers, and organizations as ways of protesting slavery. If you lived in the 1700s or 1800s, what could you have done to help the abolitionists?
4. Prepare and deliver a speech to your classmates, write a newspaper article, or describe other actions you might take.
5. Do some research on African women who campaigned for human rights and the abolition of slavery. Write a report on what they did to advance the movement.
6. Imagine that you were an enslaved African during the Revolutionary War. Tell which side you would choose to fight with, England or the colonies, and give your reasons.

REVIEW

7. Using classroom or library reference books and materials, investigate the Missouri Compromise.

    (a) What was it?
    (b) How did the North view it? How did the South view it?
    (c) How did it postpone the eventual Civil War?

8. Lake Erie was the site of a great naval battle. Do research on the Battle of Lake Erie. In your research of pictures and accounts of the battle, look for African Americans who served under Commodore Matthew Perry. Make a list of those who received his commendation.

9. The founding of the church for free Africans played a major role in their lives. Find out how the church assisted free Africans then and compare the functions of the early churches with those of today.

Reconstruction

After the Civil War, the Reconstruction (1867–1877) began. The South had been devastated by the war. The property of the plantation owners was confiscated, and the economy of the South was at a standstill. The government enacted the Reconstruction Acts, which divided the southern states into five military districts and prohibited them from voting. Southern Whites harbored much anger and frustration both against the U.S. government, and particularly against the formerly enslaved Africans. Many felt that Africans were inferior to them. People who felt this way were (and still are) called "White supremacists." At this time a decision had to be made about the fate of the newly freed Africans. The issue of how to deal with the southern states that had seceded also had to be addressed.

The Fate of Newly Freed Africans

When the Civil War began, the question of what would happen to Africans in the South if the North won was not an issue for President Lincoln and the Congress. After the Union victory, however, the needs of these newly freed Africans became a reality of major proportions. How would they support themselves since they would no longer be living on their former owners' land?

Various proposals were discussed in Congress. One proposal was to send all Africans back to Africa, but this proposal never really received much support. Still, there was a need to establish some plan to help the Africans living in the Confederate States when the war ended.

Although there had been discussion about sending Africans back to Africa or to Central America, as Lincoln had suggested, there was no big movement to do so. Most Africans were not inclined to go elsewhere after paying such a high price in life and labor in America. Some people did choose to emigrate and went to Sierra Leone. In fact, Paul Cuffe sailed 38 people there. Others, such as James Holly, emigrated to Haiti. Those Africans who went to Haiti, however, returned, frustrated by the economic conditions and differences in culture and language. Another problem that existed was the fact that the Emancipation Proclamation affected only the Africans in bondage in the Confederacy. Africans in the border states that did not secede were still enslaved and Africans were, in general, not yet considered Americans. This situation was changed by amendments to the Constitution.

Reconstruction's Constitutional Amendments

Important constitutional amendments were passed during the period known as Reconstruction (1867–1877). These amendments appeared to provide some hope that Africans might take great steps toward eventual equality. In 1865, the **Thirteenth Amendment** to the Constitution was passed. This amendment outlawed enslavement. However, this did not mean anything to many people. Those people, known as White supremacists, would not accept freedom for the Africans. They used a clause in the Thirteenth Amendment to imprison Africans and make them work on plantations as prisoners. Many southern Whites simply ignored the Thirteenth Amendment and spent their rage about losing their property by physically attacking and killing African people.

In May 1866, a race riot broke out in Memphis, Tennessee, and another followed in New Orleans two months later. Many Africans were killed and others wounded. The attacking southern Whites were angry because they were denied the right to vote as a result of their rebellion against the Union. They attempted to take out their frustration on African men and women.

Amendment XIII

Passed by Congress January 31, 1865. Ratified December 6, 1865.

Note: A portion of Article IV, section 2, of the Constitution was superseded by the 13th amendment.

Section 1.
Neither slavery nor involuntary servitude, except as a punishment for crime whereof the party shall have been duly convicted, shall exist within the United States, or any place subject to their jurisdiction.

Section 2.
Congress shall have power to enforce this article by appropriate legislation.

In 1868, the Fourteenth Amendment was enacted, which made Africans citizens of the United States. It also prohibited states from interfering with any citizen's right to equal protection under the law. The second part of the amendment, however, permitted states to not allow African Americans the right to vote. In addition, Whites found a way to make this law almost meaningless. The Supreme Court ruled that there were two kinds of citizenship, state and federal and that the Fourteenth Amendment referred to federal citizenship only. The court did not define the rights associated with federal citizenship but did say that civil rights come from the states; therefore they were not covered under the amendment.

African Americans soon began to protest for the right to vote. In 1870, the Fifteenth Amendment was ratified. It guaranteed the right to vote for all African American males. Yet when they went to vote, they had to face angry White southerners who attacked them. Later, the Civil Rights Bill of 1875 was enacted, which gave African Americans equal access to public facilities. Although it took a while for Congress to pass, it gave African Americans access to public transportation, accommodations, schools, and churches. But because of the Supreme Court's ruling about federal and state citizenship, states were free to enact "Jim Crow" laws. The name "Jim Crow" came from an African American minstrel song from the 1830s, and the laws by this name, segregated the very facilities that the Civil Rights Bill attempted to make available to African Americans.

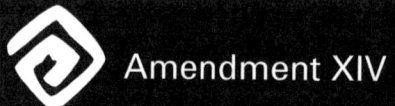

Amendment XIV

Passed by Congress June 13, 1866. Ratified July 9, 1868.

Note: Article I, section 2, of the Constitution was modified by section 2 of the 14th amendment.

Section 1.
All persons born or naturalized in the United States, and subject to the jurisdiction thereof, are citizens of the United States and of the State wherein they reside. No State shall make or enforce any law which shall abridge the privileges or immunities of citizens of the United States; nor shall any State deprive any person of life, liberty, or property, without due process of law; nor deny to any person within its jurisdiction the equal protection of the laws.

Section 2.
Representatives shall be apportioned among the several States according to their respective numbers, counting the whole number of persons in each State, excluding Indians not taxed. But when the right to vote at any election for the choice of electors for President and Vice-President of the United States, Representatives in Congress, the Executive and Judicial officers of a State, or the members of the Legislature thereof, is denied to any of the male inhabitants of such State, being twenty-one years of age, and citizens of the United States, or in any way abridged, except for participation in rebellion, or other crime, the basis of representation therein shall be reduced in the proportion which the number of such male citizens shall bear to the whole number of male citizens twenty-one years of age in such State.

Section 3.
No person shall be a Senator or Representative in Congress, or elector of President and Vice-President, or hold any office, civil or military, under the United States, or under any State, who, having previously taken an oath, as a member of Congress, or as an officer of the United States, or as a member of any State legislature, or as an executive or judicial officer of any State, to support the Constitution of the United States, shall have engaged in insurrection or rebellion against the same, or given aid or comfort to the enemies thereof. But Congress may by a vote of two-thirds of each House remove such disability.

Section 4.
The validity of the public debt of the United States, authorized by law, including debts incurred for payment of pensions and bounties for services in suppressing insurrection or rebellion, shall not be questioned. But neither the United States nor any State shall assume or pay any debt or obligation incurred in aid of insurrection or rebellion against the United States, or any claim for the loss or emancipation of any slave; but all such debts, obligations and claims shall be held illegal and void.

Reconstruction

The Freedmen's Bureau

In 1865, the government established the Freedmen's Bureau as a temporary means of addressing economic and social needs. Its formal name was the Bureau of Refugee, Freedom and Abandoned Lands. For five years, the Bureau assisted both poor African Americans and Whites. The agency did not have a budget, therefore it was limited to the use of funds from the Department of War. This arrangement did not provide enough financial aid. However, while it was in operation, it distributed food and clothing. The Bureau also assisted in locating family members, helped freedmen legalize marriages, and provided other legal representation. It supervised labor contracts and even investigated racial confrontations. The Bureau set up hospitals, and provided medical aid to more than a million freedmen. It also established a variety of schools including day and night schools, industrial schools and colleges. Many of the Black colleges received funding.

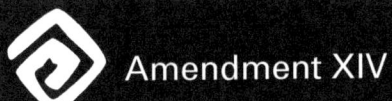

Amendment XIV

Passed by Congress February 26, 1869. Ratified February 3, 1870.

The right of citizens of the United States to vote shall not be denied or abridged by the United States or by any State on account of race, color, or previous condition of servitude—

The first commissioner of the Freedmen's Bureau was Oliver Otis Howard and he set up four divisions. There was Government-Controlled Lands, Records, Financial Affairs, and Medical Affairs. Education was a part of the Records division. The Bureau was also divided into 11 districts that covered the 11 states that had rebelled. The border states of Maryland, Kentucky, West Virginia, and Washington, D.C. were included, and each had an assistant commissioner. John W. Alvord was appointed inspector of schools and later the title was changed to general superintendent of schools for the Freedmen's Bureau. Anderson (1988) writes that Alvord's job was to record the educational activities he found. Alvord was surprised to learn of a system of self-education that had been established prior to the creation of the Bureau. Alvord called these "native schools" and estimated that there were at least

500 schools in operation in 1866, throughout the South. These native schools were what were called "common schools," meaning that they taught basic subjects, such as reading, writing, and arithmetic. There were also Sabbath schools which operated at night or on the weekend which also taught the basic elementary subjects.

According to Anderson (1988) northern missionaries and benevolent societies who came to the South expected to find terrible conditions. In fact they expected to find that the negative effects of slavery would had left African Americans almost "uncivilized." What they found was that not only were African Americans civilized, but that they had set up their own schools. Anderson (1988) goes on the say that Blacks had a strong desire to learn how to read and write, and they wanted to be self-reliant by sustaining and controlling their own schools. Southern Blacks strongly pushed for universal education, or education for all at taxpayer expense. The ex-slaves funded their own schools, and used their labor to build and sustain them. They also organized committees that were responsible for supervising the schools that were founded.

The Freedmen's Bureau funded these schools and the others that it had established with federal funds and by collecting taxes. While African Americans accepted and appreciated funds from the northern philanthropists, Blacks refused to allow anything that would undermine their own self-reliance or allow interference. It was not long before the Bureau withdrew financial aid and schools were left to support themselves as they had always done.

African Americans operated Sabbath schools, which in many cases, were in existence prior to the "native schools" These schools were not included in the reports made by Alvord. Some of the Sabbath schools had sponsorship by church societies, others did not. Anderson (1998) states that in some places in the South the Sabbath schools were the only means for instruction. Sabbath schools continued to grow long after Reconstruction. These types of schools were encouraged by the African Methodist Church (AME) who enrolled thousands of students.

For all of the efforts of the Freedmen's Bureau, however, the greatest need of the freedmen was in finding some way to make a living. Since most of them had been laborers on farms and plantations, they needed their own land on which to work. The Bureau was underfunded, understaffed, and lasted just a few short years after its start.

Forty Acres and a Mule

Thaddeus Stevens, a Pennsylvania Congressman, suggested that African Americans be given "40 acres and a mule." The suggestion was defeated in 1866. The Freedmen's Bureau was only able to distribute a limited amount of land to African Americans in the South because only a limited amount of land was available. Following the war, southern plantation owners, once viewed as the enemy, managed to regain ownership of their land through a presidential pardon. Most of the freed African Americans, however, were now on their own, and the Freedmen's Bureau was not able to meet their massive needs. The only lasting contribution of the Bureau was the establishment of schools. The Freedmen's Bureau was never able to solve the major problem of distributing southern land. This was because, in an effort to appease the former slaveholders of the Southern states, President Andrew Johnson pardoned them and returned their land. Even today, there is a movement by some African Americans for reparations. This movement for reparations is essentially the demand by African Americans for past years of free labor.

The End of Reconstruction

Reconstruction lasted from 1866 until 1877. After the passage of the 13th, 14th, and 15th Amendments, African Americans enjoyed some civil liberties, such as the right to vote. At that time some African Americans were elected to public office. They were also protected from violence by the presence of troops. The presidential election of Rutherford B. Hayes, however, brought a swift end to Reconstruction. Hayes ended Reconstruction and the military oversight of the states that had seceded, in a deal to become President. Hayes had lost the popular vote so he made a deal with the southern Democrats in Congress. So as to not be challenged, he agreed to end Reconstruction quickly as a condition for the presidency. The protections African Americans enjoyed gave way to Black Codes and the rise of the Ku Klux Klan.

Sharecropping: The New Agricultural Slavery

Instead of "40 acres and a mule," African Americans got another option. It was called sharecropping. Sharecropping came into existence partially because of the failure of the Freedmen's Bureau to distribute land to newly freed Africans. In order to support themselves and their families, they only had a few choices. Many did not want to work for their former owners because the owners had little money, so they paid poorly. Therefore, African Americans resorted to sharecropping, which they hoped would provide some economic stability.

Under the sharecropping system, African Americans would farm or otherwise cultivate a portion of landowners' land. The landowner would provide them access to housing, tools, and other supplies they needed. In return, the African American farmers gave half of their harvests to the landowners as a form of payment or rent.

At first, it seemed that sharecropping might work. It started out on a positive note but soon took a turn for the worse. The landowner found ways to keep the African American farmer in perpetual debt. He required that the farmer buy his supplies from him. But the landowner's bookkeeping often was "rigged" so that it always showed the farmer in debt. The debt constantly grew, so the farmer could never make enough to pay it off. The landowner owned all of the supplies and controlled the prices of the items sold. The landowner often used this system to cheat African Americans out of whatever they made. Many African Americans grew weary of this one-sided situation. A great many of them decided to migrate to other places. They migrated to the North but also to the West.

Freedmen and the Move West

Under the Homestead Act of 1865, millions of acres of land were given to Whites who went West. The requirements were that people who wanted land would register with the government and pay a fee of $12.00. It was expected that they would live on the land, build a home, and make improvements. After that had been done, homesteaders could then "prove up." This meant they had to get two of their neighbors to vouch that they had met the requirements. Finally, they had to pay another $6.00 for the total amount of $18.00 to get their official documents.

Most African Americans did not have the money to homestead officially, but that did not stop them. People such as Benjamin "Pap" Singleton and Henry Adams helped to form homestead associations to assist African Americans. Pap Singleton headed the Tennessee Real Estate and Homestead

Association. But African Americans still met with the same unfair discrimination and prejudice that they had experienced in the East. Often when they would arrive in an area, Whites would come and run them off, so they had to pack up and move on.

Nevertheless, thousands of African Americans settled in Kansas, Nebraska, and Oklahoma during 1870s. Encouraged by the Northwest Ordinance of 1787, which prohibited enslavement northwest of the Ohio River, African Americans saw what they thought was a way out of their situation. There was a mass exodus of African Americans in 1789. One of the first of these communities established in the West was in Nicodemus in Kansas. Another community was in Dearfield, Colorado. Others moved on to what was called the "Indian Territory" of Oklahoma and built towns such as Boley and Langston. Sometimes thriving communities were built. One of these was in Tulsa, Oklahoma, which came to be called the "Black Wall Street" of the West in the early 1900s.

The people who traveled west were called "exodusters" because they perceived themselves to be on an exodus from the poor economic conditions, discrimination, and injustices suffered in the South. To be sure, life was not easy in these towns. Most of the time, White homesteaders had taken the best land and African Americans were left with poor land in desolate places. Life was hard, but still they came.

African American Institutions: Building Community

There are two main entities that are the foundation for African American institutions and they are the school/college and the church. Both of these have a significant impact on the African American community in terms of social, economic, political, education, and civil rights. Education—or more specifically, schooling—was important for African Americans from the very first. The term "schooling" is used here to mean activities associated with reading, writing, and mathematics. Shujaa (1994) describes the term "education" as not limited to academics but includes all learning within communities and society in general.

Even when it was prohibited for African Americans to engage in academic studies, such as reading, they found ways to overcome it. During the period of Reconstruction, African Americans began a great campaign to establish churches and schools. African American churches began to push for literacy through Sabbath Schools. This is commonly known today as Sunday Schools. Bible literacy was related to general literacy in early Black churches. African Americans felt that by learning to read, write, and calculate, they would be better able to navigate the economic structure they were in and not find themselves at a disadvantage or cheated out of what they worked for. It was this push for a formal educational system that started the idea of universal schools or state-funded schools. The modern public schools originated from the push of southern African Americans for universal schools. The Freedmen's Bureau helped to establish 4,000 schools but many African Americans started their own. They constructed the school buildings and paid the teachers themselves.

Northern philanthropists, such as Samuel Armstrong, provided money for some of these schools. There was a condition, however. They had to be vocational schools. The schools had to teach a curriculum that would lead to jobs that would not compete with jobs held by White southerners. This discussion about the type of curriculum would eventually spread to colleges and would spark the disagreement between W.E.B. Du Bois and Booker T. Washington known as the "Great Debate."

The earliest colleges were all private. They were built by northern missionaries or by African American churches to which they were attached. According to Benjamin Quarles, an African American historian, the Methodist Episcopal Church started six colleges in the period of 1870 to 1886, and the Colored Methodist Episcopal Church started four colleges between 1875 and 1902.

The Black Church

Black churches started to organize both in the North and the South. The churches in the North were led by Absalom Jones and Richard Allen who started the Free African Society. Allen started an independent African Methodist Episcopal church after he witnessed discrimination in the White church. He was followed by Jones who started the African Methodist Episcopal Zion Church in 1795 before the start of the Civil War. These churches had more independence in Philadelphia and Boston as opposed to the South.

In the South slaves were slow to accept Christianity. Some White Baptist and Methodist preached that every Christian was equal in the sight of God.

Since they also encouraged the African practices of religion, Blacks began to respond. Then there were those preachers who gave a message to both free and slave alike that encouraged the institution of slavery, and for slaves to obey their masters, etc. Slaveholders liked this type of evangelical preaching and even encouraged it. They did not mind that Africans would gather to hear these messages because it was always under White supervision. According to Raboteau (1992) Christianity began to be accepted in the slave community. It should be stated, however, that not all slave-holders believed in enslaved Africans participating in church. Some did not think Black people had souls. These slave holders forbade them from attending church and others felt that the enslaved Africans might get the idea that somehow they were free.

Many Africans, however, did not accept this idea about obedience to masters and developed their own views, which can be documented in the spirituals with their double meanings (Maffy-Kipp, 2001). They formed their own informal and illicit prayer meetings. These types of meetings were forbidden. The only kind of church service that slaves could attend were those organized by the plantation owner or his family. In that way, Whites could oversee what was being discussed. African American preachers (not licensed) had to walk a fine line in order to not cross the boundaries of their conscious and the orders of the master, (Raboteau, 1991). Many enslaved Africans converted to the evangelical religions (Methodist, Baptist).

In any case slaves were only allowed to go to White churches so that they could be controlled. Eventually after the Civil War between 1865 and 1900, Black churches started to grow through the efforts of northern Black church leaders. The Presbyterian White churches, like the Congregational and Episcopal churches, also sent missionaries to the South where they started schools and assisted in the general welfare of Blacks. However, Blacks joined independent Black denominations like the Methodist Episcopal (AME) and the African Methodist Episcopal Zion (AMEZ) churches (Maffy-Kipp, 2001). These churches became the center point of political activism, social and educational outreach, throughout its history especially during the political movement of the Civil Rights era.

Today the Black church has grown in its various denominations. Some feel that the focus has changed and that they have become so big that the outreach to the less fortunate is not there. For example, where is the activism in the schools and the education of young people, or the health issues facing the African American community? This is not to say that there is no attention to the social, economic, and political issues, but there does not seem to be the vigor of the past. The Black church remains an integral and important part of Black communities.

The Founding of Historically Black Colleges and Universities (HBCUs)

Black colleges have been the incubator and repository for Black intellectual thought, research, and politics. Their impact cannot be underestimated in the current and past political, social, and economic climate. African Americans were not allowed to attend colleges or universities with Whites in most of the schools in the South. They had only limited opportunity elsewhere. Their attendance was based on a quota system. HBCUs, however, graduated more than half of all the professionals including doctors, and lawyers. This was the incubator for the middle class that was to follow.

Some of the colleges and universities established were Johnson C. Smith University, Fisk University, Spelman College, Hampton University, Morehouse College, and Bennett College. Others included Benedict College, Bethune-Cookman College, Virginia Union University, and Tuskegee Institute, which was established and run by Booker T. Washington. These schools and others became known as "historically Black colleges." Most of these colleges were established in the South. Howard University was established by the federal government. The colleges in the North, Cheyney University, and Ashmun Institute, which later became Lincoln University, were founded in the 1850s in Pennsylvania. The other HBCU in the North is Wilberforce University in Ohio. The loss of Historically Black Colleges and Universities would represent a threat to the fundamental constructs of Black intellectualism.

The Rise of Black Political Power in the "Old South"

Bennett (1988) states that because of the ten years of the Black Reconstruction (1867–1877) it appeared that African Americans were making, what seemed like, great progress. Because of the 13th, 14th and 15th Amendments, many African Americans were elected to public office. They served as officers of state legislatures. Two of these men, Hiram Revels and Blanche K. Bruce, served in the U.S. Senate representing the state of Mississippi. Revels was selected to fill the seat of Jefferson Davis, who had lost his seat when he became the leader of the Confederacy. Bruce was the only African American to serve a full six years in the Senate. Others were elected to the House of Representatives of the United States. Many of these elected officials were highly educated. By the end of this period, 16 African Americans had served in the Congress, and over 600 served in state legislatures. Many others had served in other offices as secretaries of state, lieutenant generals, or even mayors in smaller towns.

Many southern White leaders, however, began to dismantle the political gains that African Americans had made. They quickly organized to discredit, disenfranchise, and reduce African Americans to a state of near-enslavement. Southern Whites first attacked the newly elected African American politicians. They claimed that they were not intelligent and, worse, that they were mishandling public funds. Many were put out of office.

Terrorist groups such as the Ku Klux Klan, along with other White supremacist groups, had been organized to intimidate, commit violent acts, and otherwise drive African American politicians from office. In the end they succeeded. These terrorists, mainly the Ku Klux Klan, intimidated people and kept them away from the polls. African American politicians were afraid to seek office. In addition, the state legislatures of the South passed laws to keep African Americans from voting. So African Americans had no voice in government.

Although African Americans held political office from 1867 into the early 1900s, African American voters were systematically disenfranchised. Eventually the previous gains in the political process were diminished. Finally, they disappeared completely, as did the right to vote.

The Party of Lincoln

Much of the opportunity for African Americans to rise to governmental positions was through the cooperative efforts of African Americans and the Republican Party. The Party had been established because of the division among political groups on the issue of enslavement and the distribution of land. The Kansas-Nebraska Act had the possibility of extending enslavement, depending on whether the people in the new territories decided to allow it. The Republican Party represented the interests of northern abolitionists. The abolitionists merged the two issues of free land, and the prevention of the spread of enslavement. In the period of Reconstruction, organizations were established that supported African American candidates for political office. All of this political activism helped African Americans gain considerable power in the state legislatures and in the Congress in South Carolina, Mississippi, and Louisiana during Reconstruction.

The Fall of Black Political Power and Jim Crow

Black Codes

By the late 1870s, there was a backlash against African Americans. Although they had gained the right to vote, many Whites ignored that fact. Southern states enacted laws as early as 1865 that discriminated against African Americans. New laws, known as Black Codes, replaced the old slave codes. They prevented African Americans from owning guns or city property. African Americans also could not testify in court and they could be arrested for "insulting" Whites. In many states, special rules prevented African Americans from voting.

The poll tax was a way to exclude all African Americans and poor Whites from exercising their right to vote. The poll tax required a payment that was usually more than the poor could afford. Literacy provisions required that would-be voters read a certain passage before being allowed to vote. The "grandfather clause" was a section of some voting laws that stated that anyone who was able to vote in 1867 or was descended from someone who voted in 1867 did not have to pay the poll tax or pass the literacy test. Since African Americans did not gain the right to vote until 1870, this clause reinforced their non-voting status.

African Americans referred to these laws, or other practices that discriminated against them, as Jim Crow laws. This term came to symbolize the legal segregation of African Americans from Whites in everyday life. Jim Crow laws became a way of life in the South and remained until the Civil Rights Movement of the 1960s.

Ku Klux Klan and White Supremacists

In 1866, Confederate general Nathan Bedford Forrest met with other Confederate soldiers and formed the Ku Klux Klan. This occurred in Pulaski, Tennessee. This terrorist group and other hate groups, such as the Knights of the White Camellia and the White Brotherhood, were organized based on hatred toward certain ethnic and religious groups. They wore masks and carried out acts of violence against African Americans and Whites who opposed the Jim Crow laws. In many cases, members of these terrorist groups would run people off their land, so members of the group could take the crops. They burned homes and murdered many people. The main targets of the Ku Klux Klan's activities were African American teachers, elected officials, and successful farmers.

The Repression of Constitutional Rights

The U.S. government did not oppose these attacks by the Ku Klux Klan, which violated the 13th, 14th, and 15th Amendments to the Constitution. Southern states and local governments eventually passed laws that resulted in home rule. African Americans in those states were no longer under U.S. military protection, and African Americans soon lost the right to vote. Lynching, or hanging, became a common act of terrorism against African Americans who sought to exercise their citizenship rights. By the late 1800s, public sentiment turned against the Ku Klux Klan because of its excessive violence. Unfortunately, this group did not cease to exist. By the 1920s, the Ku Klux Klan emerged as a national terrorist organization. The Klan still exists in many areas of the United States, as well as other racial hate groups as part of the far Alt-right.

Freedom and New Achievements in Post-Civil War America

Despite the racism, prejudice, and injustices that African Americans endured, their creative genius could not be suppressed. Several people distinguished themselves by inventing devices that improved the quality of life. One of these persons was Howard Lewis Latimer (1848–1927), who was in the Navy during the Civil War. He began to work with Alexander Graham Bell in 1876 and drew all the plans for the first telephone. Latimer later worked with Thomas Edison. He invented the carbon filament for the light bulb that enabled it to burn for a long time. This made light bulbs affordable and practical for home use. Latimer improved on the incandescent light that was invented by Thomas Edison in 1874.

George Washington Carver (1864–1943) went to Tuskegee Institute, where he became a scientist. Dr. Carver invented hundreds of products using the peanut. His research greatly improved the production of certain crops in the South. Jan Ernst Matzeliger (1853–1889) was an African who had immigrated to America from Dutch Guiana. He went to work in Massachusetts at a shoe factory. It did not take him long to design a machine that would attach the upper part of the shoe to the sole. His invention was called the "shoe lasting machine" that made it possible to produce a greater number of shoes.

Granville T. Woods (1865–1910) invented many electrical devices that he sold to Bell, Edison, and Westinghouse. Many of his inventions were designed for use in the railroad and electrical industries. One of his inventions was a telegraph system that permitted telegraph messages to be sent between moving trains. He also invented the automatic air brake for trains. In 1887, the *American Catholic Tribune* called him the "greatest electrician in the world."

Have you ever heard the term the "real McCoy"? This is a reference to an invention of Elijah McCoy (1844–1929). In 1872, he invented a device that fed oil to parts of machinery while the machine was still running. It was called a lubricating cup. This device was so helpful that people would always ask for the "real McCoy" for trains and other machinery with moving parts.

Madam C. J. Walker (1868–1919) was a pioneer in the development of cosmetics for people of African descent. She was born Sarah Breedlove in Louisiana but grew up in St. Louis. Over time, she experimented with various substances for her hair, and the product she created worked so well she began to sell it. Soon she created other beauty products for African American women and opened several beauty parlors under the name Madam C. J. Walker. She was an accomplished businesswoman and the success of her cosmetics and hair products allowed her to open a bank. It was the first bank ever to be opened by an African American woman. Madam Walker became the first female millionaire in the United States. She gave money for a school in West Africa and contributed to many other charitable causes.

Summary

African Americans have had a long and bitter struggle, first to gain freedom, then to keep it. There was a time under Reconstruction when African Americans played a role in the government of the United States. The passage of amendments to the Constitution began to pave the way for them to make better lives for themselves. But southern Whites were determined to keep African Americans in as much servitude as possible. Even with the new laws, African Americans were not given those rights that were guaranteed under the Constitution, the Amendments to the Constitution, and the Civil Rights Bill of 1875. Their constitutional rights were challenged with the Black Codes, and they were even denied the opportunity to make a decent living or have decent housing. Unfortunately, the U.S. government was a party to this, because it allowed the states to enforce home rule and Black Codes. It allowed hate groups, such as the Ku Klux Klan, to steal from, intimidate, and murder thousands of innocent people.

Despite these circumstances, African Americans were determined to establish schools and universities. They even took the risks of traveling to desolate areas and to Indian Territory to build a better life for themselves away from racism and White supremacy. Although African Americans still faced discrimination and unfair treatment no matter where they went, they did not give up. They made great contributions to the lives of all Americans. The next chapter will highlight some of these pioneers and settlers who traveled West despite adverse circumstances and made their mark on American history.

References

African American records: Freedmen's Bureau. (2016, September 19). National Archives. https://www.archives.gov/research/african-americans/freedmens-bureau

American Reconstruction: People and politics after the Civil War. Accessed 2019. http://www.digitalhistory.uh.edu/exhibits/reconstruction/section2/section2_12.html

America's Story. http://www.americaslibrary.gov/jb/recon/jb_recon_howard_1.html

Anderson, J. D. (1988). *The education of Blacks in the South, 1860–1935.* Later Printing edition. University of North Carolina Press.

Asante, M. K. (1993). *The Afrocentric idea.* Revised and expanded edition. Temple University Press.

Asante, M. K. (1993). *Historical and cultural atlas of African Americans.* Macmillan Publishing.

Asante, M. K. (2001). *African American history: A journey of liberation*. Peoples Publishing Group, Inc..

Bennett, L., Jr. (1993). *Before the Mayflower: A history of Black America*. 6th edition. Penguin Books.

Bridges, R. *Betrayal of the Freedmen: Rutherford B. Hayes and the end of Reconstruction*. Accessed 2018. https://www.rbhayes.org/hayes/betrayal-of-the-freedman-rutherford-b.-hayes-and-the-end-of-reconstruction/

Freemark, S. (2015, August 20). *The history of HBCUs in America*. Accessed 2018. http://www.americanradioworks.org/segments/hbcu-history/

Joseph, P. E. (2015, June 19). Why the Black church has always mattered. *The Root*. Accessed 2018. https://www.theroot.com/why-the-black-church-has-always-mattered-1790860217

Library of Congress. *Reconstruction and its aftermath, African American odyssey*. Accessed 2018. https://memory.loc.gov/ammem/aaohtml/exhibit/aopart5.html

Maffly-Kipp, L. F. (2001, May). *An introduction to the Church in the Southern Black community*. University of North Carolina at Chapel Hill. Accessed 2018. https://docsouth.unc.edu/church/intro.html

Raboteau, A. J. (1992, February). The Secret Religion of the Slaves. *Christian History*, 11(1), 42. EBSCOhost

Shujaa, M. (1994). *Too much schooling, too little education: A paradox of Black life in White societies*. Africa World Press.

Slavery and the making of America: The slave experience: religion. (2004). WNET/Thirteen. Accessed 2018. https://www.thirteen.org/wnet/slavery/experience/religion/history2.html

United States v. Cruikshank, 92 U.S. 542 (1875). Justia Opinion Summary and Annotations. Accessed 2018. https://supreme.justia.com/cases/federal/us/92/542/

The Westward Movement

African American Pioneers

African Americans were involved in the westward expansion of the United States. Some of them were enslaved and others were free. These people had many skills that were necessary for building and surviving in the West. They were explorers, trappers, hunters, and fighters. They helped to protect the people who went to the frontier, and they were especially skilled at establishing friendly relationships with Native Americans.

Explorers

One of these enslaved African Americans, named York, traveled with the Lewis and Clark Expedition (1804–1806). York was very important to the success of this expedition, yet he is a lesser-known figure. He was skilled in fishing, hunting, and swimming. York won the friendship and admiration of the Native Americans he met along the way, which made life much easier for Lewis and Clark. York also assisted the party's young Shoshone guide, Sacajawea, as an interpreter. When the party arrived in Oregon and held a vote to decide where to spend the winter, Sacajawea and York were included.

It was the first time in American history that a woman or a slave had ever been allowed to vote. After the expedition returned, York asked for his freedom. Ten years later, Clark finally gave it to him. Eventually, York became a leader of a Native American community.

Stephen Dorantes or Estevanico ("Little Steven"), as he was also known, was an early explorer. He was born in Morocco and was the enslaved servant of a Spanish owner. In 1528, both he and the slaveowner were part of an expedition to explore the Gulf of Mexico. But most of the men died due to disease, starvation, unfriendly native people, and other misfortunes. Only four people survived.

Estevanico learned the language of the native people easily and was an intermediary for the others. The small party that survived went on to the territory held by Spain at that time, called Mexico. When they finally arrived in Mexico, Estevanico was chosen to lead an expedition through what are now the states of Arizona and New Mexico.

Fur Trappers

Like York, many African Americans rose to positions of leadership among the Native American nations. James Beckwourth (1798–1866) was one of them. He had many skills. Beckworth was a fur trapper, army scout, and was skilled with guns and knives. Those talents were essential for protection in the Wild West. By far Beckwourth's greatest accomplishment was the discovery of a mountain pass through the Rocky Mountains. The pass made it much easier and quicker to get to California. The pass was named after him, although that information is usually not included in textbooks. He also became a leader of the Crow Nation.

Jean Baptiste Du Sable, a trapper and fur trader, is considered to be the founder of Chicago. He was born in Haiti to an enslaved African mother and European father. After his mother's death, his father took him to France to be educated. Du Sable worked on his father's ships until he was shipwrecked near New Orleans. Du Sable traveled west in 1765 and began to build businesses which he established on the Chicago River.

Cowboys

Most people know about White cowboys of the West, who herded cattle and who were excellent horsemen and, sometimes, gunfighters. Few people, however, know about Black cowboys. There were African American cowboys who rode the same trails with White cowboys and who participated in the same rodeos, shows, and contests.

Some of these cowboys became famous. Nat Love was one of them. He reportedly got the name "Deadwood Dick" after a performance in Deadwood, South Dakota, where he won contests for roping and shooting.

Another of these cowboys was Bill Pickett. He invented the rodeo act of "bulldogging," the act of wrestling a bull down to the ground by twisting its horns. He became so famous for it that it was featured in Buffalo Bill's Wild West Show. There is a bronze monument dedicated to Pickett in Fort Worth, Texas.

Nat Love was born into enslavement in 1854. When his family was freed, he went out west to find work as a cowhand. He became very skilled. Love won a contest for his roping and shooting skills in a town named Deadwood, South Dakota. From that time on, he used the name "Deadwood Dick."

African American Women in the West

Women were also present in the West and some were almost as famous as the men. One of these women was Mary Fields. She was as rough and tough as any man. At that time, the only way to get mail to the West was by stagecoach or pony express. Fields got a job with the U.S. postal service as a stagecoach driver and had the distinction of being the first Black woman to ever carry the U.S. mail. She opened a laundry a few years after leaving the mail delivery business in Cascade, Montana.

Elvira Conley was another woman who lived in the rough times of the early West. She lived in Sheridan, Kansas, a railroad town without much law and order. Conley managed to make a living for herself by opening up a laundry. It is said that two of her best customers were Wild Bill Hickok, who was a scout for the army, and Buffalo Bill. William Loren Katz's book, *The Black West*, is full of stories about African Americans in the West.

Buffalo Soldiers

After the Civil War, many African Americans were sent West as part of the U.S. Army. The government's policies and unfair treatment of the Native Americans caused much conflict, especially when it allowed White settlers to claim their land. The U.S. Congress authorized the organization of the 9th and 10th Cavalries in 1866, and the 24th and 25th Infantries were organized in 1869. These four units, made up of African Americans, were formed to keep the peace in the West.

These four military units became known as Buffalo Soldiers, a name they got from the Native Americans whom they encountered. Historians are not sure if they got this name because of their hair or because of the buffalo skin covering that they used. Buffalo Soldiers were sent to the West to protect White settlers from Indian attacks, to force Indians back onto the reservations, and to keep law and order. Katz points out that although they were there to protect Whites, they were often subjected to hostility by the very people they protected. The 9th and 10th Cavalries made up one-fifth of the mounted troops assigned to the frontier. Two of their European American

Mary Fields was one of many African American women who traveled west. She, however, was unique in that she could hold her own against any man, black or white. She landed a job with the United States Postal Service and became the first woman to carry the U.S. mail.

scouts were Kit Carson and Wild Bill Hickok. Several men in these units earned the highest military honor awarded by the U.S. government, the Congressional Medal of Honor. The Buffalo Soldiers also served with Teddy Roosevelt at a major battle, the Battle of San Juan Hill, in the Spanish-American War.

During this time, only White officers commanded the Buffalo Soldiers. Promotions were not permitted. Even so, twenty African Americans entered West Point military academy. Unfortunately, due to the harassment and hostility of other cadets and the prejudices of instructors, only three graduated. They were Henry O. Flipper, John H. Alexander, and Charles Young.

African American Californians

Not only were African Americans important to the westward movement, but some were also wealthy. William Alexander Leidesdorff sailed to California aboard his 160-ton schooner. He was responsible for several "firsts." One was the introduction of the first steamboat to California. Leidesdorff also organized the first horse race, built the first hotel, and set up the first public school in San Francisco. In 1845, he became the first African American diplomat from the United States when he was appointed as U.S. sub-consul to California, which was under Spanish rule.

Maria Rita Valdez was an American of African and Spanish descent. Her African American grandparents were among the founders of Los Angeles. She owned Rancho Rodeo de las Aguas, which is known today as Beverly Hills. Another African-Hispanic American, Francisco Reyes, owned the San Fernando Valley, which he sold in the 1790s. Later he became the mayor of Los Angeles.

When gold was found in California in 1852, many Whites went to seek their fortune. Some African Americans also went to California during what was called the "gold rush." Most were enslaved, but some were free. One woman who became a Californian was Biddy Mason. She was an enslaved African who traveled with her White owner to California when gold was discovered. At that time many enslaved Africans were arriving in California with their owners. The miners who were already there resented the presence of nonWhites whether they were African, Mexican, or Chinese. They imposed taxes on nonWhites, who worked in the mines. They also were resentful toward other Whites who had brought enslaved Africans and some were forced to leave. Some of these Whites felt that Africans were skilled at finding gold, and they did not want anyone competing with them.

Biddy Mason was more fortunate. Despite the risks of working in the mines, she was able to buy her freedom and the freedom of her three daughters in 1856. She remained in California. The amicable relationship between the Mexicans and Africans who lived there made it possible for African Americans to make a living and become prosperous in California. Mexicans generally accepted Africans who were early explorers as well as those who escaped enslavement.

Settlers

Many of the African Americans who traveled West were part of the "exoduster" movement of 1879. Although most headed for Kansas, many went on to Nebraska, Colorado, Texas, and Nevada. African Americans also went to Oklahoma, the territory that the government had set aside for Native Americans and African Americans. The U.S. Army marched thousands of Native Americans and many Africans on what is now referred to as the "Trail of Tears." Many Native Americans died en route to Oklahoma. Africans hoped that Oklahoma could also be their escape from racism and prejudice, and more than two dozen Black townships, such as Langston and Boley, were started there.

Unfortunately, African Americans would not find the peace and freedom from oppression in Oklahoma. When Whites demanded more land to settle, the government violated the treaties with Native Americans and opened the territory for Whites to claim. When Oklahoma was admitted to the United States, it too began to make laws that favored Whites and discriminated against African Americans. By 1888, most of the towns populated by the exodusters were in decline due to underpopulation or because of the racist White farmers who drove Blacks away.

Summary

When the U.S. government sanctioned the movement of settlers into the West, African Americans were among those who went. African Americans who traveled West included cowboys, settlers or homesteaders, and Buffalo Soldiers. White settlers needed protection from Native American tribes.

Buffalo Soldiers were recruited to provide that protection; but they were still subjected to discrimination in the ranks by White officers. It is ironic that the Buffalo Soldiers turned against the Native Americans and fought them. This is particularly ironic since so many African Americans found safety with the Native peoples. However, the Buffalo Soldiers did so in an effort to be patriotic and to gain the same rights and privileges as other Americans.

There were also many prosperous people of African and Spanish descent. Primarily this was because California was already their home before it was annexed to the United States. Furthermore, Africans participated in the "gold rush," and some were able to buy their freedom and make a good living for themselves. Although the racism of the East awaited many African Americans when they went West, some were able to make contributions.

The problems of the previous century followed African Americans into the 1900s. These problems were experienced everywhere, not just in the South including lynchings and race riots. The next chapter explores some of these problems, in terms of their impact on African Americans in the early 1900s.

Bill Pickett

Bill Pickett was a cowboy of the old West. He invented a popular rodeo event called "bulldogging" in 1908. A bronze statue was erected in his honor in Fort Worth, Texas.

References

Amspacher, S. (2020, April 1). *Stagecoach Mary Fields*. Smithsonian National Postal Museum. postalmuseum.si.edu/stagecoach-mary-fields

Appiah, K., & Gates, H. L. (Eds.). (1999). *Africana: The encyclopedia of African and African American experiences*. Basic Civitas.

Asante, M. K. (1993). *The Afrocentric idea*. Revised and expanded edition. Temple University Press.

Asante, M. K. (1993). *Historical and cultural atlas of African Americans*. Macmillan Publishing.

Asante, M. K. (2001). *African American history: A journey of liberation*. Peoples Publishing Group, Inc.

Bennett, L., Jr. (1993). *Before the Mayflower: A history of Black America*. 6th edition. Penguin Books.

Blakemore, E. (2017, September 14). *Meet Stagecoach Mary, the daring Black pioneer who protected Wild West stagecoaches*. History. https://www.history.com/news/meet-stagecoach-mary-the-daring-black-pioneer-who-protected-wild-west-stagecoaches

Everett, G. (2006, June 12). *Mary Fields, a rough and tough Black female pioneer*. HistoryNet. www.historynet.com/mary-fields-female-pioneer-in-montana.htm

Franklin, J. H., & Moss, A. A., Jr. (2000). *From slavery to freedom: A history of African Americans*. Knopf.

Gates, H. L., Jr., & Higginbotham, E. B. (Eds.). (2004). *African American lives*. Oxford University Press.

Hine, D. C. (Ed.). (2005). *Black women in America*. 2nd ed. Oxford University Press.

Katz, W. L. (1993). *The Black west*. Open Hand Publishing Inc.

Katz, W. L. (1974). *Eyewitness: The negro in American history*. Pitman Learning, Inc.

Lewis and Clark. Inside the Corps. The Corps. York. (2019). PBS. https://www.pbs.org/kenburns/lewis-clark/

Parks, S. (2018, March 8). York Explored the West with Lewis and Clark, but his freedom wouldn't come until decades later. *Smithsonian Magazine* https://www.smithsonianmag.com/history/york-explored-west-lewis-and-clark-his-freedom-wouldnt-come-until-decades-later-180968427/

Trotter, J. W. (2001). *The African American experience*, Volume I and II. Houghton Mifflin.

Review

I. Checking What You Have Read

1. Why was the Freedmen's Bureau established?
2. What did it accomplish?
3. What problem did it fail to solve?
4. Explain how Reconstruction affected African Americans.
5. In what ways were the Black Codes similar to the slave codes? What were Jim Crow laws?
6. Explain what the 13th, 14th, and 15th Amendments to the Constitution were designed to do.
7. Many African Americans were involved in the westward expansion of the United States. Name two of these important African Americans and tell what they did.
8. What was important about the 9th and 10th Cavalries and the 24th and 25th Infantries of the army?
9. What was the Great Migration of 1879?
10. What did Thaddeus Stevens propose be done with the newly freed Africans?
11. Why did African Americans join the Republican Party?
12. Name some ways in which African Americans were prevented from making a decent living for themselves. Explain.
13. What were the people called who went to Kansas and points west? Why?
14. The territory that became the state of Oklahoma was originally set up for whom and why?
15. In the 1700s and 1800s, African Americans contributed to the development of American society, especially in the area of science and invention. Match the following people with their accomplishments.

    (1) Madam C. J. Walker   (a) developed a procedure to store blood plasma
    (2) Granville T. Woods   (b) developed cosmetics for African Americans
    (3) Benjamin Banneker   (c) invented the carbon filament in light bulbs
    (4) Dr. Charles Drew   (d) invented many electrical devices that were sold to Bell, Edison, and Westinghouse
    (5) Lewis Latimer   (e) designed the city of Washington, D.C., after memorizing the plans

16. Compare the Civil Rights Act of 1875 with the Civil Rights Bill of 1964.

II. On Your Own

1. Discover the names of some of the other African American settlers and cowboys who were involved in the westward movement. Discuss some of their accomplishments.
2. Find the names of some of the Native American groups who welcomed Africans.
3. Look in your current American history book and find the account of the Lewis and Clark expedition. See whether York is mentioned. If he is not, ask yourself why not, and explain why he should be included. If he is mentioned, explain why it is important to have correct information about the contributions of all people.
4. See if you can figure out how landowners might have kept the African American sharecropper in debt.
5. Think about what it might have been like to live in the West with the cowboys. What kind of jobs did they do, and what hardships might they have faced?
6. Use the Internet and other resources to learn about other Black towns that were founded in the West during the western migration of the late 1870s.
7. Lewis Latimer was most significant in the development of the telephone. He also was responsible for many other important contributions to American society. Read a biography of Latimer and give a report to your class.
8. Use library materials and encyclopedias to discover more information about the life and work of Granville T. Woods. Copy a drawing of one of his inventions and explain it, either in a written report or an oral presentation to the class.

New Century, Old Problems

The beginning of the 20th century was an exciting time. The Pan-American Exposition, a world's fair, opened in 1901 in Buffalo, New York. It was a spectacular showcase that highlighted a wide array of new inventions, particularly the use of electric lights. The exposition featured an electric tower, which was lit with thousands of colored bulbs. The Expo stretched from one part of town to another and featured various attractions on the midway. Some of the states had their own buildings, as did some South American countries. Although it was a new and exciting beginning to a new century, old racism and White supremacy continued. The White supremacy of the South had now spread to the North.

There were two attractions on the midway that upset many African Americans. "The Old Plantation" and the "Darkest Africa" exhibits portrayed stereotypical and bigoted ideas about African Americans. The plantation exhibit portrayed African Americans as being happy in enslavement. The Africa exhibit portrayed Africans as primitive, strange, or exotic. It was as if all the accomplishments of African people from the time of the West African Empires were forgotten. Even the achievements of people such as Lewis Latimer, George Washington Carver, and Elijah McCoy were simply ignored. Some African Americans, such as Mary B. Talbert, met with others

CHAPTER 8

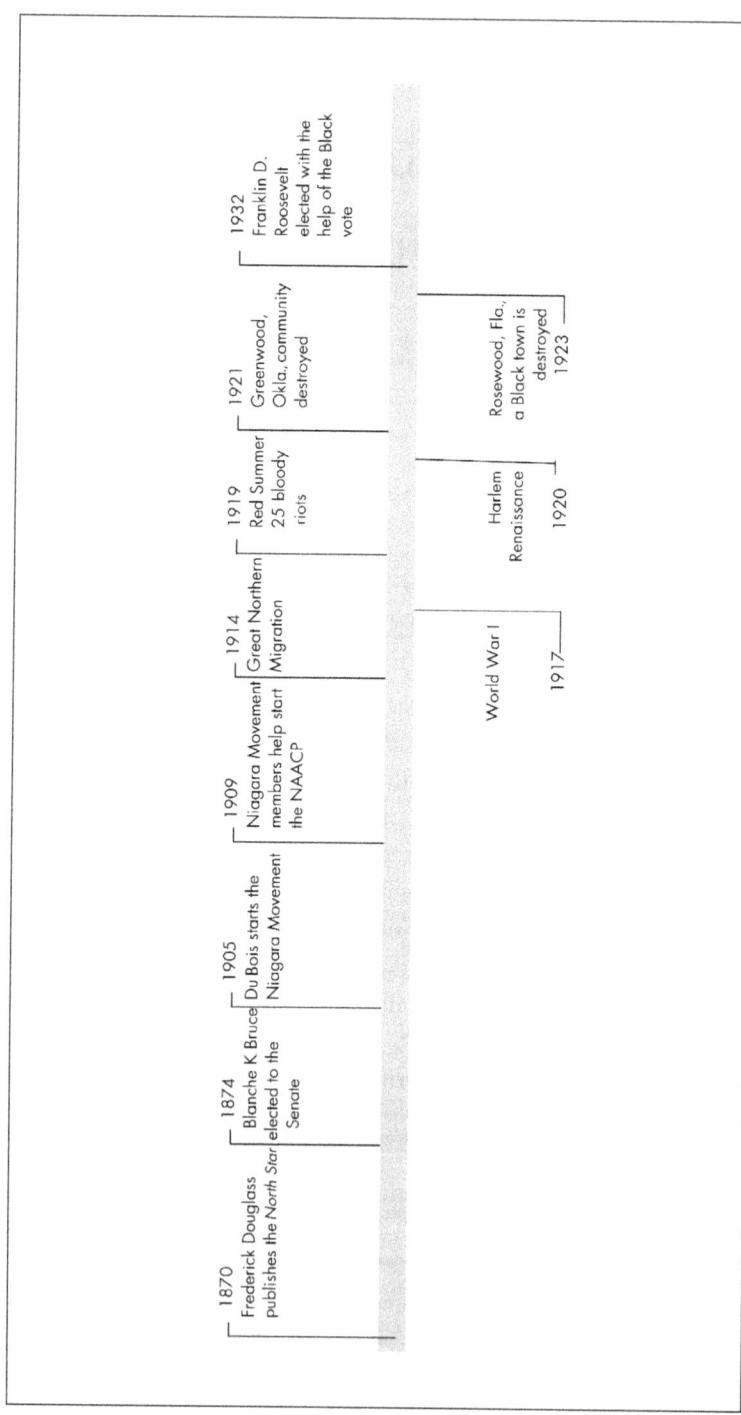

African American History 1870–1932

to protest the exhibits. She wanted to present an exhibit similar to the one that Booker T. Washington had done in 1895 in Atlanta, Georgia.

The city of Atlanta sponsored the Cotton States and International Exposition of 1895. It was quite remarkable in that it included a woman's building and a "Negro" building. In the Negro building the accomplishments of African Americans since the time of Emancipation were highlighted. Fifteen states participated. One of the exhibits showcased items constructed at the Tuskegee Institute. Some items included furniture for bedrooms, parlor, and kitchen to name a few, as well as clothing.

The Pan-American Exposition was also the scene of a tragic event, the assassination of President William McKinley. The person who shot him was Leon Czolgosz. An African American named James "Big Ben" Parker, who happened to be there, captured the assassin. Unfortunately, he was not allowed to testify at the trial of Czolgosz. In fact, the people in charge of protecting the president (the FBI and Secret Service) attempted to discredit his heroic act. To some African Americans, it seemed that these law-enforcement people were upset because not only had they failed to protect the president, they had not even captured the assassin. Still, there were eyewitnesses to the assassination, and local African American residents met to honor Parker. The report of his heroism was carried in six newspapers, including the *Buffalo Times*, and the *Atlanta Constitution*, and the *Cleveland Gazette*. This information is not usually found in history books, however.

The Eye of the Storm

The early 1900s also issued in an era of increased violence against people of African descent. African Americans suffered from many forms of oppression, racism, discrimination, and violence, from Whites—but especially southern Whites. Strong negative attitudes by Whites against African Americans could be found everywhere in the United States, from the president's office to small communities. Government officials passed laws that officially promoted segregation. Informal alliances were made among Whites to segregate African Americans in jobs and housing. White supremacy even affected the media.

Birth of a Nation was a racist movie that was produced in 1915. The movie promoted White supremacy by presenting distorted information and negative stereotypes about African Americans. It is unfortunate that the first great cinematic achievements in movie technology were used in such a negative manner. President Woodrow Wilson, however, thought that the movie was a great accomplishment.

President Wilson's racist policies are a matter of record, but historians do not include this information in their texts. Many scholars/authors/historians such as Loewen (1995), Trotter (2001), and Asante (1993), however, have discussed the racist policies of President Woodrow Wilson. For example, James Loewen in his book, *Lies My Teacher Told Me*, cites how President Wilson broke with the tradition of his Republican predecessors who usually appointed African Americans to certain positions, such as postmasters, particularly in southern towns. President Wilson appointed Whites to those positions that had been traditionally reserved for African Americans. In fact, he acted to eliminate any and all African American representation at the federal level. Other authors have reported the same. Loewen also reports that Wilson had legislation submitted that was designed to reduce the civil rights of African Americans.

Considering Wilson's racist policies, it is also not surprising that there were more race riots during his term in office than in the previous history of the United States. Whites initiated race riots in St. Louis in 1917, and many more riots during the summer of 1919. There was a riot in Greenwood, a community in Tulsa, Oklahoma, known as the Black Wall Street. Two years later, violence struck Rosewood, Florida.

Race Riots and Lynching

Lynching followed Reconstruction in the South. It is estimated that lynchings averaged about 100 a year during the 1880s and 1890s (Trotter, 2001). Bennett (1993) cites the race riot of 1866 in Memphis, Tennessee, where 46 African Americans were killed, and the riot in New Orleans, just two years later, where mobs killed almost 50 African Americans and injured another 166.

In 1898, a race riot broke out in Wilmington, North Carolina, over the right to vote. In that riot, 24 people died and hundreds of others fled to the North. Other riots broke out in New York City in 1900; in Atlanta, Georgia, in 1906; in Springfield, Illinois, in 1904 and again in 1908. This was the way in which Whites tried to control African Americans. Many African Americans were killed or injured. Property was looted and destroyed and often the police would join in the violence. Then came the bloodiest time of all, the summer of 1919.

The Red Summer of 1919

The summer of 1919 is commonly known as the "Red Summer." That name came about because of the numerous race riots that took place that year in the United States. Racial hatred and violence escalated to a new level. There were 89 lynchings that year. Some of those lynched were African American veterans, who were hanged in their uniforms. Others were burned alive. Tensions rose dramatically and hostilities broke out. Some African Americans fought back, but in the end many more African Americans than Whites were killed. There were 25 race riots during a period of seven months and more than 300 African Americans and 178 Whites were injured. The longest one lasted 13 days in Chicago, Illinois. In the Chicago riot, 15 Whites and 24 African Americans were killed.

The media conducted a powerful campaign against African Americans during this period. African Americans were characterized as stupid or foolish in cartoons, in movies, and on the radio. They also were portrayed as lazy, dishonest, primitive, and even savage. African Americans were given distorted facial features in advertising and on boxes of merchandise. These distorted and stereotypical images could also be found in the newspapers and magazines of the time, such as the *Atlantic Monthly* and *Harper's*. These images were also produced as statuettes and other souvenirs. Ultimately, they shaped the attitudes of Whites about African Americans by promoting White supremacy and the hatred of African Americans.

Black Wall Street

In 1921, racial trouble came to a prosperous Black community in Tulsa, Oklahoma known as Greenwood. This community had come to be known as the Black Wall Street of the West. The residents of the community understood full well the treatment they received under Jim Crow laws. They knew that Whites did not want to do business with them, and when they did, they often cheated them. African Americans had fashioned a community where they relied on each other. The townspeople built hundreds of successful businesses. Some estimate that there were over 200 businesses, and others say there were as many as 600. There were restaurants, grocery stores, churches, and schools. Greenwood had two movie theaters, a hospital, a bank, and a post office. In a state that had almost no airports for Whites, at least six African American residents owned their own private airplanes.

Unfortunately, the prosperity of the Greenwood community did not go unnoticed by the White population. One day the White residents who, from all accounts, were already jealous of the success of the African Americans, got their chance. A White girl named Sarah Page claimed that an African American boy, Dick Rowland, attempted to assault her in an elevator. Shortly thereafter, a mob of Whites went to lynch him. African Americans who had armed themselves prevented that from happening. But that night the sheriff deputized a mob, which included members of the Ku Klux Klan, and went into the community, threatening the Black residents. By this time, the mob had grown to 2,000 people. Shots were fired and two African Americans and ten Whites were killed.

The next morning, about 10,000 Whites came with guns and other weapons. Some estimate that about 300 African Americans were killed. The mob burned and otherwise destroyed businesses and homes alike. Of the 15,000 residents, only 7,000 were left. The others had fled. Those who were left were rounded up at gunpoint and put in detention centers. Their homes were looted and then burned.

The business buildings that comprised the commercial district of the Greenwood community were never rebuilt. The insurance companies refused to pay the residents for their losses. The Tulsa Race Riot Commission was created in 2001 to study the incident. Although it made several recommendations, the one recommendation for reparations or payments to the survivors did not occur. However, the Oklahoma legislature did set up a scholarship fund for the descendants of the riot victims who were college-bound. The legislature also appropriated two million dollars for a memorial.

In February 2003, a team of lawyers, including Charles Ogletree and the late Johnny Cochran provided their services, free of charge, to five elderly survivors who sued the city and state for reparations. This appeal was dismissed because it was beyond the statute of limitations of the law. In other words, it was too old. Currently the site is part of the Greenwood Historical District and is home to Oklahoma State University-Tulsa and Langston University-Tulsa.

Rosewood

Violence struck Rosewood, Florida, two years after the terrible destruction of Greenwood. Rosewood was an African American town that was close to Sumner, a prosperous White town. Again, Whites accused an African American man of assaulting Fannie Taylor, a White woman. About 20 to 30 White men went to confront one of the African American men whom they had targeted. Sylvester Carrier shot two of the White men and wounded four others in the shootout. The next evening, the White men returned with about 200 Whites from Sumner. They came to the town armed with guns and torches. First they went to Carrier's house, and after another shootout, went in. They found the bodies of Carrier's mother, who had been shot by Whites on the previous evening, and a Black man whom they assumed to be Carrier. (His identity was never proven.) From there the men went through the town burning houses and other buildings and even killing livestock.

Two sympathetic White men helped the African American women and children escape to Gainesville. The riot in Rosewood received national attention but, again, disappeared in the history books. In 1994, the Florida state legislature voted to give reparations to the descendants of the Rosewood incident. It awarded over two million dollars to the survivors and created a scholarship fund for their descendants.

A Red Record

Just before the turn of the twentieth century, between 1882 and 1901, Tuskegee's paper, the *Negro Yearbook*, reported that the number of recorded lynchings had reached over 3,000. Of that number, nearly 2,000 were African Americans, including 40 women. Often, African Americans were dragged from their homes and accused of false offenses, many of which alleged to be against White women or for testifying against a White in court. They were then mutilated and hanged. In most cases, there was no justification for the charges.

Many people spoke out against racial injustice and cruelty, particularly the mutilation and lynching of African Americans. One of these people was an African American woman journalist named Ida B. Wells-Barnett. She was born in Mississippi and attended Rust College for several years. Wells-Barnett had to leave her home in the South because people did not like her anti-lynching editorials. She moved to Chicago and continued her protest against lynching. According to her records, about 10,000 people were killed between 1878 and 1898. *A Red Record* was published in 1895 in which she documented the lynchings of African Americans. It was the first published record of lynchings in the United States.

The Great Northern Migration

After Reconstruction, African Americans in the South had few options for providing food, shelter, and clothing for their families. They could work for planters, sometimes their former owners, by sharecropping, and fall deeper and deeper into debt. African Americans could also work at other jobs and be paid very low wages. In either case, they barely made enough money to feed and take care of their families. Laws were passed to keep this system in place. According to Bennett, African Americans had the dirty or "Negro" jobs until Whites were in need. When Whites found themselves hungry, jobs were reclassified, so that Whites could replace African Americans in these jobs. Some southerners even found a way of getting free labor. Local law enforcement officials would arrest African Americans for vagrancy (not having a job) and put them in prisons to work on chain-gangs. These chain-gangs were loosely formed collaborations with companies and private individuals to extort free labor from unsuspecting poor Blacks.

Even when people from the North built factories in southern towns, African Americans were subjected to the hardest and dirtiest jobs. They were also given jobs such as brick-making, road building, and shoveling coal for train engines. African Americans were kept out of some factory jobs altogether, such as the cotton and textile industries.

Then southern Whites introduced segregation, which was a way to keep African Americans and Whites separated and prevent them from having the same political, economic, and social opportunities as Whites. Segregation affected everything from swimming pools to churches. There were White water fountains, swimming pools, stores, cemeteries, and even White Bibles. The same thing was true for African Americans, except that their facilities were in poor and dilapidated condition.

Segregation was also known as Jim Crow. As previously discussed, it started out as a term used to describe a type of song-and-dance routine. The routine was copied by a White minstrel performer wearing "blackface" (black makeup). The term later came to mean segregation.

By 1914, many African Americans had had enough of the South. They could accept the new bondage of sharecropping, or they could exercise another option: They could work in the factories of the North. The North, particularly after the start of World War I, needed workers for the war industries. When the war began, restrictions on immigration were put into place. The influx of immigrants from other countries, who had originally filled the need for workers in the industrial economy, greatly declined. It is estimated that nearly two million African Americans migrated to the urban areas of the North, West, and Midwest.

Southern Whites naturally did not want their source of cheap and nearly free labor to leave. They tried to discourage southern African Americans by telling them that the weather in the North was too harsh and that they would die from the severe cold. White southerners even passed laws to prevent African Americans from leaving. These laws made it illegal to recruit African Americans away from the South. Southern Whites tried to make it difficult for northern companies, who sent recruiters, by charging high fees to recruit Black workers. In the end, the South, with all its racist and segregationist policies, forced millions of people to the North. The migration started with World War I but continued through the 1920s.

The North and More Problems

Just like southern towns and cities, urban centers in the North and Midwest had their own set of racial problems that African Americans soon realized. Whereas segregation was less pronounced in the North, and African Americans were not subjected to outright hostilities and violence, discrimination continued. It took a subtler form, by becoming "de facto" (real but not official) segregation. Whites created informal agreements among themselves to limit job and housing opportunities for African Americans. African Americans could vote but had little political voice. There were very few African American elected officials, and White officials ignored them.

Although African Americans could earn more money in the factories, there was discrimination in hiring. "Last one hired and first one fired" was a term that was well known in African American communities in the past—and also in the present. In good economic times, factories hired African Americans. However, when the economy took a downturn, they were the first to be let go. In addition, African Americans were given jobs with dangerous working conditions. Some of these jobs exposed them to intense heat and fumes in the factories. Sometimes these conditions could cause injury or death, particularly in the steel industry. Whites, however, enjoyed the higher-skilled and better-paying jobs.

African Americans from the South often came to live with relatives or friends in the North or Black-owned rooming houses. With little money, many lived in overcrowded conditions in ramshackle buildings. Racially segregated communities grew rapidly due to discrimination in housing. Prejudice and racism became rampant. Realtors sought to contain African Americans and Jews in certain neighborhoods. Landlords charged outrageous rents for dilapidated housing.

The Unions and African American Workers

At one time, African Americans dominated the building and other artisan trades. It is important to remember that Africans who had been brought from the continent had many different skills. They perfected these skills as carpenters, bricklayers, and metal workers both during their enslavement and after emancipation. As stated earlier, free African Americans, particularly in New Orleans but also in other areas, could hire themselves out. Many of them did so and also taught their trade to others. But in the postbellum (post-Civil War) South of the 1890s, Whites had begun to replace the African American artisans. Southern Whites formed guilds that refused membership to African Americans. In many places, one had to be a member of a guild in order to work, and by refusing membership to African Americans, Whites effectively kept them unemployed.

In the North also, a worker had to be a member of a trade union in order to be hired. When African Americans attempted to join the White labor unions, they were denied. So African Americans decided to form their own organizations to fight for better wages and working conditions. One of the first labor organizations was the Colored National Labor

African Americans were not permitted to join white unions; therefore they formed their own labor unions to deal with economic discrimination in the early 1900s.

Union in the late 1870s. It did not survive, but it represented the determination of African Americans to organize for better jobs and wages.

In the early 1900s, there were thousands of African American carpenters, electricians, and plumbers. These skilled tradesmen were rarely allowed membership in White unions. The Knights of Labor was one of the first that allowed African Americans to join. At its peak, it had 60,000 African American members. It, too, did not last, and the American Federation of Labor, the AFL, came into existence. It was made up of many affiliated craft unions, and each union was allowed to make its own rules about admitting African Americans. Most did not admit Black workers. African Americans, however, did not wait for the White unions to admit them. Other unions followed. One very important union that was established was the Brotherhood of Sleeping Car Porters in 1925. Its founder was A. Philip Randolph.

A. Philip Randolph

There were many people working to improve the conditions of African American people. A. Philip Randolph was one of them. He focused on the discrimination in the unions. His motto was "service not servitude." He proved to be a very skilled organizer within the African American community and actually threatened to organize a march on Washington in 1941. All of this helped in the fight against discrimination in the trade unions and government agencies.

A New Labor Union

During the 1930s, a new organization was in the making. Some Whites came to realize that a new labor movement was necessary, one that addressed the needs of both African American and White workers. One of the proponents of this new philosophy was John L. Lewis. The Committee for Industrial Organization broke away from the AFL in 1935. The Committee began a vigorous campaign for a broader and more diverse membership. It was renamed the Congress for Industrial Organization, or CIO, in 1938. The members of this organization recruited and organized across craft and race lines. It targeted the larger companies that were involved in mass production. These larger companies included the meat-packing, automobile, and steel industries.

Many African Americans were skeptical about joining unions. They were afraid that unions would only make them pay dues but would not fight for their rights. Other African Americans had to convince the masses of African American labor workers to join. CIO organizers faced resistance from employers who used various tactics to intimidate Black union organizers. Some were beaten and viciously assaulted. In the South, it was especially difficult to organize. Patterns of racial segregation and hostility were entrenched. But that did not stop both southern White and African American workers from organizing labor groups such as the Inland Boatman Union, the Mine Mill, and Smelter Union in Alabama. The NAACP and Urban League worked with the organizers of these new unions.

World War I

At the beginning of the century, state issues turned to international affairs. The American government, while avowing a policy of non-involvement in world turmoil, not only got involved in policy, but in war as well. World War I started out among European countries: Austria and Serbia went to war over the assassination of Archduke Franz Ferdinand of Austria, and soon Germany, Russia, and France joined in. Eventually Britain joined the war on the side of France. When Germany sank several American ships, with passengers, on the way to England, President Wilson asked Congress to declare war on Germany.

The United States government instituted the draft to get men to serve in the war. Unlike today, when serving in the armed forces is voluntary, the draft was mandatory. There was no choice about it. Over two million African Americans registered for the draft. African Americans made up about 10 percent of the population but 13 percent of all the draftees. This registration pattern has continued in all of the subsequent wars that have been fought by U.S. military personnel. African Americans were not allowed to enlist for the Marines or the Coast Guard. They were only allowed to work in the kitchen in the Navy. African Americans were also used as stevedores, people who load and unload ships. Eventually, after a nationwide campaign by students for officer training programs, a camp to train African American officers was started in Des Moines, Iowa. It produced 106 captains and 533 first and second lieutenants.

Despite some advancement, however, there was President Wilson to contend with. He was no friend to African Americans, although many voted for him. In fact, he was considered a racist by many (Loewen, 1995; Asante, 1993; Bennett, 1993). Wilson often demonstrated his belief that African Americans and Whites should not have the same rights. He encouraged the racist treatment of African American soldiers. His policies kept the armed services segregated.

African Americans who served in World War I were often discriminated against in military camps. About 200,000 African Americans served in the war, but only about 42,000 served in combat duty. They were most often used as kitchen helpers, cooks, or road-builders. African Americans were rarely promoted and often mistreated. If they resisted their abusive treatment, they were subject to arrest and punishment.

African Americans Distinguish Themselves

Although most African Americans saw little battle action in World War I, some distinguished themselves. One of these units was the 369th Regiment, also known as the Hellfighters. African Americans who were in uniform were special targets for racist attacks, particularly in the South. Unfortunately, many of the training camps were in the South, where there were constant attacks by Whites against African American soldiers. This is what happened to the 15th Regiment, later renamed the 369th Regiment.

The 369th Regiment ("Hellfighters")

The 15th Regiment was in Spartanburg, South Carolina, when an incident occurred against some of its members. In order to prevent any more trouble, the regiment was renamed the 369th and sent immediately to France in 1918. They fought in several battles of the war and held their ground. None of the members of the regiment was captured, and the men never retreated. The Regiment lost 851 men though. In fact, the entire regiment received the French Croix de Guerre for bravery under fire. They also received the French Legion of Honor. White officers were not as appreciative, however. The White officers tried to keep the French people, especially the women, away from the African American troops. The French people were told not to be friendly toward African Americans. The officers said that that would offend the U.S. policy that called for the separation of the races.

When the African American soldiers returned, they were not treated any differently than when they had left. They did not receive the welcome that the White soldiers did, but they did face the same racism and discrimination they had previously endured even though the African Americans had defended their country with their lives and were treated as heroes by the French.

Summary

The 1900s ushered in a new century for America. It brought a great exposition full of wonder and invention but also one full of negative stereotypes about people of African descent. The new century also brought a new wave of oppression and injustice against African Americans. Jim Crow laws and segregation had been implemented in the South, and the same negative feelings and perceptions about African Americans began to filter across the nation. The end of the 1800s and early 1900s were periods in which many bloody riots occurred. It was a time when African Americans were killed for attempting to vote. African American communities were looted and burned by jealous Whites, as in Greenwood, Oklahoma, or simply burned because of mean-spirited people who looked for any reason to destroy what little African Americans had managed to build for themselves, as in Rosewood, Florida.

It was a time when many African Americans migrated to the North in search of better times, only to find themselves discriminated against in terms of jobs and housing. Still, they found that life in the North was better than life in the South. This was particularly true when the United States entered World War I. The war industry created many jobs and many workers were needed. African Americans supported the war production industry of the United States in many ways. The unionization of African Americans finally began and continued all across the country.

When they were needed, African Americans did not hesitate to answer the call to defend their country. But their efforts were not always welcomed.

References

African-Americans in Combat | *History Detectives*. PBS. Accessed 20 Mar. 2021. https://www.pbs.org/opb/historydetectives/feature/african-americans-in-combat/

Appiah, K., & Gates, H. L. (Eds.). (1999). *Africana: The encyclopedia of African and African American experiences*. Basic Civitas.

Asante, M. K. (1993). *The Afrocentric idea*. Revised and expanded edition. Temple University Press.

Asante, M. K. (1993). *Historical and cultural atlas of African Americans*. Macmillan Publishing.

Asante, M. K. (2001). *African American history: A journey of liberation*. Peoples Publishing Group, Inc.

Bennett, L., Jr. (1993). *Before the Mayflower: A history of Black America*. 6th edition. Penguin Books.

Franklin, J. H., & Moss, A. A., Jr. (2000). *From slavery to freedom: A history of African Americans*. Knopf.

Gates, H. L., Jr., & Higginbotham, E. B. (Eds.). (2004). *African American lives*. Oxford University Press.

Loewen, J. W. (1995). *Lies my teacher told me: Everything your history textbook got wrong*. Touchstone.

The 1921 Tulsa Race Riot Memorial of Reconciliation Design Committee. http://wyomcases.courts.state.wy.us/applications/OCISWeb/DeliverDocument.asp?CiteID=264071

Trotter, J. W. (2001). *The African American experience*, Volume I and II. Houghton Mifflin.

The Early Struggle for Human Rights

The Problem of the 20th Century

In his book *The Souls of Black Folk,* W.E.B. Du Bois stated that the problem of the 20th century was the problem of the color line. His book was published in 1903, but little did Du Bois know how true these words would prove to be. American society was divided by the founding fathers based on skin color. That divisive legacy has brought no end to issues of unfair discrimination, racism and human misery right into the present.

There have always been differing ideas among African Americans of how to treat the problems of racist oppression. Some people have advocated civil disobedience and others the use of violence when necessary. In the period following the Civil War, some African Americans also advocated emigration to Africa or other places. One such person was Dr. Martin Delany, one of the first African American physicians. The idea of emigration, however, did not gain widespread support by most African Americans, although Marcus Garvey revived it again in the early 1900s.

Political and Social Activists

At the beginning of the 20th century, there were many people involved in the question of what to do about the "race problem." Some prominent people included Marcus Garvey, W.E.B. Du Bois, Booker T. Washington, and Carter G. Woodson. Women such as Mary B. Talbert were also prominent and had their own way of approaching racism and discrimination against African Americans.

Marcus Garvey

Although they were many years apart, Marcus Garvey and Martin Delany had similar philosophies. They both advocated the resettlement of African Americans in Africa as a solution to the human rights struggle in the United States. Garvey was from the island of Jamaica in the Caribbean and was largely self-educated. He formed the Universal Negro Improvement Association (UNIA) while in Jamaica. The purpose of the organization was to promote Black pride and to encourage people of African descent to work together to build a better life.

Marcus Mosiah Garvey was born in Jamaica in 1887. He organized the Universal Negro Improvement Association in 1914. Garvey immigrated to the United States in 1916 and continued his campaign for African Americans to have pride in their history and culture, a concept called Black Nationalism.

Garvey came to the United States in 1916, during World War I. Garvey also believed in collective economics. This meant putting the money of many people together to start a business. In fact, he was so good at organizing that he was able to raise enough money to start several businesses, including the Black Star Line of ships.

Garvey urged African Americans to be proud of their skin color and to study their African heritage. His program was the first major effort that stressed ethnic pride and national identity. Garvey ultimately wanted to buy land in Liberia, Africa, and build a nation there with other African Americans who shared his dream. Garvey was harassed by U.S. law enforcement agencies, notably the FBI. In 1925, he was arrested and charged with mail fraud. Garvey served two years in prison, after which the president of the United States pardoned him. He was deported to Jamaica and later died in England in 1940. Today, Garvey is recognized as the national hero of Jamaica and is widely honored throughout the African world as a great thinker and freedom fighter.

Monroe Trotter

Like Du Bois, Monroe Trotter was from New England. He was influenced by the old abolitionists. Trotter started a newspaper called the *Boston Guardian* in the same building where William Lloyd Garrison had published the *Liberator*. Like Du Bois, Trotter was in direct opposition to Booker T. Washington and his policies. He lashed out at Washington in article after article. Washington responded by paying another newspaper to counter what Trotter published. Washington also initiated lawsuits against Trotter. Lawsuits were very time-consuming, though, and not very effective against Trotter.

Mary B. Talbert

Mary Burnette Talbert was born in Ohio, where she attended school. She earned her college degree, taught for a few years, then moved to Buffalo, New York, as the wife of William H. Talbert, a wealthy businessman. Talbert was a member of the Michigan Baptist Church and was quite involved in the African American community. She also was instrumental in getting Du Bois and 27 other activists to meet near Buffalo, New York, in 1905. This was the beginning of what became the Niagara Movement, the forerunner of the National Association for the Advancement of Colored People (NAACP). Talbert lectured widely both in the United States and abroad on race relations and women's rights.

The "Great Debate"

Other African Americans had other ideas on what to do about the "race problem." What came to be called the "Great Debate" occurred between Booker T. Washington and W.E.B. Du Bois. The debate centered on what each man thought would be best for African Americans. Washington wanted African Americans to accept what little they had and Du Bois wanted full rights and citizenship. Washington wanted industrial or vocational education and Du Bois advocated liberal arts or academic education.

Booker T. Washington was born enslaved in Virginia about 1856. He had learned to read and write while he was working in a coal mine in West Virginia. Washington was admitted to Hampton Institute when he was sixteen. He believed in industrial education and when he left Hampton he founded Tuskegee Institute. As a result of his work as an educator and public speaker, Washington became influential in business and politics. Many whites saw him as the spokesperson for African Americans. White philanthropists gave him money to support his projects.

Booker T. Washington was a former enslaved African in Virginia. He taught himself to read and worked his way through Hampton Institute. Washington founded the Tuskegee Institute in Alabama in 1881 and became its first president. The purpose of the school was to train African Americans in industrial arts so that working in the fields would not be their only means of earning a living.

Washington made a favorable impression on European Americans. He became friends with very important and rich people, such as John D. Rockefeller. They were willing to support what he advocated, and several of them gave him money in support of his educational projects. Many Whites saw him as the spokesperson for African Americans. Even the president of the United States

The Early Struggle for Human Rights

consulted him on matters concerning African Americans.

Washington was often described as an "accommodator." He advised African Americans to accept segregation, work hard for the friendship of Whites, and achieve economic equity. Washington also advocated industrial education. This is where the great controversy and subsequent debate began.

Although Washington believed that others should accept segregation, he himself did not follow the Jim Crow laws. He told others to forget about politics and the right to vote, while he directed much political power through his friendship with wealthy northern Whites.

William Edward Burghardt Du Bois was born in 1868 in Great Barrington, Massachusetts. He received his bachelor's degree in 1890. He then earned a master's degree and a doctorate from Harvard University in 1895. He was the first African American to receive a Ph.D. from Harvard. Du Bois disagreed with Booker T. Washington about schooling and the "proper place" for African Americans in American society. He was against Washington's message of political accommodation in favor of economic progress. He eventually emigrated to Ghana, West Africa, where he died.

W.E.B. Du Bois strongly disagreed with the ideas and methods of Booker T. Washington. Du Bois was born free in Great Barrington, Massachusetts, to intellectual parents. He was a bright student and was encouraged to attend college. He was the first African American to earn a Ph.D. from Harvard University. He also studied at the University of Berlin.

Du Bois was an intellectual, and his great ability allowed him to appreciate what Washington had accomplished but object to his policies. He demanded equal political rights for African Americans, and he stressed pro-active methods of attacking unjust discrimination. He also felt a college education was important and that African Americans should have access to it. Du Bois also believed in the "Talented Tenth," those African Americans who would have the responsibility of leadership. They would be well educated and act as the social, political and economic conscience of African Americans. Eventually, Du Bois came to the conclusion that Whites would not respect African Americans despite their academic training. He became a central figure in the Niagara Movement and, later, the National Association for the Advancement of Colored People (NAACP).

Du Bois was a prolific writer, having published more than 2,000 works of literature and commentary. He also published 21 books. One of his most popular works was *The Souls of Black Folk*, in which, with one simple statement, he summed up all the social, economic and political issues for generations to come. Du Bois said "the problem of the 20th century was the problem of the color line."

The Normal/Industrial School Model

Despite the disagreement between Booker T. Washington and W.E.B. Du Bois, many schools were founded to train teachers. These schools were called "normal" schools. Typically the students who attended these schools came with poorer elementary training. Anderson (1988) describes the typical normal schools as providing a course of study that was two to three years in length. Students received the equivalent of a tenth grade education. They did not receive a bachelor's degree but could qualify for a common school certificate. Both the Hampton Institute and Tuskegee were typical normal schools. However, both stressed manual labor, as did other types of schools at that time. Unfortunately, for the schools to get funding from the northern philanthropists, they had to emphasize industrial education. Therefore, both became trade or technical schools.

Many southern Whites were opposed to schooling for African Americans. Southerners knew that they could not stop the growth of schools for African Americans. Other Whites knew that also. Samuel Armstrong, a northern philanthropist, devised a plan to steer education in a direction that would place African Americans in a subordinate position. His plan was to disenfranchise southern African Americans while preparing them for the lowest forms of labor. The students received low-level trade training but also had to work long, hard hours for little pay on various jobs. In fact the pay

The Early Struggle for Human Rights

Hampton's curriculum began to focus increasingly on vocational studies or industrial education. A major area of study was agriculture at Hampton. Pictured here are Hampton Institute male students studying plants in a greenhouse.

they received went to pay for the expenses of their schooling. It was not enough to cover tuition, room, and board so students found themselves working more than they were attending classes in order to pay.

Many northern philanthropists bought into these ideas. Even Booker T. Washington, who was a student of Armstrong, willingly participated in Armstrong's idea. Now, it can be said of Washington, that in order to get support for schools and funding to run them, he had to go along with the wishes of his benefactors. Washington made many influential friends and got money for his projects. In any case, this was the Hampton/Industrial model.

The Niagara Movement

In 1905, with the encouragement of Talbert, Du Bois called a meeting of African American scholars, professionals, and reformers. This meeting, held in Fort Erie, Ontario, near Niagara Falls, resulted in the beginning of the Niagara Movement. The formation of this organization troubled Booker T. Washington, however. Up to this point, he had been the one who wielded power. It was on his approval that schools or educational projects got

Both Hampton Institute and the Tuskegee Institute started as "normal" schools which prepared women for teaching. Pictured here are women students marching in rows on the campus.

funding. His word could make or break newspapers and affect the lives of countless people. Washington must have perceived the Niagara Movement as a threat to the power and influence that he held with rich and important Whites. He sent people into the organization to act as informants. These people reported to him about what the organization was doing or preparing to do. The movement did not last long, but some of the members of the Niagara Movement later played an important role in the founding of the NAACP in 1909.

The National Association for the Advancement of Colored People (NAACP)

The NAACP was a joint effort of a few White liberals who opposed the increase in violence against African Americans and some African Americans who had formed the Niagara Movement. Several Whites, Mary White Ovington, William English Walling, Dr. Henry Moskowitz, and Oswald Garrison Villard organized a conference in New York. Among those African Americans who were invited to attend were Du Bois and Ida B. Wells-Barnett. Monroe Trotter was invited but indicated that he did not trust White people to do the right thing, so he declined. It was the first interracial organization of its kind. After its formation, Du Bois became the editor of its magazine, called *The Crisis*. The NAACP set up a legal committee headed by Arthur Spingarn. This began its long history of legal defense for people of color.

The National Urban League

In 1911, another interracial organization was formed. It began as the Committee on Urban Conditions Among Negroes. It was later named the Urban League. It was begun by an African American, Dr. George Edmund Haynes, a graduate student in social work, and a White woman, Ruth Standish Baldwin, Jr. Mrs. Baldwin was a wealthy widow who was sympathetic to the suffering of African Americans. During this time, the living conditions of African Americans in urban areas were terrible. The organization focused on helping to train African American social workers, provide education, and broaden job opportunities for African Americans. It also attempted to overcome discrimination in the workplace. The Urban League emphasized industrial training, the type of training that Booker T. Washington promoted. In fact, some of the supporters of the Urban League were Washington, Julius Rosenwald, a philanthropist, and Kelly Miller, Howard University dean.

 **Charles Hamilton Houston (1895–1950)**

Very little has been written about Charles Hamilton Houston, but he was the NAACP legal director. Prior to that he was the vice-dean of the Howard University Law School. Houston greatly influenced Thurgood Marshall. Houston argued several important civil rights cases before the U.S. Supreme court, including one having to do with segregation in universities.

The Pan-African Movement

Pan-Africanism is another term for Black Nationalism. It is a term that focuses on Black people sharing a common African culture and world view.

Many African Americans have advocated it. As stated earlier, both Delany and Garvey urged African Americans to return to Africa to make a home there. Although most African Americans did not intend to emigrate, the idea of unity with African people on the continent continued to be discussed. Du Bois also began "to develop a nationalist and internationalist consciousness within the African American community." Du Bois brought Pan-Africanism into focus in 1919 when he helped to organize a Pan-African conference in Paris, France. It was attended by representatives from 16 countries and colonies and delegates from the United States.

Summary

The beginning of the 20th century marked the start of a strong drive against racist oppression and unfair discrimination. It was also a time when race pride and Black nationalism became a focus through the efforts of Marcus Garvey. The early 1900s, with all of the violence and race wars, sharpened the focus on gaining not only civil rights but human rights as well. African American leaders did not want to "go along to get along" with Whites but demanded equity. W.E.B. Du Bois and Monroe Trotter strongly questioned the methods and ideas of Booker T. Washington, and each took different approaches to challenge him.

There was the formation of two interracial organizations, the Urban League and the NAACP. They were the first organizations of their kind in which both sympathetic Whites and African Americans joined to help people of color. The NAACP developed into a major force in the fight for civil rights. The Urban League focused on urban social issues. These organizations continue to address issues of unfair discrimination and racism, because, although Du Bois stated the color line was a problem in the 20th century, it is still a problem in the 21st century. African Americans still face discrimination and racism, whether it is subtle, as in housing discrimination, or blatant, as in racial profiling.

It was no doubt due to the discrimination and racism that African Americans banded together to build a sense of community. Many African Americans moved from the South to the North and West, bringing their music and ingenuity with them.

The next chapter will examine the revolution in the arts and music called the Harlem Renaissance and the inventors of the early 1920s.

References

Anderson, J. D. (1988). *The education of Blacks in the South, 1860–1935*. Later Printing edition. University of North Carolina Press.

Appiah, K., & Gates, H. L. (Eds.). (1999). *Africana: The encyclopedia of African and African American experiences*. Basic Civitas.

Asante, M. K. (1993). *The Afrocentric idea*. Revised and expanded edition. Temple University Press.

Asante, M. K. (1993). *Historical and cultural atlas of African Americans*. Macmillan Publishing.

Asante, M. K. (2001). *African American history: A journey of liberation*. Peoples Publishing Group, Inc.

Bennett, L., Jr. (1993). *Before the Mayflower: A history of Black America*. 6th edition. Penguin Books.

Franklin, J. H., & Moss, A. A., Jr. (2000). *From slavery to freedom: A history of African Americans*. Knopf.

Gates, H. L., Jr., & Higginbotham, E. B. (Eds.). (2004). *African American lives*. Oxford University Press.

Hine, D. C. (Ed.). (2005). *Black women in America*. 2nd edition. Oxford University Press.

Shujaa, M. J., & Shujaa, K. J. (Eds.). (2015). *The Sage encyclopedia of African cultural heritage in North America*. 1st Edition. Sage Publications.

Trotter, J. W. (2001). *The African American experience*, Volume I and II. Houghton Mifflin.

Review

I. Checking What You Have Read

1. What is meant by the term "Red Summer"?
2. What was the Niagara Movement? Which woman played a major part in establishing it?
3. Why did Booker T. Washington feel that the Niagara Movement posed a threat to him?
4. There were several ideas suggested by African Americans to combat increased racism and unjust discrimination. Choose two of the following and discuss each individual's beliefs and ideas.

   Martin Delany   W. E. B. Du Bois
   Monroe Trotter   Marcus Garvey
   Booker T. Washington

5. What was the Black Wall Street? Why was it called by that name and what happened to it?
6. Explain several types of discrimination faced by African Americans in the armed services.
7. Who was "Big Ben" Parker and what did he do?
8. Why did African Americans migrate to the North and Midwest?
9. During the great migration during World War I, what was the reaction of southern Whites?
10. Explain the realities that people had to face when they moved to northern cities.
11. Who was A. Philip Randolph?
12. What is meant by the "Great Debate"?
13. Why was Marcus Garvey important? What philosophy made him different from previous leaders?
14. Name two interracial organizations that were founded during the early 1900s and tell why and how they were started.
15. Who threatened a march on Washington in 1941? Why?

II. On Your Own

1. Booker T. Washington and W.E.B. Du Bois differed in their beliefs about the role of African Americans in society. Read the poem "Booker T. and W.E.B." by Dudley Randall and discuss the two different points of view.

2. Mary B. Talbert was an important figure in the Niagara Movement. Imagine what it was like to be an African American woman during this period. Write a short paragraph about it.

3. Conduct some research on the Pan-American Exposition of 1901 that was held in Buffalo, New York. What kinds of exhibits were there? Find out more information on the two African American exhibits. Explain to your classmates why they were so offensive.

4. Monroe Trotter founded one of the first African American newspapers. Do some research about the newspaper and what happened to it. Make a report to your classmates.

5. The NAACP started a legal defense fund to aid people of color. Find out about some of the prominent lawyers who volunteered their time to the organization and write a report about them.

10

African Americans in American Society

The early 1900s were filled with violence against African Americans, but that did not dampen their resolve for justice or stifle their creativity. In fact, a new perspective and attitude were beginning to emerge. Some important events had begun to usher in a new mood and began to challenge the status quo of bigotry in American society. One of these events of this new era was the success of Jack Johnson, an African American prizefighter. What became known as the Harlem Renaissance quickly followed on the heels of Johnson's rise to fame and notoriety.

Jack Johnson won the heavyweight championship from a White contender, Tommy Burns, in 1908 in Sydney, Australia. The fact that an African American had beaten a White man affected the moods of many people. To most Whites, this was unacceptable. They were fearful that African Americans would begin to challenge inequities and injustices, and they did not want African Americans to challenge their subordinate position or the power that Whites held over them. African Americans, however, were proud of Johnson's accomplishment, even though some were upset by Johnson's flamboyant behavior, particularly out of the ring. Later, he defeated Jim Jeffries, another White, who was looked upon as the "great White hope." This victory by Johnson in 1910 caused Whites to attack African Americans. Race riots broke out all across the country, but it could not change the fact that he had beaten another White contender.

Johnson's victories were won during a time when African Americans were being lynched and laws were being passed to separate African Americans and Whites. Johnson challenged all of the rules of the White establishment and power brokers, including the rule against associating with White women. His associations with White women were particularly problematic, especially considering the time in which he lived. Eventually, his relationships with White women proved to be his downfall. He fled the United States when he was charged with violating the Mann Act of 1910, a federal law that made it illegal to transport women across state lines for immoral purposes.

Johnson lost his championship while in exile in Cuba. Some say that he deliberately lost the fight in order to divert attention away from himself. When he returned to the United States, he was arrested and sent to prison in Leavenworth, Kansas. Some people said that Johnson was unjustly accused. Johnson died in 1946. He was granted a posthumous pardon in 2018 by the Trump administration.

During this era, there was a proliferation of African American publications. Two of the oldest and best known were *The Crisis*, edited by Du Bois, and the *Boston Guardian*, edited by Trotter. Du Bois' magazine appealed to the intellectuals and Trotter's newspaper appealed to those with more combative ideas about how to respond to racism and injustice. While these two papers were both important, other newspapers and journals were in the making. Newspapers such as the *Chicago Defender* started new publishing models. This paper was founded by Robert Abbott. The *Chicago Defender* appealed to the masses, or the general population, of African Americans. The paper focused on the everyday issues that affected African Americans, especially the conditions in the South. It is said that the *Chicago Defender* played a significant part in the great Northern migration.

Newspapers played a major role in highlighting a period of great creative talent of African Americans. *The Crisis* magazine of the NAACP and the *Opportunity* magazine of the Urban League did the same by sponsoring literary contests. This great outpouring of talent was known as the Harlem Renaissance.

Early Literary Achievements

The early 1900s was not the only time that the creative talents of African Americans had been displayed, though. An early figure in the field of literature was Phillis Wheatley, an enslaved African who was born in Senegal, West Africa. She had published a book of poetry in 1773, the first book to be published by an African American woman. But before that, Jupiter Hammon, also an enslaved African, was the first African American male to publish a poem as a broadside. He wrote *An Evening Thought: Salvation by Christ with Penitential Cries,* which was published in 1760.

William Wells Brown (1814–1884) was the first African American to write a novel. It was called *Clotel: or, The President's Daughter,* and was published in 1853. He was also the first African American playwright. His play, *The Escape,* was published in 1858.

Later, in the late 1890s, African American writers, such as Charles Chesnutt (1858–1932), Paul Laurence Dunbar (1872–1906), and James Weldon Johnson (1871–1938), became prominent.

Charles Chesnutt was one of the greatest writers of his day. He wrote several novels, but his talent lay in attacking White supremacy with even more skill than his White peers. Chesnutt critiqued the racial injustices in American society, such as sharecropping, convict labor, and other unfair practices against African Americans.

Paul Laurence Dunbar wrote three novels and several volumes of poetry. His work used dialect—in this case, how African Americans from the South spoke—as a

Paul Laurence Dunbar was born 1872 in Dayton, Ohio. He was a prolific writer who preceeded the Harlem Renaissance and produced short stories, novels, librettos, plays, songs and essays as well as the poetry for which he became so well known. He was the first African-American to gain national eminence as a poet. Dunbar lived to be only 33 years old.

means of expression. Although his work reinforced the stereotypical "happy" enslaved African, his skills in writing dispelled the notion of the inferiority of the African American intellect.

James Weldon Johnson wrote about the experiences and perspectives of emancipation. He was also the author of what has come to be known as the Black national anthem, "Lift Every Voice and Sing." Johnson also worked for the NAACP and taught art and history.

The Harlem Renaissance

The 1920s was a time of Black consciousness, thanks to people such as Marcus Garvey, W.E.B. Du Bois, and others. It also a period in which there was a creative and artistic explosion called the Harlem Renaissance. From 1920 to 1929, a small group of African American writers, poets, artists, and intellectuals began to gather in Harlem in New York City. James Weldon Johnson commented that when African Americans first moved into that community in Manhattan, in 1903, they went unnoticed. Johnson is also given credit for crafting the Black National Anthem, "Lift Every Voice and Sing." As other ethnic groups moved into upper east side of Manhattan, White flight began. New York City's population of African Americans increased by 66 percent between 1910 and 1920. New York City even attracted people of African descent from the Caribbean, such as Cubans, Puerto Ricans, and Haitians.

There was a growing sense of pride and Harlem represented a place full of excitement and opportunity for African Americans. Their lives centered on social and political clubs, churches, theater, and music. This historic movement became known as the Harlem Renaissance, a term that is synonymous with cultural and artistic expression.

The best of the artists, writers, jazz and blues musicians, and actors could be found in Harlem. Alain Locke used the term the "New Negro," to describe this new group of African Americans with such a store of talent and training. Locke was an outstanding example of an intellectual. He was born into a well-to-do family in Philadelphia. He became a Rhodes scholar, an honor awarded by Oxford University in England. Locke was the first African American to receive such an honor. He and Jessie Fauset, who wrote for *The Crisis* magazine, helped to guide the course of the Harlem Renaissance, and they both became well known during this period. Fauset, who was also a graduate of Cornell University, encouraged young writers and highlighted their work in *The Crisis* magazine.

Writers

As the number African American creatives grew, several outstanding writers and artists emerged as the "stars" of the Harlem Renaissance. Some of the most significant writers were Countee Cullen (1903–1946), Langston Hughes (1902–1967), Zora Neale Hurston (1891–1960), and Claude McKay (1889–1948).

Countee Cullen was one of Harlem's favorite poets. He was born in New York City and graduated from New York University. He received his master's degree from Harvard University. His works appealed to the elite and not only appeared in Black publications but in White publications as well.

Langston Hughes is possibly the most famous African American poet. He was born in Joplin, Missouri, in 1902. While on a trip to visit his father in Mexico, he wrote a poem entitled "The Negro Speaks of Rivers." He was only a teenager, and little did he know how famous he would become because of this poem. *The Crisis* published it in 1922. Hughes went to New York City, where he attended Columbia University for a year.

Langston Hughes was a prolific writer of the Harlem Renaissance. He wrote 16 books of poems, two novels, three collections of short stories, four volumes of "editorial" and "documentary" fiction, twenty plays, children's poetry, musicals and operas. He also authored three autobiographies, a dozen radio and television scripts and dozens of magazine articles. Hughes was a very popular author. He also captured the life, language, and culture of ordinary African Americans. Hughes is pictured here (left to right) with sociologist Charles Spurgeon Johnson, historian E. Franklin Frazier, doctor and author Rudolph Fisher, and legislator Hubert Delaney.

Zora Neale Hurston is famous as an author, however, she was trained as an anthropologist. She used this training to write about the culture and folklore of African Americans of the South. A famous book of hers is *Their Eyes Were Watching God.*

In 1926 his first volume of poetry, *The Weary Blues,* was published. Hughes continued to write many works, including a two-volume autobiography.

Langston's fiction included novels, short stories, children's books, and sketches about his Harlem character, Simple. Hughes also published at least 16 volumes of poetry, which eloquently expressed the day-to-day life of ordinary African Americans. His appeal was to ordinary people, not necessarily the elite or emerging African American middle class.

After Zora Neale Hurston graduated from Howard University, she attended Barnard College, where she earned her graduate degree. Hurston was trained as an anthropologist. She used this background to write fiction based on the folklore of African Americans throughout the United States. One of her most famous works was *Their Eyes Were Watching God.*

Harlem attracted people of African descent from many places, including the Caribbean. Claude McKay was born in Clarendon Parish in Jamaica. His work was representative of the militant mood of some African Americans. McKay was very direct and defiant in his writings. One of his works of poetry was "Harlem Shadows."

Visual and Performing Arts

African American painters and sculptors also emerged and received recognition. Aaron Douglas was the most famous African American painter of that period. He painted wall murals that were inspired by African themes. His paintings were featured on the walls of the Fisk University library, the

Harlem Branch YMCA, and the Sherman Hotel in Chicago. Richard Barthe was a sculptor who won recognition for his work *FluteBoy*. He sculpted two other famous works of art, *African Dancer* and *Feral Benga*.

Popular Music

There was a range of music that encompassed jazz, blues, spirituals, Latin beats such as the rumba, and ragtime. Music such as the blues, jazz and spirituals was uniquely inspired by African Americans as an expression of their hopes, dreams, even hardships. The blues, in particular, emerged during the late 1800s and eventually provided the foundation for ragtime and finally jazz.

The Blues

The blues is a uniquely African American musical creation. It is a special kind of music that tells the story of hardships and personal experiences, particularly from the antebellum work songs of the South and the Mississippi Delta region. W. C. Handy is usually credited with making the blues popular. Some White entertainers, such as Mae West adopted it and brought it to a wider-audience popular. The blues provided the foundation for ragtime and finally jazz. There were many blues greats such as Leadbelly, Robert Johnson, John Lee Hooker, and Muddy Waters.

The music of the early 1900s produced new dances such as the Lindy Hop, a type of swing dance that uses jazz music. This explosion of musical talent and expression produced some of the best that could be found in blues and jazz. Many of the musicians who had lived in places such as New Orleans followed the great migration to Kansas City, Memphis, Chicago and New York. Artists such as ragtime jazz pianist Jelly Roll Morton, bandleader Louis Armstrong, and blues singer Bessie Smith were some of the people who became famous during that time.

Big Band leaders also came into prominence and became popular with Whites and African Americans alike. Big Band artists included people such as Duke Ellington and Count Basie. Whites would come to Harlem, to the famous Cotton Club on Lenox Avenue or the Savoy Ballroom at 140th and

141st Streets, to hear these artists. What was so ironic and sad was that African American performers entertained White audiences, but African Americans were not allowed to sit in the audience. A few places, such as Smalls Paradise, did allow mixed groups of African Americans and Whites.

Some people refused to perform for segregated audiences, however. Josephine Baker was one of these people. She was a civil rights activist and worked against racism and discrimination while in the United States. She was born in St. Louis, Missouri, and later became a world-famous singer and performer. Baker eventually emigrated to France because of the racism she was subjected to in the United States. While in France, she did undercover work for the French Resistance during World War II, for which she was decorated. Baker was the first American woman to receive military honors. She died in 1975 in France.

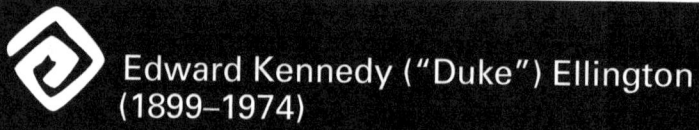

Edward Kennedy ("Duke") Ellington (1899–1974)

There were many musicians who made their own unique contribution to jazz. Duke Ellington was not only a musician, he was a master composer. He was born in Washington, D.C. Ellington studied the piano and played jazz as a teenager. He moved to New York where he became a bandleader. There, he helped to create the Big Band sound of the "swing dance" era.

Duke Ellington was the most prolific composer of the twentieth century because he composed so many pieces in a variety of forms and settings.

He wrote music for the ballroom as well as the nightclub, for the movie house as well as the theater.

Classical Performance

Marian Anderson and Roland Hayes were two famous classical concert singers. In 1930, Anderson went to Europe, where she sang for government leaders. In the United States, however, the Daughters of the American Revolution prevented her from singing at Constitution Hall in Washington, D.C. There was such a public outcry that she was invited to sing from the steps of the Lincoln Memorial in 1939 by the Secretary of the Interior, Harold Ickes.

Jazz

African Americans have influenced the music of America through their unique forms and styles. Jazz started around 1895 in New Orleans. It combines marching band music, blues and elements of ragtime. One major way in which jazz differs from traditional American or European music is that in Western music, all the musicians try to play what is written on their music sheets. In jazz, however, there is improvisation, and the musicians create their own musical score, which becomes an entirely new piece.

Jazz moved with the Great Migration to places such as Chicago, Memphis and Kansas City. In New York City, the "Big Band" movement incorporated jazz.

Roland Hayes sang with the Fisk Jubilee Singers early in his career. He, too, had to go to Europe to gain recognition. When he returned to the United States, though, he was signed up to sing in Boston, Massachusetts, thus breaking the color barrier for African American concert singers of classical music.

Theater

Paul Robeson was an actor and singer. He was also a person of great intellect, an all-American athlete in college, and law school graduate. When he played the lead role in Shakespeare's *Othello*, his performance was called one of the greatest events in the history of the American theater. It still is. Like Baker, however, Robeson eventually moved to France because of the racist treatment he received in the United States.

Vaudeville was another form of theatrical stage entertainment. Florence Mills began her acting career in vaudeville. She later landed a role in *Shuffle Along*. She played in several other roles but won international acclaim in the musical *Blackbirds*, which traveled to London and Paris.

All of these artists gave expression to the African American experience and by doing so gave expression and shape to American culture. Many of the music and art forms have become an intrinsic part of American culture. One in particular is jazz, an African American art form. This period came to an end, however, with the Great Depression because people could no longer afford to support artists by coming to shows or even by publishing the work of African American writers.

Scholars and Scientists

The early 1900s was a time of intellectual growth and discovery for African Americans. The Harlem Renaissance was in full swing also. There was a new determination to fight against the oppression of White supremacy and racism. There were many great writers, intellectuals, creative people and academic leaders in that period. One of the personalities who was very important to both the intellectual and the ordinary person was Carter G. Woodson. A new sense of academic curiosity and of scholarship began to grow based on the contributions that Black scholars made in various academic disciplines.

Carter G. Woodson

Carter G. Woodson is considered the father of Black history. In 1915, under his encouragement, the Association for the Study of Negro Life and History was founded. In his book *The Mis-Education of the Negro,* Woodson explained that African Americans do more harm to themselves than Whites do to them. He said this because he felt that African Americans had been taught to despise themselves and to be inferior. Woodson felt that they had been taught to think that they had no history of which to be proud, that they had been taught to look to Whites and their history for what was worthwhile. They did not know their own history, so they had no pride in the accomplishments that it held. What was worse, he felt, was that the schools and colleges for African Americans deliberately attempted to keep them in mental servitude. These schools, with their curricula that focused on European achievements, promoted the idea of the superiority of European culture. This would lead African Americans to deny their own art and cultural achievements. Unfortunately, Woodson was right. Even today, too many African Americans know too little about their history, and most schools are making very poor efforts to teach it.

Woodson's book, published in 1933, caused quite a sensation. Woodson was a man ahead of his time. He founded the *Journal of Negro History* and, in 1926, he started Negro History Week. It was expanded to Negro History Month, or, as it is known today, Black History Month, in 1976.

 Carter G. Woodson (1875–1950)

Carter G. Woodson is known as the "Father of Black History." He founded the Association for the Study of Negro Life and History, from which was published the *Journal of Negro History*. His book, *The Mis-Education of the Negro*, caused quite an uproar when it was published. In his book Woodson wrote that "When you control a man's thinking you do not have to worry about his actions." He published five textbooks and several other major works during his lifetime.

Ernest Just

Ernest Just was an African American scientist from Charleston, South Carolina. He was a biologist, zoologist, and research scientist, and his work focused on the study of cells, or cytology. Just was the first person to receive the Spingarn Medal from the NAACP for his scientific achievements. The Spingarn Medal is awarded to an African American with the "highest and noblest achievement" for the preceding year or years.

Benjamin Quarles

Benjamin Quarles, an African American historian, was born in Boston in 1904. He taught at Shaw University in North Carolina and was also the chair of the history department at Morgan State University in Maryland. Quarles formally introduced the study of African American studies into schools at a time when Whites did not think there was sufficient history to merit it or that African American writers could be objective. It is interesting that White historians often do not produce balanced history even in the 21st century. Quarles proved them wrong by documenting just such historical information.

The Schomburg Collection

Arthur Schomburg was born in Puerto Rico in 1874. He was well educated and led a rich public life. He worked at several different occupations, including law clerk, journalist, and editor. What makes Schomburg so important was his huge collection of books, letters, artwork, and Black culture about African Americans. The Carnegie Foundation bought his collection and gave it to the New York City Public Library. The collection became known as the Schomburg Center for Research in Black Culture.

The Negro Baseball Leagues

Since African Americans were barred from participating in every area of social and cultural life, they found ways to provide these outlets for themselves. One major area was in sports. African Americans formed what were known as the Negro Leagues. The first recorded baseball league began just after the Civil War. There was a game between the Uniques of New York City and the Excelsiors of Philadelphia in 1867. But when African American players attempted to join the National Association of Baseball Players, the first organized league in the country, they were refused. This did not stop them, though. In 1885, Frank P. Thompson organized the first professional Negro team, called the Cuban Giants. It was very successful—but White teams refused to play them. Other independent teams were formed, such as the Philadelphia Orions, the Lord Baltimores, the St. Louis Black Stockings, and the Cuban X Giants, to name a few.

The new century brought a new wave of Black teams. In 1920, Rube Foster, owner of the Chicago American Giants, met with other independent owners and founded the Negro Baseball League. Unfortunately, Foster became ill and was unable to continue in his leadership role, and the Great Depression devastated the economy, not only for Whites but particularly for African Americans. People could no longer afford to attend games and this severely diminished this creative period. Eventually, the League folded.

Other leagues were formed after the Great Depression. Two of these were the Kansas City Monarchs and the Homestead Grays. Out of these leagues came outstanding baseball players, such as Josh Gibson and Buck Leonard. Jackie Robinson was the baseball player who integrated the National White baseball leagues. When he was signed to play with the Brooklyn Dodgers, he was harassed and even booed, but that did not stop his resolve to play. He continued, and became a great hero to many. When the integration of baseball teams ultimately came, it marked the end of the old Negro Baseball Leagues. Other players such as Satchel Paige began to follow in the steps of Jackie Robinson.

Summary

The Harlem Renaissance reflected a new attitude of African Americans. It greatly affected the cultural development of the United States, while it presented the artistic and intellectual talents of African Americans to the rest of the world. It highlighted the writings of such people as Langston Hughes and Zora Neale Hurston. It produced a new type of music called jazz and introduced the blues and even new dances, such as the Lindy Hop, or swing dancing. The Harlem Renaissance also served as a forum for African Americans to express their aspirations for human rights and self-determination.

This renaissance produced the "New Negro," according to Alain Locke, one who was self-confident, assured of creative talents, and determined to fight for equal rights. It was also a time when Carter G. Woodson urged African Americans to take a closer look at themselves, their history, and the education they were receiving.

Racism forced African Americans to form their own baseball teams and other forms of entertainment. The "color line" was broken in baseball when Jackie Robinson was signed to play with the Brooklyn Dodgers in 1947. It was a milestone for sports, but Robinson suffered much abuse in the way of booing crowds and name-calling. It was also the end of the Negro Leagues.

However, this was a time when African Americans could point with pride to the accomplishments arising out of their ranks. The artists of the Harlem Renaissance experienced a major advancement up the ranks of society. Unfortunately, this celebration of African American artists was not to last. A Great Depression descended upon America. The next chapter will discuss the effects of this Depression, a second world war, and the rise of an African American middle class.

References

Anderson, J. D. (1988). *The education of Blacks in the South: 1860–1935*. Later Printing edition. University of North Carolina Press.

Appiah, K., & Gates, H. L. (Eds.). (1999). *Africana: The encyclopedia of African and African American experiences*. Basic Civitas.

Asante, M. K. (1993). *The Afrocentric idea*. Revised and expanded edition. Temple University Press.

Asante, M. K. (1993). *Historical and cultural atlas of African Americans*. Macmillan Publishing.

Asante, M. K. (2001). *African American history: A journey of liberation.* Peoples Publishing Group, Inc.

Bennett, L., Jr. (1993). *Before the Mayflower: A history of Black America.* 6th edition. Penguin Books.

Domonoske, C. (2018). *NPR choice page.* www.npr.org/sections/thetwo-way/2018/05/24/614114966/legendary-boxer-jack-johnson-gets-pardon-105-years-after-baseless-conviction

Franklin, J. H., & Moss, A. A., Jr. (2000). *From slavery to freedom: A history of African Americans.* Knopf.

Gates, H. L., Jr., & Higginbotham, E. B. (Eds.). (2004). *African American lives.* Oxford University Press.

Hine, D. C. (Ed.) (2005). *Black women in America* (2nd ed.). Oxford University Press.

Morgan, T. (1996). *Jazz: The first thirty years.* Accessed May 24, 2004. http://www.jass.com/jazzo.html

Morse, B. (2020). *When a Black heavyweight boxer's victory terrified a US president.* CNN. https://www.cnn.com/2020/07/03/sport/jack-johnson-fight-of-the-century-110-anniversary-boxing-cmd-spt-intl/index.html

Simon, Scott. (2021, March 27). How Black players propelled Cleveland's baseball team to win the 1948 World Series. NPR. https://www.npr.org/2021/03/27/979683299/how-black-players-propelled-clevelands-baseball-team-to-win-the-1948-world-serie

Shujaa, M. J., & Shujaa, K. J. (Eds.). (2015). *The Sage encyclopedia of African cultural heritage in North America.* 1st edition. Sage Publications, 2015.

Trotter, J. W. *The African American experience*, Volume I and II. Houghton Mifflin, 2001.

Old Problems, New Deals, and Continued Hard Times

The Great Depression

Within the period from 1929 to 1939, America had to confront serious national problems that included two wars, an economic recession and racial strife. America fell into terrible economic times during the 1930s, and at the end of World War II. In October 1929, the stock market crashed, and many Whites who had invested in the market lost all of their money. Some people were so devastated by their losses that they committed suicide. Businesses closed, and, at the peak of what came to be called the Great Depression, there were 15 million people out of work. It is estimated that 25 percent of the workforce population was unemployed at that time.

The economy for African Americans was even worse than Whites. The Depression ended the Harlem Renaissance and brought even harder times than before. The phrase "last one hired and first one fired" had a new and terrible meaning to most African Americans. Most unions would not help them. Unions wanted only to assist Whites with getting whatever jobs were available. Many people, both White and African American, had to wait in soup lines set up to help feed those who were jobless and homeless. However, twice as many African Americans as Whites needed public assistance by

CHAPTER 11

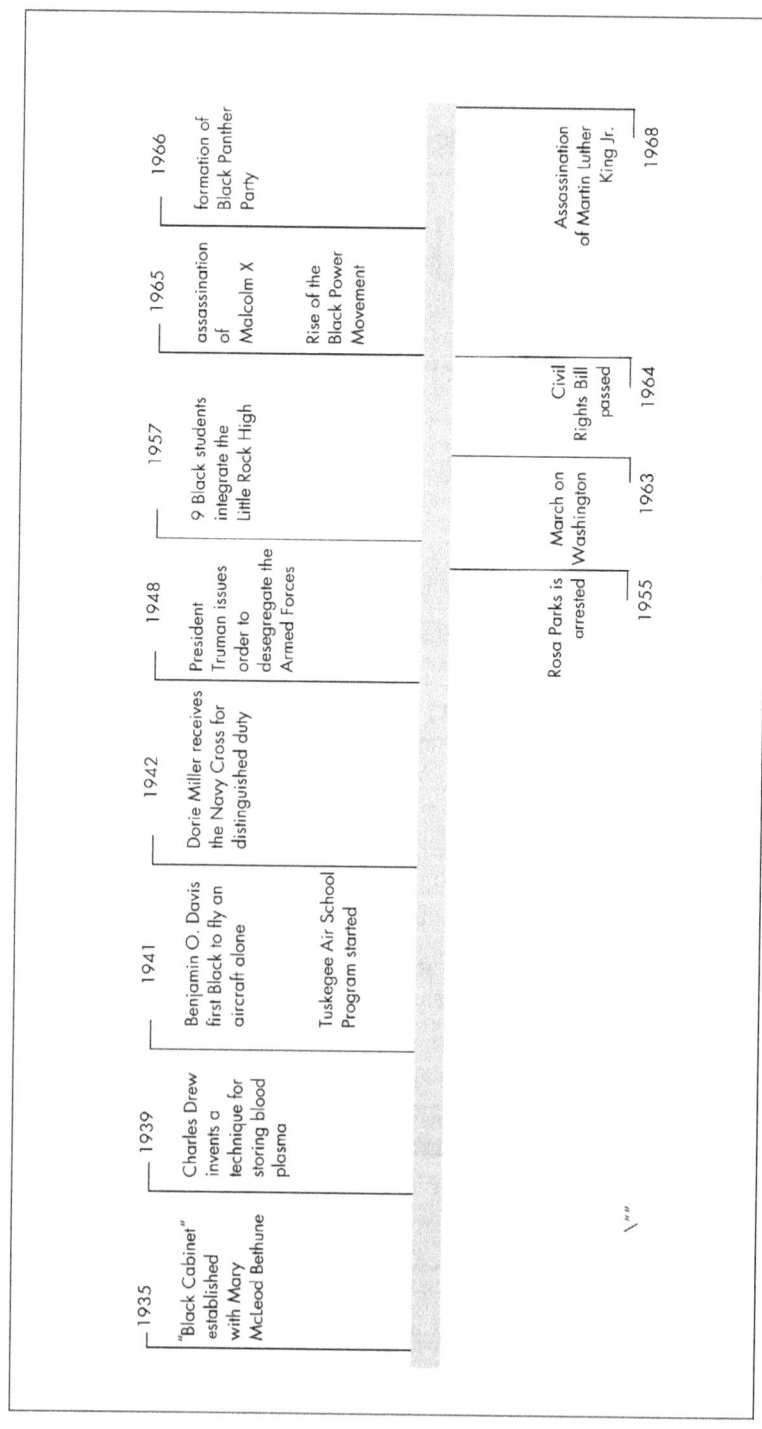

African American History 1935–1968

the mid-1930s. Some historians state that one out of four African Americans was on public relief by 1935. Suddenly, African Americans, who had begun to see a modest improvement in their living conditions, became the largest group in need of public assistance.

African Americans in the rural South were perhaps the worst off, because of the reduced demands for farm labor with the collapse of cotton prices and with the added use of machines. So African Americans tried to help themselves in whatever ways they could. They had rent parties, sold dinners, and helped one another to survive.

Often, the African American church was where one could find help. Many churches started relief programs. In 1931, Rev. Adam Clayton Powell Sr., the pastor of the Abyssinian Baptist Church, raised over $2,000 in a call to help fellow African Americans. The church was soon able to feed and clothe more than 2,000 people a day in its soup kitchen.

Leaving the Party of Lincoln

Up until the Great Depression, African Americans, when allowed, voted for candidates from the Republican Party. This was the party that had previously fought to prevent the spread of slavery. It was also the party of Lincoln, who had issued the Emancipation Proclamation. Finally, during the years of Reconstruction, the Republican Party organized to get African Americans elected to public office.

African Americans voted for Republican candidates on a national level. But allegiance to the Republican Party began to decline, particularly in local elections, where African Americans constituted large populations of the urban North. During the Depression, Herbert Hoover, a Republican, was running against Franklin Delano Roosevelt, a Democrat, for the presidency. Hoover's "trickle down" policy of relief did not trickle down sufficiently or swiftly enough for African Americans. The New Deal of Roosevelt seemed to have more appeal. The new Democrats promised to take the necessary steps to provide relief to people affected by the Great Depression. Their programs, according to Bennett (1993), at least recognized the problems that urban African Americans faced. African Americans voted for Roosevelt in record numbers. It is estimated that Roosevelt received about one-fourth of the African American vote in northern cities.

 **Mary McLeod Bethune (1875–1955)**

Mary McLeod Bethune was an educator. She founded Daytona Normal and Industrial Institute for women. It later merged with Cookman Institute to become the Bethune-Cookman College. She was a member of the Federal Council of Negro Affairs, known as the "Black Cabinet" in the Franklin D. Roosevelt administration.

The New Deal

Roosevelt was elected upon the promise of relieving Americans from the economic devastation of the Great Depression. There were some inherent problems with Roosevelt's policies and programs, but, given the alternative, African Americans chose him. Roosevelt did nothing to challenge civil rights issues, although he did initiate programs that made it easier to get relief. Getting jobs, however, was a different issue. Despite this, his administration established housing projects and agencies to deal with the problems brought on by the Depression. Some of these agencies were the National Youth Administration (NYA), the Works Progress Administration (WPA), the Civilian Conservation Corps (CCC), and the Public Works Administration (PWA). Roosevelt also instituted the Tennessee Valley Authority (TVA), a hydroelectric project that provided cheap electric power, and the Social Security Administration.

The PWA provided low-income housing and African Americans occupied about one-third of the housing units. The CCC provided jobs for African Americans on various projects. The WPA provided educational and cultural programs as well as vocational training. It also employed many writers, actors, and artists.

Even though Roosevelt never challenged the civil rights issues and the blatant violations of the Constitution by White southerners, there was still a backlash against him and his programs. At first, southern Whites liked the New Deal programs because they were helped. But when they thought that the programs would substantially help African Americans, they became threatened and organized a campaign to defeat Roosevelt. In the end, it was World War II that brought an end to the Depression, not the programs of the New Deal.

Two Influential Women

During this time, a dialogue was opened between African Americans and President Roosevelt. He created the Federal Council of Negro Affairs or the "Black Cabinet." Mary McLeod Bethune was a very influential member of this cabinet. She was born in 1875 in South Carolina, where she attended a mission school. Later, she attended Scotia Seminary in North Carolina and Moody Bible Institute in Chicago. Bethune had previously led African American women's grassroots organizations in the 1920s and 1930s. Bethune also started a normal (or teacher training) and industrial school for girls in Florida in 1904. It merged with the Cookman Institute of Jacksonville and became co-educational. Bethune became the director of Negro Affairs of the National Youth Administration (NYA) in 1935 and organized two conferences on "The Problems of the Negro and Negro Youth."

Although women's activist groups were emerging up to this point, women played a very small role in the politics of the nation. Eleanor Roosevelt influenced some of the programs on the behalf of women and youth. She managed to get women appointed to posts in the Roosevelt administration and she influenced programs such as the NYA. Most important, however, was her support for African Americans. Eleanor Roosevelt was acutely aware of the problems that Blacks faced from southerners and northerners alike. Her biggest crusade on behalf of African Americans was related to anti-lynching. She prodded her husband FDR to take a more proactive stance against "lynch laws." She befriended Mary McLeod Bethune and Walter White, executive secretary of the NAACP. Eleanor Roosevelt, working with Mary McLeod Bethune, became sympathetic to the conditions of African Americans and gradually increased her support on civil rights issues.

Unrest and Protests: The New Deal

The New Deal programs instituted during the Great Depression helped but did not address racism and discrimination against African Americans in the workplace. African Americans renewed their protest against unjust treatment in the workplace. They organized picket lines and boycotted places that had only White workers. The protests started in Chicago and spread to other places. The purpose of the protests was to force White employers to hire Black workers, especially in places that depended on African American customers. African Americans picketed lunch counters, movies, bakeries, and other such businesses. These protests proliferated across Black America. Their slogan was "Don't Buy Where You Can't Work."

Adam Clayton Powell, Jr.

One place that felt the impact was Harlem. A young preacher by the name of Adam Clayton Powell, Jr. brought the struggle into focus. Powell was born in New Haven, Connecticut, in 1908. He and his parents moved to New York City, where his father, Rev. Adam Clayton Powell, Sr., established one of the largest congregations in the country. In 1932 the younger Powell administered the extensive relief program that provided food and clothing for the needy that was started by his father.

Powell was a charismatic leader. He organized and led a four-year campaign that targeted a variety of businesses. He led protest marches against utility companies, bus lines, department stores, and even hospitals. It is estimated that he added 10,000 jobs for African Americans to the workforce. Powell went on to become the pastor of his father's church. The victories that he secured made him very popular among the Harlem residents, both middle class and poor. He was eventually elected to the Congress of the United States.

 Adam Clayton Powell Jr.

Adam Clayton Powell was as controversial as he was charismatic. During the Depression, Powell established himself as a successful civil rights leader by using picket lines and mass meetings to demand reforms. He was elected to the New York City Council in 1941 and then to Congress in 1944. His voice was often the lone one against the injustices perpetrated against African Americans.

A Renewed Focus on Civil Rights

In the spring of 1933, civil rights activist Joel Spingarn held a three-day conference at his estate in Amenia, New York. The purpose was to decide how the NAACP could best focus its attention against social injustice. The NAACP filed suits covering a number of civil rights issues and won Supreme

Court decisions banning the "grandfather clause" and residential segregation. Its campaign in the courts had a great effect on the issues of segregation.

One case that focused the attention of many was in Scottsboro, Alabama, where nine African American young men were charged with the alleged rape of two White women. The problem started when a fight broke out between the African American youth and some White youth on a freight train in 1931.

Both groups were "catching" a ride on a freight train headed south. The African American youth claimed that the White youths initiated a fight and that they were defending themselves. In any case, the White youth either jumped off the train or were put off, but they got their revenge. They reported the incident to the authorities. When the sheriff went to arrest the African Americans, there were two White women on board the train also. The women were afraid of being arrested, so they claimed that the young African American men had raped them.

The young African Americans were given a speedy trial and all but one sentenced to the electric chair. The young men did not receive proper legal representation and would have lost their lives if the Communist Party had not intervened. They mounted a nationwide campaign to call attention to the situation. They also provided legal defense that took the case all the way to the Alabama Supreme Court, which upheld the convictions. The outrage over this decision caused numerous demonstrations and marches. Finally, the Supreme Court overturned the convictions and ordered new trials. The last of the young men were not released until after World War II.

Despite that setback, however, there were victories. The NAACP became more focused. It began to concentrate on challenging inequality in graduate schools of various colleges and universities. Charles Hamilton Houston and Thurgood Marshall led these challenges. In 1935, Houston became the first African American to argue a case before the U.S. Supreme Court. The court overturned the conviction of a man accused of murdering a White in the case of *Hollins v. State of Oklahoma*. It was overturned because African Americans had been illegally excluded from the jury. In other words, the decision held that Hollins had been denied due process under the Fourteenth Amendment law. This was just the first in a series of court challenges and victories for the NAACP. While the NAACP fought court battles, Eleanor Roosevelt continued to prod President Franklin D. Roosevelt to get more involved in the Negro problem. This created a two-pronged strategy to deal with the problems of African Americans at this time. Through the courts a formal assault through legal challenges was waged. With the aid of influential White political and social reformist, and the use of back door channels, President Roosevelt was persuaded to take more action to help Negros.

World War II

The New Deal programs provided some relief for Americans during the Depression, but hard economic times persisted until World War II. The war began between the Axis powers of Germany, Italy, and Japan against the Allied forces of France, Great Britain, the United States, and Russia. After war broke out, the United States began supplying material aid to its European allies. The increase in material production began to revitalize the devastated U.S. economy. Then, on December 7, 1941, Japan attacked the American armed forces stationed at Pearl Harbor in Hawaii. President Roosevelt declared war on Japan and the United States entered the actual fighting. Economically, this created an even greater boost to the economy because of wartime industries.

Discrimination in Employment

Despite the creation of new jobs, African Americans were refused employment at plants with government contracts. A. Philip Randolph, who had previously organized the Brotherhood of Sleeping Car Porters, threatened a march on Washington to protest job discrimination in the defense industries and in the military. He had proven to be an effective organizer. Randolph threatened to have 100,000 African Americans march in protest. President Roosevelt and others called Randolph to Washington and tried to dissuade him, but he was adamant about the march. President Roosevelt then convened a meeting with African American leaders and, in the end, issued Executive Order 8802 on June 25, 1941. This order banned discrimination in the war industries. It set up the Fair Employment Practices Commission. This was a significant milestone for African Americans, because this was the first presidential order that directly affected them since the Emancipation Proclamation.

 France Attracts African Americans

France has held a great attraction for African Americans. Its history has included the presence of Blacks for centuries. France also participated in the slave trade as well as the development of racist ideology. Despite these issues, in the late 1800s, the country developed an appeal to many African Americans who either visited or relocated. It became the home of painter Henry Ossawa Tanner in 1891. Sculptor Meta Vaux Warrick Fuller studied there for two years. Abolitionists Frederick Douglass, Mary Church Terrell, and actor Ira Aldridge visited during the late 1800s. Booker T. Washington, and W.E.B. Du Bois visited in the early 1900s. The interest shown by these prominent African Americans contributed to the perception that France was color-blind.

During World War I (1914–1918) African American troops were stationed in France. Soldiers introduced jazz to the French people. That introduction paved the way for Black entertainers and writers to find an audience for their art. During the early 1900s, writers such as Claude McKay and Countee Cullen visited France and entertainer Josephine Baker settled there. During the 1950s, writers such as Richard Wright, James Baldwin, Chester Himes and jazz drummer Kenny Clark settled in France. Jazz singer Nina Simone, who died in 2003, moved to France in 1974.

Service in World War II

Although Randolph also demanded equality in the armed forces, it was more difficult to achieve. Yet there were some changes in military practices. The government no longer prohibited the induction of African American volunteers as it had in World War I. It actually increased the number of recruits to reflect the African American population, and it increased the number of slots allotted to African Americans who commanded all-African American units. The government also prohibited discrimination in the selection and training of military personnel because of race.

At the beginning of the war, African Americans were barred from the Marines, the Army Air Corps, and the Coast Guard. By 1942, these restrictions had been lifted. African Americans were permitted to join the Marine Corps and Navy for general service. In 1948, President Harry S. Truman issued Executive Order 9981, which ended segregation in the armed forces. It called for "equality of treatment and opportunity" in the military.

An African American Naval Hero

The Navy only used African Americans as cooks. But when the Japanese bombed Pearl Harbor, one African American proved to be more than a cook. He was Dorie Miller from Waco, Texas, who served as a mess attendant on board the battleship *Arizona*. He came to the aid of wounded sailors, including the ship's captain, Mervyn Bennion, by moving them out of danger. Because there was a restriction against African American naval personnel, Miller had never been trained in the use of weapons of any kind. Even so, he manned an anti-aircraft gun and shot down several Japanese planes before he was ordered to abandon ship. Miller was one of the first heroes of the war, and he was the first African American sailor to receive the Navy Cross. He was killed in battle in 1943, but his heroism is remembered by many.

Benjamin O. Davis, Jr. (1912–2002)

Benjamin O. Davis, Jr. graduated from West Point in 1936. It was difficult for him there. No one spoke to him for four years except on official business. Upon graduation, he was initially assigned to the infantry. He became one of only two Black line officers in the U.S. Army. The other officer was his father. He became a lieutenant colonel commanding the 99th Fighter Squadron in combat. Davis was awarded the Distinguished Flying Cross after his flying mission in which he led 39 Thunderbolts that were escorting B-24 bombers to targets in Munich, Germany.

Davis rose first to the rank of brigadier general in 1965 and then to lieutenant general in 1970. He was the first African American in the entire military to rise to that level. After a distinguished career, he retired as a lieutenant general in 1970. In civilian life, he served in the Nixon administration as Assistant Secretary of Transportation for Environment, Safety, and Consumer Affairs. In 1998, President Bill Clinton awarded him a fourth star, bringing him to the rank of a full general.

The Tuskegee Airmen

African Americans also served in the air force. The most famous were the Tuskegee Airmen. In 1940, a civilian pilot training program was started for African American college students at Tuskegee Institute in Alabama, the school begun by Booker T. Washington. In 1941, the program was expanded into a military flight school to train pilots for the war effort. At one point, Eleanor Roosevelt visited the school to see how the program was going, and, when invited to take a flight with an African American pilot, she accepted.

Benjamin O. Davis became the first African American officer to fly a plane solo in the Air Corps. Over time, more than 1,000 African American pilots were trained. They distinguished themselves in World War II and flew missions in Germany, France, Poland, Romania, and Africa. The Distinguished Flying Cross was awarded to more than eighty African American pilots, including Davis.

The Red Ball Express

Although some African American soldiers served in fighting units, many others were given menial duties in labor battalions. In both cases, the units were segregated. But whatever duty they were given, they performed admirably. One of these duty situations involved the famous Red Ball Express. This was a unit of mostly African American soldiers who were charged with supplying ammunition and other supplies to the soldiers who were fighting on the front lines. This company was made up of drivers, mechanics, and administrative clerks, of which three-fourths were African Americans. There were not enough trucks or drivers when units such as these were organized. Often, African Americans were pressed into these units because they had no training with weapons, but, unfortunately, they were also inexperienced drivers. Even so, this did not stop them from completing their missions. The members of these units had to accept the discrimination that they received, and they were warned not to have any associations with the White soldiers, in order to avoid problems. Dwight D. Eisenhower acknowledged their service when he wrote that the successful campaign in France was due as much to the men of the Red Ball Express as it was to those who drove the tanks.

African Americans in the Midst of Combat

There were many other war campaigns in which African Americans distinguished themselves. They were among the first to land with the Coast Guard at Okinawa. During this time, African American soldiers, Marines, and sailors were deployed throughout the South Sea Islands and the Pacific.

They helped to build the Ledo/Stillwell Road from Assam, India, to China through the Himalayan mountains, and they fought Japanese forces all along the way.

Despite the obstacles put before African Americans in the military, they put their lives as well as their labor on the line. By the end of the war, over a million African American men and women had served their country, 6,000 of them as officers. Still, they returned to a largely ungrateful American citizenry.

Josephine Baker (1906–1975)

Frequently African Americans emigrated to other countries in order to live and work in dignity and for freedom from racism and segregation. One of these people was Josephine Baker.

Baker was thirteen when she began dancing in vaudeville and then on Broadway. Baker performed in a Broadway review called Shuffle Along in 1922 and was virtually a star by 1924. In 1925, Baker went to Paris, where she became famous for her performances in the Revue Negre at the Theatre des Champs-Elysees.

Baker did undercover work for the French Resistance during World War II in 1940. The French rewarded her with the Croix de Guerre and Medal of the Resistance.

She was a civil rights activist and refused to perform for segregated audiences and because of this policy integrated nightclub shows in the Las Vegas, New York and Boston. Baker adopted twelve children from around the world whom she called her "Rainbow Tribe."

She died in Paris and was buried in Monaco. Baker became the first American woman to receive French military honors at her funeral.

Trouble on the Home Front

Return to the Racist Nation

African American women also attempted to join the war effort, and they, too, faced discrimination. There was a quota on the number of African Americans accepted into the Army and Navy Nurse Corps. A campaign was waged by Mabel K. Staupers to integrate these services, yet it was only when there was a shortage of White nurses that the quota on African American nurses ended. More than 4,000 women served in the Women's Army Corps (WACS), and the Women Accepted for Volunteer Emergency Service (WAVES), a branch of the Navy.

Although African Americans answered the call to defend their country, they were subjected to racist treatment in the armed forces, and segregation was rigidly enforced. African Americans were still denied entry into some programs. African American men were subjected to discrimination on a routine basis in training camps in both the North and South. Sometimes fights broke out between White and African American soldiers, and African American soldiers were also often subjected to random attacks. African American women were also subjected to assaults, intimidation, verbal abuse, and sexual harassment. William Hastie, an African American civilian aide to the Secretary of War, resigned in protest because of continuing racist policies of the military.

The Blood Bank

The American Red Cross practiced segregation by separating the blood drawn from African Americans from that drawn from Whites. This was ironic considering that it was Charles Drew, an African American, who discovered the method of preserving blood plasma. Drew (1904–1950), who was from Washington, D.C., attended Amherst College, then went on to receive his medical degree from McGill University in Montreal, Canada. He pioneered a system for storing blood and was employed by the British to set up a model for the mass distribution of blood. This became the model that was used in Europe and England.

When the United States entered into the war, he was hired to head a project to do the same. Charles Drew became the first director of the blood plasma project of the American Red Cross in 1941. The American Red Cross refused to accept blood drawn from African Americans, however. When it finally did so, it was on a segregated basis. Although transfusions are based on blood type, not skin color, still racists did not want blood from African Americans to be given to Whites. Dr. Drew resigned his position because of this discriminatory practice.

Resistance and Riots at Home

When World War II began, almost two million African Americans from the South moved to the North to work in the war industries. Housing then became a bigger issue than ever. Many White workers did not want African American families moving near them. Often, African American families were met with violence in the form of evictions and arson. The race problem was becoming deeper and more dangerous.

Tensions rose to the point that hostilities broke out in several cities. The summer of 1943 was, in many ways, similar to the "red summer" of 1919. Race riots broke out in New York; Detroit, Michigan; Mobile, Alabama; and Beaumont, Texas. Often, African American soldiers faced more danger at home, in America, than in the war in Europe. There were lynchings of African American veterans in various states. In Walton County, Georgia, not only were two veterans lynched, but their wives were lynched as well. These atrocities fueled protests and tensions. Following these events, many committees on race relations and human relations were set up, but they did very little to solve the problems. President Truman established a Civil Rights Committee, but the report that was published was filed and forgotten.

Notable Figures of the Period

During the Roosevelt administration two events occurred in 1936 that did more to raise the pride of African Americans than anything else. The first was the victory of track star Jesse Owens at the Berlin Olympics in 1936. The second was the success of boxer, Joe Louis.

Jesse Owens

Jesse Owens was born in Alabama, one of eight children, to poor sharecropping parents. When the family moved to Cleveland, Ohio, Owens attended public schools, where he ran track. He attended Ohio State University, where he broke the world track records for the 220-yard hurdles, the broad jump, and the 220-yard dash. He set several new American records as well.

Owens was made team captain, the first African American ever to hold that position on any Ohio State team. He won a position on the American Olympic Team in 1936. The Olympic Games were held in Berlin, Germany, where Adolf Hitler aimed to prove the superiority of Germans, specifically, what he called the "Aryan" race. This race included only certain White people and left out German Jews and non-Germanic ethnic groups.

Owens crushed Hitler's theory by winning four gold medals. Owens won the 100 meter sprint, the 200 meter sprint and two other events at the Olympic Games. He broke two world records, tied one world record and helped his 400-yard relay team set another world and Olympic record. Owen had left for Germany simply as an African American athlete but returned aboard the *Queen Mary* as a hero to all Americans. Many people gathered at the docks and over 1,000 got passes to board the ship before it docked. It was the first time that both African Americans and Whites united in their praise of one individual, who just happened to be an African American.

Jesse Owens was born in Alabama but moved to Cleveland, Ohio, in 1921. He made history when he won four gold medals in the 1936 Olympics held in Berlin, Germany. Owens also set two Olympic records and one world record. His long jump record lasted for 25 years. This he did in the face of racial discrimination.

Joe Louis

There was another boxer who became as famous as the infamous Jack Johnson. Joe Louis, also known as "The Brown Bomber," was a source of great pride for African Americans. He, like Jesse Owens, was born in Alabama. His family moved to Detroit, where he became a Golden Gloves fighter. He held the amateur light heavyweight championship for ten years before turning to professional boxing. Joe Louis fought the Italian, Primo Carnera, a former heavyweight champion, but he became famous when he beat Max Baer.

Louis went on to meet the German heavyweight champion, Max Schmeling in 1936. To the disappointment of many, he was defeated in the 12th round, the first defeat Louis had suffered. Still, he went on to win the heavyweight championship from James Braddock in 1937. But Louis would not consider himself a champion until he could fight and defeat the only boxer who had defeated him. He got his chance in 1937, when he met and knocked out Schmeling in the first round. It was another defeat for Hitler's so-called superior race. Again, an African American became a hero to all Americans, especially African Americans. They had something to be proud of and something that again disproved the theory of the superiority of one race over another. Joe Louis retired as the undefeated heavyweight champion of the world in 1949.

Louis was very generous and gave much of his money to charity. Unfortunately, he owed back taxes so, at one point, he attempted a comeback to the ring to pay them. His comeback was not successful, though, and when he retired for a second time, he was broke. Louis was forced to work as a host in a Las Vegas nightclub. Joe Louis had been the source of much pride for many Americans, regardless of color, and some people felt the government had punished him too severely. But despite his financial situation, when he died Louis was buried in Arlington National Cemetery.

The African American Middle Class

The Multifaceted Issues of Class in African American Society

The rise of the African American middle class has had its starts and fits, its movement forward, or sometimes not at all. The one thing that can be said is that it is not monolithic. There is no such thing as one community of African Americans. This was especially demonstrated in the 2016 presidential election. The Black vote, no matter the class, cannot just be taken for granted. The Black middle class is as diverse as White groups who live in America. There are groups within the African American communities who have different backgrounds and origins. They are made up of native born African Americans, or those who arrived through slavery, and immigrants from different countries. The experiences of native born African Americans are different from those African people who have emigrated from other countries, including the Caribbean.

The Origins and Development of the Black Middle Class

In order to understand the diversity of African American class structure one has to look at the history of the lives of people during the various time periods. To do this one must start with the period of slavery. In the South, during the founding of America there were distinct segments of the Black population. This slave regime included the house slave and the field slave. One was subjected to harsher and crueler realties. They included also Africans who became free through manumission, which was the voluntary emancipation of an enslaved African by the slave owner. They were people such as Peter Salem in the North. Some Africans bought their freedom, such as Salem Poor, although that became very difficult to do as the practice of slavery continued. There were also free Africans who had never been enslaved such as John Chavis, Aggripa Hull, and William Flora in the South. These two groups, free and slave, made up one part of the American social and class system.

Free Africans lived in both the North and the South. Many of those who lived in the South, continued to live there despite the practice of enslavement. According to USHistory.org, these Africans were highly skilled artisans, business people, writers, musicians and inventors. Although they lived under a slave regime and their civil rights were severely limited (similar to Black Codes), they were able to make a living for themselves. These Africans, however, were forbidden to learn how to read and some laws forbade them from returning if they went out of state to do so. With the skills they had, however, they had the basis for forming a better life for themselves.

Blacks in the North were already active participants in American society (African American Odyssey). Some free Blacks bought and owned other slaves (whom they freed). Others owned land, fought in America's first wars such as Salem Poor and were active in the fight against slavery. These Blacks also spoke out in newspapers such as *Freedom's Journal*. In addition northern Blacks founded churches that also provided a setting for economic, social and intellectual activities. Out of this combination of Blacks came the first glimmer of a community that had different backgrounds, and different means to self-sufficiency.

The third group consisted of were those who arrived from the Caribbean and elsewhere such as John Baptist DuSable, who had been shipwrecked near New Orleans, and became a fur trapper and explorer. He is credited with the founding of Chicago. In fact, in the area near New Orleans, there were a number of Blacks who had come to America of their own free will as immigrants. As for this third group of Blacks within the African American community, the Caribbean Africans, one cannot assume that they identified with native born Blacks. In many cases the experiences of their cultural heritages were different.

Other than the society that existed during the period of enslavement and antebellum, the next period of the development of a middle class occurred during the early 1900s. It was a part of a larger movement that focused on serving the needs of and providing services for African Americans. There was a huge increase in the African American population in the cities of the North and Midwest. The continued policy of segregation provided the conditions that allowed for the significant increase of African American-owned businesses. As stated earlier, African American newspapers were on the rise. They advertised and promoted African American businesses. African American banks and insurance companies were started as well. The Negro Baseball Leagues were organized into successful commercial businesses, and they attracted large crowds of people.

There also was a growth in professional services. These new professionals included teachers, doctors, nurses, lawyers, and social workers. As opportunities for professionals grew, a wealth of information was directed to this new middle class. Furthermore, the early 1900s saw the establishment of fraternities and sororities on college campuses. Alpha Phi Alpha was the first Greek-letter organization for African American men on a college campus. It was founded in 1906 at Cornell University in Ithaca, New York. In 1908 Alpha Kappa Alpha became the first organization for women. This Greek-letter organization was founded on the campus of Howard University in Washington, D.C. These organizations also were a part of the growing middle class. They sought to not only survive in the hostile racial atmosphere of the times in which they were established, but sought to provide a means to enrich social and intellectual college life as well. Over time, seven other African American sororities and fraternities were established.

Then during the early to mid-century (1916–1970) there was the Great Migration when millions of African Americans left the South because of unsatisfactory working conditions and segregation. Included among this group were those came from the South and settled in Harlem becoming a part of the Harlem Renaissance. Then there were workers who moved to urban areas for work. Some of the Black newspapers that were started included the *Chicago Defender*, the *Dallas Post Times*, and the *Washington Informer*. Black magazines were started such as *Ebony* magazine which was started in 1945 by John H. Johnson. The possibility for better economic conditions was a function of the industrialization of the North and the rise of global trade.

The next part of this wave was during the 1960s and 1970s. Those families that had moved had begun to see a modest elevation in their economic conditions. The ability to work in factories and other industries provided African American workers with better wages. African Americans also had better access to schools. These educational opportunities were also available for their children. Out of these opportunities came the white collar professionals such as teachers, nurses and others. The African American middle class played an important role in the fight for equality of civil and human rights. They were outspoken in their opposition to segregation, were role models for many, and provided funding for these causes.

This new wave of African American middle class coincided with the presidency of Jimmy Carter. The African Americans of the 1970s moved into the professional middle class. Those in the labor jobs lost out, however. That ground was lost when plants closed. The professional class held onto civil service, health care and education careers and entrepreneurial endeavors. The emergence of the middle class can be compared to the successful community that was built by African Americans but destroyed by Whites in Greenwood, Oklahoma. The difference was that these new communities could be found in many cities and towns all over America. They could not all be destroyed as Greenwood had been.

The outlook for the truly disadvantaged in the Black community is dire in today's society. There are three basic reasons. One, it is a function of the industrialization of the workforce and the rise of global trade and technology. The economic centers of opportunity have shifted to the suburbs where there is limited public transportation (Wilson, 1996). Secondly because of the requirements for prior experience as the prerequisite, many jobs are no longer available. A third reason that career opportunities for Blacks have decreased is because of overly zealous background checks that have no relationship to career opportunities. These arbitrary and capricious background checks have nothing to do with the job at hand, but serves to keep Black workers out.

Race and Distinctions Within the African American Community

As of 2020, the gains that African Americans have made, in many instances do not compare with that of their White counterparts according to the Pew Research Center. Many African Americans in the middle class, as defined by education, occupation, housing value and income, still have a long ways to go in terms of socialization with the greater White community. While one may have the money to mingle with various entities in White American society, true acceptance is illusive.

In terms of Africans from other countries or the Caribbean, some authors point to the disdain that some Afro-Caribbean's have towards African Americans and the perception that they are somehow better. Things such as having a better education or a perceived better work ethic, and more respect for authority are among some of qualities cited in one report. The political and historical background of Black Caribbean people is also cited. One author discusses the lengths that some will go through to identify themselves as separate from African Americans. However in the long run, it makes little difference in America. Their lived experiences and heritage, which may be different from native born African Americans, have no bearing. The color of one's skin in America makes these perceived differences of little worth in terms of treatment. This was the structure in the early founding of America and continues to this day.

There is a perceived divergence among African Americans in terms of treatment. Given the way the so-called middle class developed, it can be said that they do not all think the same way. Some reach back to help others in their communities. Others Blacks move away from the communities in which they were raised. Black wealth does not equal to White wealth as is reported by some agencies. In the end, money can mitigate treatment against some of disadvantages in society, but it does not insulate the Black middle class from racism. Blacks of all class standing and ethnic heritage have the same threats as those "privileged" few who deem themselves as separate from those others. Blacks have distinctness but not separateness.

Summary

The prosperous years of the Harlem Renaissance came to an end with the Great Depression. All of America felt the economic pressures. African Americans fared the worst because Whites were given preference for jobs while programs to help them were few. However, African Americans helped each other. The churches started relief programs. The promise of a New Deal sent many African Americans from the Republican Party to the Democratic Party, but it was not until World War II that African Americans began to recover.

New leaders emerged, such as Adam Clayton Powell, Jr., who helped lead the fight against discrimination in jobs and education. Although African Americans in the military served on all fronts of World War II and distinguished themselves in several battles, they served in segregated units and were discriminated against. Discrimination even went as far as the blood bank established by Dr. Charles Drew. Even so, there were triumphs, such as the accomplishments of athletes Jesse Owens and Joe Louis, which made them heroes to all Americans, not just African Americans. This period also saw the development and growth of a Black middle class of professionals all across the country and the rise of the modern civil rights era.

The next chapter will focus on some of the events that precipitated the civil rights movement of the 1950s and 1960s. It will look at the court cases and the various non-violent strategies used by the leaders of the civil rights movement.

References

Alpha Kappa Alpha Sorority Inc. Founders. Accessed 2018. http://aka1908.com/about/founders

Bamford, T. (2020). *African Americans fought for freedom at home and abroad during World War II*. The National WWII Museum. https://www.nationalww2museum.org/war/articles/african-americans-fought-freedom-home-and-abroad-during-world-war-ii

Bennett, L., Jr. (1993). *Before the Mayflower: A history of Black America*. 6th edition. Penguin Books.

Durant, Jr., T., & Louden, J. S. (1986). The Black middle class in America: Historical and contemporary perspectives. *Phylon* (1960–), 47(4), 253–263. Clark Atlanta University.

Eichenlaub, S., Tolnay, S., & Alexander, T. (2010). Moving out but not up: Economic outcomes in the Great Migration. *American Sociological Review*, 75(1), 101–125. https://journals.sagepub.com/doi/abs/10.1177/0003122409357047?journalCode=asra.

Eleanor Roosevelt's battle to end lynching. (2016, 12 February). Forward with Roosevbelt. https://fdr.blogs.archives.gov/2016/02/12/eleanor-roosevelts-battle-to-end-lynching/

Free Blacks in the Antebellum Period. The African American Odyssey: A Quest for Full Citizenship. Accessed 2018. https://www.loc.gov/exhibits/african-american-odyssey/free-blacks-in-the-antebellum-period.html

Harding, L. (2009, April 12). *Alpha Phi Alpha Fraternity (1906–)*. BlackPast. Accessed 2018. https://blackpast.org/aah/alpha-phi-alpha-fraternity-inc.

Hughes, E. C. (1956). American Sociological Review. *American Sociological Review*, 21(3), 383–384. JSTOR, www.jstor.org/stable/2089298.

Johnson, T. *John Chavis (1763–1838)*. BlackPast. Accessed 2018. https://blackpast.org/aah/chavis-john-1763-1838

Kindig, J. The Scottsboro Boys trial and defense campaign (1931–1937). BlackPast. https://blackpast.org/aah/scottsboro-boys-trial-and-defense-campaign-1931-1937

Moore, K. (2008, December). Class formations: Competing forms of Black middle-class identity. *Ethnicities*, 8(4) 492–517.

Nash, G. (2008, July 2). *Agrippa Hull: Revolutionary patriot*. BlackPast. Accessed 2018. https://blackpast.org/perspectives/agrippa-hull-revolutionary-patriot

Pells, R. H., & Romer, C. D. (2019, January 10). *Great Depression | Definition, History, Causes, Effects, & Facts.* Encyclopædia Britannica. www.britannica.com/event/Great-Depression

Rollock N., Vincent, C., & Gillhorn, D. (2013). 'Middle class by profession': Class status and identification amongst the Black middle classes. *Ethnicities*, 13(3), 253–275. https://doi.org/10.1177/1468796812467743

1775–1900: The history of the Black soldier. (1999). Novelguide.com. Accessed 2018. http://www.novelguide.com/reportessay/history/american-history/1775-1900-history-black-soldier

Swartz, E., & Lessie, R. (1985). *The role of Black Americans in the development of the United States: A supplement to our country's history.* Rochester; City School District.

The archives of historic Black newspapers are going digital. Smithsonian. Accessed 2018. https://www.smithsonianmag.com/smart-news/explore-archives-historic-black-newspapers-180969292/

Thernstrom, A., & Thernstrom, S. (1998, March 1). *Black progress: How far we've come, and how far we have to go.* The Brookings Institute, Accessed 2018. https://www.brookings.edu/articles/black-progress-how-far-weve-come-and-how-far-we-have-to-go/.

Trotter, J. W. *The African American experience*, Volume I and II. Houghton Mifflin, 2001.

Wilkerson, I. *The long-lasting legacy of the Great Migration.* (2016, September). The Smithsonian. Accessed 2018. https://www.smithsonianmag.com/history/long-lasting-legacy-great-migration-180960118/.

Wilson, W. J. (1996). *When work disappears. The world of the new urban poor.* Alfred A. Knopf.

Review

I. Checking What You Have Read

1. The Harlem Renaissance was a period of cultural and artistic expression for many African Americans. Explain the importance of each of the following figures of the movement.

    (a) Zora Neale Hurston   (b) Langston Hughes   (c) Alain Locke

2. Who was Carter G. Woodson? Why did he say African Americans were miseducated?
3. How did Woodson's writings differ from those of Claude McKay?
4. Research the many talented African Americans who participated in the Harlem Renaissance, such as Claude McKay, Jean Toomer, Arna Bontemps, and Countee Cullen. Read samples of their work and present a group project for an exhibit in the hallway of your school.
5. Name at least three musical or theater celebrities of the Harlem Renaissance and tell what each was famous for.
6. What brought the Harlem Renaissance to an end? Why?
7. Who was Jack Johnson and why was he a hero for many African Americans?
8. What was Arthur Schomburg most famous for?
9. How did African Americans deal with discrimination in baseball?
10. Why did African Americans leave the party of Lincoln?
11. Are the difference between the segments of today's African American community with its different ethnic components superficial or meaningful? Explain
12. Explain the Great Migration. Give at least two major reasons for it and the results.

II. On Your Own

1. Scenario: Imagine you are an African American soldier who has just returned from war in Europe. Upon return to the United States you experience bigotry, racism, and discrimination after fighting the Nazis.

    (a) What would be your reaction to American discrimination vs. Nazi discrimination?

(b) If you were an African American would you fight for American Freedom although you have limited civil political and economic opportunities? Explain.

2. During the early 1920's there were photographers who captured the middle class in photos. One of these persons was James Vandersee. Who was he and why was he important during that time?

The Modern Struggle for Civil Rights

The Civil Rights Era

During the 1950s and 1960s, African Americans continued to face injustices. Hangings, or lynchings, were common. In an effort to address these injustices and secure civil rights for all people, organizations such as the National Association for the Advancement of Colored People (NAACP) were formed. "Civil rights" refers to the rights of all citizens to fully participate in society and be afforded equal and fair treatment under the law. The NAACP had begun an aggressive campaign in the early 1930s aimed at ending segregation, particularly in higher education. Roy Wilkins became its leader in the 1960s, but it was the 1954 Supreme Court decision *Brown v. Board of Education* that was a turning point in the modern civil rights movement. This suit was brought by the NAACP and was argued before the Supreme Court by Thurgood Marshall on behalf of the plaintiffs.

In this case, a little Kansas girl named Linda Brown had to be bused five miles across town to attend a school for African American children when another school was just four blocks from her home. The problem was that the closer school was for White children. Her parents filed suit against the Board of Education in Topeka, Kansas.

The Supreme Court Decision that was rendered in this case said that separate schools for African Americans and Whites were unconstitutional. It said that people who had to attend separate schools because of race were "deprived of the equal protection of the laws guaranteed by the 14th Amendment." This ruling reversed *Plessy v. Ferguson* and meant that segregated schools would have to integrate, in the court's words, "with all deliberate speed." Many schools in the upper part of the South complied, but those in the lower part of the South refused.

Three years after this decision, the Civil Rights Act of 1957 was passed. This was the first legislation that had addressed civil rights since Reconstruction. It established the Civil Rights Commission and gave it the power to investigate violations to civil rights.

Emmett Till

The 1950s were dangerous times for African Americans. They were particularly dangerous for those who traveled to the South to visit with relatives, especially if they were unaccustomed to Southern social rules. In 1955, Emmett Till, who was fourteen, was visiting relatives in Mississippi. He was from Chicago, Illinois and he was not accustomed to the severe segregation of the South. Till was supposed to have said something to a White woman in a store and later they found his beaten body in the river. His murder received national attention, but his murderers were acquitted.

Nearly 60 years later the case was re-opened in light of new evidence about the 1955 murder. The accuser Carolyn Bryant Donham admitted in 2007 that she had lied about the assault, supposedly committed. Even though the case was reopened, the Justice Department did not bring charges that would have led to convictions on state and federal civil rights crimes. The case was quietly closed.

Martin Luther King, Jr.

The Civil Rights Movement of the 1950s and 1960s produced some philosophies and forms of protest that differed from the previous human rights ideologies. Martin Luther King, Jr., is one of the best-known leaders of the African American human rights struggle during the 1950s and 1960s. King, a Baptist minister, was a graduate of Morehouse College in Atlanta, Georgia, and Boston University, where he received his Doctor of Divinity degree.

The Modern Struggle for Civil Rights

He was impressed with Mohandas Gandhi's use of nonviolence to implement social change. Gandhi believed in passive resistance as a means to obtain freedom for the people of India, who were under British domination. King adopted Gandhi's strategy. He coupled resistance with the idea of non-violence and devised a way to protest injustice. He saw boycotting as a technique that could be used as economic pressure to achieve equal treatment.

The Montgomery bus boycott of 1955 was the first example of this tactic and was perhaps the beginning of the modern civil rights movement. In Montgomery, Alabama, an African American woman named Rosa Parks was arrested for refusing to give up her seat in the front of a bus to a White man. Parks was a well-respected member of the community as well as an official of the local NAACP. Her action earned national publicity and inspired others in the fight against segregation.

King had been elected president of the Montgomery Improvement Association (MIA). This group organized and led African American citizens in protest. African Americans boycotted, or refused to ride, buses until segregation ended. During this time, the homes of several of the African American leaders were bombed, including the home of King while his wife and child

Martin Luther King, Jr. was born in Atlanta, Georgia. He was a major leader of the Civil Rights Movement. Dr. King was elected president of the Montgomery Improvement Association, the organization that was responsible for the successful Montgomery Bus Boycott in 1955. Dr. King led the March on Washington in 1963. He was assassinated in Memphis, Tennessee, on April 4, 1968.

were inside. Later, King was arrested for violating an anti-boycott law, along with about 100 other African Americans. But this did not stop his determination. The buses were desegregated a year later. The boycott proved to be a powerful way of drawing attention to the injustices that African Americans faced, because it got national attention.

James Baldwin (1924–1987)

Another African American artist who went to France to escape racism was Baldwin. He was born in Harlem, New York in 1924 as the oldest of nine children. His family was poor and he looked for a way to improve his circumstances. Baldwin was a preacher in a small revivalist church from the age of 14 to 16. In 1944 he moved to Greenwich Village in New York City, where he met the well-known writer Richard Wright. Wright helped Baldwin get a fellowship to write his first novel.

Baldwin was bothered by the racial injustice in America. He left for France in 1948. Although Baldwin made his home in France, he often returned to the United States to lecture or teach and to participate in the civil rights movement. He was an important literary voice during the civil rights era of the 1950s and 1960s. In the early 1960s he traveled throughout the South and authored an explosive work about Black identity and the state of the racial struggle. *The Fire Next Time* (1963) was a most powerful civil rights statement. Baldwin basically said that African Americans and Whites must come to terms with the past and make a future together. The alternative was to face destruction.

Baldwin also wrote plays. He wrote *Blues for Mister Charlie*, which was produced in 1964. He also wrote *Going to Meet the Man* (1965) and *Tell Me How Long the Train's Been Gone* (1968). These plays provided powerful descriptions of racist oppression of African Americans.

The Southern Christian Leadership Conference (SCLC)

After the success of the Montgomery Bus Boycott, southern African American ministers formed the Southern Christian Leadership Conference (SCLC). Dr. King was elected president and Ella Jo Baker was elected executive director. The practice of boycotting was used in other places, such as Tennessee, Florida, Arkansas, and Georgia. They took place throughout the 1950s and

1960s and resulted in a number of positive changes for African Americans. But things changed abruptly and tragically when King was assassinated in Memphis, Tennessee, on April 4, 1968.

Reverend Ralph Abernathy was another important leader. He worked with King to bring about desegregation. Rev. Abernathy took over the leadership of the SCLC after King's death, but without King, the movement foundered.

Ella Jo Baker (1903–1986)

Ella Jo Baker was born in Norfolk, Virginia in 1903. Most of her childhood was spent in Littleton, North Carolina. She attended Shaw Academy and Shaw University.

Ella Jo Baker was a very important woman in the Civil Rights Movement of the 1950s and 1960s. She worked as an organizer for 50 years, behind the scenes. Baker was the Director of various branches of the NAACP. She was also instrumental in forming the Southern Christian Leadership Conference. Baker also assisted the students in the Greensboro sit-ins.

The Desegregation of Schools

The Little Rock Nine

An important focus for the NAACP was school desegregation. Although *Brown v. Board of Education* had been won, many places in the South simply ignored the ruling. In 1957, nine African American students in Little Rock, Arkansas, attempted to enroll in Central High School, an all-White school. Daisy Bates was the leader of the local NAACP who prepared the students for the threats and abuses they would receive for attempting to integrate the school. Her life was threatened, but she persisted. At the time, Dwight D. Eisenhower was president and Orval Faubus was governor of the state of Arkansas. Faubus refused to comply with the desegregation orders of the Supreme Court. He said that his state had the right to decide its own affairs (states' rights).

 Daisy Bates (1914–1999)

There were many noteworthy people during the Civil Rights era. One of those people was Daisy Bates, a courageous civil rights leader. Bates was born in Huttig, a tiny town in Arkansas. Her mother had been murdered by three White men who had attempted to rape her. The men were never brought to justice and her father left town right after that happened. The people whom she had come to think of as her parents were actually friends of her real parents.

Daisy eventually married and she and her husband established a newspaper, *The Arkansas State Press*. She and her husband had been members of the National Association for the Advancement of Colored People (NAACP) in Little Rock, Arkansas since 1952. The paper that she and her husband started became an avid voice for civil rights even before a nationally recognized movement had emerged and enjoyed a large readership.

Daisy Bates is best known as the person who mentored nine high school students in preparation for the desegregation of Central High in Little Rock, Arkansas in the fall of 1957. When the decision was made to integrate the school, the NAACP went into action. Daisy Bates became the advisor for the Little Rock Nine. The students would gather at her house, and she advised them on how to handle the taunting and other insults that they would receive for attempting to desegregate the high school. She died in 1999.

The governor called out the Arkansas National Guard and ordered them to stand guard in front of the school to prevent African American students from entering. A petition was filed by the Justice Department to force him to comply, but Faubus defied the order. President Eisenhower, however, sent units of the U.S. Army to Little Rock. He also federalized the Arkansas National Guard. This meant that the guard was now under the command of the president of the United States. Eisenhower ordered the National Guard to enter the school and protect the students. On September 23, 1957, federal troops escorted the students through a side door and into the school. Unfortunately, the tensions between the Whites and the African Americans did not go away. Officials in Little Rock closed the public schools for two years. When the schools were finally reopened, they were desegregated.

James Meredith and "Ole Miss"

Colleges and universities had been the major focus of the NAACP. In 1950, the Supreme Court made some major rulings. Bennett (1993) cites three cases that made a major difference in desegregating schools. They were the Sweatt (Texas), McLaurin (Oklahoma), and Henderson (Maryland) cases. The first case desegregated the University of Texas law school. The second case prevented African American students from being segregated after being admitted to state universities. The third case desegregated dining cars on trains. Although this third case (the Henderson case) was not related to the desegregation of schools, it helped paved the way for future desegregation efforts by the NAACP.

Then the *Brown v. Board of Education* (1954) case was ruled upon by the Supreme Court. The previous civil rights cases had focused on discrimination in areas such as labor and housing, dining facilities, and discrimination in state universities. This suit, however, was aimed at secondary and elementary schools. It set the legal basis for the desegregation of all public schools.

In 1962, James Meredith, a 29-year-old air force veteran, attempted to enroll at the State University in Mississippi. The governor of the state, Ross Barnett, announced to the television cameras and media around the world that he would go to jail before he would let an African American attend the school. He even stood and physically barred the way. He was found guilty of contempt of federal court and was ordered to leave. When federal marshals arrived to escort Meredith into the university, the governor himself did not attempt to prevent them from entering. But a mob of several thousand Whites started to riot and attack the marshals and troops.

Two men were killed and several hundred people were wounded, and some property was destroyed. The government sent in 12,000 federal troops and national guards to restore order. Meredith was escorted to classes by 300 soldiers.

Unfortunately, although the members of the mob could be readily identified from television films, they went unpunished. This was true of all mobs that had committed violence against African Americans since the end of the Civil War. These were acts of terrorism, but nothing was done to punish those who committed those acts.

The Congress of Racial Equality (CORE)

While the NAACP focused on desegregating schools, the Congress of Racial Equality (CORE) turned its attention to desegregating public facilities. This organization was established in 1942, in Chicago, Illinois. James Farmer was one of its founders. He, like King, also used non-violent methods. CORE had chapters in many northern cities in the United States. The organization helped four college students in Greensboro, North Carolina organize their campaign to desegregate lunch counters in 1960. Members of CORE continued their efforts at desegregation in the South by organizing other sit-ins and freedom rides.

The Student Non-Violent Coordinating Committee (SNCC)

As its name suggests, the Student Non-Violent Coordinating Committee (SNCC) was founded for students. It was organized at Shaw University in 1960 in Raleigh, North Carolina. Its purpose was to coordinate student sit-ins, but it soon began to organize freedom rides and voter registration. When SNCC was first organized, many of its members joined with CORE and participated in the freedom rides that took place in the South.

The organization did not last, however. But before it ended it helped to turn the spotlight on the injustices suffered by African Americans, and it helped to bring about change.

The Mississippi Freedom Summer Project

During 1963 and 1964 several civil rights organizations teamed up to initiate the Mississippi Freedom Summer Project. Among the organizations participating were the SCLC, the NAACP, and members of SNCC. Its purpose was to get African Americans in Mississippi, mostly in rural areas, registered to vote and to provide education. A number of Freedom Schools and community centers were established. This project was a very dangerous undertaking, especially in the deep South. Students were subjected to arrest and shootings, but many participated anyway, including increasing numbers of Whites.

In 1964 the nation's attention was focused on events involving three young men who had disappeared near Philadelphia, Mississippi. One was an African American named James Chaney and the other two were White,

Andrew Goodman and Michael Schwerner. All three were students who had volunteered to work in the project. They disappeared on their way back to the CORE office in Meridian, Mississippi. Their disappearance drew a great deal of national attention to the Civil Rights Movement—and its dangers—in Mississippi. The FBI was sent to find out what had happened. They discovered that the deputy sheriff, Cecil Price, had arrested the men. Then, they were released, only to be confronted by a mob of Whites. Members of the Ku Klux Klan murdered all three; their bodies were hidden in a swamp. There was an outcry across America from both White and African American citizens, and many people felt that now there was no turning back.

Many members of SNCC began to question the effectiveness of nonviolence. They began to carry guns. One of these people was Stokely Carmichael, who went on to join the Black Panthers.

Sit-Ins, Freedom Riders, and Marches

Despite the changing attitude toward non-violence among some groups, King's followers still advocated peaceful protest. King's form of non-violent protest grew all over the South, wherever injustice was encountered. Many of those who participated in non-violent protest were college students.

Boycotting was one form of non-violent protest. It was powerful because businesses depended on people using their services, and when business was disrupted, the impact was felt by merchants. But it also caused merchants to become angry and even attack those who demonstrated against them. Angry Whites often hit, kicked, and spat on protesters, and even turned vicious dogs on them. But, still, those protesting would not fight back.

Besides boycotting, there were other forms of non-violent protest. These included sit-ins and freedom rides.

Sit-Ins

One form of protest was the sit-in. In 1960, four students from North Carolina Agricultural and Technical College in Greensboro staged a sit-in at a White lunch counter at a Woolworth's store. These four students, Izell Blair, Jr., Franklin McCain, Joseph McNeil, and David Richmond were told that they would not be served, so they sat until the store closed. They were advised by some African American leaders to contact CORE so that their

Fannie Lou Hamer was born into a poor sharecropping family in Mississippi. She went through some life-threatening circumstances, when she was evicted for attempting to vote and later, when shots were fired into the home where she was staying with friends. Hamer was also badly beaten for attempting to use a whites-only restroom. She joined the Student Non-Violent Coordinating Committee's (SNCC) voter registration campaign. The Mississippi Freedom Democratic Party that was formed by SNCC ran her as a candidate for the Democratic Party. Although the delegation was not seated, the Democratic Party passed a resolution to ban segregated delegations.

next attempt would be organized and well planned.

The sit-ins were planned so that when one group of students got up, another group took its place. In this way, the White lunch counter seats were always filled, but the stores were not making any money. The students remained until they were arrested. Beginning in the 1960s, thousands of students, both African American and White, started to do the same with other stores all over the South. This approach began to work.

This new means of protest got media attention and many people began to protest segregated facilities. The protesters then moved from stores to other public facilities such as libraries—and then on to trains and bus stations.

Freedom Riders

Another area where discrimination was practiced was in public transportation. Most African Americans were at the lower end of the economic ladder, and, because they could not afford cars, they depended on public transportation to get to work. But African Americans, such as Rosa Parks, had to sit in the back of the bus—although Rosa Parks refused to on that important day. Furthermore, it was not only public transportation within city limits that was segregated; interstate transportation was segregated as well.

In the South, the bus stations were segregated with separate waiting rooms, ticket counters, and toilets for African Americans and Whites. African American passengers who were traveling from one state to another were refused service at lunch counters at rest stops. Again, college students got involved and were joined by members of the Student Non-Violent Coordinating Committee (SNCC). White students from the North joined them, and they rode buses through southern states. The students were met with violence and mobs that threatened their lives. The farther into the South they rode, the more severe the violence they met, especially in Georgia, Alabama, and Mississippi. Sometimes the mobs blew up the buses in which the students were riding. The mobs, many of which included the Ku Klux Klan, often stopped buses and pulled the riders off and beat them with lead pipes. Police and other officials did nothing to stop the mobs. But eventually, the students won. The "Whites only" signs came down.

This time in American history is often referred to as the Second Reconstruction, because of all that was happening to change things in the South, particularly to end the Jim Crow laws. The First Reconstruction changed the social, political and economic conditions of African Americans after the Civil War. It was intended to help African Americans gain equal opportunities, which included voting and the use of public facilities. The Second Reconstruction, although focused on the South with the March on Washington, also intended to rectify racial injustices for all African Americans and put them on an equal footing with White America. Both were met with defiance and violence by most southern Whites.

Marches

Another means of protest that was used by civil rights activists was the freedom march. Perhaps the most famous of these was the March on Washington in 1963 that was organized by Dr. Martin Luther King, Jr. It drew a crowd of more than 250,000 Americans, both African American and White. It was a peaceful demonstration to call attention to the new civil rights bill that was in the Congress and to encourage its passage. This was where King delivered his famous "I Have a Dream" speech. The Civil Rights Act was passed in 1964, but it didn't seem to matter to the Whites in Alabama.

One march was not as positive as the March on Washington. It was the march from Selma to Montgomery, Alabama, on March 7, 1965, which

The black codes that were instituted in the South segregated African Americans from southern whites. Everything was segregated from public transportation including buses/railways, restaurants, toilet facilities, drinking fountains, the military, libraries, schools, even to books. African Americans were denied access to parks, beaches, and picnic areas. They were also barred from many hospitals.

came to be known as "Bloody Sunday." At that time, the majority of African Americans in Alabama could not vote, and there were rules that prevented them from getting registered. For example, they were given material to read that was so difficult that even the people in charge of registration could not read it. African Americans were threatened with the loss of their jobs or told that they would not be able to purchase what they needed from Whites to keep their small farms going. Their lives were even threatened. Many African Americans decided they didn't want to put their lives or meager livings in jeopardy for what they considered the "White man's business."

Some African Americans, however, were not content or afraid. They organized the Montgomery March to protest their disenfranchisement. And even when state troopers and local police met the marchers at the Edmund Pettus Bridge and ordered them to turn back, they did not. The police beat, clubbed, and gassed the marchers, and drove their police horses into the crowd, which forced them back across the bridge. At least 70 people were hospitalized as a result.

King, who was in Atlanta on that day, went to Alabama. He called for African Americans to unite to complete the march. And they did. The 54-mile walk was completed fourteen days later. The marchers had to get an order to prevent the police from interfering, and President Johnson had to federalize the Alabama National Guard to protect the marchers. While difficult and dangerous, these marches brought into focus the great need for voting rights and a new law that would ensure and protect those rights.

The James Meredith March

Several groups worked together during the early part of the fight for civil rights. One of these occasions was when James Meredith, who had previously attended the University of Mississippi, began a 220-mile "March Against Fear" from Memphis, Tennessee, to Jackson, Mississippi, in June 1966. He was shot by a Klansman and was not able to go on. The march continued with the help of civil rights leaders, but it marked a turning point in future joint efforts between groups such as the NAACP, CORE, and SNCC.

The more combative members of SNCC were becoming unwilling to accept the help of Whites. They were also more willing to arm themselves for protection. The marchers who walked with James Meredith used the slogan "Black power." This was the beginning of the Black power movement.

The Civil Rights and Voting Rights Acts

The sit-ins, freedom riders, and boycotts had an effect on the nation. The March on Washington in 1963 had also focused attention on civil rights legislation. In the end, the Congress of the United States passed the Civil Rights Act of 1964, the 24th Amendment to the Constitution. Once again, the law stated that it was illegal to discriminate and to violate the rights of any U.S. citizen, regardless of color.

Even so, this did not mean much to most Whites in the South. "Bloody Sunday" had demonstrated that. The determination of states such as Alabama and Mississippi to deny African Americans their rights, including the right to vote, needed to be addressed specifically. Therefore the Voting Rights Act of 1965 was passed, which made it a federal crime to prevent African Americans from voting.

Unfortunately during this period, President John F. Kennedy had been assassinated and a new president, Lyndon B. Johnson, sworn in. At first, many did not have confidence in Johnson. But when he signed the Civil Rights Act of 1964, it brought hope.

Summary

The United States entered a Second Reconstruction beginning with the 1950s and the court rulings won by the NAACP. African Americans used nonviolent means to protest violations of their civil rights. It was a time of peaceful marches, freedom riders, sit-ins, and boycotts—but also a time of vicious and violent behavior by many Whites. Although they were attacked, the protesters did not fight back.

The mid-1960s saw desegregation of schools, including universities, mostly under violent circumstances. It saw a massive March on Washington and the subsequent passage of two new laws, the Civil Rights Act of 1964 and the Voting Rights Act of 1965. It saw the assassination of John F. Kennedy. However, his successor Lyndon B. Johnson continued in his footsteps and signed the Civil Rights Act of 1964.

It was also a time when the more forceful members of civil rights groups began to look for a different response. The slogan "Black Power" was beginning to be heard more frequently as the Civil Rights Movement took another direction. People began to question the use of non-violent protest as a means

During the 1960s African Americans had waged a costly battle for civil rights. It had taken its toll with many lives. The assassination of John F. Kennedy made many African Americans worry as to whether the new president, Lyndon Baines Johnson, would be sympathetic to their cause.

to gain equal rights. The next chapter will explore other ways in which African Americans responded to the fight for civil rights and the push toward pride in heritage, history, and culture.

References

Appiah, K., & Gates, H. L. (Eds.). (1999). *Africana: The encyclopedia of African and African American experiences.* Basic Civitas.

Asante, M. K. (1993). *The Afrocentric idea.* Revised and expanded edition. Temple University Press.

Asante, M. K. (1993). *Historical and cultural atlas of African Americans.* Macmillan Publishing, 1993.

Asante, M. K. (2001). *African American history: A journey of liberation.* Peoples Publishing Group, Inc.

Bennett, L., Jr. (1993). *Before the Mayflower: A history of Black America.* 6th edition. Penguin Books.

Blinder, A. (2018, July 12). U.S. reopens Emmett Till investigation, almost 63 years after his murder. *The New York Times.* https://www.nytimes.com/2018/07/12/us/emmett-till-death-investigation.html

Franklin, J. H., & Moss, A. A., Jr. (2000). *From slavery to freedom: A history of African Americans.* Knopf.

Gates, H. L., Jr., & Higginbotham, E. B. (Eds.) (2004). *African American lives.* Oxford University Press.

Hine, D. C. (Ed.). (2005). *Black women in America.* 2nd edition. Oxford University Press.

Pérez-Peña, R. (2017, January 28). Woman linked to 1955 Emmett Till murder tells historian her claims were false. *The New York Times.* https://www.nytimes.com/2017/01/27/us/emmett-till-lynching-carolyn-bryant-donham.html

Shujaa, M. J., & Shujaa, K. J. (Eds.). (2015). *The Sage encyclopedia of African cultural heritage in North America.* 1st Edition. Sage Publications.

The Voting Rights Act. Accessed August 24, 2004. http://www.votescount.com/ votrights.htm

Topeka 50 years later: The real story behind the Brown in *Brown v. Board of Education.* (May 2004). *Ebony, 59*(7), 114–116, 118.

Trotter, J. W. (2001). *The African American experience*, Volume I and II. Houghton Mifflin.

U.S. Constitution. *Civil Rights Acts.* http://www.usconstitution.com/CivilRightsActs.htm

The Black Power Movement

Other Means of Protest

While the efforts of earlier civil rights activists addressed the inequities in American society, more was needed. During the 1960s, an approach to Black disfranchisement emerged. The problem of unequal civil rights was experienced throughout the North and South, alike. Some African Americans began to feel that there were deeper issues of equality that needed to be addressed. Many African Americans were particularly frustrated at how they were treated under the law. Activists took a more confrontational stance towards securing civil rights. In 1965, less than a week after the signing of the Voting Rights Act, civil unrest broke out in Los Angeles. It occurred in an African American community called Watts, a section of South Central Los Angeles.

The Watts civil unrest began over the tactics used by the police to stop and detain a young African American man. Today, that police policy is known as "stop and frisk." The police and members of the African American community exchanged "heated" words and, eventually, unrest ensued. Many businesses were burned or looted. After that, people such as Stokely Carmichael began to advocate the armed self defense when necessary for self-defense. Some activists responded to the denial of human rights by organizing direct confrontation groups such as the Black Panther Party for Self Defense. The members of these groups did not hesitate to arm themselves and demonstrate their willingness to fight to protect their families and communities against racist violence.

Black Power and Black Pride

Carmichael, who had been jailed during the freedom rides, became the chairman of SNCC. He was frustrated at the slow pace of the non-violent movement and, unlike his predecessors, he felt that violence should be retaliated against. He also felt, like Marcus Garvey, that African Americans should have pride in themselves. He coined the phrase "Black is Beautiful." Carmichael also adopted the term "Black Power," which had been used by the members of the James Meredith March. It became the slogan for many. Carmichael also led the organization toward separatism, not integration.

Carmichael's position on Black power and the use of weapons to protect and retaliate against injustice made him and his organization incompatible with groups with which King had worked. Whereas King was willing to include poor Whites, SNCC and other groups were not. And, whereas King believed in non-violence, others no longer accepted it as the way to equality and justice. Carmichael eventually left SNCC and joined the Black Panthers.

The Black Panther Party for Self Defense

Two university students, Huey Newton and Bobby Seale, founded the Black Panther Party for Self Defense in Oakland, California, in 1966. It came into existence just after the assassination of Malcolm X, who had been the national spokesperson for the Nation of Islam. When Malcolm severed his ties with the Nation, he formed another organization.

Greatly influenced by the teachings of Malcolm X, Newton and Seale's philosophy was to promote Black pride and help poor people of color. They had a ten-point plan that called for decent housing, full employment, an end to brutality and repression, the ability to decide the destiny of the African American community, and an education that revealed the truth about America's history, among other things.

The Black Power Movement

The Black Panthers brought much-needed programs into the inner city. They started free breakfast programs (a model that the government later adopted), ran free health clinics, and food programs. They also started schools. But critics of the Black Panthers focused not on these programs, but on the fact that they armed themselves with guns. The Black Panthers felt that under the law they had the right to bear arms to protect themselves, and they always had their guns in full view. They also felt that the government wanted to destroy them and what they stood for—and they had good reason to believe this. Local and state police working with federal marshals, and the FBI conducted covert attacks against Black Panther Party chapters and leaders. Law enforcement also conducted armed raids against local Panther headquarters across the country and jailed individuals for political affiliations and on bogus charges.

The Black Panther Party was eventually crushed by the government. However, there is a new movement, which calls itself the "New Black Panthers." It has no affiliation with the original group. However, it claims to promote many of their ideals.

Other Activist Groups

US Movement

Separatist movement groups came into existence during the 1960s as well. Some of these were the US Movement, the Revolutionary Action Movement (RAM), and the Republic of New Africa (RNA). The US Movement was started by Maulana Karenga in 1965. Karenga, who was attending the University of California in Los Angeles as a doctoral student, felt that African Americans needed a cultural basis from which to operate in order to guide their actions. His organization emphasized African culture and heritage and, most important, working together to help each other. He established the tradition of Kwanzaa in 1966 as a celebration to reaffirm African culture and heritage.

Revolutionary Action Movement (RAM)

Max Stanford was the founder of the Revolutionary Action Movement (RAM). He had been a member of the National Youth Movement and the

Students for a Democratic Society in the early 1960s. Stanford merged the philosophy of Malcolm X with that of Robert Williams. Williams believed in arming oneself for self-defense and wrote a book about why this was necessary. But Williams was seen as a radical and before he could be arrested on false charges, he fled the country.

RAM was based on the idea of Black nationalism, which was established in 1963. Black nationalism for the group meant the right to arm oneself for self-defense. It also meant self-determination. The group knew that people in the urban areas were ready for a revolution against their conditions and treatment. Then, in 1964 and 1969, race riots broke out across the country—initiated this time by African Americans in urban ghettos. The FBI and police politicized the riots and violence, placing the blame on RAM and other activist groups. Members of RAM were arrested and held in jail on unsubstantiated charges. Eventually the organization was disbanded. One of the members of this group was Huey Newton, who went on to co-found the Black Panthers in Oakland, California.

The Republic of New Africa (RNA)

The Republic of New Africa (RNA) was another organization formed to better the conditions of African Americans. Its purpose was to establish a Black nation in the South. The first meeting was held at Wayne State University in 1968. Its leaders went on to declare Mississippi a Black nation, which set the stage for an invasion. They knew the government would react—and it did. The FBI and the police, using armored cars, raided the headquarters in Jackson. The FBI arrested Imari Obadele, the leader, and ten others. They were charged with treason against Mississippi, murder, and assault.

Young people on college campuses founded all of these organizations. They all focused on achieving better conditions for African Americans. But all of these organizations were met with retaliation. Their members were detained by illegal means in jails and the organizations were finally crushed.

COINTELPRO

In the 1960s federal law enforcement had a focus on Black protest movements such as the Black Panthers, SCLC, freedom riders, and anti-Vietnam protesters. The FBI and other law enforcement agencies targeted a forceful campaign against the Black Panthers. The FBI, under the leadership of J. Edgar Hoover, devised a program called COINTELPRO. This was a counterintelligence program designed to infiltrate the Black Panthers with paid informers to spy and report back to authorities. They would spread lies, rumors, and misinformation to, and cause conflict among, members of the group to destroy the organization from within.

Fearful that they might unite, the FBI used these same tactics on similar groups. They would cause confusion, mistrust, and dissension in order to pit the groups against each other. For example, the FBI would write and send letters to the Black Panthers attacking their leader, Eldridge Cleaver, and they would sign Maulana Karenga's name to it. They would then do the same to Karenga. This caused tensions between groups. The FBI wanted to keep the groups, the US Movement and the Panthers, from joining forces. They did not want any groups to unify into a Black national movement.

J. Edgar Hoover ordered many people arrested on false charges. He wielded great power and had unlimited resources at his disposal, which he abused by violating the rights of many African Americans. Hoover especially targeted African American officials and group leaders. He also kept files on them. These groups included the SCLC, CORE, and SNCC. Hoover was especially consumed with the destruction of Dr. Martin Luther King, Jr. right up until King's assassination. He targeted any African American who was a leader or had the potential to become one. In addition, he kept files on anyone whom he thought he could turn to his own use. Hoover's racist views represented a dark period of the FBI.

In the years following this period, other events have occurred. Under the Trump presidency and led by Attorney General, William Barr, BlackLivesMatter groups were viewed as left wing violent insurrectionists. Protests were responded to by force and intimidation by U.S. Marshalls. However, Biden's approach toward matters of race and rights is significantly different than Trump's. The Justice Department and the FBI have refocused its priorities towards domestic threats. Those threats include homeland terrorism, White supremacists and anti-government groups.

The Nation of Islam

Another organization that stressed Black power and Black pride was the Nation of Islam. Founded in 1930 in Detroit, Michigan, by Wallace D. Fard, it is a religious group that bases its teachings on Islam.

Elijah Muhammad

Elijah Muhammad, a student of Fard Muhammad, became the leader of the Nation of Islam in 1934. Like SNCC, the Nation of Islam also favored the idea of separatism. Members wanted the United States to set aside territory for a separate self-ruling nation for African Americans. Elijah Muhammad maintained that in this way, conflict between African Americans and European Americans would be diminished. Elijah Muhammad attracted a considerable number of followers, among them the remarkable Malcolm X, also known by his religious title El Hajj Malik el-Shabazz.

Malcolm X

Malcolm X, previously known as Malcolm Little, had been a thief and a peddler of illegal drugs. While in prison in the late 1950s, he learned of the teachings of Elijah Muhammad. Malcolm converted to the Muslim faith, which changed his life. Upon his release from prison, he became an important

Malcolm X was born Malcolm Little in Omaha, Nebraska, to the son of a Baptist minister, who was an avid supporter of Marcus Garvey. Malcolm got in trouble with the law, but when he was released from prison, joined the Nation of Islam, where he became the national spokesperson. He advocated militancy where necessary. He was assassinated in New York City while giving a speech.

advocate for Black power. Like Marcus Garvey, Malcolm X did not feel that European Americans would ever, as a whole, live with African Americans on a basis of equality. He agreed with Elijah Muhammad that African Americans should have their own separate nation. He did not want African Americans to integrate into the American system. Elijah Muhammad also stressed that African Americans should take pride in themselves and their African heritage. Malcolm X became the spokesperson for the Nation of Islam. Eventually, however, he broke away and formed his own group, the Organization of African Unity. In February 1965, while giving a speech in New York City, Malcolm X was assassinated.

Malcolm X presented a powerful image. At times his persona seemed to be as powerful, if not more so than, King's. Many people might not have agreed with King, for whatever reason, but were more willing to deal with him rather than Malcolm X. This is all the more curious when one considers that the Nation of Islam does not arm its members. It is only the perception of power through the unity of its members that appears to pose a threat to some people.

Louis Farrakhan

The Nation of Islam was not without its own problems, however. With the death of Elijah Muhammad, the Nation of Islam underwent a transition period. The successor to Elijah Muhammad was his son, Warif Deen Muhammad, who moved away from the teachings of his father. Two years later, Louis Farrakhan returned to the Nation of Islam and became its leader. Many people criticize Farrakhan today because of the stance he takes on many issues. Some say that he is anti-Semitic and hates Whites. Others say that he hates injustice, no matter who perpetrates it. Some people feel that he is the only African American who will say publicly what many other African American leaders think but are afraid to say. Nearly everyone has an opinion about him. Yet none can dispute the platform on which he stands: empowerment for African Americans. His program emphasizes self-help and self-restraint, condemns the use of drugs and alcohol, and encourages individuals to better their conditions.

CHAPTER 13
A New Cultural Renaissance

During this period, African Americans, spurred on by the Black power movement, began to reclaim the African past that had been forgotten due to the institution of enslavement. African Americans came to understand they had a great culture and history. They became aware of, and began to celebrate, the African genius. In many ways, this new awareness was reminiscent of the philosophy of Marcus Garvey, who also emphasized the importance of having pride in one's cultural heritage.

One such leader of this era, who can be compared to Garvey, is Maulana Karenga. He felt that African Americans needed to form their ideas around an African-centered (or Afrocentric) culture and not a European (or Eurocentric) one. The celebration of Kwanzaa, which he started, focuses on the achievements of people of African descent all over the world. The seven principles of Kwanzaa are unity, self-determination, collective work and responsibility, cooperative economics, purpose, creativity, and faith. It is celebrated from December 26 through January 1.

Kwanzaa

Kwanzaa is an African American holiday that is celebrated from December 26 through January 1. The name comes from the phrase "matunda ya kwanza" which means "first fruits" in the African language Swahili. The celebration originates from the first harvest celebrations in Africa.

Its founder, activist and scholar Maulana Karenga, believed that people of African descent needed to reaffirm their culture and heritage. Although it is observed during the Christmas holiday, it is not a substitute for Christmas. The seven principles of Kwanzaa are Umoja (Unity), Kujichagulia (Self-Determination), Ujima (Collective Work and Responsibility), Ujamaa (Cooperative Economics), Nia (Purpose), Kuumba (Creativity), and Imani (Faith).

The Black Arts Movement

Amiri Baraka was one of the most important leaders of the Black Arts Movement. This cultural awakening of African Americans was present in almost every part of the arts. There was great creativity among new writers, particularly women. Some of these included Maya Angelou, Nikki Giovanni, Sonia Sanchez, and Toni Morrison. It was also reflected by African American theater groups and in jazz and other music of the times.

The artistic world was not the only place that people began to take pride in their cultural heritage. It was also evident in hairstyles, such as the Afro, and the wearing of African clothing, such as the dashiki shirt and woven Kente cloth.

Kente Cloth

A trend for many African Americans today is the wearing of Kente cloth. Kente, however, is more than a trend, it has an interesting origin and cultural significance. Kente is a special cloth that dates back to 12th-century Africa, in the country of Ghana. The cloth is usually woven in colors of bright yellow, green, blue, and gold with traditional symbols depicted in the designs. Each Kente pattern was unique and had its own name and deep symbolic meaning. At that time, certain designs were specifically made to be worn by the royals and important figures of state in Ghana's society.

Later, when economic conditions improved, other non-royal people also wanted access to the cloth. It is hand woven and is therefore expensive and considered a treasure by those who possess it. In the West African culture, Kente is a festival cloth. It is worn mainly during the annual and seasonal festivals, which celebrate happy occasions. Kente is the national cloth of Ghana.

Today these cloths are not only used for festive occasions but are worn on such important events as marriage, death, and religious worship. It is quite appropriate for outsiders to wear it for religious and festive occasions and also for inspiration and to express pride in one's African heritage.

American Popular Culture

Much of the cultural revolution that was created by African American artists is evidenced in America's popular culture. It was celebrated by African American artists such as singers James Brown, who popularized the song "Say It Loud, I'm Black and I'm Proud" and Aretha Franklin, with her soul-searching songs. It was, and continues to be, the Philadelphia sound and Motown. It is evident in the work of African American literary artists and filmmakers as well.

African American History or Black Studies

Starting in the late 1960s, college students on campuses around the country began to demand courses in Black Studies. Many schools responded and began African American history programs or departments. There also was a demand for more African American faculty. Some of these programs became courses offered at colleges and universities; others grew into departments. Programs such as these offered students the opportunity to learn about African American culture and history. They also offered a history that was not just about enslavement but about Africa's great history and cultural past.

Black Power and Politics

Up to this point African Americans had only enjoyed a brief period of political influence. That was just after the Civil War during the time known as the Reconstruction of the South. Many African Americans were elected to public office. Two of these people were Hiram Revels and Blanche K. Bruce, who served in the Senate. Other African Americans served in the House of Representatives. The end of Reconstruction brought an end to African American involvement in public office as well. This state of affairs, coupled with Jim Crow laws and rising violence against African Americans who attempted to vote, brought African American participation in government to a standstill. This changed during the 1960s, when protests focused on equal rights through political power.

Black political power began to grow as a result of the civil rights movement and particularly the voter registration drive. As more African Americans gained the right to vote, they began to organize to put more elected officials in office. At first most of the elected officials were from the northern states, where there were large numbers of African American voters. The noted exception was Senator Edward Brooke, who was from Massachusetts, a state in which the majority of the voters are White. In 1966, he was the first African American senator elected by popular vote since Reconstruction. Brooke also was awarded the Presidential Medal of Freedom in 2004. African American mayors were elected in several cities. Richard Hatcher became the first African American mayor of Gary, Indiana, and Carl Stokes became

The Black Power Movement

the first African American mayor of Cleveland, Ohio. There were others in other major cities.

The Congressional Black Caucus

In the late 1960s, a national movement started that focused on increasing the political power of African Americans. One strategy to enhance African American political power and Black voter engagement was through the use of Black Power conferences. This approach was initiated by activists like Amiri Baraka. The thrust of the conference was to galvanize support for Black candidates at all levels of government. The number of African American elected officials rose from about 100 in 1965 to about 3,500 in 1975. They were state legislators, mayors, judges, and law enforcement officials. An offshoot of this effort to increase Black elected officials resulted in the founding of the Congressional Black Caucus. Representative C. Diggs of Michigan sought to bring together the Black members of Congress. He founded the Democratic Select Committee. Eventually the Committee grew to 13 African Americans and it was thought that a more formal structure was needed to address the concerns of African Americans. The organization was formalized during the 92nd Congress, in 1971–73, becoming the Congressional Black Caucus.

Congresswoman Shirley Chisholm announcing her candidacy for presidential nomination (Photo: [TOH]. O'Halloran, Thomas J., photographer)

Women in Politics

During this time, men were not the only ones who were being elected to public office. Shirley Chisholm, from New York, was the first African American woman elected to the House of Representatives and also the first one to run for president of the United States. Barbara Jordan was a state senator from Texas. She was the first African American to be elected to the Texas Senate. Then in 1972, she was elected to the House of Representatives. Yvonne Burke was elected in 1973 from California. The first African American woman elected to the United States Senate was Carol Moseley Braun from Illinois. She served with Senator Edward Brooke of Massachusetts. Numerous Black women have served in Congress. Most have served in the House of Representatives, but only a few have served in the Senate.

The Rainbow Coalition

Just prior to the assassination of Martin Luther King, Jr., the movement had taken a new turn. King had begun to include poor Whites, and some of the groups within the movement disagreed with this. They felt that if this happened the focus on racial equality would be forgotten. This issue grew to an even greater debate when King was killed.

Reverend Jesse Jackson was an activist and became a full-time organizer for the Southern Christian Leadership Conference in 1965. He worked with Dr. Martin Luther King, Jr. in the civil rights movement. He later went on to form Operation PUSH, an organization for economic empowerment and the expansion of educational, business and employment opportunities in 1984. He formed the Rainbow Coalition and also ran for president of the United States in 1984.

After King, no new leader emerged from the civil rights movement until Rev. Jesse Jackson. Jackson had been an associate of King's, and he believed in the ideals that King had promoted. Jackson had marched with him and had been with him at the March on Washington when King delivered his "I Have a Dream" speech. Jackson founded the organization called People United to Save Humanity, or PUSH, to work for affirmative action. This organization advanced the same ideals that King had held, and it included many diverse groups of people. Jackson then formed the Rainbow Coalition in 1984. The Rainbow Coalition was composed of an assortment of political and social activists of different races and ethnicities. Its agenda mirrored the old progressive coalitions of the FDR era with Native Americans, Asians and all people of color. With support from the Rainbow Coalition, he ran for president of the United States, but was unsuccessful. Although he was not the first African American person to run—Shirley Chisholm and Dick Gregory ran previously—he was the first African American who many felt could be a serious candidate for the office.

Summary

Unlike today, when many young people choose to sit in the back of the bus, it was a different issue in the 1960s. It is one thing to have a choice of where to sit and another to be told where to sit on penalty of arrest.

The 1960s witnessed a new way to protest for civil rights. The National Association for the Advancement of Colored People (NAACP), along with the Urban League, the Congress of Racial Equality (CORE), and similar groups, concentrated on non-violent protest and other tactics to change laws and bring about human and civil rights for African Americans.

Yet some African Americans demonstrated that they were not afraid to take up arms to defend themselves. Groups such as the Black Panthers represented the anger and desperation of a people too long mistreated. These groups were regarded as a threat to the mainstream of White American society. Consequently, they were suppressed by various governmental agencies to the point of extinction. Although groups such as the Black Panthers of the 1950s and 1960s were crushed, they serve as a reminder that people who are sorely oppressed will react. Today, there is a resurgence of activist-type groups in the form of the "new Black Panthers."

The Black power movement began a cultural awakening for African Americans. This awakening fostered pride in African American culture and was manifested in music, theater, styles of dress, and attitude. Black power conferences also mobilized voters with the purpose of voicing the concerns of African Americans on many issues.

One of the issues that severely tested many Americans in the 1960s was the Vietnam War. It was a problem for African Americans as well as Whites.

However, it was only one of several others that were fought. The next chapter will examine the wars since World War II and the role of African Americans.

References

African-American Baseline Essays. Portland Public Schools, 1987.

African American Senators. (2018, July 27). U.S. Senate. www.senate.gov/pagelayout/history/h_multi_sections_and_teasers/Photo_Exhibit_African_American_Senators.htm

Anderson, J. D. (1988). *The education of Blacks in the South, 1860–1935.* Later Printing edition. University of North Carolina Press.

Appiah, K., & Gates, H. L. (Eds.). (1999) *Africana: The encyclopedia of African and African American Experiences.* Basic Civitas.

Asante, M. K. (1993). *The Afrocentric idea.* Revised and expanded edition. Temple University Press.

Asante, M. K. (1993). *Historical and cultural atlas of African Americans.* Macmillan Publishing.

Asante, M. K. (2001). *African American history: A journey of liberation.* Peoples Publishing Group, Inc.

Austin, S. (2020). *A Record Number of Women Will Serve in the 117th Congress, Including at Least 51 Women of Color.* The Conversation. Accessed March 20, 2021. https://theconversation.com/a-record-number-of-women-will-serve-in-the-117th-congress-including-at-least-51-women-of-color-149736

Bennett, L., Jr. (1993). *Before the Mayflower: A history of Black America.* 6th edition. Penguin Books.

Congressional Black Caucus. https://cbc.house.gov/history/

Franklin, J. H., & Moss, A. A., Jr. (2000). *From slavery to freedom: A history of African Americans.* Knopf.

Gates, H. L., Jr., & Higginbotham, E. B. (Eds.). (2004). *African American lives.* Oxford University Press.

Gurman, S. G., & Viswanatha, A. (2021, February 22). Garland looks for Justice Department to tackle domestic extremism. *Wall Street Journal.* Accessed March 20, 2021. https://www.wsj.com/articles/garland-to-make-case-for-new-era-at-justice-department-11613989802

Loewen, J. W. (1995). *Lies my teacher told me: Everything your history textbook got wrong.* Touchstone.

Mission & Priorities. (2019). Federal Bureau of Investigation. www.fbi.gov/about/mission.

Morgan, T. (2018, August 31). The NRA supported gun control when the Black Panthers had the weapons. History. https://www.history.com/news/black-panthers-gun-control-nra-support-mulford-act

Muhammad, T. (Ed.) (1996). *Chronology of Nation of Islam history*, Unknown Binding.

Predicting the enforcement priorities of the Biden DOJ. (2021). *The National Law Review*. Accessed March 20, 2021. www.natlawreview.com/article/predicting-enforcement-priorities-biden-doj

Shujaa, M. J., & Shujaa, K. J. (Eds.). (2015). *The Sage encyclopedia of African cultural heritage in North America*. 1st Edition. Sage Publications.

Trotter, J. W. *The African American experience* (2001). Volume I and II. Houghton Mifflin.

Review

I. Checking What You Have Read

1. What was the Black Arts Movement? How did it affect American culture?
2. What events took place to desegregate high schools in Little Rock, Arkansas?
3. Who was Daisy Bates?
4. The Vietnam War did much to increase the violence and militancy of the civil rights movement in the 1960s and 1970s. Explain the connection.
5. What was COINTELPRO and what was its function?
6. What is Kwanzaa and how did it start?
7. How did the terms "Black Power" and "Black is Beautiful" start?
8. How did the Black Panthers differ in their approach to civil rights from the NAACP?
9. Who was Stokely Carmichael?
10. Who started the Black studies movement and why?
11. Where was SNCC started and what was its purpose?
12. Discuss James Meredith and his connection to the civil rights movement.

II. On Your Own

1. Ask your library media specialist to help you find information on one of the following:

Huey Newton	Richard Claxton Gregory	Angela Davis
Stokely Carmichael	Fannie Lou Hamer	Bobby Seale

    Do a report (oral or written) for the class on the person you have selected.
2. Do some research to find out what were the first colleges or universities that became desegregated because of lawsuits filed by the NAACP.
3. There were many tragic incidents during the struggle for civil rights in the 1960s. One was the murder of Emmett Till and another was the murder of Medgar Evers. Find out what happened in these cases and whether the murderers were ever brought to trial.

4. What kind of issues has the Congressional Black Caucus addressed? Research this topic and write a report for your class.
5. Find information about Amiri Baraka and tell how he influenced the Black Arts movement.

African Americans and Military Conflicts

The Asian and Middle Eastern Conflict

Following World War I and World War II, the United States became involved in foreign conflicts that started in the 1950s. One was the Korean War, which is sometimes referred to as the "Forgotten War." The other was the Vietnam War, which was an extremely unpopular war. There was Desert Storm or the liberation of Kuwait and the Afghan War on "terror." These were both fought because of the threat of communism after the USSR (Soviet Union) and China became a superpower and a threat to U.S. interests.

The Korean Conflict

Not long after World War II, America went to war again. The Korean Conflict began in 1950 and seems to have occurred because of "unfinished business" related to World War II. It was unfinished because at the end of World War II, the two superpowers at the time, the United States and the Soviet Union, had some lingering issues. The Japanese had dominated Korea for 40 years. When Japan surrendered at the end of World War II, the Soviet Union and the United States were supposed to oversee the surrender of Japanese

CHAPTER 14

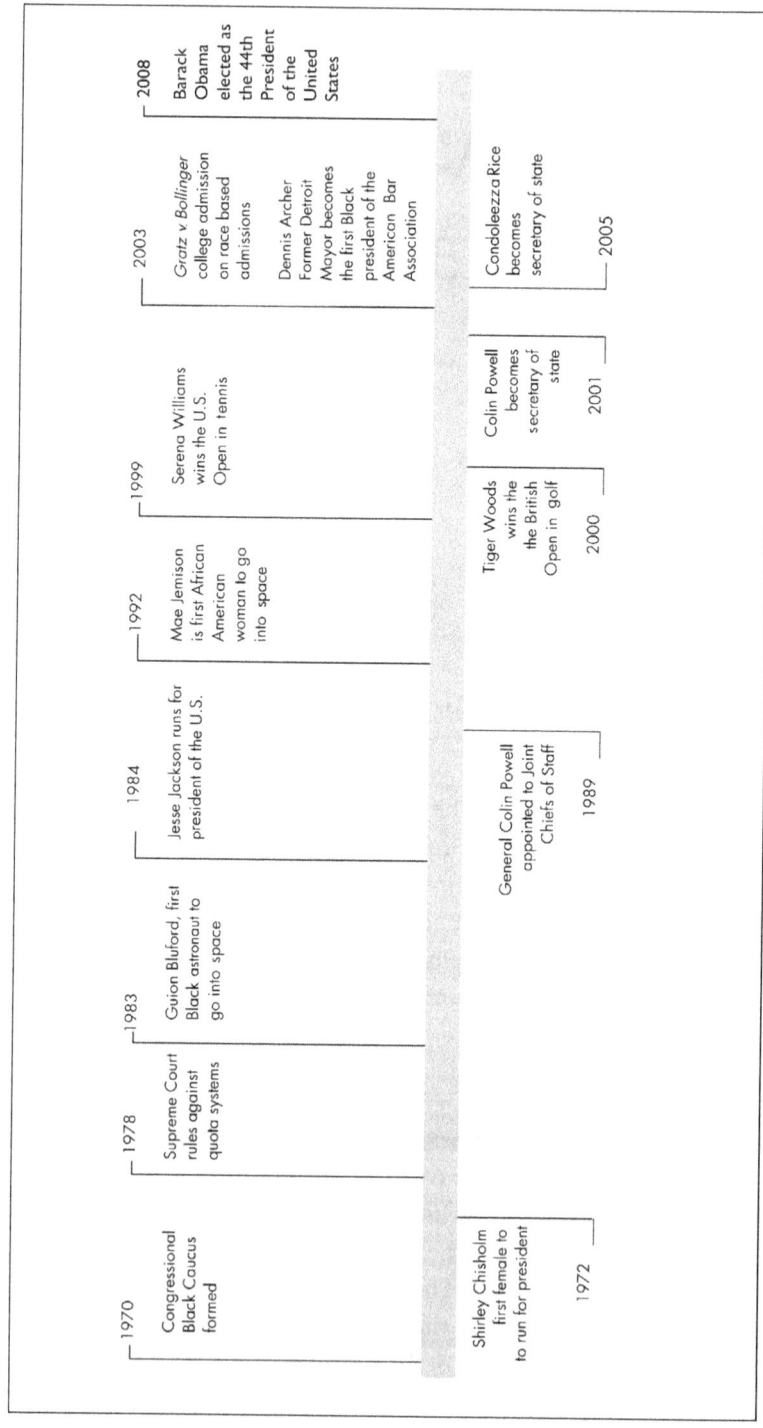

African American History 1970–2005

troops. In order to do this, the United States proposed that Korea be divided into two administrative parts. The Soviet government agreed. The Soviets would ensure the withdrawal of the Japanese from the partition of Korea. The United States would do the same for South Korea. The 38th Parallel became the dividing line of the Korean peninsula.

North Korea invaded South Korea in 1950. The Communist Chinese government also helped the North Koreans. The government of South Korea, however, was democratic and favorable to the United States. The United States did not want communism to spread into South Korea and possibly other areas, so it stepped into the conflict. Many American soldiers were sent to Korea. Just two years earlier, in 1948, President Truman had issued Executive Order 9981 that desegregated the armed forces. The order called for "equality of treatment and opportunity" in the military. It took some time, but eventually all of the African American units were disbanded, including the 25th Infantry, which had been known as the Buffalo Soldiers.

When the Korean Conflict broke out, African Americans enlisted again. This time when African Americans went to fight for their country, it was within ethnically integrated units. As the pressure of the war grew dramatically, so did the need for male recruits. This led to the increase in African American participation in the Korean Conflict. African Americans made up approximately 8 percent of the fighting forces. The Korean Conflict ended in July 1953.

The Vietnam War

The Vietnam War was an universally unpopular war. Vietnam had been a colony of France for 100 years. It became divided when the Vietnamese fought the French to liberate themselves. The French lost a decisive battle at Dien Bien Phu, which forced them to seek a peace settlement in 1956. The Geneva Peace Accord was signed. It provided for the temporary partition of the country and that elections be held in 1956 to reunify the country. The Accord was a face-saving move for France, which had been soundly beaten.

A civil war broke out in 1958 between the communists of North Vietnam and the South Vietnamese, who were backed by the French. Fearing a communist takeover of the South the U.S. government sent military advisors to help the South Vietnamese. Many more U.S. advisors were sent after that, raising concerns about increased involvement. These advisors were U.S. soldiers who provided troop support to the South Vietnamese.

Finally, in 1964, the North Vietnamese attacked an American warship in the Gulf of Tonkin. This gave President Johnson a reason to ask Congress for the authority to retaliate against North Vietnam. Congress passed the Gulf of Tonkin Resolution and thousands of soldiers were sent to war. While there was general opposition to the war by many groups of people, there were some major concerns by African Americans. Although the armed forces had been integrated, it became apparent that racism and discrimination were at work in other ways. One example was that the number of African American officers was far below the percentage of enlisted men in each branch of the armed services. A second issue was the high number of African American casualties

The administrative division of Korea, however, turned into a political division as the Cold War between the Soviet Union and the United States began. A leader was installed in North Korea who was backed by the Communists' ideology and weapons. In South Korea, a president who had been educated in the United States was elected. Neither the Soviets, Chinese, nor the United States recognized each other's authority. Each wanted the reunification of Korea but on their own terms.

In 1965, the first fighting troops went to Vietnam. There was a high rate of casualties among African American soldiers. Often, they were placed in the deadliest war zones, although some sources say that African Americans volunteered for these dangerous missions. Other people, however, felt that African Americans were expendable, which was why they were placed in these most dangerous areas. Whether some chose these high-risk combat positions or not, the fact remains that African Americans died at a higher rate. Some historians state that almost 20 percent of the casualties in 1965 were African American (Goodwin, 2017).

According to some reports, African Americans made up about 14 percent of the total of enlisted men in the Vietnam War. One source points out that at that time, Blacks only made up 11 percent of the young male population of the nation (American War Library website). Two years later in 1967, the percentage of deaths dropped to about 12 percent. This was due to the intervention of President Lyndon Johnson because of the protests by Black leaders (American War Library website).

Another issue was the draft, known as military conscription, itself. It was started during World War II, but with the escalation of the war, many more men were needed. The greatest number of draftees came from the working class or poor. Although the draft law provided deferments or exemptions from military service because of attendance in college, most young Black men did not qualify because they could not afford to go to college. Young men could also qualify for moral or religious reasons as conscientious objectors. More Whites were able to get deferments than African Americans were. Twice as many African Americans as Whites were drafted. During 1967, 64 percent of African Americans were eligible for the draft, compared to 31 percent of Whites.

Opposition to the War

Both the Student Non-violent Coordinating Committee (SNCC) and the Congress of Racial Equality (CORE) were opposed the Vietnam War as early as 1965. The rise of Black Nationalism focused attention on the conditions of African Americans and on a cultural identity that was opposed to war. The opposition to the war by these groups made them targets for surveillance by the FBI. Martin Luther King, Jr., the Southern Christian Leadership Conference (SCLC), and the Black Panthers also came under scrutiny because of their opposition to the war.

The tactics of the FBI did not lessen the opposition, however. Anti-war feelings grew throughout the country and gave impetus to the rise of more activist protests in the African American community. Many people also felt that the millions of dollars being spent on a war that was rapidly losing support could be better spent to alleviate urban problems such as joblessness, poor housing, and inferior education.

Muhammad Ali and the Conscientious Objection

One controversial case where an individual was denied an exemption as a conscientious objector was that of Muhammad Ali, formerly Cassius Clay. He had won the light-heavyweight boxing title in 1960 and went on to win the heavyweight championship in 1964. Ali also converted to the Islamic faith and became a member of the Nation of Islam. He requested an exemption because of his religious views but was denied. Ali won the heavyweight championship again in 1967 but was arrested for refusing to join the Army. His title was taken away from him and he was sentenced to five years in prison. Ali was also fined $10,000.

In 1971, the Supreme Court reversed its decision about Ali's conviction, and he went on to win the title two more times before retiring. Ali's conviction was controversial for many people because it seemed to be political and racist. This conviction was viewed as political because the Nation of Islam was also a target of the FBI. It appeared to many that any group that attempted to empower itself became a target. It was viewed as racist because White conscientious objectors were given exemptions, whereas often African Americans were denied. Ali's flamboyant behavior was reminiscent of Jack Johnson in 1910. The difference was that Ali did not associate with White women as Johnson had. The government jailed Ali just as they had Jack Johnson, but the rest of Ali's life turned out much better than Johnson's did.

The Persian Gulf Wars

The United States engaged in two other foreign wars during the end of the 20th and the beginning of the 21st century. This time soldiers were sent to fight in the Persian Gulf. Both times the target was Iraq and its leader, Saddam Hussein.

The Persian Gulf War (Desert Storm)

The countries of Iraq and Kuwait in the Middle East had a dispute about oil production. Iraq accused Kuwait of overproduction, and Saddam Hussein sent troops into Kuwait in July of 1990. As a result, several nations around the world implemented economic sanctions against Iraq. Iraq responded by annexing, or taking over, Kuwait. The ruler of Saudi Arabia invited American troops to his country, apparently for protection from Saddam Hussein. President George Bush sent troops to Saudi Arabia, but it was not long before he sent troops into Iraq.

The United Nations declared the annexation of Kuwait by Iraq to be invalid. President Bush got support from the members of the United Nations to use whatever political and military actions were necessary. He was able to do this because many of the members of the United Nations were opposed to what Saddam Hussein had done. They were also concerned for economic reasons primarily, the control of the oil fields of Kuwait. Kuwait has one of richest supplies of oil in the world.

These nations, however, were reluctant to send troops, but Iraq did not back down. President Bush got the Security Council of the United Nations to pass a resolution setting a deadline of January 15, 1991, for Iraqi troops to withdraw from Kuwait. The United States led air and ground war activities beginning the next day. When Hussein refused, American troops were sent in on February 24 to begin the ground war called Desert Storm. Other troops came from the participating countries of the United Nations. After four days of combat, the war ended. The terms for a ceasefire were discussed on March 3, 1991, and an official ceasefire was signed on April 6, 1991.

The Iraq War

The war against Iraq, however, did not end with Desert Storm. In March 2003, President George W. Bush, the son of the former President George Bush who initiated Desert Storm, sent troops into Iraq. He said he did so because Iraq posed a threat to the United States. He also said the Iraqi government was not abiding by an arms agreement made during Desert Storm.

President Bush asserted that Iraq had nuclear arms and had the ability to conduct chemical warfare. Weapons inspectors went to Iraq to verify whether Hussein had any of these illegal weapons. The weapons inspectors found no such arms or chemicals. When the United States invaded the country, no chemical warfare was used against the U.S. military and no chemical weapons were found.

President Bush also said that Iraqi leaders were connected to terrorism. Yet, 15 of the 19 terrorists who led the attack on the United States on September 11, 2001, were from Saudi Arabia, not Iraq. Unlike Desert Storm, the war that George W. Bush's father had pushed America into, the Iraq War had only one other ally, Britain. Other countries were unwilling to support the United States, and two countries, France and Russia, were very outspoken against the actions of the United States.

Iraq is an oil-rich country. There were reports that the war was as much about the oil as it was about Saddam Hussein. Members of the Bush administration, including President Bush himself—a former oil executive— have ties to "big oil" and its production and control. Many Americans felt, and still feel, that the war that was started by George W. Bush was about economics, namely oil. It was a pre-emptive strike. This means that the United States sent troops into a country that had not attacked or threatened them.

Many people would agree that Saddam Hussein was a tyrant, and that he should not have stayed in power. It is said that he committed many human rights violations against his own people. But it becomes a problem when the most powerful country in the world attacks another without provocation against its citizens. This was the first time in history that the United States initiated a preemptive attack against another country. It made the United States look like a bully to many countries and caused fear and strained relationships around the world.

Who Fights in These Wars?

The young people who are sent to fight in these wars are mostly poor, African American, and other people of color. During the first Iraq War, African Americans made up 22 percent of the armed forces but only 12 percent of the American population. The United States does not have a military draft any longer. It ended in 1973 and was replaced with an all-volunteer military. Many of those who have joined the military did so to serve their country. Many also wanted to have an opportunity to further their education, thereby gaining skills to make better lives for themselves. In addition, professionals such as teachers and police officers have also joined the reserve units of the military. While supporters point to the fact that the all-volunteer military is more professional, better motivated, and more stable than before, there are problems.

Young people who join the military may understand that the main reason for doing so is for the defense of their country. However, it stands to reason that given deployment to war zones may be more likely given the new "war on terror." Some of the people who have enlisted have had to spend a longer time in the war zone than they expected. The military extended the length of service of men and women who were in Iraq. In addition, U.S. troops are deployed in other areas, such as Afghanistan. The military capacity of the United States is stretched. Other issues with the voluntary military is that people may not choose to enlist. Without replacements, how long can military personnel endure the hardships associated with war?

Many think that the draft will have to be reinstated because many more people are needed than the few who enlist voluntarily when the country is fighting a war. The idea of reinstating the draft is also a way to ensure equity in terms of which Americans fight in these wars. Representatives Charles Rangel from New York and John Conyers from Michigan are members of the

Congressional Black Caucus. They voiced support for the draft. The congressmen maintain that the burden of defending America should not fall disproportionately on the poor and people of color.

Global War on Terror

The terrorist attack on the United States in 2001 presented a new reality for its citizens. The destruction of the Twin Towers, the financial icon, in New York City and coordinated attacks at other sites, launched a new offensive for America. For the first time, foreign nationals invaded the United States and launched an attack against its citizens as well as its political and economic icons. The attack was undertaken by 19 foreign nationals who had been trained by Al-Qaeda under the Taliban regime. The response by the U.S. government was to launch an attack against the Taliban that was very broad in scope and sequence. It was also comprehensive and carried out on several fronts.

According to Jackson (2018) and others, the "war on terror" turned into an endeavor that included war in Iraq and Afghanistan. There were also operations in Yemen and conflict in Syria. It also meant large-scale military assistance for those friendly Middle Eastern countries willing to assist America, and more intelligence sharing with other nations. While many leaders of Al-Queda were arrested, or eliminated unfortunately, the war never ended. Even the elimination of Osama bin Laden by the Obama administration did not dampen or slow the "war." One criticism of the "war on terrorism" is that it also seemed to be an opportunity to seize the oil rich countries of the Middle East. Another is that America's current policies almost justify going to war in various countries without the consent of Congress, which is also a problem.

For Americans, the USA Patriot Act was put into place that affected their rights. A new security agency was created called Homeland security. There have been increased security measures for airports among other measures have been instituted. America's "war on terror" has been compared to the Cold War era, 1945–1991. This era was a time during nuclear proliferation, when Russia and the United States were at heightened tension and fear of outright aggression by either country. While that era has passed, it has been replaced with the "war on terror" which has not slowed but continues with each new flare-up on the geopolitical map.

Summary

Until 1948, African Americans served in a racially divided military. They were not permitted to be members of certain units in the Army and were segregated from White soldiers until President Harry Truman desegregated the military through an executive order. Nevertheless, more than a million African Americans entered the U.S. armed forces during World War II. Once again, despite this military service, African American men and women often faced racism and discrimination, both in military training camps and when they returned home. African Americans also served in the Korean War, during a period that finally saw the end to segregation in the armed services.

Despite the constant struggle to gain their human rights, African Americans have consistently defended the United States and unfailingly taken part in America's wars. They even fought in wars about which they had some trepidation or concerns. They served on the western frontier in the early days and in the Spanish-American War, World War I, World War II, the Korean War (when the last unit of the Buffalo Soldiers was dismantled), the Vietnam War, and Desert Storm.

The "war on terror" has actually brought the threat of physical dangers and harm to the American people. The Cold War ended during the administration of former President Ronald Reagan. However, there are new threats that all Americans face, for which everyone should be vigilant.

African Americans have repeatedly demonstrated their patriotism and willingness to fight for the freedom of all Americans and the right to "life, liberty, and the pursuit of happiness." These ideals, as stated in the Declaration of Independence, have been difficult to achieve. African Americans have been discriminated against in all the wars and conflicts conducted by the United States.

Still, the hope exists for African Americans that, one day, America will live up to its Declaration and that it will include all of its citizens. Much of this hope stems from the enactment of laws that provided for civil rights of African Americans. People of all colors helped fight for and defend America from threats foreign and domestic despite the limits and restrictions placed on African American. Throughout history and modern times Black soldiers have fought in every conflict of the past 50 years and served with high distinction. While many of these laws have been helpful, others were not. The next chapter focuses on some of the laws that have helped African Americans as well as those that created many problems for them.

References

Aron, N. R. (2018, April 27). Muhammad Ali wouldn't go to war for a country that didn't value Black lives. *Medium.* Accessed March 13, 2021.https://timeline.com/muhammad-ali-wouldnt-go-to-war-for-a-country-that-didn-t-value-black-lives-9bf6e3f7d766

Butler, J. S. (1999). African Americans in the Vietnam War. In *The Oxford Companion to American Military History.* Oxford University Press.

Coffey, D. (1998). African Americans in the Vietnam War. In S. C. Tucker (Ed.), *Encyclopedia of the Vietnam War: A Political, Social, and Military History.* ABC-CLIO,

Coleman, M. (2015). *Women in the military.* Rosen Publishing Group, ProQuest Ebook Central, https://ebookcentral.proquest.com/lib/daemen/detail.action?docID=5142704

Eldridge, L. A. (2001). *Chronicles of a two-front war: Civil Rights and Vietnam in the African American press.* University of Missouri Press.

Ferraro, M. (2002, May 12). Black grads take top posts in the Army. *Poughkeepsie Journal.*

Goodwin, G. (2017, July 18). Opinion: Black and White in Vietnam. *The New York Times.* https://www.nytimes.com/2017/07/18/opinion/racism-vietnam-war.html

Hiro, D. (2007, September). How Bush's Iraqi oil grab went awry. *The Nation.* Accessed 2018. https://www.thenation.com/article/how-bushs-iraqi-oil-grab-went-awry/

History.com Editors. (2019, 30 April). *Muhammad Ali refuses army induction.* History. www.history.com/this-day-in-history/muhammad-ali-refuses-army-induction

Holmes, S. A. (2003, April 6). Is this really an all-volunteer army? Accessed 2004. http://www.csudh.edu/dearhabermas/warbk25.htm

Jackson, R. (2018, November). *War on terrorism: United States history.* Encyclopedia Britannica. Accessed 2018. https://www.britannica.com/topic/war-on-terrorism

Juhasz, A. (2013, April). Why the war in Iraq was fought for big oil. CNN. Accessed 2018. https://www.cnn.com/2013/03/19/opinion/iraq-war-oil-juhasz/index.html

Katz, M. N. *What exactly is the war on terror?* Middle East Policy Council. Accessed 2018. https://www.mepc.org/commentary/what-exactly-war-terror

Krishnadev, C. (2016, June 4). When Muhammad Ali refused to go to Vietnam. *The Atlantic.* www.theatlantic.com/news/archive/2016/06/muhammad-ali-vietnam/485717/

Nathan, A. (2004). *Count on us: American women in the military.* National Geographic Society.

135 thousand troops to remain in Iraq. (2004, May 4). CBS/AP. Accessed May 4, 2004. http://www.cbsnews.com/stories/2004/05/05/iraq/main615669.shtml

Powell, C., & Davidson, J. (2004). "The general gets specific." *Crisis (00111422), 111(5),* 38–41. America: History & Life database.

Reams, J. E. (2003, September). Is our all-volunteer army dying? Accessed 2003. http://www.americandaily.com/article/3122

Rothschild, M. (2006, October 12). *So now Iraq is for oil, Bush admits*. The Progressive, Accessed 2018. https://progressive.org/dispatches/now-iraq-oil-bush-admits-d2/

Schimmel, B. (2004, April). *Restart the draft*. Accessed 2004. http://citypaper.net/articles/2004-04-15/canon.shtml

Taylor, A. (2011, September 8). 9/11: The day of the attacks. *The Atlantic*. Accessed 2018. https://www.theatlantic.com/photo/2011/09/911-the-day-of-the-attacks/100143/

Trotter, J. W. (2001) *The African American experience*, Volume I and II. Houghton Mifflin.

Vietnam war deaths, by race, ethnicity and natl origin. (2020). The American War Library. http://www.americanwarlibrary.com/vietnam/vwc10.htm

Wallsten, P. (2008, November). Red and blue, Black and White. *The Los Angeles Times*. P. A11. Accessed 2008. https://www.latimes.com/archives/la-xpm-2008-nov-05-na-assess5-story.html

Westheider, J. E. (1997). Front Matter. In *Fighting on two fronts: African Americans and the Vietnam War* (pp. i–vi). NYU Press. http://www.jstor.org/stable/j.ctt9qfvsp.1

From a Legal Point of View

Civil Rights and Legislative and Judicial Milestones

Every society makes laws that help people govern themselves. These laws affect all members of that society. Over the years laws made by the Congress of the United States and state and local governments have greatly affected the lives of African Americans. Some of these laws have hurt African Americans and resulted in the unjust treatment. Others have helped African Americans gain civil and human rights.

Laws and Amendments That Hurt

There were many laws that hurt the cause of African Americans. This section will highlight only a few of them. It should be noted that these laws directly affected the provision of civil liberties and rights that other American citizens enjoyed but which were denied to African American citizens.

The Three-Fifths Compromise

The Three-Fifths Compromise and the slave codes were harmful to African Americans. In 1776, following the Revolutionary War, a group of colonists

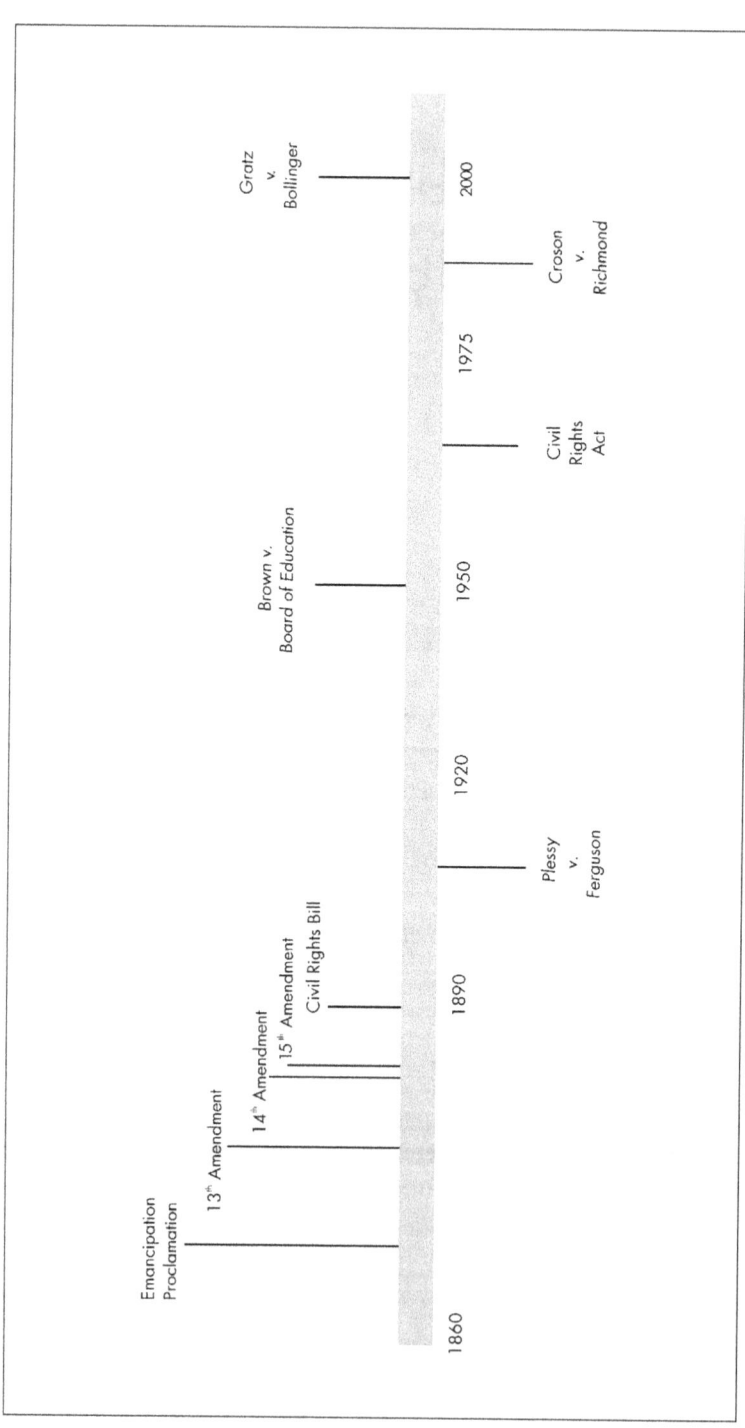

Legislative and Judicial Milestones

met in Philadelphia to convene the Constitutional Convention to set up the new government. After much debate, it was decided to have a Congress made up of two parts, a Senate and a House of Representatives. The Senate would have two representatives for each state. The number of representatives in the House would depend on the number of people who lived in that state. Although Africans lived in both the North and the South, the southern states had a great deal more. So, in order to prevent them from having an advantage, it was decided that the southern states would be allowed to count three-fifths of their enslaved Africans as the basis for representation in Congress.

Slave Codes to Black Codes and Jim Crow

The "slave codes" are other examples of laws that hurt African Americans. As the enterprise of enslavement grew to such enormous proportions and became so profitable, slave codes were enacted, which took away the rights of the Africans. Simple rights that we take for granted now were disallowed. These included the right to assemble, to learn how to read, or to get married (because marriage was a contract and enslaved persons could not enter into legal contracts).

After the Civil War and the Emancipation Proclamation, African Americans were free. Other laws were enacted that were supposed to provide African Americans the same treatment and protection as White citizens in such areas as education, housing, medical treatment, and political rights. Southern states simply ignored the federal laws that were enacted. They cited states' rights and enacted their own laws. These laws were called Black Codes or Jim Crow laws. The laws prevented African Americans from voting and from owning guns, which was a carry-over from the old slave codes. They were not allowed to do the jobs they used to as carpenters, mechanics, and metal working. African Americans were then prevented from obtaining training as craftsmen by the unions. They were also prevented from working in industries such as textile mills.

Plessy v. Ferguson

In 1896, the Supreme Court handed down the *Plessy v. Ferguson* decision. The lawsuit in this case was over the seating arrangements in railroad cars, which called for separation of Whites and African Americans. Homer Plessy sued, saying that this separation violated the 13th and 14th Amendments. But the Supreme Court upheld the constitutionality of state laws that provided "separate but equal" accommodations for African Americans. In other words, they said that the amendments pertained only to interstate railway travel. The argument was made by human rights activists that accommodations for African Americans were usually never equal, but this was to no avail.

Laws and Amendments That Helped

After the Civil War, laws were passed that were to give African Americans equal status and treatment and were supposed to reverse years of abuse and oppression. One of the major legislative acts was the passage of the 13th, 14th, and 15th Amendments to the Constitution. The 13th Amendment made enslavement illegal. The 14th Amendment made Africans citizens. The 15th Amendment gave African Americans the right to vote. These Amendments are examples of laws that benefited African Americans.

Following the passage of the Reconstruction Amendments a new Supreme Court Decision was made which was intended to support them. The Cruikshank Case Decision was rendered in 1876 because of the Colfax Massacre where armed Whites murdered over 100 Black men. It dealt specifically with the 14th Amendment. Among the provisions of the Decision was the right to assemble, a freedom that the Black Codes forbade. The Decision also dealt with the right to bear arms for a lawful purpose and to have the full and equal benefit of the law. However, the Cruikshank Decision also set the precedent that states would not be required to enforce federal protective legislation of African Americans. Cruikshank required that federal protections be enforced by the federal government not the state. While this Decision provided civil rights at the federal level, it could only be litigated by federal authorities and was ignored by state officials.

The Early Civil Rights Acts

After the passage of the 13th Amendment, the Civil Rights Act of 1866 was passed because, although slavery was abolished, African Americans still did not have rights. In fact, there have been a total of seven civil rights acts enacted. Four civil rights acts were passed in the 1800s and three others during the 1900s. One would think that the Amendments and perhaps one civil rights bill would have been all that was needed, but this was not the case.

There were the Civil Rights Acts of 1866, 1870, 1871, and 1875, which were intended to give African Americans legal and political rights. The first three gave African Americans the right to own property, to sue and be sued, and attempted to eliminate registration fraud in elections. The Civil Rights Act of 1875 gave freedom of access to public facilities and the right to sue for personal damages. It was never enforced, though, and in 1883, the Supreme Court overturned this Act. The court cited that it violated states' rights. African Americans soon saw that these amendments and laws still were not enough to protect them and ensure their rights.

Southern Whites passed their own laws that nullified the federal law, saying that states' rights allowed them to do so. Since the federal government withdrew the troops who provided protection after Reconstruction and refused to force the states to implement federal law, Jim Crow laws took away the rights that African Americans had worked and fought so hard to gain.

Although laws were passed to help African Americans, court interpretation of the laws resulted in unjust treatment. Most often, when African Americans went to court to have laws enforced, the courts interpreted these laws in such a way as to make them meaningless. For example, the Supreme Court ruled that there were two categories of citizenship, state and federal. The Supreme Court further stated that the 14th Amendment pertained only to the rights under federal citizenship. Encouraged by these and other decisions of the Supreme Court in the civil rights cases of 1883, individual states continued to pass and enforce Jim Crow laws.

The Early Education Cases

As noted, the NAACP began an aggressive drive to bring about equal education opportunities for African Americans. Other members of the organization wanted to bring about equal accommodations and access to public facilities; a decision was made to focus on schools. As early as 1935, the Maryland Supreme Court ruled against segregation in the *Murray v. Pearson* Law School case. In that case Donald G. Murray had been denied admission to the University of Maryland Law School. The Maryland Court of Appeals ordered that either a separate school should be established or that Murray was to be admitted to the existing one. The two civil rights lawyers who argued the case were Thurgood Marshall and Charles Houston. This was Marshall's first major victory.

Other decisions included *McLaurin v. Oklahoma* and *Sweatt v. Painter*. In 1950 McLaurin was denied admission to the University of Oklahoma's doctoral program in Education. As a result of the lawsuit, McLaurin was admitted but forced to sit in segregated areas of the school. He appealed and won. The *Sweatt v. Painter* case not only focused on admittance to the Law School but the equity and quality of the facilities provided. In this case, the University of Texas was given a period of time in order to provide "substantially equal facilities" for African Americans who wanted to attend law school. The university opened a separate law school, but it was of substandard quality and Sweatt refused to enroll.

During the mid-1900s, the NAACP also looked to desegregate K–12 schools. Several suits were filed during this period until a very important case came before the Supreme Court. This suit was known as the 1954 *Brown v. Board of Education* decision in Topeka, Kansas. It was an important one for education, which had become the major focus of the NAACP.

Brown v. Board of Education

The plaintiff in *Brown v. Board of Education*, for whom the case was named, was Oliver Brown on behalf of his daughter. Linda Brown was a third grader who had to walk past a White school a few blocks from her home to a school for African Americans that was in another part of town. She had to go through a railway switchyard and cross a busy street to get to a bus stop to go across town to the school. When her father tried to enroll her in the nearby White school, he was refused. Oliver Brown went to the NAACP in Topeka, Kansas, for help.

It started out as a single case, but the lawyers asked Oliver Brown to be a part of a larger suit that included four other cases. These cases were from the states of Delaware, South Carolina, and Virginia, and the District of Columbia. The *Brown* case represented nearly 200 plaintiffs and was named after Oliver Brown, who was the only male plaintiff. It was the strategy of the NAACP to have a man at the head of the roster and to include a state that was from somewhere other than the South.

Before *Brown v. Board of Education*, schools were segregated. Pictured here is a reading lesson in a Negro school in Washington, D.C.

In *Brown v. Board of Education*, the Supreme Court ruled that "maintaining schools for White and colored children is in direct conflict with the Equal Protection Clause of the 14th Amendment." In other words, it was unconstitutional to have separate schools for African Americans and Whites. Some schools in the South complied with the ruling; others did not.

One of the lawyers who worked for the NAACP on this case was Thurgood Marshall. He later went on to be appointed the first African American member of the Supreme Court. Some Whites were so opposed to *Brown* that they resorted to violence to keep it from being implemented. This was the case in Little Rock, Arkansas, where the governor of the state sent the National Guard to Little Rock's Central High School in 1957 to prevent African American students from entering the school.

Americans felt that it was a great victory. It held great promise. Their children could attend schools on a nonracial basis in their districts. At last their children would have access to good schools. The fact is that it did not miraculously create integrated schools or provide access to good education. *Brown* proclaimed that separate was not equal, but it did not prescribe how or the means by which this would happen. *Brown et al. v. Board of Education, Topeka et al.* (1995) left desegregation to the very people who had tried so hard to keep African Americans from participating in an equal society. It

Thurgood Marshall was the chief attorney for the NAACP. He argued the *Brown v. Board of Education* case which ended legal segregation in schools. He was appointed to the Supreme Court in 1965.

left the school districts to comply and required them to submit a desegregation plan.

Also, not considered was what would happen to the African American educators in those schools that were desegregated. One major outcome was that many teachers and principals lost their jobs. This was not intended, but indeed it was a part of the aftermath. Another outcome has been residential segregation, particularly in the north. This happens when Whites move into other residential areas that are essentially White, thereby avoiding integration. These issues could not have been foreseen or addressed by the *Brown II* ruling. It could only achieve what laws do and that was to put it on the record. In May 2004, the 50th anniversary of *Brown v. Board of Education* was commemorated in Topeka, Kansas.

Civil Rights Legislation of the 1900s

As stated earlier, several additional Civil Rights Acts were passed during the mid-1900s. They were the Civil Rights Acts of 1957, 1960, 1964 and 1991. In addition the Civil Rights Act of 1968 is known as the Fair Housing Act. The Civil Rights Acts of 1957 and 1960 were the first to be passed since 1875. They established the Civil Rights Commission and the Civil Rights Division of the Department of Justice. Unfortunately, the Civil Rights Act of 1960, which was intended to stop discrimination in the voting registration process in the South, was unenforceable.

The law that is most commonly thought of when discussing the civil rights movement is the Civil Rights Act of 1964. That law made it illegal to discriminate against a person because of race, color, religion, or national origin, in all public accommodations. It also banned discrimination in employment, funded school desegregation, renewed the Civil Rights Commission for another four years, and banned the use of federal funds for programs or schools that discriminate. The last two, the Civil Rights Acts of 1968 and 1991, addressed fair housing and the reversal of previous Supreme Court decisions that had limited certain civil rights.

In addition to the Civil Rights Acts mentioned above, Congress passed a Voting Rights Act in 1965. This act put in place enforcement procedures. It was renewed in 1970, 1975, and 1982. In 2006, the Voting Right Acts, which was also named the Fannie Lou Hamer, Rosa Parks, Coretta Scott King Act, was reauthorized by President George W. Bush.

Voting Rights

As part of the great society of Lyndon Johnson and the murder of civil rights workers in Mississippi and across the South, the federal government became actively involved in voter protection. Southern states had enacted numerous barriers and arbitrary methods to prevent African Americans from voting. These included literacy tests, poll taxes, and other nefarious requirements that were not applied to White voters. Efforts to increase minority voting were met by force, intimidation, hostility and economic reprisals. The federal government under Presidents Kennedy and Johnson addressed the issue of Black voter intimidation through legislation. The Voting Rights Act of 1965 set forth two important policies that made free elections possible. The first policy by the federal government was uniform federal guidelines for elections and voting. The second policy was federal oversight by monitoring and providing remedy for the states that had demonstrated historic biased voting practices and procedures.

Affirmative Action: A Tool of Opportunity

Despite the passage of the various civil rights laws and legislative acts, discrimination against Blacks persisted. Then in 1961, President John F. Kennedy introduced the term "affirmative action" in his Executive Order 10925. Affirmative action was introduced as a method to redress the persistent discrimination against Blacks (Holst, 2006). President Lyndon B. Johnson went on to enforce it after Kennedy's assassination. Although, the policy and set of initiatives originally focused on discrimination in employment and education, it was expanded into other areas including housing, medical and health services. Affirmative action also eventually included other ethnic groups, women, and the disabled.

The push to enforce affirmative action was in full gear by the end of the 1960s. In 1969, President Nixon set hiring goals for federal contractors and in 1972 affirmative action was extended to include colleges and universities. Since the purpose of affirmative action was to increase the number of underrepresented groups of people in various areas, employers and schools looked for ways to comply. There are different ways of approaching affirmative action, one of which is the use of quotas and/or set asides. A quota reserves a certain number of jobs or positions. Another way is to eliminate the barriers that keep people from being treated equally. Affirmative action is generally not to be based on quotas or used to give preferences to unqualified candidates according to Froomkin (1998). In fact, the use of quotas is prohibited by law; however, affirmative action is still associated with preferential treatment by race.

There are many vocal opponents of affirmative action who see it as reverse discrimination. They feel that they are not to blame for the many years of discrimination against African Americans. They do not see it as a way of "leveling the playing field" but as providing preference programs for unqualified minorities. However, several writers state that if one chooses to discuss affirmative action in the context of preference programs, then there are other types of preference programs which should also be discussed. Berube (2005) and Antwi-Boasiako and Asagva (2005) point out that there are other types of preference programs that are rarely discussed which also focus on specific groups as Michelle Obama learned when she attended Harvard University (Interview with Gayle King, 2018).

These include legacy set asides in colleges and universities, star athletic set asides, or nepotism in government and employment. A legacy set aside is a preference program for the children of the school's alumni. Student legacies exist in most of the Ivy League universities and they make up 10–15 percent of every class (*The Economist*, 2005). Cose (1995) writes that there have been no angry protests or movements against colleges who offer admission to star athletes or sons or daughters of alumni, notwithstanding their qualifications for college admission. He further states that, although these preferences may not be liked, people go along with them because they "understand that academic merit is not the only relevant consideration" (Cose, 1995).

Nepotism is a type of preference that usually involves politics and the workplace. It is where relatives offer other relatives positions or jobs regardless of qualifications. Reeve and Sheridan (2003), as well as others, also cite instances of this occurring but again there is little discussion about it (Padgett & Morris, 2005; *The Economist*, 2004).

Many of those who oppose affirmative action have mounted successful campaigns against it. Laws were passed that began to destroy what meager gains had been made. Opponents of affirmative action were successful in striking down the use of a quota system in California in the 1978 *Bakke* case. Then, in 1995, the University of California stopped its commitment to affirmative action. The state of Washington eliminated its preferential treatment of minorities in 1998. When that happened, the number of African American and other ethnic minorities attending college dropped significantly. This backlash was also felt in employment.

Croson v. Richmond

Then in 1989, in the *Croson v. Richmond* case in Richmond, Virginia, African Americans received a setback in the gains they had made in obtaining jobs. It was ruled that a percentage of city contracts could not be set aside for minorities. In this case, as in others during the terms of Presidents Reagan and Bush, a law that was designed to remove injustices suffered by African Americans was overturned. It affected other areas, including education, across the United States.

Bakke v. Regents of the University of California

The practice of setting aside a number of places for minorities in colleges and universities received a setback in the *Bakke v. Regents of the University of California* decision. Allan Bakke, a White man who was denied acceptance to medical school, sued the University of California–Davis, stating that his rights were violated because minority students whose scores were lower than his were admitted while he was not. Although the California Supreme Court ordered that he be admitted, the Supreme Court intervened, granting part of the decision and denying another part. The Supreme Court stated that Bakke could be admitted because the university could not prove that he would have been denied even if the school did not have this special program. However, it also allowed the special admissions program to continue. The courts decided that race could be a factor in choosing a diverse student population, but it also stated that the use of a quota was not permissible.

University of Michigan

In 2003, affirmative action came into the spotlight again and marked a victory for African Americans and other people of color. In the *Gratz v. Bollinger* and the *Grutter v. Bollinger* cases, White students claimed that their civil rights had been violated by the university's point system used for entrance to undergraduate school and law school, respectively. They claimed that the system gave African Americans an unearned advantage and violated their rights.

Two of the laws that the students used to argue their case were the 14th Amendment and Title 6 of the Civil Rights Act of 1964. That the 14th Amendment was used is especially interesting since its intent was to provide citizenship for African Americans after the Civil War and to grant *them* equal protection under the law. It was the basis for lawsuits for the civil rights cases brought forward by the NAACP. It was a mixed victory, although the Supreme Court overturned the case. While the court did not fully agree with the university's point system, it did maintain that race can be used in determining whether a student is admitted.

Fisher v. University of Texas

Abigail Fisher, a White woman sued the University of Texas at Austin for race discrimination. She claimed that the admission policy violated the Fourteenth Amendment against White and Asian students. The argument was that she was not afforded equal protection under the law. Fisher claimed that the university was admitting Blacks who had lower grades than her. The Court upheld the use the race in a holistic program if it cannot achieve diversity otherwise (Bouie, 2015). Interestingly in Texas there are three ways in which one can attend the University of Texas at Austin. One option is to score in the top 10 percent of your high school class. A person can also try for one of the non-top 10 slots. Finally, a person with weak grades could attend a satellite campus and transfer if that person has good grades and a strong course load.

Her suit failed because she did not fall within the boundaries of any of the options. While her grades were good, they were not of the level necessary. Unfortunately, four of the justices on the Supreme Court are against affirmative action. That is an ominous situation for future African Americans, who again make up only approximately 13 percent of the population of the United States. However, it is even more unfortunate given all of the set asides given to legacy applicants (those whose parents attended), student athletes, and others who arrive in college with less than stellar high school grades. These other students are provided an educational opportunity based on their circumstances, White privilege, not necessarily on grades, so why the pushback for race conscious college admission?

Summary

Many laws have been passed since the formation of the government of the United States. It is documented that many of them directly related to the enslavement of African people and the dominance of Whites over African Americans. At first there were laws to keep people enslaved. Later, although slavery had ended, and laws were passed to ensure the civil rights of African Americans, such as the right to vote, due process, equal opportunity, they were ignored.

When people reflect on the 1960s and the struggle of African Americans, the Civil Rights Act of 1964 comes to mind. While this legislation was an important step to make social progress for African Americans, the Voting Rights Act and Affirmation Action legislation are equally important. During the sixties these three legal instruments set the foundation for greater equality within the legal political, social, economic, and housing fabric of contemporary society. President Johnson's vision of a Great Society needed the protections and methodology of legal due process to become reality. The impact of the sixties era legislative and policies were tools that opened the doors of opportunity for African Americans, women, the people with disabilities.

There have been many civil rights laws passed—and violated prior to the sixties. It is noteworthy that so many civil rights laws were passed, but it was not until the 1960s that they were enforced. The right to vote is basic and important but something that many people now take for granted in American society. Many young people do not realize the cost in human life that it took to secure that right. It is a right that African Americans, in particular, should exercise regularly.

Early on, the NAACP had some victories. A landmark victory was the *Brown v. Board of Education* decision, where the courts ruled that schools were to be desegregated. In the University of Michigan, and the University of Texas case it's ironic that the 14th Amendment of the Reconstruction period was used to argue the case, especially since it was clear that the law pertained to African Americans. It is interesting how the law can be maneuvered to benefit those who already have privilege and opportunity because of their skin color. The struggle for civil rights has been ongoing since emancipation. It has been a never-ending campaign. Other concerns which are very much related to civil issues are those that involve unequal justice, economics, and education. These issues present dilemmas for many African Americans. The following chapter will examine these issues more closely.

References

Antwi-Boasiako, K. B., & Asagba, J. (2005). A preliminary analysis of African American college students' perceptions of racial preferences and affirmative action in making admissions decisions at a predominantly White university. *College Student Journal.* 39(4), 734–748.

Berube, M. (2005). And justice for all. *The Nation.* 280(3), 27–31.

Bouie, J. (2015, June). Easy AA. The Supreme Court might destroy Affirmative Action because this White woman's grades weren't good enough. *Slate.* Accessed 2018. https://slate.com/news-and-politics/2015/06/fisher-v-university-of-texas-the-supreme-court-might-just-gut-affirmative-action-this-time.html

Civil rights: Law and history. Find Law. Accessed May 2009. https://civilrights.findlaw.com/civil-rights-overview/civil-rights-law-and-history.html

Civil rights acts. Prentice Hall Documents Library: Civil Rights Acts. Accessed May 2004. http://cwx.prenhall.com/bookbind/pubbooks/dye4/medialib/docs/civrit.htm

Cose, E. (2004, May 16). 50 years after *Brown:* The struggle for equality of opportunity must proceed to a new level. *Detroit Free Press.* http://www.freep.com/voices/sunday/ecose16_20040516.htm

Cose, E. (1995). The myth of meritocracy. *Newsweek,* 125(14), 34.

The curse of nepotism. (2004). *Economist,* 370(8357).

Ever higher society, ever harder to ascend. (2005). *Economist,* Vol. 374, Issue 8407.

50 years of diversity: *Brown v. Board* anniversary. (2004, May). *Ebony,* 59(7)105–106.

Froomkin, D. (1998, October). Affirmative action under attack. *The Washington Post.* Accessed 2004. https://www.washingtonpost.com/wp-srv/politics/special/affirm/affirm.htm

Gates, H. L., Jr., & Higginbotham, E. B. (Eds.). (2004). *African American Lives*. Oxford University Press.

Harding, V. (1993). *There is a river: The Black struggle for freedom in America*. Harcourt Brace.

Holst, S., et al. (2006). *Affirmative Action*. Affirmative Action—Federalism in America. http://encyclopedia.federalism.org/index.php/Affirmative_Action

Jim Crow Laws—Time Marches On. www.nku.edu/~taylorann/jimcrownotes.htm

Liptak, A. (2016, June 23). Supreme Court upholds affirmative action program at University of Texas. *The New York Times*. Accessed 2018.https://www.nytimes.com/2016/06/24/us/politics/supreme-court-affirmative-action-university-of-texas.html

Kegu, J. (2019, January 1). Michelle Obama interview with Gayle King—full transcript. *CBS News*, CBS Interactive. www.cbsnews.com/news/michelle-obama-book-interview-gayle-king-becoming-michelle-obama/

Menand, L. (2020, January 20). The changing meaning of Affirmative Action. *The New Yorker*. https://www.newyorker.com/magazine/2020/01/20/have-we-outgrown-the-need-for-affirmative-action

Newsweek Staff. (1995, April 2). The myth of meritocracy. *Newsweek*. Accessed March 9, 2021. https://www.newsweek.com/myth-meritocracy-181478

Obama, M. (2018). *Becoming*. Crown.

Padgett, M. Y., & Morris, K. A. (2005, Winter). Keeping it "All in the Family": Does nepotism in the hiring process really benefit the beneficiary? *Journal of Leadership & Organizational Studies* (Baker College), *11*(2), 34–45, 12p, 1 chart.

Reeve, R., & Sheridan, G. (2003). "Nepotism: Is it back?" *New Statesman, 132*(4657).

Risjord, N. (1986). *History of the American people*. Holt, Rinehart and Winston.

U.S. Constitution, Civil Rights Acts. (n.d.). US Constitution. http://www.usconstitution.com/CivilRightsActs.htm

United States v Cruikshank: Reconstruction and the Constitution. *Constitutional Law Reporter*. https://constitutionallawreporter.com/2016/12/13/historical-united-states-v-cruikshank/

Review

I. Checking What You Have Read

1. African Americans have always taken part in armed conflict in America. List five wars and/or conflicts in the 20th century in which African American men and women distinguished themselves.
2. The Vietnam War did much to increase the violence and militancy of the Civil Rights Movement in the 1960s and 1970s. Explain the connection.
3. What happened in the University of Michigan law case?
4. Why do some African Americans think that the United States should provide aid to Liberia?
5. What law reversed the *Plessy v. Ferguson* decision?
6. Why were many people upset about the United States starting the Iraq War?
7. Explain the "war on terror" that has become the new Cold War for America. Explain the Cold War.
8. Summarize the Supreme Court decisions of *Plessy v. Ferguson* and *Brown v. Board of Education*. What effect did each decision have on African Americans?
9. What did the Supreme Court rule in *Croson v. Richmond*?
10. What did the Civil Rights Act of 1984 accomplish? What did affirmative action laws try to do?
11. What was the Court's decision in the *Fisher v. University of Texas* ruling?
12. Why did the ruling in *United States v. Cruikshank* have both positive and negative effects?

II. On Your Own

1. Ask your library media specialist to help you find information on the Vietnam War. Find information on who served during that war. Find out the ratio of officers to enlisted men. See if they reflect the general population. Do a report (oral or written) for the class on what you found.
2. Do some research to find out which colleges or universities were the first to became desegregated because of lawsuits filed by the NAACP.

3. Find out why America's war against Iraq was, and still is, so controversial. Give at least three points to illustrate.
4. It is argued that the 1946 *Mendez v. Westminster* case set a precedent for the *Brown v. Board of Education* decision. Find out why that is stated.
5. Contrast the difference between civil rights and human rights. A chart might help you organize your ideas.
6. Compare and contrast the Civil Rights Law of 1875 and the Civil Rights Law of 1964. Why was the second law necessary?
7. Review the University Case, *Grutter v. Bollinger* and *Fisher v. University of Texas* and locate the reasons for the decision that were given by the Justices. Write your own explanation of what they said in their briefs.

Achievement Against the Odds

Black Creativity Redefines American Culture

In spite of the obstacles African Americans have faced, they have been able to establish a remarkable record of achievements and meaningful participation throughout American life and culture. The talents of African Americans have been demonstrated repeatedly. African Americans are prominent among inventors and scientists in the United States. They have contributed to the arts and humanities as actors, singers, playwrights, writers, musicians, and artists. African Americans are also active and highly regarded in such fields as law, medicine, education, sports, and politics for their accomplishments.

African Americans have influenced every aspect of American society. Their influence is notable in "popular culture." It is that part of culture that appeals to the masses of people. It is ever changing and is influenced by many things outside the main culture.

Entertainment

There are numerous individuals that have influenced American arts and culture that it is impossible to mention them all here. Some examples in entertainment include Ossie Davis, Denzel Washington, Ruby Dee, Sidney Poitier, Halle Berry, comedian Bill Cosby, and Oprah Winfrey. There are movie directors, such as Spike Lee and John Singleton. August Wilson was a well-known playwright who won two Pulitzer Prizes for his work.

The music of America is very much influenced by Quincy Jones and the Motown sound created by Berry Gordy Jr., where Marvin Gaye, Stevie Wonder, Gladys Knight, Aretha Franklin, the Temptations, and the Miracles were produced. Classic great jazz musicians such as Count Basie and Louis Armstrong and modern jazz artists such as Wynton Marsalis have also influenced American culture. Hip Hop and Rap became major musical genres in the mid-80s. Others have had a profound influence on literature in the 20th century. Early writers included Langston Hughes and Zora Neale Hurston. More contemporary writers such as James Baldwin, Alice Walker, and Toni Morrison chronicled African American life in fiction.

Sports

When given the opportunity, African Americans have also excelled in sports. The old Negro Baseball Leagues were some early examples. African Americans have excelled in baseball, football, and basketball. Take, for example, Jackie Robinson, who was the first African American to break the color barrier and be signed by the Brooklyn Dodgers. After he left baseball, he was active in the civil rights movement. Other sports figures include Hank Aaron, who played for the Atlanta Braves, Reggie Jackson of the New York Yankees and countless modern players.

There are numerous basketball and football athletes, including former players such as Kareem Abdul-Jabbar, Bill Russell, Walt Frazier, and more current athletes such as Michael Jordan and Shaquille O'Neal. There are football players such as Jim Brown, Walter Payton, Herschel Walker, and Deion Sanders. African Americans have followed in the footsteps of Jesse Owens and have excelled at the Olympic Games. Consider Jackie Joyner-Kersee, who won three gold medals, one silver medal, and one bronze medal at the Olympics.

African Americans have participated in virtually every area of the sports world. Olympian Althea Gibson was an early pioneer in both tennis and golf as early as 1950. Arthur Ashe was the first African American tennis player to play on the U.S. Davis Cup Team. He led the way for sisters Venus and

Achievement Against the Odds

Serena Williams. Serena won the 1999 U.S. Open Singles, making her the first African American woman to do so since Althea Gibson. She was 17 years old. A year later, her sister Venus won the Wimbledon's women singles. The two sisters went on to win the women's Wimbledon's doubles crown. It was the first time in history that two sisters had accomplished such a feat.

Calvin Peete was the precursor to Tiger Woods. Tiger Woods won the 1997 Masters and the 1999 PGA golf championship. In 2000 and 2005 he won the British Open and became the youngest player to do so. These are just a few of the people who have made their mark on American culture. They have made their mark in other areas, too, such as horse racing. The first jockeys were African Americans. During enslavement, they cared for the horses and, between the Civil War and the beginning of 1900, were the ones who raced horses in the Kentucky Derby. In fact, Oliver Lewis rode the first Kentucky Derby winner. Racism eventually forced them out of horse racing, however.

Jackie Robinson played for the Kansas City Monarchs in the Negro Baseball Leagues. He broke the color barrier when Branch Rickey signed him to play for the Brooklyn Dodgers in 1945. Robinson became the first African American to play for a major league baseball team. What is so important about him was not only his great talent and ability, but his perseverance and endurance of the verbal and physical abuse he received from opposing teams and spectators.

Law

Prominent in the area of law was Charles Hamilton Houston, the vice-dean of the Howard University law school. He served as special counsel for the NAACP and won several civil rights cases against the "separate but equal" doctrine. He was also the legal mentor to former Supreme Court Justice Thurgood Marshall. Houston is credited with the legal strategy for pioneering cases leading to *Brown v. Board of Education*. In the aftermath of the Civil Rights cases Dennis Archer became president of the American Bar Association, some years later. He was the first African American to hold that position and also the first African American mayor of Detroit, Michigan.

Education and Government

Condoleezza Rice was the first African American woman to become Secretary of State of the United States. She was confirmed in January 2005 in the George W. Bush administration after General Powell resigned. Colin Powell served one term in the Bush cabinet. Rice was the second African American and the second woman to hold that post.

Rice was born in Birmingham, Alabama, in 1954. Her father was a Presbyterian minister and counselor and her mother, a science teacher. She was eight years old when her school friend, Denise McNair, was killed in the bombing of the Sixteenth Street Baptist Church by White supremacists. Rice's parents attempted to shield their daughter from the violence connected with the Civil Rights Movement. According to some writers, while they supported the goals, they disagreed with the methods, particularly when it put a child in harm's way.

Reverend Rice emphasized the need for Black people to prove they were worthy of advancement. He also stressed that Black people would have to be twice as good to overcome the inherent injustices in the system (Jackson, 2002). In Rice's words, "I was going to be so well prepared, and I was going to do all of these things that were revered in White society so well, that I would be armored somehow from racism" (Russakoff, 2001). Her parents eventually moved to Denver, Colorado where she completed her doctorate at the University of Denver. After graduate school, Rice joined Stanford University in 1981 as an assistant professor in political science. She cultivated an interest in Russian and East European studies. Eventually Rice was promoted to full professor status and appointed provost at Stanford making her the youngest person to ever hold the position.

Rice had distinguished herself as an expert on Soviet affairs and was no stranger to political life. In 1986 she served as the special assistant to the director of the Joint Chiefs of Staff and in 1989 joined the administration of

George H. W. Bush as a special assistant to the president for national security affairs. This was during the period of the fall of the Berlin Wall and the final demise of the Soviet Union from 1989 until 1991. After her service she went back to Stanford to teach. It was not for long.

Rice's expertise was also noted by George W. Bush. When he decided to run for the presidency, he tapped several of the same people who had served in his father's administration, Rice was one of them. She was asked to be his foreign policy advisor and she accepted. After Bush was elected, she was subsequently appointed as the national security advisor. Rice was appointed and confirmed as Secretary of State in 2005 following the resignation of General Powell.

Rice became a Republican in 1984 after the Democratic National Convention. She stated that during the convention she noticed how the Democratic Party's speeches to "women, minorities, and the poor" really meant "helpless people and the poor." Rice said she would rather be ignored by the Republican Party than be patronized by the Democratic Party (Jackson, 2002). As Bush's National Security Advisor and then Secretary of State, Rice came under much criticism over her support of the Iraq invasion and for the assertive foreign policy stance of the Bush administration. She has also been criticized as simply being a mouthpiece for President Bush. However, King (2005) proposes that there is nothing in Rice's background that suggests that she is "a mindless follower." He states that she appears to be just the opposite and that the Bush administration's policies and hers are one and the same. In any case, the policies were unpopular to some in the Congress. In her confirmation hearings for secretary of state, she was questioned particularly about the misstatements and misleading information concerning the necessity of going to war with Iraq. Nevertheless, she was confirmed and continued the policies of the Bush Administration.

Some have portrayed Rice as race indifferent. Race indifference is a theory that holds that factors other than race and ethnicity are more important to achieving equality. However, France (2008) suggests that conservatives and Black women's organizations reacted by supporting Rice and demanded that the racist and sexist portrayals of her stop. This surprised many liberals because they did not expect the backlash. The explanation given for Rice's support is that while many of these Black women's groups perceived many of the policies of the Bush administration as racist, they were also keenly aware that he had appointed a number of African Americans to key positions. Black women groups saw this as the struggle to be faced by women of color in a White, male dominated society. Rice returned to Stanford to teach, give lectures and pursue her music.

In 2020, Kamala Harris was elected as Vice President of the United States. Harris became not only the first woman, but the only Black woman to do so. She is of Jamaican and East Indian lineage. Harris was formerly the Attorney General of California. She was then elected to the Senate of the United States. Harris became one of the few women who have ever served in the Senate.

Harris first campaigned for President on her own. There were a number of candidates running for the Democratic nomination. Eventually, she ended her bid for the nomination. Harris was asked by Joe Biden to be his running mate for the upcoming 2020 election, which they won.

The Military

Blacks have continued to distinguish themselves and rise to powerful and important positions. One of the first people to do this was General Colin Powell. He has had a distinguished career both as a soldier and a statesman.

Colin Luther Powell was born in New York City of Jamaican immigrants. After graduating from City College of New York he accepted a commission in the Army as a second lieutenant. He was sent to Vietnam as a military advisor by President Kennedy in 1962. General Powell suffered injuries in both of his two tours of service in Vietnam, and he also earned several medals including the Purple Heart and the Bronze Star. When Powell returned, he earned a Master's in Business Administration in 1971 from George Washington University and began a long term of political service to the country. He was promoted to major and won a White House fellowship, serving in the Nixon administration. Powell rose throughout the ranks and eventually became a general in 1971. He was the youngest person to attain the rank of general at that time.

Powell alternated between active duty and political service and served in the administration of several presidents. General Powell has a number of firsts among his accomplishments. Powell served as the head of the National Security Council in 1987 in the Reagan administration. He became the first African American to serve as Chairman of the Joint Chiefs of Staff in the George H. W. Bush administration in 1989. This is the highest military position in the Defense Department and he was the youngest person to ever serve (at 52). He also became a four-star general and in charge of the Desert Storm forces in 1991. Powell spent 35 years as a professional soldier before retiring in 1993. In 2000 he was appointed by President George W. Bush as the first African American secretary of state. During Powell's term as secretary of state, he came under criticism for his role in pleading the case for the invasion of Iraq. Powell, according to some reports, had some doubts about a weapons development program. His testimony, however, was a major factor in persuading many members of Congress to support military action against Saddam Hussein. When no weapons of mass destruction were found, he came under harsh public criticism. Eventually Powell announced his resignation as secretary of state in November 2004.

Colin Powell served as National Security Advisor in 1987 and Chairman of the Joint Chiefs of Staff in 1989. He was appointed the Secretary of State by President George W. Bush in 2001.

Powell declared his affiliation with the Republican Party after he had written his biography. However, in October 2008, Powell announced that he would endorse Barack Obama for president of the United States. He cited the Republican Party's move to the far right and the negative tone that the McCain campaign had taken as his reasons. Powell has been vocal and has openly criticized the George W. Bush administration on a number of issues. He is in demand as a speaker but offers his services free of charge to schools, prisons, and veteran's hospitals.

Entrepreneurship

The future of African Americans may be related to "economic liberation" issues. According to Jesse Jackson, the civil rights struggle of African Americans throughout the history of the United States can be divided into three parts. The first was to abolish enslavement. The second was to end legal segregation. The third was to assure all Americans the right to vote.

The issue for Jackson and others is economic progress and stability. There are two major ways this is accomplished. One is by access to jobs. But the most powerful way is through ownership of one's own business or entrepreneurship. It is only through owning one's own business that one can determine one's destiny.

Reginald Lewis (1942–1993)

Reginald Lewis was one of the most successful African American entrepreneurs in history. He was born in Baltimore, Maryland, and after high school attended Virginia State University. Lewis graduated on the Dean's List in 1965. He attended Harvard Law School, where he received his law degree in 1968. He and two other African American attorneys created the first African American law firm on Wall Street.

In 1983 he bought the McCall Pattern Co. for $22.5 million and later sold it for $90 million in 1987. In October of the same year he purchased Beatrice Foods international division. It became the largest African-American-owned business in the United States. By 1992 the company's sales rose to over $1.50 billion.

Forbes magazine estimated his net worth at $400 million, putting him on the magazine's 400 list of wealthiest Americans.

The Reginald F. Lewis Foundation was established in 1987. Before his death in 1993, he had given away millions of dollars to various schools and community and civil rights organizations.

The early 1900s gave rise to an increase of various small businesses to serve the needs of the newly established African American middle class. During that period, African Americans owned banks, insurance companies, stores, and hotels. Newspapers also grew and promoted these businesses. Some of those who were involved during this time were people such as

Madam C. J. Walker in 1915 and Marcus Garvey in the 1920s. Garvey was one of the first to organize an economic development program that focused on developing businesses, such as his Black Star Line Shipping Company. His organization also opened restaurants and grocery stores.

More contemporary examples of individuals who have made their mark in the world of entrepreneurship include people such as Reginald Lewis, the first African American to own a multibillion-dollar organization. It also includes Dempsey Travis, the president of Travis Realty Company, and television celebrity Oprah Winfrey. Another successful African American is Robert Johnson, who founded the Black Entertainment Television in 1980. At one time, the company published three magazines. It was sold to Viacom in 2000.

Science and Invention

African Americans have contributed greatly to the world of science and invention. Many people are not aware of their contributions. Consider Otis Boykin, who invented the pacemaker, among many others. The inventions and accomplishments listed on the following pages are just a few in the sciences, government/public service, business, education, and entertainment. Race and gender barriers were broken during the space race with the National Aeronautics and Space Agency (NASA) during the 1960s. The intelligence and mathematical genius of three African American women was showcased in the movie *Hidden Figures*. Through their fortitude and determination, Katherine Johnson, Dorothy Vaughan, Mary Jackson and others overcame bias against women of color in stem related fields. Their ability to calculate, by hand, the complex planetary motions made it possible for lunar space missions.

African American Inventors

W. Johnson	Egg Beater	1884
A. Miles	Elevator	1887
R. F. Flemmings, Jr.	Guitar	1886
Sarah Boone	Ironing Board	1892
L. S. Burridge	Typewriting Machine	1885

J. L. Love	Pencil Sharpener	1897
J. A. Burr	Lawnmower	1899
Issac Johnson	Bicycle Frame	1899

For additional information, see *Blacks in Science* by Ivan Van Sertima.

Contemporary African American Scientists

Patricia Cowings	Psychologist and aerospace medical specialist; the major investigator in space medicine research at NASA
Frederick D. Gregory	Research space shuttle pilot for the U.S. Air Force; designed an automatic landing system that will allow planes to land without the assistance of the pilot
Katherine Johnson	Physicist and mathematician who has worked for NASA (the National Aeronautics and Space Administration) in the development of navigational systems to track human- and robot-controlled space missions
Robert E. Shurney	Aeronautical engineer for the Marshall Space Flight Center; designed the tires for the moon buggy used in the *Apollo* mission
Moddie D. Taylor	Chemist and mathematician; one of the scientists who helped to develop the atomic bomb
George R. Carruthers	American inventor, physicist, and space scientist
Mae Jemison	First African American woman astronaut, 1992
Annie Easley	Computer scientist, mathematician, and rocket scientist

Achievement Against the Odds

Notable Professional Black Achievers

While some career and professional opportunities for Blacks have occurred since the civil rights era, advancement beyond mid-level careers has been difficult. This career advancement has come at great cost, effort, and personal determination. It has taken more than a half century to see a small, but well-qualified group of African Americans move into the top tiers of their professions. Many Blacks gained a foothold in high profile positions because of diversity policies, mentors, and career coaches who helped them navigate organizational systems.

There is an increasing awareness of just how few peoples of color occupy high level positions in various career fields. All too often, the media presents images of greater equality than the few opportunities that Blacks and other minorities can actually avail themselves of.

Listed below is small accounting of African Americans who have achieved great professional success in leadership roles in modern America—"against the odds."

Significant Contributors to Government/Public Service

Valerie Jarrett	Senior adviser and assistant to the president for intergovernmental affairs and public engagement
Susan Rice	U.S. ambassador to the United Nations
Maxine Waters	U.S. representative for California's 35th Congressional District
Kamala Harris	Former California attorney general; former U.S. Senator; Vice President of the United States
Raphael Warnock	First African American Senator from Georgia since Reconstruction
Tim Scott	U.S. senator
Linda Thomas-Greenfield	Current U.N. Ambassador/Life-long Foreign Service Officer
Eric Holder, Jr.	First African American appointed as U.S. Attorney General (Obama Administration)

Hazel Johnson	Promoted to the rank of general in the U.S. Army, 1979
Latitia James	First elected African American Attorney General of New York State
David Dinkens	Elected mayor of New York City, 1989
Douglas Wilder	Elected governor of the state of Virginia, 1989
Ruth Simmons	First African American President of an Ivy League College (Brown University)
Carol Moseley Braun	United States attorney from the state of Illinois; first African American woman in the Senate, 1992; presidential candidate, 2004
Michael Curry	Presiding Episcopal bishop of U.S. who married Britain's Prince Harry and Meghan Markel
Rev. Al Sharpton	Presidential candidate, 2004

Media/Entertainment

Marian Anderson	Performed at the Metropolitan Opera, 1955
Nat "King" Cole	Hosted his own network TV show, 1956
Sidney Poitier	Received an Academy Award for his performance in *Lilies of the Field*, 1963
Denzel Washington	Won an Academy Award for best actor, 2002
Halle Berry	Won an Academy Award for best actress (same year as Denzel Washington, above), 2002
Carole Simpson	First African American weekend News Anchor for the ABC News Network, 1988–2003
Dean Baquet	First African American Executive Editor and Chief of *LA Times* and *NY Times*
Max Robinson	First African American Nightly News Anchor for ABC Network

Business

Clifton R. Wharton, Jr.	First Black CEO of a Fortune 500 company (TIAA-CREF); first Black career diplomat, first Black to lead two predominately White university systems (Michigan State & SUNY)
Franklin Thomas	Became president of a major American foundation, the Ford Foundation, in 1979
Mr. Rene Jones	CEO and President of M&T Bank
Ursula Burns	Former President/CEO of Xerox
Reginald Lewis	First African American to make the *Forbes* list of 400 wealthiest Americans, 1992
Rosalind Brewer	CEO of Walgreens
Marvin Ellison	President/CEO of Lowes Co.
Thasunda Brown Duckett	CEO of TIAA-CREF

Summary

Across a spectrum of disciplines, vocations, and fields African Americans have been able to distinguish themselves in creative ways that have had a lasting impact on America. Achievements by peoples of color has come through long hard struggles and challenges. They have had to overcome significant barriers, setbacks, and personal struggles. In the face of bigotry, discrimination, and ridicule the creative spirit of African Americans has flourished in science, engineering, medicine, and other technical fields. Education has been made more democratic through the bright minds of legal professionals working with education pioneers who held fast to the beliefs of the value of universal quality schooling. The Arts have catalogued the influence of people of color in dance, theater, music photography, literature, sculpture, film, inventors, and entrepreneurs.

Beyond providing expressions of cultural significance about minority communities, African Americans have impacted mainstream venues of professions and diverse achievements globally. From the design of the nation's capitol's streets by Benjamin Banneker to the exploration of space and the rise of information technology, peoples of color have been instrumental in the invention, design, development, and creative uses for many modern tools, apparatuses, and common household items. The creative spirit of African Americans' achievement emanates from practical necessity and is nourished by African American colleges, universities, and mentors.

Historically Black Colleges laid the foundation for Black intellectualism, research, and provided valuable critical pathways for the rise of inventions and medical procedures. New methods of educating children of color that embraced their heritage and learning styles were adopted. The connection between achievement, higher education, practical necessity, and commercial utility can be found in virtually every field in which African Americans have participated. Creating an inclusive society in which access and opportunity for all people has been largely influenced by civil rights leaders and government elected minority officials. Making the promises of America true, in spite of opposition and changing political views has been a central theme of African Americans in government.

References

African-American History Online. Facts on File, Inc. Accessed December 2008. http://www.fofweb.com/activelink2.asp?ItemID=WE01&iPin=EWAP0442&SingleRecord=True

African-Americans in racing. (2004, May). Accessed 2004. http://horseracing.about.com/library/weekly/aa012499.htm

Biography.com Editors. (2018, January 19). *Althea Gibson: (1927–2003)*. Biography.com. www.biography.com/athlete/althea-gibson

Biography.com Editors. (2009, February). *Colin Powell*. Biography.com. Accessed 2009. http://www.biography.com/search/article.do?id=9445708

Biography.com Editors. *Famous Black Scientists*. Biography.com Accessed 2018. https://www.biography.com/people/groups/famous-black-scientists

Coffey, D. (1998). African Americans in the Vietnam War. In S. C. Tucker (Ed.), *Encyclopedia of the Vietnam War: A Political, Social, and Military History*. SABC-CLIO.

Colin Powell. Answers. January 2009. Accessed 2009. http://www.answers.com/topic/colin-powell/

Condoleezza Rice. Search. 2009. Accessed 2009. http://www.search.com/reference/CondoleezzaRice

Condoleezza Rice. Answers. 2009. Accessed 2009. http://www.answers.com/topic/condoleezzarice

Condoleezza Rice. NNDB Tracking the Entire World. http://www.nndb.com/people/205/000024133/

Congressional Black Caucus of the 108th United States Congress. Congressional Black Caucus. May 2004. Accessed 2004. www.congressionalblackcaucus.net

France, H. (2008). Rice, Condoleezza. In L. E. Ford (Ed.), *Encyclopedia of Women and American Politics.* Facts on File, Inc.

Gorlick, A. (2009, January). Condoleezza Rice on returning to campus. *Stanford Report.*

Henry, T. T. (n.d.). *The Return of the Black Jockey?* http://www.africana.com/articles/daily/bw20030502jockey.asp

Jackson, D. Z. (2002, November 20). A lesson from Condoleezza Rice. *The Boston Globe.* Accessed 2006. http://www.freerepublic.com/focus/news/792581/posts

King, C. (2005, January). Why the crass remarks about rice? *The Washington Post.* P. A17.

McNamee, G. L. (2019). *Kamala Harris.* Encyclopædia Britannica, www.britannica.com/biography/Kamala-Harris

Powell, C., & Davidson, J. (2004). The general gets specific. *Crisis (00111422), 111(5),* 38–41. America: History & Life Database. January 2009.

Russakoff, D. (2001, September 9). Lessons of might and right: How segregation and an indomitable family shaped national security adviser Condoleezza Rice. *Washington Post Magazine.* Accessed April 2, 2007. https://www.washingtonpost.com/archive/lifestyle/magazine/2001/09/09/lessons-of-might-and-right/e3c9f9e2-5f42-420e-b86f-d33abbc7bf42/

Stevenson, K. (2005, September). *Colin Powell.* Colin Powell. Primary Search database. Accessed 2009.

Swartz, E., & Lessie, R. (1985). *The role of Black Americans in the development of the United States: A supplement to our country's history.* Rochester; City School District.

The White House. (2021, January 20). *Kamala Harris: The vice president.* The White House. www.whitehouse.gov/administration/vice-president-harris/

Van Sertima, I. (Ed.). (1983). *Blacks in science: ancient and modern.* Transaction Publishers.

The Quest for Quality Education: Past and Present

Education: The Mainstay of African Americans

Education has always been important to people of African descent. Throughout the early period of ancient and medieval history and through the time of enslavement until today, African Americans have sought it. It has been shown that African people were knowledgeable, and that they created schools and universities, both ancient and medieval as well.

During slavery, African people were willing to die in pursuit of schooling/education. The desire for schooling, as well as the journey toward achieving equal access to education is well documented.

As part of the quest for education, there has been the struggle and the methods to gain access to basic education resources, well-trained teachers, facilities, and the needed support systems essential for high effective learning. Historically, the quest for quality education has taken many different forms and methods.

Today schooling and education remain a high priority among African Americans despite setbacks, challenges, and obstacles. Good schools and universal access to higher education are important ingredients for addressing social, economic, political, and legal barriers that face African Americans and other minority groups in the United States.

Schooling vs. Education

Some scholars, make a distinction between schooling and education. According to Shujaa (1994), education is the acquisition of experiences from family involvement, knowledge of culture, community, and life experiences. Education is a continuous process that helps to form the basis for beliefs and knowledge of the world. On the other hand, schooling is narrower in its scope of learning. Schooling is related to functioning in western and American society. Other scholars go further, stating that schooling perpetuates an unequal power structure that benefits Whites more than it does African Americans. They feel that schooling prepares people for second-class citizenship.

While some scholars may debate the value and functional benefits of schooling, there is overall agreement that it does have its place. Other noted scholars such as Carol Lee, Kofi Lomotey, and Mwalimu Shujaa also recognize that there are three functions of the schooling process. The first is the acquisition of adequate skills in literacy, numeracy, the humanities, and the technologies needed for self-sufficiency. The second is citizenship, based on a realistic understanding of the political system and the fostering of critical thinking and questioning skills, as well as democratic values. The third is the provision of an accurate view of the history of the nation that would represent the contributions of all ethnic and cultural groups to human knowledge. Currently there are few, if any, American history books that give an accurate account of the contributions that people of African descent have made to the world and to America specifically. Usually, African American history must be supplemented by additional books and is relegated to Black History month, the shortest month of the year.

Generally, when people are asked about the value of an education, the reply is that it is the way to obtain jobs. Schools and education are supposed to prepare people to earn a good standard of living. In many cases, there is a gap between the labor market of available jobs and the skills for which schools train young people. Schools provide career foundation competencies and awareness of professional options even if jobs are not always readily available. Since schooling is an important part of American economic and political institutions, it is something that the country must focus on and improve for all peoples.

Early/Global Models of Education

Schools and even universities have existed for a very long time. Most societies, even ancient ones in Africa and elsewhere, developed some form of educational system, including schools. The idea of schools for the masses or everyone in society, that is, universal education, is relatively new, however. In the past, schooling was only afforded to a very few, usually the elite members of society. For example, in ancient Egypt or Kemet, it was only the boys of the royal or wealthy families who went to school. They were trained in the "mysteries" system, or Egyptian curriculum. Many of the initiates became scribes and were the only ones who could read or write. The other children learned the trades of their families. The ancient Egyptians built a place called Ipet Isut, also known as Karnak. It contained temple buildings, where the Egyptian initiates were trained. It is considered the oldest university in the world.

Later, in 700 C.E., the African empires of the Moors established schooling systems which were extended into the Iberian Peninsula. The African scholars used the Arabic language to record and transmit the various histories and sciences of the past. They added to the knowledge base that became the foundation for other European educational systems. These scholars held learning in high esteem and did not restrict it to men only. The Moors of North Africa established schools in Spain. In fact, education was universal in Moorish Spain, meaning that schools were for everyone. This was a concept that was virtually unheard of until later in Europe and then in the United States.

The Moorish tradition of schooling and education continued with the medieval West African empires of Ghana, Mali, and Songhay. During the 15th century, universities were founded that contained volumes of academic books. The largest was the University of Sankore in Timbuktu, West Africa.

Schooling in America for Blacks

Schooling for Blacks during Reconstruction was known as native and Sabbath schools. There were the vocational schools for the trades and normal schools that prepared teachers. Many of these schools were formally established just after the Civil War, during the period of Reconstruction. African Americans funded these schools themselves, but they also pushed for universal education or public schools that would be paid for by tax dollars. Schools were also established in the North during the 1700s. Often these schools were in held in homes, as was the case of Prince Hall, who started a school for free Africans.

Although African Americans made significant education progress, there are still many problems yet to be addressed in education. The struggle to gain equal schooling and quality instruction are on-gong. The early desegregation laws were aimed at physically integrating African American and White children. The *Brown v. Board of Education* Supreme Court ruling of 1954 began the process in K–12 schools. Its purpose was to end the "separate but equal" doctrine in public places, particularly schools. It was aimed at physically placing African Americans and Whites together. While *Brown* was a landmark decision, many people feel that it was not altogether successful.

The Brown Decision went a long way to address education issues, there were mixed results. The Brown decision affected hiring and promotion of Black teachers, pupil expenditures, and school facilities. Many schools in Black neighborhood that formerly existed were closed. Those skilled and well-trained teachers and principals lost their jobs. Many Black professional educators were not hired to teach in predominately White schools after Brown. Desegregation did not guarantee good schooling, quality education outcomes, nor positive, nurturing learning experiences for Black students. Examples of this were evident in the Little Rock Nine case at Central High School in Arkansas. When Black students attempted to desegregate all White schools, they experienced verbal and physical attacks.

The second ruling of *Brown et al. v. Board of Education, Topeka et al.* (*Brown II*), which was decided in 1955, allowed school districts to delay the implementation of the Court's first *Brown* ruling. Many school districts resisted desegregation. Schools were either closed or new private ones were set up. Attempts were made to use public funds or tax dollars to fund these new private schools. Many schools were still segregated in the 1970s.

A great concern of African American parents is still the quality of education their children ultimately receive. Although *Brown* struck down "separate but equal," simply moving students around did not necessarily produce better prepared individuals. The 1954 ruling on *Brown* caused many barriers to equity for African Americans to fall. Although the *Brown* decision was aimed at schools, it was more effective in ending legal segregation in public facilities than in gaining equity in schooling

Since the *Brown* Decisions, many school districts have subsequently come under unitary status. In other words, they have integrated to the extent possible given their population; thereby they were released from their court desegregation orders. Students were then free to go back to their neighborhood schools. Unfortunately, these neighborhoods became very segregated as the more affluent people simply moved away. Starting in the mid-1980s, schools began to re-segregate. They do so because of residential segregation, whereby Whites move to other areas to avoid integrated communities. When the wealthier people leave, so does the tax base, which is the means to support schools and other services. Today, according to reports schools are more segregated than ever (Naaryan, 2018; Stancil, 2018).

The tax base which urban cities depend upon does not keep pace with their expenses. The tax base declines because those who are left, in many cases, are the aged, who can least afford to pay, or those with low-paying jobs. Then there are those who rely on Social Services and receive funds from the government. This is called municipal overburden. In urban cities, the cost is high for providing services. This means that many urban cities cannot adequately fund their schools but rely on state support.

Generally, Black children who attend urban schools continue to perform below White children on standardized tests. In high-poverty schools students tend to have lower levels of academic achievement. Many children attend schools in dimly lit, and in some cases, dilapidated buildings in urban areas. Resources remain limited as well as highly qualified teachers. Research indicates that teachers are the key to successful educational programs. Teachers need to be well trained and to care about their students. They must really believe that all children can learn. Teachers who care make a great difference. Urban school districts do attract well-trained caring professionals who are dedicated to student success. Unfortunately, because of scarce resources, large class sizes, and high rates of poverty professional burnout is widespread. For the most part, more experienced teachers work in more affluent schools. With all the support and resources these teachers receive, they are less likely to experience burnout.

In addition, there is the alarming disproportionate number of children who are diagnosed with learning and behavioral problems. Consequently, this causes them to be placed in special education classes or expelled from school. Still other children simply drop out, which can fuel the school to prison pipeline (Keyes et al., 2015; Johnson, 2018).

Many African Americans have become frustrated with public schooling and its curricula. Educational researchers have noted that over the years many African Americans have come to mistrust the educational system and for good reason. Schooling, in many cases, has not met their expectations for gaining access to productive roles in society. Although school desegregation and other early efforts to enhance educational opportunities and improve schools were good first steps, they were ineffective. Further efforts were and still are needed to improve schools and student performance. Towards the beginning of the new century many changes to improve schools were launched.

School Choice

In recent years, the issue of quality schooling has led many people, including various politicians, to promote their own plans for a solution. One of these plans was formulated during the administration of President George W. Bush. This administration devised the school choice plan to deal with failing schools. School choice is not new. In the 1950s, it was primarily used to avoid desegregation. Yet who can argue with a plan to give parents more choice in schools when their children are failing? There are both opponents and supporters of these plans.

The idea of school choice is part of a larger plan to provide parents with more options on where to send their children to school. Some of the choices that parents have include tax-supported charter schools, vouchers, educational tax credit, home schooling, and private-public partnerships with school districts. School choice is implemented in different ways. Some scholars, such as Weil (2002), point out that there is private choice and public choice. Public choice is limited to public schools, whereas private choice can provide funds for private schools. For example, in some school districts, such as in Buffalo, New York, students only have a choice of attending non-failing schools within the public school district. Another variation is that in other school districts, students can attend schools outside their school districts. It depends on whether the other schools agree to participate.

In Buffalo, New York, some of these non-failing schools were once designated as magnet schools. They had specialized programs and funding and were subject to an application process. These magnet schools and other programs were made possible through the influx of money from the Federal

Government. When the money was cut, Buffalo was hard-pressed to continue the programs, as they were once conceived. In the end their special status came to an end. They have become "fair game" with the exception of a "honors" school and one technical school, which uses testing to determine admittance. Unfortunately, the magnet status has also been compromised because the district failed to financially support the special programs that were previously funded by federal money.

There are problems with magnet school approaches in urban schools, including Buffalo, New York. The number of schools that are available is one issue and the other includes the resources. There may be only a few schools in which children are achieving success. Enrolling more students from other underachieving schools causes burdens on the teachers and strains the resources of the receiving schools. Often the resources do not follow the students, and teachers are not available, which results in overcrowded classrooms. What happens then is that all the children are "left behind."

While the idea of school choice is good and something everyone can agree with, the question is—how much choice is really provided? The affluent have always had choices. Do the poor have those same options or even just good choices? School choice originated with the No Child Left Behind legislation. This legislation makes school choice a federal law. The choice of attending a private school can be far different from attending a public school which has to adhere to certain standards and assessment programs. In some places there is a two-tiered program that hold private and public schools to different standards, such as in Milwaukee.

The Policies, Practices, and New Education Initiatives

No Child Left Behind Legislation

The No Child Left Behind Act was passed in 2001. It is actually the reauthorization of the Elementary and Secondary Education Act (ESEA) or Title 1, which was begun by President Lyndon Johnson's "War on Poverty" program. It provided federal dollars to schools to improve education for low income families. With No Child Left Behind (NCLB), the federal government attempted to make school districts more accountable. In fact, there are four major provisions. First of all, states had to implement a system of accountability for student performance. Second, provisions in the Act emphasized using educational programs and practices that work to improve schools and enhance teacher quality. Third, it provided expanded parental options. Under that legislation, parents whose children attend low-performing or failing schools were free to choose among non-failing schools in the public-school sector. Fourth, it gave states and schools greater flexibility in the use of federal education funds, but schools must meet the accountability requirements. According to several research scholars (Klein, 2015; Rosales & Walker, 2015; Keller, 2005) the legislation did not provide adequate funding to carry out these mandates. The NEA reported that funding for the fiscal year of 2005 for NCLB was 9.4 billion dollars short. Nevertheless, these were the options that were provided to parents at the time. Therefore, it is worthwhile to take a closer look at some of them.

The No Child Left Behind (NCLB) legislation was a name given to ESEA by President George W. Bush in 2002, at the time when the reauthorization was due. When it was reauthorized in 2015 by President Obama, it was renamed the Every Student Succeeds Act (ESSA). The National Education Association (NEA) developed eight principles as guidelines for changing the law to help schools improve. In addition, Arne Duncan, the secretary of education under President Obama, issued a letter to state officers proposing changes to the Title I (NCLB) regulations that were previously issued by the Bush administration. Some changes to the law were suggested. One, included eliminating the Adequate Yearly Progress feature and another required multiple methods of assessment. However, the Congress that President Obama was working with made some issues controversial. One of the most controversial issues was to make the use of these funds more flexible. Previously, states could not divert federal money away from their Title I or III programs. Some feel that the new Law was watered down so much as to be ineffective.

Alternative School Choices for African Americans

Independent Schools

Early on, African Americans who became disenchanted with the dominant educational system, sought alternatives by establishing their own independently run schools, of which there are two kinds. There are schools that reflect African culture, history, and pedagogy and others that do not. Some schools have adopted the Eurocentric historical and curricula content model. The curricula and pedagogy at the elementary and secondary levels are almost indistinguishable from mainstream White schools. Most of these schools focus on high academic standards, but in many, the cultural foundation is ignored. Many of them, while producing positive results with the students who attend, struggle to survive because of financial issues. They depend on tuition.

Other independent schools reflect African culture and history. In these schools, the academics are accompanied by an emphasis on African American content and pedagogy similar to Molefi Asante's Afrocentric education model. This model originates from the African American community. It teaches the African American historical perspective and promotes the Africana cultural experience, while also paying attention to the other academic subjects.

Charter Schools

Some African Americans have turned to charter schools. These schools, which are supported by public funds, are proliferating in great numbers. They are encouraged by the legislation ESSA (formerly NCLB). They have greater flexibility in how they are run, but in exchange, students must show improvement in academic achievement. Many of these public charter schools have not been in business long enough, however, to have a record of success. Still, parents have been removing their children from traditional public schools and enrolling them in the new charter schools in the hope of obtaining better schooling.

School Vouchers

School vouchers are another outcome of the ESSA (formerly NCLB) legislation. Initially, the problem with vouchers was that they could be used for religious schools, and this, some said, would violate Amendment One of the Constitution, the separation of church and state. On June 27, 2002, the Supreme Court, however, ruled that vouchers for religious schools are constitutional. There are 15 states including the District of Columbia that currently participate in voucher programs. Some of these include Ohio, Arkansas, Maryland, Oklahoma, and Wisconsin. The oldest program is in

Milwaukee and provides public funds for private schools. In Florida there are public voucher programs which involve religious schools.

Supporters of private vouchers give various reasons for promoting the concept. One reason they cite is parent demand. They say that parents are upset at poor student performance and dissatisfied with racial discrimination against their children in public schools. Supporters also say that it forces public schools to do a better job through competition. Religious or parochial schools, in particular, would greatly benefit so they also advocate for vouchers. While no one would dispute the academic failure of students in urban areas is a serious matter, there is a question of whether vouchers will solve it.

There are also concerns associated with vouchers. The debate about them centers on the following concerns. One is that the money provided by school vouchers usually is not enough to pay the tuition for high-priced private schools. So, students are more likely to attend parochial/religious schools that usually cost less. Typically, in Cleveland as of 2016, low-income parents who would like to place their children in elementary schools receive scholarships of $4,250. The scholarship award for a high school is $5,000. This tuition assistance can be used in private schools as well as parochial ones. It has been documented that, in both Milwaukee and Cleveland, most of the funds were used to attend religious/parochial schools. The tuition received is then used to fund the schools' programs and curricula, including religious instruction. According to reports, the program in both cities is failing miserably. Most of the students who used the vouchers were not from schools that were designated as "in need of improvement."

Many people feel that vouchers represent an attempt to privatize education and will bring about the end of public schools. According to a report by Barbara Minor (2013), entire voucher schools have been established in Milwaukee. This development takes vouchers to a new level because these schools are classified as private, but they receive tax dollars. These voucher schools do not have to meet state requirements and accountability that public schools must follow. They also do not have to accept children with special needs. In fact, private and religious schools can choose whom they wish to admit. Opponents point to the fact that it takes money away from public schools, which are often in African American urban communities. The administration does not provide additional money to fund these programs but redistributes money that is already allocated to education. In the end, many opponents to school vouchers feel that America would end up with good schools for those who can pay and poor public schools for those who cannot.

The Privatization of Public School Administration and Management

Public education has come under attack by those who would change it to a form of privatization. The Trump administration was a proponent of school choice. The idea of school choice would be good if it truly provided better school choices. The Trump administration proposed to put public taxpayer money under private control. According to Barkan (2017), K–12 schools could be run by these private for-profit companies to provide minimally adequate education through school vouchers. If parents or guardians wanted further education for their children, they would have to purchase additional educational services on the free market. Some of the school entities that might receive taxpayer funds might be religious/parochial schools, private for-profit schools, private non-profit and perhaps some government schools including charters.

This program would siphon money from the public school system and put it into private for-profit hands. This plan would doom those with lower incomes and most in need. Education is the key to improving socio-economic class, but it is difficult to achieve given these circumstances. Some people have compared this model of the privatization of schools to the current privatization of federal prisons. In other words, the prison model is where private companies make money for keeping the prisons filled with mostly people of color and are assisted in the effort by judges.

The public schools' plan proposed by the Trump Administration would have eliminated the Department of Education. The Trump administration proposed to cut funds. The savings would be redirected to fund charter schools. Where would Trump get this money to fund these private schools? The Trump administration proposed to cut funds from the Every Student Succeeds Act (ESSA; formerly ESEA) and use this money to fund charter schools. Generally, schools get less than 10 percent of funding from the federal government. Those federal dollars are used for after school reading and math enrichment programs. Other activities are paid for through federal grants. There were also cuts and proposed plans that would have affected students in colleges and universities who receive federal funding for tuition.

In higher education, Trump sought to ease regulations on for-profit schools, such as ITT and others. This would have included Trump University, which was not a bonafide school, before it was closed (Tuttle, 2016). These are for profit schools that use deceptive recruiting and borrowing practices that incur student debt but don't provide students an education that will allow them to pay off these federal loans or get jobs.

The election of Biden and Harris has also brought a new Education Secretary. Miguel Cardona was the Education Commissioner in Connecticut. He is said to be a strong supporter of public education.

Higher Education and African Americans

Colleges and universities can be counted among those early schools that African Americans created. There was a time when African Americans were not allowed to attend White colleges and universities. This was due to laws of segregation that were put into place after the Civil War and Blacks being denied this higher type of education. Most of the White colleges and universities would not admit African Americans into their programs. Berea College, which was established in Kentucky, was one of the few White colleges that admitted African Americans, but was forced to discontinue the practice until the 1950s.

The development of Historically Black Colleges and Universities began in the early 1800s. The first university founded for college-level instruction for African Americans was Lincoln University in Pennsylvania. It wasn't until the second Morrill Act in 1890 that funds were provided for land grant institutions for African Americans. Historically Black Colleges and Universities were very successful during the first half of the 20th century. They produced lawyers, doctors, dentists, teachers, and other professionals during the time when segregation was the norm.

One of the missions of Historically Black Colleges and Universities was to create a pipeline for African American scholars, leaders, and professionals. An intrinsic value in attending a HBCU was that it served to create peer professional networks that would last for a lifetime. A second goal or mission was to provide access to mentors, advisors, and role models to guide first generation students through the academic process to graduate and enter their respective professional disciplines. The third mission of HBCUs was to create a sense of community responsibility, for "paying it forward," for the next generation. This was the only path for Blacks to higher education. Some well-known and successful people have graduated from HBCUs including Spike Lee, Alice Walker, Toni Morrison, Martin Luther King Jr., and Samuel L. Jackson to name a few.

The trends at HBCUs have changed. With the ending of legal school segregation with *Sweatt v. Painter* and *Brown v. Board of Education*, White schools are now available. Blacks can either go to a HBCU or an elite White university or college. Many of the students who attend HBCUs are legacy attendees, meaning that one or both of their parents attended the university in the past. However, because White institutions are now available, attendance at HBCUs is dropping. The top students are opting to go to other more "prestige" colleges. That leaves more unprepared and underprepared students who seek to attend college. More academic assistance is needed for these students, and there are other challenges.

The fact is that HBCU's are becoming more expensive. Black colleges and universities cannot compete with the financial aid given to students by White colleges and universities. They do not have the endowments to offer scholarships to students that White colleges have. There is also the lack of available internships which often leads to jobs. Additionally, HBCUs don't have broad research programs for students.

While it is recognized that many Black colleges and universities have financial and long-term sustainability problems, the role that they have played in the past and currently is still crucial. It was through those institutions that a broad segment of the African American community became college educated and subsequently part of the Black middle class. Black colleges and universities only represent about 3 percent of the available universities and colleges. However, even with the issues that Black colleges and universities face, these colleges and universities produce approximately 24 percent of Science, Technology, Engineering and Mathematic (STEM) graduates and confer 35 percent of all bachelor degrees.

Some of the premier Black colleges and universities are Meharry Medical College, Howard Law School, Hampton University, Morgan State University, and Virginia Union University to name a few. The significance of these schools is that they helped developed the African American professional middle class during the early to middle century. The colleges and universities that were located in cities became the regional learning centers for African Americans. People migrated to these cities and learning centers seeking educational opportunities. Many people stayed and not only helped to build the economy of cities like Atlanta, Richmond, and others, but established a budding middle class. Even though there are some issues for the larger Black colleges and universities, there are major issues for those that are located in rural areas. Today, some of the colleges in rural areas face very harsh economic times. These colleges are closing because the economic environment in their area cannot sustain them. There is not the economic environment that will lead to professional careers in the same way as a university or college located in a large city like Atlanta, or Washington D.C.

Remembering Their Roots

Today, there are many organizations and people who recognize the importance of schooling. Some of these people participate in self-help and charitable endeavors to assist young people. These African Americans have remembered to "give back" to the community, which is one of the principles and foundation of Black higher education. In some cases, entertainment personalities participate in these activities as well. People in the entertainment business are often highly visible and make a great impact on their television or radio audiences. This includes people such as Oprah Winfrey and Tom Joyner.

Oprah Winfrey hosted a syndicated television talk show for a number of years. She established the Oprah Winfrey Foundation, which supports the education, empowerment, and well-being of women, children, and families. The Oprah Winfrey Scholarship Program awards scholarships to students who use their education to give back to the community.

Tom Joyner hosted a syndicated radio show that is broadcast from Dallas, Texas. For years he flew between Chicago and Dallas to host two talk shows. This earned him the name of "The Fly Jock." He is to radio what Oprah is to television. Joyner had millions of listeners and highlighted the issues and concerns related to African American radio listeners. What's more important is that he did not forget where he came from. Joyner was born in Tuskegee, Alabama. After college, he went into the broadcasting business. Eventually he made his way from a small town in Alabama to a big city, Dallas, Texas. Joyner went from a radio station in Montgomery, Alabama, to host one of the most popular radio shows across the nation. However, even with his rise to fame, he reached back to help others. Joyner set up a foundation that provides financial aid for students who are attending Historically Black Colleges. Both people are examples of the underlying foundational principles of HBCUs.

Oprah Winfrey (1954–)

Oprah Winfrey came from modest beginnings to host one of the most successful television shows in America. She is one of the wealthiest people in the United States and donates a significant amount of money to various charities and education. Winfrey invested $40 million to establish the Oprah Winfrey Leadership Academy for Girls in South Africa which opened in 2007.

Winfrey's show has won several Emmys for Best Talk Show and she has been honored as Best Talk Show Host. She has also received many other awards and was named one of "America's 25 Most Influential People of 1996," therefore when she threw her support behind Barack Obama's bid for the presidency, it was significant. Winfrey had never publicly supported a political candidate for office. Although Winfrey was a supporter of Obama from the beginning, she did not use her show as a platform for his campaign. She did put her "star" power behind him and campaigned with him in the early voting states of Iowa, South Carolina, and New Hampshire. He won in Iowa and South Carolina but lost in New Hampshire.

Winfrey elicited some criticism because she decided to support Obama. Her show has great appeal to women and some saw her as a "traitor" for not supporting Clinton, if she indeed were to support anyone. Her television ratings declined for a brief time, and she acknowledged to the viewers that her choice might not be theirs, but she persisted. In the end, she was at Grant Park in Chicago for Obama's acceptance speech on Election Night. It is difficult to say whether having such a high-profile celebrity such as Oprah Winfrey helps a campaign or not, at least according to news commentators and news agencies.

Having celebrities at the various rallies and speeches seems to have been a positive factor, at least in terms of swelling the already impressively large crowds that Obama drew.

Summary

The challenges to educational opportunities for African Americans are great. There are significant educational achievement gaps between African Americans and their White counterparts. The achievement gap starts at pre-school and continues through college and graduate school.

Achieving a quality education will remain elusive for many African American learners. Some key policy makers believed that education can be achieved through vouchers, charter schools and tax credits. They saw the solution to failing schools as school choice. It is also understandable that there was and remains some suspicion about school choice, since historically it was used in order to avoid desegregation. More importantly government does not provide meaningful school vouchers for African Americans and poorer students to attend quality schools.

School funding issues for learners of color persist in post-secondary institutions that service minority and first-generation students. Disparities in government funding have created and fueled the education achievement gaps that now seem immutable, or unchangeable. Therefore, the result is that some families can choose to send their children to better schools and have the money to do so, and others cannot. Consequently, poor and minority students are stuck in failing schools, underfunded colleges with few options for remediation. There is insufficient financial aid—even with vouchers, and college financial aid—for parents to have meaningful alternatives to poor performing schools and colleges.

Real school choices allows poor students access to quality schools. School choice requires the financial support from state and federal government budgets. Whether a child is from an impoverish background in the inner-city, rural Appalachia, or from a farming community in the upper Midwest, greater contributions by the governments is required. Short of moving into a more affluent neighborhood with better education support systems, there are few ways to break the cycle of under-achievement for children of the poor and minorities. More targeted dollars devoted to under-performing school support systems that are based on evidence based practices are needed.

While President Obama sought to reauthorize the Every Student Succeeds Act (ESSA) federal program, he was met with the usual opposition of the Republican Party who wanted to water it down. In the end the new ESSA was watered down and attempts were made to divert funds from those who needed it the most. The 2015 ESSA legislation signed by President Obama scales back the Federal requirements, mandates, and degree of federal education oversight on States. One of the major changes is that it leaves the job of evaluating school success up to the States rather than the Federal government. Then there are others, such as Trump, who sought to privatize public education without an understanding of the comprehensive needs of poor and minority students. The net effect of privatizing education will significantly reduce education quality and accountability. The demise of public education and the subsequent plan to pay private for-profit companies for a minimal education portends doom for thousands of students.

While the Black college and university of the 21st century have changed, they still represent a viable and necessary part of education for African Americans. There are those who say that because of the decision of students to attend White institutions, Black colleges are no longer attracting the best and the brightest. Du Bois referred to select groups of academically gifted people as the "Talented Tenth." These people would ascend to key leadership positions in the Black community. The students, who now attend may be less well prepared. We have the failures of the public school system to thank for that. Perhaps the colleges do not have the endowments to offer scholarships, but they play an important role in providing an option for students of color. Historically Black Colleges and Universities still prepare leaders, scientists, educators, engineers, and other professionals to this day. In many cases, they offer a vital link to minority communities by providing mentors, coaches, and pathways to higher education. Education, schools and colleges build the next generation of professionals who enrich communities.

References

African American senators. (2018, 27 July). United States Senate. www.senate.gov/pagelayout/history/h_multi_sections_and_teasers/Photo_Exhibit_African_American_Senators.htm

Álvarez, B., Walker, T., Long, C., & Litvinov, A. (2018, August 3). *10 challenges facing public education today.* NEA. www.nea.org/advocating-for-change/new-from-nea/10-challenges-facing-public-education-today.

Amos, J. (2003). *House passes $10 million DC voucher program.* Alliance for Excellent Schools. Accessed 2018. https://all4ed.org/articles/house-passes-10-million-dc-voucher-program-voucher-opponents-criticize-vote-timing-set-sights-on-senate-debate/

Barkan, J. (2017). The miseducation of Betsy DeVos. *Dissent,* 64(2), 141–146.

Bryant, J. (2018, March 2). *Betsy DeVos wants to cut public education to the bone: It's hard to imagine a worse secretary of education.* Common Dreams. Accessed 2018. https://www.commondreams.org/views/2018/03/22/betsy-devos-wants-cut-public-education-bone

Catapano, J. (n.d.). *What is a voucher system?* Teach Hub. Accessed 2018. http://www.teachhub.com/what-voucher-system

BlackAmericaWeb.com Staff. (2016). *Celebrities who attended HBCUs.* BlackAmericaWeb.com. https://blackamericaweb.com/playlist/celebs-representing-hbcus/item/494650

Cheesman, F. (n.d.) *Facts about the school-to-prison pipeline.* National Consortium on Racial and Ethnic Fairness in the Courts 28th Annual Conference. National Council for State Courts. Accessed 2018. http://www.national-consortium.org/~/media/Microsites/Files/National%20Consortium/Conferences/2016/Materials/School-to-Prison-fact-sheet.ashx

Chiles, N. (2017, March 1). *HBCUs graduate more poor Black students than White colleges.* NPR. https://www.npr.org/sections/codeswitch/2017/03/01/517770255/hbcus-graduate-more-poor-black-students-than-white-colleges

Curtis, J., & Andersen, R. (2015, January). How social class shapes attitudes on economic inequality: The competing forces of self-interest and legitimation. *International Review of Social Research* 5, 1, 4–19.

D.C. voucher program gains congressional approval. (2004, January). Accessed 2004. http://www.schoolchoiceinfo.org/topics/item.cfm?id=31

Every Student Succeeds Act (ESSA). U.S. Department of Education. Accessed 2018. https://www.ed.gov/ESSA

50 Years of diversity: *Brown v. Board* anniversary. (2004, May). *Ebony, 59*(7) 105–106.

Good, T. L., & Braden, J. S. (2000). *The great school debate: Choice, vouchers, and charters.* Lawrence Erlbaum Associates.

High Court approves school vouchers, random drug tests. (2002, June 27). Fox News. www.foxnews.com/story/0,2933,56376,00.html

Holguin, J. (2002, June). *Supreme Court oks school vouchers.* CBS News. https://www.cbsnews.com/news/supreme-court-oks-school-vouchers/

Hsu, S. (2004, Fall). How vouchers came to D.C. *Education Next, 4*(4). https://www.educationnext.org/howvoucherscametodc/

Jarus, O. (2013, January 21). Timbuktu: History of fabled center of learning. *Live Science.* Accessed 2018. https://www.livescience.com/26451-timbuktu.html

Johnson, K. (2015, August 5). *5 facts about the school-to-prison pipeline.* Black Enterprise. Accessed 2018. https://www.blackenterprise.com/5-facts-about-the-school-to-prison-pipeline/

Johnson, S., Campbell, N., & Sargrad, S. (2018, February 12). *Trump and DeVos continue to undermine public education with their proposed fiscal year 2019 budget.* Center for American Progress. Accessed 2018. https://www.americanprogress.org/issues/education-k-12/news/2018/02/12/446423/trump-devos-continue-undermine-public-education-proposed-fiscal-year-2019-budget/

Keller, B. (2005, April 20). NEA files 'No Child Left Behind' lawsuit. *Education Week.* www.edweek.org/policy-politics/nea-files-no-child-left-behind-lawsuit/2005/04

Kelly, K. (n.d.). *School vouchers: What you need to know.* Understand.org. Accessed 2018. https://www.understood.org/en/school-learning/your-childs-rights/basics-about-childs-rights/school-vouchers-what-you-need-to-know

Keyes, A. W., Smyke, A. T., Middleton, M., & Black, C. E. (2015). Parenting children in the context of racism. *Zero In Three.* 35(4), 27–34.

Klein, A. (2015, April 11). No Child Left Behind: An overview. *Education Week.* www.edweek.org/policy-politics/no-child-left-behind-an-overview/2015/04

Kreighbaum, A. (2018, August 7). Winners and losers from DeVos approach. *Inside Higher Ed.* Accessed 2018. https://www.insidehighered.com/news/2018/08/07/devos-regulatory-framework-means-less-pressure-colleges-tougher-standard-student

Lee, J. (2014, May 15). Still apart: Map shows states with most-segregated schools. *USA Today.* Accessed 2018. https://www.usatoday.com/story/news/nation-now/2014/05/15/school-segregation-civil-rights-project/9115823/

Marakami, K. (2021). Biden selects Miguel Cardona as education secretary. *Inside Higher Ed.* www.insidehighered.com/news/2021/01/04/biden-selects-miguel-cardona-education-secretary

Miner, B. J. (2013, February 5). Milwaukee example of Walker's threat to schools. *The Cap Times.* Accessed 2018. https://madison.com/ct/news/opinion/column/barbara-j-miner-milwaukee-example-of-walker-s-threat-to/article_e564cc46-6cbb-11e2-8c4a-0019bb2963f4.html

Minor, B. (2003, Winter). Vouchers: Special ed students need not apply. *Rethinking Schools.*

Minor, B. (2002/3, Winter). Keeping public schools public, vol. 17, no. 2. http://www.rethinkingschools.org/special_reports/voucher_report/Tax172.shtml

Naaryan, A. (2018, March). School segregation in America is as bad today as it was in the 1960s. *Newsweek.* Accessed 2018. https://www.newsweek.com/2018/03/30/school-segregation-america-today-bad-1960-855256.html

NEA Report Identifies Funding Gaps in Federal Education Programs. NEA. Accessed March 24, 2005. https://www.nea.org/esea/fundinggap.html

O'Donnell, P. (2016, July 11). Tuition vouchers aren't helping Ohio kids learn more, new study finds. Cleveland.com. https://www.cleveland.com/metro/index.ssf/2016/07/tuition_vouchers_arent_helping.html

Prothero, A. (2017, January 26). What are school vouchers and how do they work. *Education Week.* https://www.edweek.org/ew/issues/vouchers/

Questions and answers on No Child Left Behind. (2004). U.S. Department of Education. Accessed 2004. http://www.ed.gov/nclb/overview/intro/faqs.html

Rhodes, C. *School choice facts.* Accessed 2004. http://www.schoolchoiceinfo.org/facts/index.cfm

Risjord, N. (1986). *History of the American people.* Holt, Rinehart and Winston.

Rosales, J., & Walker, T. (2015). *Congress delays debating 'No Child Left Behind,' again.* NEA. Accessed March 9, 2021. www.nea.org/advocating-for-change/new-from-nea/congress-delays-debating-no-child-left-behind-again

Salter, D. *Robert F. Williams (1925–1996).* (2007). BlackPast.org. www.blackpast.org/african-american-history/williams-robert-f-1925-1996/

Sanchez, C. (2017, May 19). *Lessons from the nation's oldest voucher program.* NPR. https://www.npr.org/sections/ed/2017/05/19/527429292/the-nations-oldest-voucher-program-beacon-of-hope-or-failed-experiment

School-to-prison pipeline. (n.d.). ACLU. Accessed 2018. https://www.aclu.org/issues/juvenile-justice/school-prison-pipeline.

Shujaa, M. (1994). *Too much schooling, too little education: A paradox of Black life in White societies.* Africa World Press.

Stancil, W. (2018, March 14). School segregation is not a myth. *The Atlantic.* https://www.theatlantic.com/education/archive/2018/03/school-segregation-is-not-a-myth/555614/

Strauss, V. (2019, February 11). There's a blacklash against charter schools. What's happening and why?. *The Washington Post.* Accessed 2019. https://www.washingtonpost.com/education/2019/02/11/betsy-devos-loves-charter-schools-theres-little-love-lost-lots-places-whats-happening-why/?utm_term=.23ee505c07a4

Trotter, J. W. (2001). *The African American experience*, Volume I and II. Houghton Mifflin.

Turner, C. (2015, December 10). President Obama signs education law, leaving 'No Child' behind. NPR. Accessed 2018. https://www.npr.org/sections/thetwo-way/2015/12/10/459219774/president-obama-signs-education-law-leaving-no-child-behind

Tuttle, I. (2016, February 26). Yes Trump University was a massive scam. *National Review.* https://www.nationalreview.com/corner/trump-university-scam/

Types of school choice: What are school vouchers? EdChoice. https://www.edchoice.org/school-choice/types-of-school-choice/what-are-school-vouchers-2/

Weil, D. (2002). *School vouchers and privatization: A reference handbook.* ABC-CLIO, Inc.

Winerip, M. (1985, May 13). School integration in Buffalo is hailed as a model for U.S. *The New York Times.* Accessed 21 Mar. 2021. www.nytimes.com/1985/05/13/nyregion/school-integration-in-buffalo-is-hailed-as-a-model-for-us.html

Yoshida, H. (2013, March 14). *Barbara Miner on the struggle to protect Milwaukee public schools.* NEA Today. Accessed 2018. http://neatoday.org/2013/03/14/barbara-miner-on-the-struggle-to-protect-milwaukee-public-schools-2/

Review

I. Checking What You Have Read

1. What does "school choice" mean?
2. What is culture and why do we need to respect the culture of other peoples?
3. African Americans have made major contributions to our lives. Name two and explain how their contributions specifically affect your life and/or your future plans or the life of someone close to you.
4. What does Tom Joyner do that shows his commitment to the African American community?
5. Explain the difference between charter schools and voucher programs.
6. What kinds of inequities do African Americans still face?
7. Why is choice for schools such a controversial issue?
8. Why do some people say that voucher schools do not really provide choice of quality education for Blacks or the poor?
9. In the movie *Hidden Figures* there were three women who were portrayed as contributing greatly to the NASA space program. Identify who they were, what they did and which of them was awarded the Presidential Medal of Freedom by President Barack Obama in 2015.

II. On Your Own

1. Find an example that demonstrates that African Americans still suffer from discrimination in the media today (e.g., newspapers, magazines, television, radio). Be prepared to explain your reasons to the class.
2. The first jockeys to ride horses in races were African American. See if you can discover who were some other African American jockeys.
3. Otis Boykin invented the pacemaker. Find out what other inventions that he is credited with inventing. Make a list and discuss each invention.
4. Select any area that interests you (science, art, sports, music, etc.) and make a list of famous African Americans in that field. Be sure to identity each person's accomplishments.

5. The super soaker water gun was invented by an African American. Find out who he was and his occupation.

Barack Obama: The 44th President of the United States

Barack Obama became the 44th president of the United States of America on January 20, 2009. History was made on that day because this was not just another ordinary election but one in which Obama became the first African American president of the United States. His campaign and subsequent election were historic and remarkable. Obama had worldwide appeal and was particularly popular with young people. He was an unknown entity; many people had never heard of the junior senator from Illinois. So, when Obama threw his hat into the ring for the presidential election, he was met with surprise and curiosity. He was a certainly a long shot.

The President and His Lineage

Obama was born in Hawaii of mixed parentage. His father was an African from Kenya: his mother was a White woman from Kansas. Interracial marriages were rare, at this time, in the United States. In some states in America, it was illegal. Obama's White grandparents were originally from Kansas but moved four times until they settled in Hawaii. Their daughter, Stanley Ann Dunham, met Obama's father, Barack Obama Sr. at the University of Hawaii in Honolulu, where he was an exchange student. They fell in love, were married and in 1961, Barack was born. Stanley Ann did not stay in Hawaii but took her infant son and moved to Seattle, Washington, according to her biographer, Janny Scott (2011). When she returned to Hawaii, two years later, she and Obama Sr. divorced.

Obama Sr. was awarded a scholarship to Harvard University to pursue a Ph.D. in economics. He left Hawaii and went to Boston, but he did not complete his degree. According to the Associated Press and public immigration records, the college was concerned about Obama Sr.'s personal life and finances. They claimed he was already married to a woman in Kenya. The college looked for a way to dismiss him from the program. They found it by saying that although the academic work of Obama Sr. was fine, the funds were not available. His request for an extended stay to complete his studies was denied. Obama Sr. went back to Kenya, and never completed his degree.

Eventually, Stanley Ann married Lolo Soetoro, an Indonesian exchange student. When Soeharto, a military leader, came into power in 1966, there was political unrest. All exchange students were recalled to Indonesia. Stanley Ann went on to earn her Ph.D. in anthropology. She then joined her husband in Jakarta, Indonesia. That is where Barack Obama's half-sister, Maya was born. According to his memoirs, Obama (2004) attended school there with his mother supplementing his education with additional information, with particular attention to the "civil rights movement, the recordings of Mahalia Jackson, [and] the speeches of Dr. King" (p. 50). She wanted her son, Barack to have a good command of the English language and have a strong educational background that would serve him later in life.

Obama's mother supported his education as much as she could. Therefore, four years after the birth of Maya, Barack was sent to live with his maternal grandparents, Madelyn (Toot) and Stanley Dunham (Gramps) in Hawaii to continue his schooling. He was enrolled in Punahou School and finished high school in Hawaii. His mother returned to Hawaii for a short period of time, however, she spent most of her life in Indonesia. Stanley Ann Dunham died of cancer in 1995.

Higher Education and Career

Obama left Hawaii after high school to attend college in Los Angeles in 1979. He enrolled in Occidental College where there were only four other Black students. During his years at Occidental College, Obama was always seeking his identity. Having roots in both the White and Black worlds was difficult. Obama was comfortable with his international friends because of his familiarity with Asia and having lived in Indonesia. He blended well with his Pakistani friends, where he was known as Barry not Barack. Obama could easily move from one cultural group to another as well as from one political group to another, according to Maraniss (2012), a biographer. After two years at Occidental College, Obama decided to apply to Columbia University in New York City.

When Obama attended Columbia University, he made different kind of attachments than he had made at that small liberal arts college in Los Angeles, writes Maraniss (2012). While at Columbia, Obama immersed himself in advanced courses, and took as many as he could. His interests were in political science and literature, and Obama was also an astute listener. He was reluctant to join into a conversation until listening to what others had to say and deliberating on it. It was still a struggle for Obama to find a world in which he could best fit. Obama worked his way through college and upon graduation found temporary employment for a couple of years. After this Obama decided to become a community organizer in Chicago in 1985, according to Kovaleski (2008). He was not quite sure of what a community organizer was but knew that some choices had to be made in order to seek his place and fit into some community or station in life.

The Roots of Community Activism

Obama's desire to become a community organizer led him to accept an offer to work for the Developing Communities Project (DCP). This was a church-based organization that was originally comprised of eight Catholic parishes in a section of Chicago. A grassroots community organizer is someone who helps empower people at the local level in neighborhoods and he was very successful at this. Both of Obama's parents had been involved in community work, so this seemed to be a natural fit.

Kovaleski (2008) wrote about Gerald Kellman's encounter and subsequent interview with Barack Obama in Chicago (2008). Gerald Kellman, a community organizer, interviewed Obama and thought that his understanding of how it was to be an outsider would help him relate and work with others who were also outside of the system. He was not immediately accepted, at first, in the Black community. Obama faced scepticism by some

Black pastors who thought he was some sort of conspiratorial agent working for the Catholic churches or the Jews, to make money off the African American community, according to Kovaleski (2008). These were the only groups who embraced him, at first.

Living in Chicago also had a profound effect on Obama, giving him quite a different experience in the Black community than he had either in Indonesia or Hawaii. According to Galluzzo, a community organizer, Obama found himself in one of the most complex Black communities in America (Warren, 2010). Eventually, with his easy manner and the way he used his listening skills to interact with Blacks in the community, more trust was earned. As director of the organization, Obama helped to set up a job training program and a college preparatory tutoring program, among other accomplishments.

Obama wanted to do more, so three years later, he applied and was accepted at Harvard Law School. He was selected as an editor of the *Harvard Law Review* in his first year, and in his second year became its president. This accomplishment resulted in national media attention because he was the first Black president of the *Harvard Law Review*. Obama was encouraged to write about his experiences and was offered a publishing contract and book advance. While in law school, Obama would return in the summers to work in the Chicago law firms of Sidley, Austin, Hopkins and Sutter, respectively. It was during this summer employment that Obama met his future wife, Michelle. They eventually married and had two children.

After graduation, Obama was recruited by the University of Chicago Law School to their faculty. They offered to provide him with a fellowship and an office in which to write his book. That book became *Dreams from My Father*. Obama says it took longer to complete the book than he anticipated, but in any case, he finished it. Obama taught constitutional law for twelve years at the university and practiced civil rights law in the small law firm of Sidley and Austin.

Early Political Career

Obama's political career began in 1996 when he was elected to the Illinois State Senate. He had studied the 1983 political campaign of Harold Washington who went on to become Chicago's first African American mayor. Mayor Washington's election may have even served as a catalyst for Obama's future plans. Obama ran, was elected, and served three terms in the Illinois State Senate, from 1997 until 2004. In 2000, he campaigned for a seat in the House of Representatives but failed to win election. In July 2004 Obama delivered the keynote address at the Democratic National Convention in Boston, and this speech, according to various accounts, propelled him into the spotlight. In 2004, he campaigned for a seat in the United States Senate, which he won. Obama became the junior senator from Illinois in 2005 and was the only senator to become a member of the Congressional Black Caucus. The other members are all Congressional Representatives. Obama also became only the fifth African American to hold a Senate seat since Reconstruction and only the third to be elected.

Personal Struggles and Search for Identity

While Obama's political life is a matter of record, there are much deeper issues when attempting to learn more about the person. The questions that many people had about him were related to his belief system, his values, and his culture. What were the experiences that shaped Obama? Who was this fast-rising star on the political scene with the audacity to run for president of the United States after only two years as a U.S. senator? How did his upbringing as a biracial child affect him? Many African Americans wanted to know if Obama was Black enough. In other words, could he relate to the experiences and realities that they felt and faced daily? Simply stated, Obama's ancestors did not necessarily have the same background of American enslavement as most other Black Americans. Even his upbringing was different, having lived in Indonesia and then Hawaii. These views were expressed by some, such as Walters (2007) who said Obama's cultural heritage and perhaps his realities were not the same as those of Blacks in America. Walters quotes Dickerson (2007) stating the following, "'Black' in our political and social reality means those descended from West African slaves. Voluntary immigrants of African descent (even those descended from West Indian slaves) are just that . . . with markedly different outlooks on the role of race in their lives and politics" (Walters, 2007, p. 2).

Other questions also arose. Both Whites and Blacks wondered who was this upstart and how dare Obama challenge Senator Hillary Clinton for the presidency of the United States? Some, television commentators, charged that he was an "angry Black man." There were others on the conservative side who linked him with Reverend Jeremiah Wright, whose church the Obama family had formerly attended. Reverend Wright had made some statements in a sermon that the media claimed portrayed him as angry and against American society. Some, including, Obama, said the comments were taken out of context. However, some media and the organizers of the Republican campaign took the opportunity to link Obama with Reverend Wright's statements, as if to say, they were indicative of Obama's position.

Candidate Obama had a fine line to walk, and eventually gave a speech about race in Philadelphia, Pennsylvania. In this speech he outlined his ethnic background and acknowledged that perhaps he was not the most conventional candidate. Obama also said that there was "no other country on Earth where [his] story was even possible" (NPR, 2008). He said that race cannot be ignored. It had been a part of America since its founding. Obama said that the Founding Fathers had produced an unfinished document (the Declaration of Independence) and that "what would be needed were Americans in successive generations to do their part . . . to narrow that gap between the promise of our ideals and the reality of their time" (Obama, 2008).

President Obama also discussed his association with the Reverend Wright. Wright had made some inflammatory racial remarks some years earlier while Obama was a member of his church. He acknowledged Reverend Wright was a product of his experiences and that there is anger in the Black community, from Wright's generation as well as from the current generation. That anger stems from the history of racial injustice which is still manifested in inferior schools, discrimination in housing, and lack of economic opportunity and was part of what fuelled Reverend Wright's frustration. Obama, however, noted that those remarks were divisive, and that unity was needed instead. More importantly, Obama, spoke of solving the challenges that America faces together and in making America a better place for all its citizens. He called on the African American community to not become victims of the past but insist on justice and work with all Americans for better health care, schools and jobs (NPR, 2008). Obama's speech on race was historic as the first or even the best one on race given by a president.

The memoirs of Obama provide a great deal of insight into the turmoil he experienced within himself as a biracial child. He described the search for his own cultural identity as well the bigotry he experienced even in Hawaii. Obama commented that his bouts with bigotry were not as severe as they could have been if he had lived on the mainland. He stated, in his memoirs, that he would remind his high school friend, Ray, that they "weren't living in the Jim Crow South." They "weren't consigned to some heatless housing project in Harlem or the Bronx." Obama reminded his friend that living in Hawaii, they did not have to sit in the back of the bus and could eat where they pleased. Their White friends treated them okay, for the most part.

However, even with living in Hawaii and his White middle class upbringing, he could not hide the color of his skin (Obama, 2004, p. 82). In his book, Obama remembers the conversations about race with some of the Black students at Punahou School, especially when they discussed "White folks" in disparaging ways. The discussions were difficult for him, especially because his own grandparents were "White folks." Obama says "the term itself was uncomfortable in my mouth at first" (pp. 80–81). He points out that he would find himself saying "White folks, this and White folks that" to his friend Ray. Obama went on to say that "I would suddenly remember my mother's smile, and the words that I spoke would seem awkward and false" (p. 81).

Obama's friend, Ray, said his grandparents were "cool." So, young Obama finally decided that the term "White folks" was just a "tag." It was similar to the word bigot which was explained to him by his mother. However, young Obama came to understand that some Whites could obviously be exempted from the distrust that his friends equated with the term, "White folks." Still he could not understand why he felt uncomfortable if, in the middle of the conversation, a White girl mentioned how much she liked Stevie Wonder or asked if he played basketball. Young Obama tried to fit in but it was difficult. In the end, he would move between his White world and his Black one, learning that each provided its own language, customs, and meanings. Eventually they would merge into his personality and behaviors (Obama, 2004). One of Obama's early struggles was a clear sense of his racial identity.

There was his desire to know about his father. Obama had only seen his father once, when he was ten, before he died in a car accident in 1982. Before entering Harvard Law School, Obama travelled first to Europe for three weeks and then to Kenya, his father's home. He stated that although he found the countries in Europe to be beautiful, he could not relate to them. He did not have a sense of belonging. He was met by his half-sister in Kenya and experienced a homecoming that is customary and typical of African people.

CHAPTER 18

The Presidential Campaigns

The 2008 Election

The presidential campaign of Barack Obama was unique and remarkable in several ways. The campaign organizers made use of digital media in a way that had never been done before. According to writer Wasow (2008), Obama built a bottom-up Internet machine. The campaign organizers were able to sign up millions of supporters using the Internet. They built a database of millions of email addresses, utilized YouTube and cell phones as methods of delivery. Obama's team even developed a Facebook site. Obama engineered his own social network with My.BarackObama.com. Using the digital media, he was able to raise more funds than his opponents. Many of those donations were small amounts by people who might not have donated otherwise. Obama even collaborated with major recording artists such as Stevie Wonder, Lionel Ritchie, John Mayer, Sheryl Crow and others to create a CD. The CD, *Yes, We Can: Voices of a Grassroots Movement* was paid for by the Obama Victory Fund, a joint fundraising committee authorized by Obama for America and the Democratic National Committee.

Senator Obama faced stiff competition for the democratic nomination. His major opponent for the party's nomination was Senator Hillary Clinton. In the general election he faced the long-term, popular, Arizona Senator John McCain. Both of his competitors had tremendous national political experience, political action networks, and influential friends in high places. Obama remained steady in his message of change where the other candidates vacillated. Although his opponents would point out his inexperience, his message of change resonated with many people. The campaign was exciting, innovative, and appealing, especially to young people. College students joined grassroots organizations and got out the vote. In the presidential debates, Obama was the only one who discussed issues related to higher education and schools in general. Senator Obama had previously made his opposition to the war on Iraq known and his plan was to bring American troops home in a responsible way. His other issues of health, jobs, alternative energy resources, and middle-class tax cuts also found willing listeners, as well as support.

The economic crisis that the country had fallen into during the last few months of the presidential campaign was also a factor. The economic downturn began early in 2008 and grew progressively worse. Observers and news commentators noted that many voters felt that the Republicans were at fault and that there was a lack of an effective action to address the issues. There was also little confidence that the Republicans could fix the problems. Obama's campaign slogan of change was appealing (Wallsten, 2008). Senator McCain's choice of a running mate, Sarah Palin, for the vice-presidential post was also seen as a poor choice. While she was a surprise pick and even for a few weeks boosted McCain's flailing campaign, the excitement wore off as she began to appear and give interviews in public. While there were those who cited the inexperience of Obama, there were others who felt that the female governor of a state with such a small population had even less experience and was even more of a novice.

President Obama has been compared with several of his predecessors. Most notably John F. Kennedy, Franklin Delano Roosevelt, and Abraham Lincoln are mentioned. Obama is compared to Kennedy in terms of his charisma and oratory skills and compared to Lincoln for his speech-writing abilities. According to a writer (Hornick, 2009), President Obama is a Lincoln scholar and often spoke of Lincoln in his speeches. Obama launched the inaugural events with a speech from the Lincoln Memorial. The inauguration, 200 years after the birth of Lincoln, was reminiscent of Lincoln because Obama, like Lincoln, arrived by train in Washington. He travelled from Philadelphia to Delaware, where Senator Biden, his vice president, joined him on board, and then on to Washington. The theme of the inauguration, "A New Birth of Freedom," was adopted from Lincoln's Gettysburg Address, and Obama chose the Lincoln Bible for the swearing-in ceremony.

There are other similarities with both Lincoln and Roosevelt when one looks at the state of the country. When Lincoln took office, the problem was how to keep the Union together. With Roosevelt, it was how to address the serious economic challenges of the Depression. President Obama faced equally serious challenges such as the Recession. Upon his election, there was a smooth transition between the Obama and Bush administrations. The Obama administration quickly started to put cabinet members in place. Senator Hillary Clinton was confirmed as secretary of state shortly after President Obama was sworn in, and although most of his candidates for Cabinet posts had been selected, they faced close scrutiny.

2012: The Re-Election of Obama

Not only was President Obama elected to a first term, he also won a second term. It was not by as great a margin as the first election, but still it was historic. This is one of Obama's biggest successes. While he won this second term running against Mitt Romney by a margin of 3.8 percentage points in the Electoral College, he won the popular vote by 51.1 percent. Nevertheless, it is an accomplishment in and of itself that the American people were willing to elect Obama to a second term.

During Obama's second term he achieved other accomplishments, including brokering the Iran nuclear peace agreement and establishing the International Climate Change Accord with America's allies. He faced fierce opposition, with obstructionist behavior by members of the Republican Party. At this point in time the Republicans were in the majority in both the Senate and the House. According to some writers if President Obama proposed an action regarding the military, for example, the Republicans would say that it was the wrong action. If he didn't offer a proposal, then they would say "well, why not?"

President Obama had to resort to governing by the use of executive order. The use of that strategy to enact policy guaranteed that he would not be a "lame duck" president. A "lame duck" president is one who is in his final year of office and is usually limited in the policies that he can propose and have Congress pass. President Obama actually utilized the same strategy as his Republican counterparts, Reagan and Nixon. President Obama used the power of the pen to put into place a number of things on his list that he wanted to achieve. Unfortunately, these orders can be overturned by the next president because they are not ratified by Congress.

In 2012, he protected the Dreamers or Deferred Action for Childhood Arrivals (DACA immigrants) from deportation under the (DACA) program. The so-called Dreamers were protected by an executive order that he signed which allowed undocumented immigrants a two-year period in which to stay in America. This program was extended to those immigrants who were brought to America before they were 16 years old. Many of these immigrants only know America as their home. They have even grown up and joined our military to fight for the United States. They work and are contributing members of our society. Obama also oversaw the elimination of Osama Bin Laden, the mastermind of the 9/11 terrorist attack in New York City and the other American targets.

President Barack Obama, First Lady Michelle Obama, daughters Sasha and Malia, Vice President Joe Biden, Dr. Jill Biden, and the Biden family wave to the crowd as confetti rains down following the president's election night remarks at McCormick Place in Chicago, Illinois, on November 6, 2012. Courtesy Barack Obama Presidential Library.

During Obama's second term in office there were several issues that occurred that were of grave concern. Although gun violence was an issue in his first term, it escalated. There was the shooting at Sandy Hook Elementary school in Newtown, Connecticut, that killed 20 children and six school employees. Other acts of gun violence included the attack in a movie theatre in Aurora, Colorado, the Pulse Nightclub attack in Orlando, Florida. a second shooting at Ft. Hood, Texas, and the District of Columbia Navy Yard shooting, as well as others.

In addition, far too much of this gun violence was identified, as hate crimes. They included the killing of nine Black people who were attending a prayer service in a church in Charleston, South Carolina, and six people who were shot at a Sikh Temple in Oak Creek, Wisconsin. Despite the grief and outrage, President Obama was unable to push through gun control legislation. He was blocked by the gun lobbyist, activists, the National Rifle

Association (NRA), and Republicans who used the excuse that new laws would be an infringement on the Second Amendment—The Right to Bear Arms.

One should understand the timeframe and purpose for the ratification of Second Amendment in 1791. It was intended to maintain the collective right of the militias which had been established in the states, in the 1790s, to carry weapons/guns. Furthermore, individual citizens also have the right to bear arms for their own protection. This Amendment was passed in a time when there were no assault type weapons of the sort used by the modern military. Assault weapons are not usually used to protect a person's home, business, or for game hunting. These kinds of weapons are intended for use in the military and should not be available for use in the streets of America.

The rallying cry by Second Amendment advocates against regulation was that "they're trying to take away our guns." This is far from the truth but was used to instil fear, suspicion, and discord as well as to protest against any changes. The 1999 law against assault type weapons previously passed by the Congress was allowed to lapse. The opponents of this law stated that there was no correlation between the law and the reduction of gun-related crimes. Some say that loopholes contributed to the lack of its effectiveness. Other gun laws that have been proposed such as background checks to keep criminals and people with mental health issues from purchasing guns have fallen on deaf ears. Other issues that remained during President Obama's presidency had to do with the slow growth of the economy. Then, there were issues that arose concerning the sustainability of the Affordable Health Care program during Obama's second term.

The Politics of Race and Division

Race and race relations have always been difficult topics to discuss and in fact are avoided by many. People feel uncomfortable and awkward when the topic arises. With the election of the first Black president, however, race is no longer something from which the American people can hide. The election of Barack Obama put race front and center. One would think that the election of a Black president would signal a post-racial era, and that America had outgrown its old prejudices and troubled past, with regards to race. That was not the case.

Barack Obama

President Barack Obama, Ruby Bridges, and representatives of the Norman Rockwell Museum: Laurie Norton Moffatt, CEO, and Anne Morgan, President of the Board, view Rockwell's painting *The Problem We All Live With* hanging in a West Wing hallway near the Oval Office. Ruby Bridges is the girl in the painting. Courtesy Barack Obama Presidential Library.

With the election of President Obama, racial tensions increased exponentially, as did acts of aggression and violence against Blacks and people of color including immigrants. President Obama was subjected to it when he was disrespected by Republican congressman Joe Wilson of South Carolina. He took the unprecedented step to yell "YOU LIE" during the president's nationally televised State of the Union speech. It not surprising that this verbal attack would come from the Representative from South Carolina, when one looks at that state's racial history. However, it is surprising and disrespectful that Wilson felt that he could shout at a sitting president in the Congress of the United States.

There were two issues concerning race with the election of Barack Obama. First, although the people had elected a Black man as president, was Congress really going to allow him to govern within the parameters of the Constitution and the laws of the United States? The second issue was the underlying racial tensions which bubbled to the top, spilled out into the streets, and became a backlash in the form of violence against African Americans, particularly men, Hispanics, and immigrants.

Barack Obama represented an acceptable model for White Democrats. He was well educated, the editor of the *Harvard Law Review*, and well-spoken. He was also "light-skinned," according to Harry Reid, a senator from Nevada, a comment for which he later apologized. But for all of this, he was still African American. According to Coates (2017) the Republicans were not going to let him govern as president. The symbolism of a Black man in a seat of power over a nation of predominately White citizens was too potent. It became increasingly evident that the Republicans and Tea Party members of the Congress would not cooperate. This was an important time because, in order to pass a law, a majority of the votes from both the Senate and the House of Representatives were needed. In the first two years of the Obama administration, the House and Senate seats were in the hands of the Democrats.

There was one short period of about 4 months in 2009 to 2010 when both houses were held by Democrats. It was during that time period in which the Health Care Act and the Stimulus Bill to help the economy were passed. During the rest of those first two years, although the House majority was Democrat, the Senate was not. Some legislation was passed because sometimes Senate Republicans would vote with the Democrats. During the last two years, Congress was controlled by Republicans in both the House and the Senate.

The second issue of race and racial tensions was a major area of concern. During President Obama's presidency there was a rise in outright racial slurs and attacks on people of color and immigrants across the country. Although Obama appealed to many with his platform of jobs, health care, and education, several media outlets reported that the majority of African Americans were skeptical that race relations would improve. They were correct because racial violence escalated in various ways. There were suspected incidences of police brutality and the killing of unarmed African American men, in particular, but also women and children. These cases included African Americans such as Walter Scot and Sandra Bland, who died while in police custody. Michael Brown and Tamir Rice were killed by police officers. Trayvon Martin was killed by George Zimmerman, a so-called vigilante neighborhood watch person. Hate crimes escalated against African Americans in the streets of America.

The targeting of African Americans caused the formation of the BlackLivesMatter movement. This movement quickly became controversial because others twisted the term to imply that only Black lives mattered and that blue lives (the police) and other lives did not. However, it was only Black lives that were being taken disproportionately, as opposed to other groups. The BlackLivesMatter movement specifically called attention to African Americans who have historically been targeted for ill treatment by the justice system and more severe types of punishment, even death.

The Presidency of Barack Obama: Challenges and Successes

The election of Barack Obama as the first African American president of the United States was momentous. His election sent shockwaves throughout America, and the world, because it represented a change in political dynasties or the insider track to the presidency. Obama was an outsider with new views and ideas that appealed to younger people and those who had been overlooked by all the political parties. Obama's slogan "Yes We Can" represented a new inclusive spirit of American democracy and opportunity to rise above one's birth circumstances.

Many Americans, both Black and White, did not think that such a phenomenon would ever occur, at least not in their lifetimes. The shock of President Obama's election promptly caused the Senate majority leader from Kentucky, Mitch McConnell to say that his number one priority was to make sure President Obama was a one-term president. Mitch McConnell was determined in his efforts to oppose and obstruct every policy or piece of legislation that President Obama proposed. He was aided and abetted by other Republicans and Tea Party members in the Congress. The sweeping victory that President Obama enjoyed in his first election, was due in great part by his appeal to younger voters, minorities, and those with moderate incomes of $60,000 or less, according the Pew Research Center. There were a number of issues that President Obama faced when he took office. In 2008, the issue that was the most dominant was the economy.

The country was in a deep economic crisis, due to the Recession of 2008. A large part of this crisis was due to the housing market where many people lost their homes through foreclosure. This happened because banks were dealing in subprime mortgages. That is when banks, in an effort to make profits from the rising costs of homes, granted loans to people who had poor credit histories and did not have the income to pay the mortgages. In the meanwhile, the housing bubble broke and housing prices declined. In many cases, people found that their houses were valued for less than the loans they had to pay.

In addition, the stock market lost half of its value. That meant that those people who had their retirement funds invested in the market loss half of those funds. This money was what the prospective retirees relied on for their retirement. To be clear, not everyone was invested in the stock market. However, if a person has a 401-retirement account through his or her employer, those funds could be invested in stocks. The value of those stocks can rise or decrease. In any case, in 2007, the loss in the value of retirement funds meant that people who depended on the funds that they thought they had saved and were safe, could not retire.

The passage of the Dodd-Frank Wall Street Reform and Consumer Protection Act was intended to regulate the financial sector in order to help prevent the repeat of those troublesome practices that helped cause the recession. Also, during that period in 2007 leading up to the election of 2008, employment opportunities had declined and a number of investment banking institutions failed. The auto industry was also in trouble, and about to fail. This recession was also reflected in other countries because they are all interdependent on each other and a domino effect occurs in the financial markets.

President Obama inherited a financial mess and was met with opposition from the Republican Party consistently throughout his leadership that guided the country out of the recession. The Republicans were resistant to the policies that President Obama proposed, including the Dodd-Frank Act which was intended to regulate the financial markets and protect consumers. They were against his bailout of the auto industry, which, in the end, greatly assisted them in becoming financially sound again. There were other instances of obstruction, but too many to delineate here. Despite these attempts to make Obama's presidency unsuccessful, he managed to get his signature program passed, which was health care.

The passing the American Recovery and Reinvestment Act of 2009, added to the economic growth of the country. This Act was similar to Roosevelt's New Deal plan. It was important, but President Obama also wanted to address health care. In fact, this was one of his major concerns. The policies that he proposed were focused on providing affordable health care for low income people. Republicans and those known as the Tea Party members of the Congress claimed that the health care proposal would be too expensive. These conservatives wanted less government intervention and not more. In fact, they wanted to eliminate or greatly reduce entitlement programs such as Medicare, Medicaid and Social Security, Unemployment Insurance and Social Welfare.

Despite the efforts of the Conservatives, Tea Party members and other Republicans, the Affordable Care Act, also known as Obamacare was passed. It provided health insurance for those persons whose income was too high to qualify for welfare, but too low to afford to purchase health insurance at all. The Health Care Program allowed students to remain on their parents' insurance until the age of 26, and it prevented people with pre-existing health conditions from being denied treatment. President Obama also expanded the Children's Health Insurance Program (CHIP) (The White House Archive, n.d.) to cover health care for 4 million children. In terms of education, he expanded Pell Grant funding and took banks out of the Federal Student Loan Program to end wasteful loan practices.

One of Obama's notable accomplishments was to win the Nobel Peace Prize. A number of articles written about the first term of President Obama, identify his other accomplishments. Some of them include the 2010 tax cut which provided for the extension of unemployment benefits, payroll taxes, and extension of the Bush tax cuts.

The Obama Political Legacy

There have been several public opinion polls which, for the most part, agree that race relations significantly declined during President Obama's terms in office. However, there are some writers who state that President Obama is not to blame for the deterioration in race relations. It only seems that way because the election of a Black president of the United States put race front and center and forced people to confront the racism that has always been present and just under the radar. Discrimination and racist behaviors have a long-standing hold on America, although many do not want to overtly admit it. It is found in the legal and social areas, political areas, and certainly in the economic disparity in wealth.

President Barack Obama talks on the phone with pastors who offer a birthday prayer during a call in the Oval Office, August 4, 2015. Courtesy Barack Obama Presidential Library

Despite the racial issues and tension that President Obama had to endure and the increase in racial tensions overall in the nation, he managed to have some achievements and certainly leaves a legacy. For one, Barack Obama became the first African American President of the United States. Another is that when President Obama left office, he did so with dignity and honor. There had been no scandals as there had with Bill Clinton or Ronald Regan, or for that matter, Richard Nixon, who had to resign because of his involvement in Watergate. Obama thawed the frosty relations and embargo on Cuba. He was the first American President to visit Cuba since 1928.

Obama inherited an economic fiasco, but he turned the country around and passed the financial banking law. He signed an Executive Order protecting those young immigrants or DACA recipients. President Obama adhered to the "rule of law." He did not attempt to blur the lines between the three branches of the government. While President Obama did bring the United States out of the 2008 Recession, his policies for the Middle East might have had with some mixed reviews, especially with the Iran Nuclear treaty. Some say, however, that negotiating an agreement with some level of stabilization was better than nothing, and allowing Iran to continue toward becoming a nuclear power.

While some of his detractors might have wanted to insinuate that he would only assist Black people if Obama came into office, they were found to be incorrect. Obama studiously avoided the issue of race or even talking about race. The only exception was his Philadelphia speech on race during his first run for the presidency, and his mention that Trayvon Martin could have been his son. For Obama's comments of sympathy and compassion, he was verbally attacked by the conservative talk show hosts.

Obama's policies were directed toward the working poor, disadvantaged, and a demographic that included White America. In fact, many Blacks such as Cornell West, and others don't think that he did enough for Blacks. One has to acknowledge the fact that one person, even if he is the president, cannot do the job alone. That person has to work with the Congress. Unfortunately, it was especially difficult for the first African American President, since the Congress did not work with him.

While Obama, did use Executive Orders to get many of his proposals accomplished, as was stated, it only takes a successor to undo everything that he did. Indeed, Donald Trump has made it his mission to do just that, regardless if it was a good policy for the people of the United States. Perhaps if Hillary Clinton had become president, the populist agenda would have continued. She was the seen as the standard bearer for the populist left.

Summary

President Barack Obama made history when he won election as the 44th President of the United States. He had world wide appeal and his optimism, and enthusiasm encouraged many thousands of young people and African Americans to come out and vote. African Americans only make up approximately 13 percent of the entire population of the United States. As a voting block African Americans cannot elect a President merely by their votes alone. However, enough African Americans and Latinos believed in Obama and voted in higher numbers than had ever been seen. This was supplemented by the votes of younger Americans which caused a new era in American political and election history.

Obama's election and the coalition that supported him represented the best of political grassroots inclusiveness. There can be no doubt that

President's Obama's election and subsequent two terms was a source of great pride for African Americans. John McCain's concession speech, after the presidential election acknowledged this.

References

Agiesta, J. C. (2016, October 5). *Most say race relations worsened under Obama, poll finds*. CNN. Accessed 2018. http://www.cnn.com/2016/10/05/politics/obama-race-relations-poll/index.html

Anderson, S. (2017, August 6). *Oak Creek Sikh temple shooting: 5 years ago as it happened*. Oak Creek Patch. Accessed 2018. https://patch.com/wisconsin/oakcreek/oak-creek-sikh-temple-shooting-5-years-ago-it-happened

Associated Press Staff. (2011, April 29). *Obama's father forced out at Harvard*. The Associated Press. Accessed 2018. https://www.politico.com/story/2011/04/obamas-father-forced-out-at-harvard-053968

Baker, R. (n.d.). Obama the Outsider. *USA Today*, Academic Search Elite database. Accessed 2009.

Biography.com Editors. *Barack Obama*. Biography.com. Accessed 2018. https://www.biography.com/tag/barack-obama

Cable News Network. (2007, November 27). *Winfrey could help Obama draw women voters from Clinton*. CNN. Accessed 2007. http://www.cnn.com/2007/POLITICS/11/26/obama.oprah/index.html

Coates, T.-N. (2017, January). My president was Black. *The Atlantic*. Accessed 2018. https://www.theatlantic.com/magazine/archive/2017/01/my-president-was-black/508793/

Cohen, E. *Women angry over Oprah-Obama campaign: Some say Oprah is a 'traitor' for endorsing Obama and not Clinton*. ABC News. Accessed 2008. https://abcnews.go.com/politics/story?id=4167650&page=1

Dallek, M. (2008, November). The comparisons between Barack Obama and Abraham Lincoln. *US News & World Report*. Accessed 2008. https://www.usnews.com/opinion/articles/2008/11/20/the-comparisons-between-barack-obama-and-abraham-lincoln

Dickerson, D. J. (2007, January). *Colorblind: Barack Obama would be the great Black hope in the next presidential race—if he were actually Black*. Salon. Accessed 2018. https://www.salon.com/2007/01/22/obama_161/

Everding, G. (2018, January 29). *Record expansion of U.S. hate groups slows under Trump administration*. The Source: Washington University in St. Louis. Accessed 2018. https://source.wustl.edu/2018/01/record-expansion-u-s-hate-groups-slows-trump-administration/

E.W.B. *Notable biographies: Barack Obama*. Accessed 2018. https://www.notablebiographies.com/news/Li-Ou/Obama-Barack.html

Gill, K. *Political career of Barack Obama*. Thoughtco. Accessed 2018. https://www.thoughtco.com/barack-obamas-political-career-3368167

Gillin, J. (2017, January). *Congress blocked Obama's call for new gun laws after mass \ shootings*. Politifact. Accessed 2018. http://www.politifact.com/truth-o-meter/article/2017/jan/06/congress-blocked-obama-call-gun-control-mass-shoot/

Gilmore, J. (2008). *The FRONTLINE interview: Gerald Kellman—the Choice 2012*. FRONTLINE. Accessed March 12, 2021. www.pbs.org/wgbh/pages/frontline/government-elections-politics/choice-2012/the-frontline-interview-gerald-kellman/

Glastris, P., Cooper, R., & Hu, S. (2012, April). Obama's top 50 accomplishments. *Washington Monthly*. Accessed 2018. https://washingtonmonthly.com/magazine/marchapril-2012/obamas-top-50-accomplishments/

Hamby, P., & Malveaux, S. (2007). *Thanks to Oprah, Obama camp claims biggest crowd yet*. CNN. Accessed 2007. http://www.cnn.com/2007/POLITICS/12/09/oprah.obama/

Hornick, E. (2009, January 18). *For Obama, Lincoln was model president*. CNN. Accessed 2009. http://edition.cnn.com/2009/POLITICS/01/17/lincoln.obsession/index.html#cnnSTCText

Johnson, D. (2014, May 29). *Republican strategy: Obstruct, blame Democrats for obstruction's damage*. OurFuture. Accessed 2018. https://ourfuture.org/20140529/republican-strategy-obstruct-blame-democrats-for-obstructions-damage

Korte, G. (2016, June 12). 14 mass shootings; 14 speeches: How Obama has responded. *USA Today*. Accessed 2016. https://www.usatoday.com/story/news/politics/2016/06/12/14-mass-shootings-14-speeches-how-obama-has-responded/85798652/

Kovaleski, S. (2008, July 27). Obama's organizing years, guiding others and finding himself. *The New York Times*. Accessed 2018. https://www.nytimes.com/2008/07/07/us/politics/07community.html?register=google

Maraniss, D. (2012, May 25). Barack Obama: The college years. *The Guardian*. Accessed 2018. https://www.theguardian.com/world/2012/may/25/barack-obama-the-college-years

Merry, R. W. (2016, November 10). Why Obama's second term paved the way for Trump's rise. *The National Interest*. http://nationalinterest.org/feature/why-obamas-second-term-paved-the-way-trumps-rise-18359

NPR. (2008, March 18). *Transcript: Barack Obama's speech on race*. NPR. www.npr.org/templates/story/story.php?storyId=88478467

Obama, B. (2004). *Dreams from my father: A story of race and inheritance*. Three Rivers Press.

Obama heads for the convention. *Economist*. Academic Search Elite database. Accessed 2009.

Pew Research Center. (2008, November 5). *Inside Obama's sweeping victory*. Accessed 2016. http://www.pewresearch.org/2008/11/05/inside-obamas-sweeping-victory/

Roberts, D. (2017, January 5). Obama's second term: A president faces the limits of his power. *The Guardian*. Accessed 2018. https://www.theguardian.com/us-news/2017/jan/05/barack-obama-second-term-achievements-sandy-hook

S. M. (2018, February 20). Why the second amendment does not stymie gun control. *The Economist.* Accessed 2018. https://www.economist.com/the-economist-explains/2018/02/20/why-the-second-amendment-does-not-stymie-gun-control

Schlesinger, R. (2013, January). Conservatives can't win at the negotiating table what they lost at the ballot box. *U.S. News & World Report.* Accessed 2018. https://www.usnews.com/opinion/blogs/robert-schlesinger/2013/01/04/the-final-2012-presidential-election-results-arent-close

Schmidt, M. S., & Pérez-Peña, R. (2015, December 4). F.B.I. treating San Bernardino attack as terrorism case. *The New York Times.* Accessed 2018. https://www.nytimes.com/2015/12/05/us/tashfeen-malik-islamic-state.html

Scott, J. (2011, March 3). *The 'singular woman' who raised Barack Obama.* NPR. Accessed 2011. https://www.npr.org/2011/05/03/135840068/the-singular-woman-who-raised-barack-obama

Scott, J. (2008, May 18). The story of Obama, written by Obama. *The New York Times,* Accessed 2008. http://www.nytimes.com/2008/05/18/us/politics/18memoirs.html?pagewanted=all

Shear, M. D., & Schmidt, M. S. (2013, September 17). Gunman and 12 victims killed in shooting at D.C. navy yard. *The New York Times.* Accessed 2018. https://www.nytimes.com/2013/09/17/us/shooting-reported-at-washington-navy-yard.html

Silver, N. (2008, September 27). *Why voters thought Obama won.* FiveThirtyEight. Accessed 2008. https://fivethirtyeight.com/features/why-voters-thought-obama-won/

Smith, D. (2017, October). *The backlash against Black Lives Matter is just more evidence.* The Conversation. Accessed 2018. https://theconversation.com/the-backlash-against-black-lives-matter-is-just-more-evidence-of-injustice-85587

Snow, M., & Zilberstein, S. (2007, January). *Winfrey could help Obama draw women voters from Clinton.* CNN. Accessed 2007. http://www.cnn.com/2007/POLITICS/11/26/obama.oprah/index.html

Time Magazine Staff. (2017, January 20). 10 historians on what will be said about President Obama's legacy. *Time Magazine,* Accessed 2018. http://time.com/4632190/historians-obamas legacy/

The Similarities and Connections Between President Obama and President Lincoln. Accessed 2009. http:/www.reobama.com/ObamaLincoln.htm

Wallsten, P. (2008, November). Red and blue, Black and White. *The Los Angeles Times.* p. A11. Accessed 2008. https://www.latimes.com/archives/la-xpm-2008-nov-05-na-assess5-story.html

Walters, R. (2007). Barack Obama and the politics of race. *Sage Publications, 114*(3), 12–15. journals.sagepub.com/doi/10.1177/0021934707305214

Warren, J. (2010, October 16). Organizer's influence helped shape Obama. *The New York Times.* Accessed 2018. https://www.nytimes.com/2010/10/17/us/17cncwarren.html

Wasow, O. (2008, November). The first internet president: How Obama tapped netizens to transform American politics. *The Root.* Accessed 2008. http://www.theroot.com/views/firstinternetpresident

The White House. *Barack Obama*. The White House Press Office. Accessed 2018. https://www.whitehouse.gov/about-the-white-house/presidents/barack-obama/

The White House. *Improving health for all Americans*. Accessed 2018. https://obamawhitehouse.archives.gov/the-record/health-care

2016 Presidential Election: A Campaign of Polar Opposites

The United States is a democracy that is governed by a Constitution, statutes, and laws. When the United States was formed, the "Framers" intended to ensure that a well-ordered society was established and would be maintained. Without the rule of law, and the U.S. Constitution supported by a system of "checks and balances" of power between the three branches of government, chaos could ensue. In the absence of a balanced of governmental powers, the Framers feared that America would become full of strife, rebellion, and political tyranny. The rights of the few and their voices in the democratic process would be taken away by the majority. Also, the values of democracy and the rule of law would not apply equally to all Americans. Everyone needs civil order and the protections provided by just laws that insure the protections of life, liberty and the pursuit of happiness.

To promote the values within the new nation's government, the founding fathers designed the U.S. government based on the separation of powers by branches. There are three branches of government in the United States of America. There is the Legislative Branch which is made up of the House of Representatives and the Senate. There is the Executive Branch, which is represented by the president. And lastly, there is the Judicial Branch, which is composed of various courts with judges. Each branch of government was intended to be a separate entity and have separate functions and powers. After the inauguration of the new president in 2017, the independence of the three branches of government was tested. Donald Trump and his administration took an activist's role in decreasing congressional oversight and judicial scrutiny. The effect of this new level of executive power was an elevation of presidential domination of the federal government without meaningful opposition or scrutiny by the Congress.

The 2016 Major U.S. Presidential Candidates

Hillary Clinton: Democratic Insider and Operative

The role of women in politics can be described as an evolutionary process. In the history of America, the right to vote was first given to Black men through the 15th Amendment. Later, the 19th Amendment gave women the right to vote which subsequently witnessed the entrance of women on the political scene. It could be speculated that perhaps the office of the presidency could follow the same pattern, of first an African American and then a woman President.

In many ways, the 2016 presidential election was a highly anticipated election. There had only been one other time when a woman had attempted to make a bid for the presidency of the United States. In 1968, Shirley Chisholm from New York became the first African American woman to serve in Congress. Four years later (1972) Chisholm challenged George McGovern for the Democratic nomination. Chisholm lost, but became a national icon for women of color and African American electoral politics.

Some years later, Hillary Clinton became the second "major" female candidate to make a viable bid for the Democratic Party nomination for the presidency. She ran against Barack Obama in the Democratic primaries in 2008 for the nomination, but like Chisholm, she lost. In the primaries, she was forced to concede to Obama when it became apparent that he had won the majority of the primary delegate votes. Obama went on to become president, running against the Republican candidate John McCain. Not to be deterred, however, Clinton ran again and succeeded in securing the Democratic nod to become its candidate in 2016. It was the first time that a woman had become the candidate of a major political party. In addition, she was the only First Lady, the wife of a president, to run for the presidency.

Many people thought that Senator Hillary Clinton would win her second bid for the presidency. Her political credentials were impressive and diverse. Not only had she been a U.S. senator but also secretary of state. As Obama's secretary of state, she gained significant experience in foreign affairs. Those experiences provided her with the credentials to seek the presidency.

Hillary Clinton was born in Chicago, Illinois, but graduated from Yale University Law School. She married Bill Clinton and moved to Arkansas. Her husband Bill Clinton went on to become Arkansas' governor and later a two-term president of the United States. After President Clinton's term in office, his family moved to New York. The Clintons planned to campaign for the upcoming "open" Senate seat of Daniel P. Moynihan.

Even with her vast credentials, and experience, Hillary Clinton had many detractors. There were several reasons for this. For example, some analysts say that White working-class voters did not feel that she was looking out for their interests. Indeed, the Democratic Party appeared to be more focused on college educated voters rather than the working class. Traditionally African Americans have voted with the Democrats, since the Civil Rights movement of the sixties. However, Black voters had become disenchanted with the Democratic Party due to feelings of neglect.

A 2017 survey presented to the Congressional Black Caucus found that 63 percent of Black Americans felt that the Democratic Party took them for granted. In addition, the percentage was even higher for Black women, age 50 and over. Some writers and analysts noted that when politicians are running for office, in both local and national elections, they frequently show up at Black churches on Sunday mornings looking for support. African Americans rarely see their issues addressed after major elections, however. These analysts also point out that although Democrats will hire Blacks during their campaigns, they are not offered jobs in the administration. African Americans had grown tired of being pawns and having their vote taken for granted. This is especially true when the new administration's agenda does not prioritize Black concerns.

Senator Bernie Sanders: Independent and "Insurgent Progressive"

Hillary Clinton's major opponent for the 2016 Democratic primary nomination was Bernie Sanders, a senator from Vermont. Some felt that he was an unlikely opponent; others liked his socialist-democratic platform. Sanders was especially appealing to younger voters. His socialist-democratic views were very different from prior campaigners. Some say his views were the opposite of capitalism. Socialist democrats believe that the government should have programs that assist the poor, and the working class with education. They should also subsidize health care, such as is found in Canada and other countries. Capitalists, on the other hand, do not think the government should be in the business of providing social welfare assistance to the poor. They feel that government does not utilize its economic resources efficiently. The emphasis, for capitalists, is on individual profit rather than society and workers, as a whole. In looking at Sander's background, one can see how his views on policies and politics were formed.

Sanders was born into a working-class Jewish family from Brooklyn, New York. He attended the University of Chicago, after which he settled in Vermont. He became the mayor of Burlington, Vermont, an office in which he served for four terms. Finally, Sanders ran as an Independent for the House of Representatives, and later for the Senate. He is the longest serving Independent in the Congress. In his earlier life, Sanders was involved in the Civil Rights Movement of the sixties, even marching with Dr. Martin Luther King, Jr. in the March on Washington. It can be noted that since Sanders was from a working-class family, he understood the issues they faced. Perhaps this is one of the reasons for Sander's appeal to so many people.

College bound people liked Sanders' proposals for free tuition at public colleges and universities, single-payer health care, and a $15.00 minimum wage. Sanders supporters were characterized, by some writers and analysts, as being college attendees or college graduates who were concerned about school debt and income inequality. Supporters were also concerned about the lack of jobs in the fields that met their qualifications after college.

In some ways, Sanders' young supporters were also compared to Trump voters. This was because Sanders' supporters were also interested in issues that personally affected them. Being concerned about issues that affect one's life is also the case for African Americans. They, too, are interested in issues that affect their immediate situations. In the 2016 election, while a vote for Clinton did not necessarily mean that their lives would be better any time soon, African Americans were truly skeptical of Sanders. While many of the issues that he proposed were ones that were important for them, some felt that he did not speak to them in a way in which they felt he connected with them.

On the other hand, Hillary had one advantage, her husband Bill, who was popular with African Americans. Ultimately, Sanders lost the Black vote, especially in the South. Clinton, too, found that even with the popularity of her husband Bill, it just was not enough to sway minority voters. Many Blacks simply did not come out to vote at all for either Sanders or Clinton. According to analysts, there was a lower turn out of Black voters in 2016 than in either the 2008 or 2012 election of Barack Obama. The excitement of the Obama elections did not carry over to either Clinton or Sanders. In the end, Bernie Sanders lost the nomination to Hillary Clinton who went on to face the Republican nominee, Donald Trump in the general election.

The irony of the voter disconnect is that neither Sanders nor Clinton understood how to gain the vote of African Americans. Black voters are not monolithic. In other words, politicians just cannot take for granted that African Americans are going to automatically vote for Democrats. As is the case for other groups, African Americans will vote for those who they feel will work in their best interest. African Americans have shifted political parties because of issues that affect them, as is evident from the past.

Blacks have not always affiliated with the Democratic Party. During the time around the Civil War, African Americans were Republican, which was the party of Lincoln. The shift away began in the 1930s with the Great Depression. Many of them voted Democratic during the presidency of Franklin Roosevelt and the New Deal. During the Civil Rights Movement of the 1960's African Americans made another big move. They left the party of Lincoln in huge numbers when it became apparent, through the speeches of Barry Goldwater, who ran for President, that the Republicans were against civil rights.

The Republican Candidates

For the 2016 Republican nomination there were 17 initial candidates. Since there were so many candidates, the Republican debates were divided into two tiers. The first tier was composed of candidates who had won a major primary. The second tier was mainly composed of candidates who met the baseline qualifications to run in the presidential primary elections. However, they had no significant intra-party appeal. This second tier of candidates had also raised less money and received less votes. They, therefore, participated in, what might be described, as the minor debates. The minor debates did not receive as much of the spotlight and television coverage.

The candidates in the major debates included Donald Trump, Jeb Bush, Chris Christie, Ted Cruz, Marco Rubio, John Kasich, Ben Carson, Rudy Giuliani, Rick Perry, Lindsey Graham and some others. The tier one debates were full of drama with people calling others unflattering names or trying to belittle them. Most of name-calling was done by Donald Trump towards the other candidates, although some of the other candidates responded in similar fashion. As time passed, most of the second-tier debaters left the race. The field of candidates dropped to three, Trump, Kasich, and Cruz. In the end, they too dropped out and the Republican Party nominated Donald Trump as their candidate.

Donald Trump: Nativist, TV Reality Personality, Republican Nominee

Donald Trump's background provides a clear picture of his background and beliefs. His parents were German immigrants and he grew up in Queens, New York. His family became involved in real estate development amassing great wealth. Trump's father, Fred, often ignored the rules, and used illegal means to conduct business. Fred Trump got into trouble with the Senate Banking Committee in 1954 because of fraudulent property and business deals, according to researchers, Mahler and Eder (2016). Fred Trump eventually brought Donald into his business and later assisted him in beginning his own. Donald Trump graduated from the Wharton School of Business at the University of Pennsylvania. Trump claims that he received an estimated $50 million gift from his father and, he too, entered into the real estate business. Trump later branched out into Casino ownership.

After working in real estate and casinos, Trump turned his attention to a reality-based television show. He became the executive producer and star of *The Apprentice*. The show was very popular and ran for nearly two decades. Trump recouped some of the losses from his casino businesses and continued with the development of golf courses and the branding of his businesses with his name. Trump was also the owner of the Miss Universe pageant, which included Miss USA and Miss Teen USA. He has been both a Democrat and a Republican and has contributed to candidates of both parties. He claimed that his business dealings demonstrated his business acumen. However, the *New York Times* reported differently (Barstow, Craig, and Buettner, 2018). The article stated that Trump claimed he used the laws to do a great job for his company and family, but an analysis of court records, and regulatory review showed that Trump put very little of his money into these deals. As a result of the *New York Times* article, Mr. Trump was viewed with suspicion about his business practices.

While there are many areas in which Trump is different from the Democratic candidates, Sanders and Clinton, the most egregious is his record of discrimination against minority groups. Donald and Fred Trump were named as defendants in a housing discrimination lawsuit by the Justice Department in 1973. The Justice Department sued both Donald and his father, Fred for housing discrimination against Blacks in Brooklyn and Queens. Instead of settling the claim, Trump retaliated saying that the government was attempting to force him to rent to welfare recipients. He turned the whole incident into a long, ugly battle.

Eventually, Trump was ordered to desegregate his properties. He signed a consent decree, which allowed him to settle the case without admitting guilt. Trump, then went on to declare a victory in the case. He used "coded words," such as welfare recipients, to mean Blacks. However, the fact is that there are more White welfare recipients than Black recipients. The reason is simply because, according to the U.S. Census Bureau, the overall number of White Americans outnumbers Black Americans as well as other minorities in the United States (U.S. Census, 2017).

The 2016 Presidential Campaign

The presidential campaign started out with Hillary Clinton, the Democratic insider and Donald Trump, the Republican outsider. Some sources state that the Democrats had not fully embraced the policies of Barack Obama. The Republicans, on the other hand were dead set against anything that President Obama had done while in office. They found their champion in Donald Trump. On campaign issues, Sanders was very vocal that he felt the economy benefited millionaires and billionaires. Clinton said the same but perhaps not as vociferously. To be sure, the economy was an issue even though it had begun to improve through the interventions of President Barack Obama. However, the economy still needed improvement and there were other issues.

Some Major Campaign Issues

While the economy was a main issue, there were other voter concerns. They included immigration, health care, foreign affairs, and soaring drug prices. There was also the issue of gun control and the school and church killings which involved, children. There were Whites, Hispanics, the LGBT community and African Americans also shot by lone gunmen. Then, there was the rise in police violence against Blacks and the formation of the Black Lives movement. There was the concern over climate change as well as the energy policy that included fracking or drilling deep in the earth for gas and oil that could pose a danger to the environment. Other major issues included cyber security, which had to do with surveillance of citizens, as well as the hacking of American websites by the Chinese; and the hacking into Hillary Clinton's email by the Russians during the 2016 campaign.

Immigration

Conservatives and Republicans rallied their supporters by launching a barrage of insults against Mexicans. Mexicans were described in disparaging ways and racist overtones. The Republican platform had the goal of stopping the flow of illegal immigrants and building a wall between the United States and Mexico. The Republicans vowed to make Mexico pay for this wall. However, Enrique Peña Nieto, the President of Mexico at the time, rebuffed this notion.

After the Republicans took office, Nieto cancelled a scheduled meeting with Trump, no doubt because of the assertions made by Trump. Trump then, wanted to put tariffs on goods coming into the country from Mexico, but that would only hurt American consumers. Companies who purchase these overseas goods would simply raise prices on those imported goods. In the end it would fall on Americans to pay for the proposed wall. Trump also questioned the ability of a judge, who was of Mexican descent, to rule fairly. Judge Curiel presided over the Trump University case, where it was found that the university defrauded many of its students.

During the presidential campaign, Trump rallied his supporters against Muslim Americans and even insulted a gold star family who had lost their son fighting for America. The promise of stopping illegal immigration was a main goal. The administration, especially wanted to limit immigration from African countries, the Caribbean, Muslim, and other Third World countries.

Affordable Health Care

An issue, almost equal to the economy was health care and the soaring prices of drugs. The Democrats wanted better health care and had passed the Affordable Care Act prior to Trump's election. It was not without flaws, but it covered people who would not have had it otherwise. Under the Affordable Care Act people with pre-existing health conditions were covered and young people could remain on their parent's insurance until age 26. Most Republicans wanted to repeal it and had attempted to do so several times during President Obama's term.

As for Medicare, the national insurance program for people over 65, some Republicans wanted to restructure it, raise the age of eligibility, or charge wealthy seniors more. Others wanted to privatize it and have people buy their own or give the states subsidies in the form of block grants. According to some analysts, the costs for Medicare will rise significantly by 2025. The Republican plan continues to shift, but the main thing is that they are looking for ways to pay for the big tax cut that was given to the wealthy in 2017. There is also the high cost of prescription drugs, which Trump has somewhat addressed. The plan is intended to improve competition and transparency, but in incremental steps over a period of time. The main idea of lowering drug prices was not addressed, however.

The Medicaid program is a public health insurance program for the poor and people with disabilities funded by the federal and state government. It is referred to as a socialist program, which both Sanders and Clinton favored. The Republicans are against this type of socialist program. They would leave the poor to do the best they could with the little they have. Trump was in favor of undoing everything President Obama championed.

While Congress does not have free health care, according to researchers, they only have to pay 27 percent of the costs. If the Affordable Care Act were repealed, they would see an even bigger savings, but 20 million Americans would not. That old congressional plan was called the Federal Employees Health Benefits Program (FEHBP). What is most interesting is the people who depend on these programs are the GOP base. According to the Center on Budget and Policy Priorities, the federal programs, slated for reduction, helped reduce poverty for the White working class, or blue-collar workers. These federal programs assist Blacks also. However, given the overall population of the United States, Blacks and other minorities are only a small percentage when compared to Whites.

Gun Violence

Gun violence is a significant problem in the United States. It not only encompasses every community but has taken its toll on the young and the old. In addition to schools and churches, gun shootings have occurred at concerts or even night clubs. It is also present among gang members in various communities. Some say the issue is making gun laws stronger, closing loopholes, enforcing background checks, and preventing those with mental illness from purchasing firearms. The National Rifle Association (NRA), however, is against any proposal to gun safety. They lobby against any laws proposed.

BlackLivesMatter

The BlackLivesMatter movement started soon after the shooting of Trayvon Martin and Michael Brown, both young Black men. The BlackLivesMatter marchers were protesting the murder of unarmed Blacks, and in some cases the brutality against Black women. This protest was met with negativity with some saying that "blue lives matter" or "all lives matter." The fact is, however, the police are seldom on the receiving end of an attack, brutal beating, or shooting. This is not to say that the job of the police is not dangerous; it certainly is. It is hard to imagine a society where there was no law and order as well as an entity to enforce the laws. Without someone to keep the peace, there would be chaos, however, the objection is targeting someone because of their race or because of someone's racist views. The police have all the power and control and when racism, or bias is added, it becomes a dangerous recipe for African Americans, especially Black men.

For those who say "All Lives Matter" they seem to be working from the assumption that this nation is color blind. It certainly is not. People see color in the world and in the people they meet. Perhaps some are more accepting of others, but there are others who are not. Those people are racists and no matter what, they have preconceived notions and biases against people of color, and particularly African Americans, due to the legacy of slavery.

Some prominent athletes also protested about the violence against African Americans. One such person was Colin Kaepernick. Trump tweeted insults and said he should be fired. He caused such a stir that the NFL owners made new rules as to what players could do when the National Anthem is played. This controversy was highlighted with the Philadelphia Eagles. Trump had invited the Philadelphia Eagles to the White House, however, he subsequently disinvited them. Those players that he disinvited did not kneel during the opening ceremonies, but many said they were not coming for the photo opportunity with Trump. He then scheduled a military ceremony, instead.

It should be noted that being a professional athlete does not make one immune to attacks by the police. In 2018 two incidents involving Black professional athletes were publicized. Desmond Marrow, a former NFL player, was approached, slammed to the ground, and beaten unconscious according to reports. The police claimed he had a gun. NBA player, Sterling Brown, who played for the Milwaukee Bucks, was slammed to the ground in a parking lot. The police said he resisted arrest when they tried to put handcuffs on him. According to the article, Brown did nothing that warranted the harsh treatment that he received. Brown went on to say that this is what Blacks face in their community every day.

Cyber Security

The need for cyber security is recognized, so it is necessary to have surveillance. The attack on the World Trade Center on September 11, 2001, caused certain security precautions to be enacted. The question is how much security is too much before it infringes on the civil liberties of individual citizens? In addition, it was learned that the Chinese had hacked American businesses and government sites in 1999. Not only were the Chinese doing this, it was learned that in 2016, the Russians had hacked into the emails of the Democratic National Committee. The Russian cyber hacking caused the most problems. The Republicans did not want to believe this was happening. Reports from the FBI, CIA, and NSA could not be refuted, however. In this instance both Republicans and Democrats were mostly on the same page.

The results of the 2016 election made Donald Trump the 45th president. The Russian hacking and interference in the 2016 election is reported to have had the effect of assisting Trump in the election. It was also reported that the Russians targeted Blacks and other groups through the use of social media on issues related to African Americans. The Russians used fear mongering, disinformation, and other strategies to engender distrust and encourage division between racial and religious groups.

Summary

The 2016 U. S. presidential election represented fundamental changes in the social, legal, and political fortunes for not only African Americans, but many other peoples. Eligible voters neglected to exercise their right to vote in numbers comparably to 2008 and 2012. Voters lacked enthusiasm according to many writers. In terms of African Americans, they also did not feel that the Democratic Party had their best interest at heart. Some analysts stated that the Democrats failed to recognize that African Americans are not a monolithic group. Their vote cannot be taken for granted. It cannot be assumed that they will side with the Left, according to Troy (2016), a columnist.

In any case, Blacks were not drawn to Sanders either. Many shared some of the same concerns that he expressed about the economy, etc., but he did not know how to connect with them or empathize. Sanders was not on the same page as they were, mainly because he knew too little about African Americans. Unfortunately, other American citizens did not feel the Democrats or the Left had their backs either. They turned to Bernie Sanders and while they were enthusiastic about Sanders, it was not to be. In the end, Sanders threw his support to Clinton. Many of Sanders supporters were upset and some columnist say either voted for Trump or stayed at home.

The 2016 U.S. presidential election appears to have represented a major shift in the political parties that was fuelled by anti-establishment sentiment. Like Barack Obama who was a fresh face on the political landscape, Donald Trump appealed to the electorate who had grown weary of "business as usual" politics. It is doubtful that any old guard, traditional politician could have captured the presidency in 2016.

For African-Americans, the political climate of "making America great again" is viewed with scepticism and concern. There will have to be a genuine effort by Trump to attract minority voters. Sincere efforts will be needed to expand his base beyond staunch supporters of his "make America great again" philosophy. Bringing real life and meaning to the words "we the people" must include all the peoples of the United States regardless of race, religion, ethnicity, sexual orientation, or political ideology.

References

Aleem, Z. (2018, March). *Trump still wants Mexico to pay for the wall. He also wants tariffs. He can't have both.* Vox, Accessed 2018. https://www.vox.com/world/2018/3/12/17109282/trump-border-wall-mexico-tariffs

Ayers, W. (2016, November). *Donald Trump's electoral victory highlights the long-term challenges facing the GOP.* U.S. News & World Report. Accessed 2018. https://www.usnews.com/opinion/articles/2016-11-28/how-trump-lost-the-popular-vote-and-won-the-2016-election

Barabak, M. Z. (2017, November). Trump vs. Clinton: Why are we still obsessed a year later?" *LA Times.* Accessed 2018. http://www.latimes.com/politics/la-na-pol-trump-clinton-hangover-20171108-story.html

Barstow, D., Craig, S., & Buettner, R. (2018, October). Trump engaged in suspect tax schemes as he reaps riches from his father. *The New York Times.* Accessed 2018. https://www.nytimes.com/interactive/2018/10/02/us/politics/donald-trump-tax-schemes-fred-trump.html

Belson, K. (2018, April). Colin Kaepernick is not going away. *The New York Times.* Accessed 2018. https://www.nytimes.com/2018/08/31/sports/colin-kaepernick.html

Berson, S. (2018, April). I'm not even fighting back! Ex-NFL player thrown to ground during arrest, video shows. *Ledger-Enquirer.* Accessed 2018. https://www.ledger-enquirer.com/news/state/georgia/article209961214.html

Biography.com Editors. *Hillary Clinton.* Biography.com. Accessed 2018. https://www.biography.com/people/hillary-clinton-9251306

Biography.com Editors. *Bernie Sanders.* Biography.com. Accessed 2018. https://www.biography.com/people/bernie-sanders-02032016

Binelli, M. (2016, March). Hillary Clinton vs. Bernie Sanders: The good fight. *Rolling Stone.* Accessed 2018. https://www.rollingstone.com/culture/culture-news/hillary-clinton-vs-bernie-sanders-the-good-fight-177834/

Black Party affiliation. BlackDemographics.com. Accessed 2018. http://blackdemographics.com/culture/black-politics/

Black Lives Matter. (2013). Black Lives Matter. Accessed 2018. https://blacklivesmatter.com/about/

Brownstein, R. (2017, February 16). Federal anti-poverty programs primarily help the GOP's base: Republicans want to shrink government. But their core voters benefit from assistance, like the supplemental nutrition assistance program, the most. *The Atlantic.* Accessed 2018. https://www.theatlantic.com/politics/archive/2017/02/gop-base-poverty-snap-social-security/516861/.

Cillizza, C. (2018, June). *5 takeaways from the Supreme Court's monumental ruling in support of Trump's travel ban.* The Point, CNN. Accessed 2018. https://www.cnn.com/2018/06/26/politics/scotus-travel-ban-donald-trump/index.html.

CNN. *2016 Presidential campaign hacking fast facts.* CNN. https://www.cnn.com/2016/12/26/us/2016-presidential-campaign-hacking-fast-facts/index.html

Day, E. (2015, July). #BlackLivesMatter: The birth of a new civil rights movement. *The Guardian*. Accessed 2018. https://www.theguardian.com/world/2015/jul/19/blacklivesmatter-birth-civil-rights-movement

Dilanian, K., & Pollen, B. (2018, December). *Russians favoured Trump, targeted African Americans in election meddling reports say*. NBC News. Accessed 2018. https://www.nbcnews.com/politics/politics-news/russia-favored-trump-targeted-african-americans-election-meddling-reports-say-n948731.

Donald Trump. Biographynytimes. Accessed 2018.

Eilperin, J., & Camerson, D. (2017, March 24). Trump is rolling back Obama's legacy *The Washington Post*. https://www.washingtonpost.com/graphics/politics/trump-rolling-back-obama-rules/?utm_term=.860178a20959.

FiveThirtyEight. (2015, November). *The big issues of the 2016 campaign and where the presidential candidates stand on them*. FiveThirtyEight. Accessed 2018. https://fivethirtyeight.com/features/year-ahead-project/#part1.

Gambino, L., & Rushe, D. (2017, May). Republican healthcare plan will cost 23 million people their coverage, CBO says. *The Guardian*. Accessed 2019. https://www.theguardian.com/us-news/2017/may/24/trump-republican-healthcare-plan-cbo.

Goozner, M. (2017). The many consequences of repealing Obamacare. *Challenge*, 60:2, 122–140. DOI: 10.1080/05775132.2017.1294865.

History.com Editors. (2019, March 7). *Donald Trump*. HISTORY, www.history.com/topics/us-presidents/donald-trump

Johnson, J. (2016, April). Donald Trump to African American and Hispanic voters: 'What do you have to lose?' *Washington Post*. Accessed 2018. https://www.google.com/search?q=Donald+Trump+to+African+American+and+Hispanic+voters%3A+%E2%80%98What+do+you+have+to+lose%3F&rlz=1C1GGRV_enUS751US752&oq=Donald+Trump+to+African+American+and+Hispanic+voters%3A+%E2%80%98What+do+you+have+to+lose%3F&aqs=chrome..69i57j69i60l3.3263j0j9&sourceid=chrome&ie=UTF-8.

Krogstad, J. M., & Lopes, M. H. (2017, May). *Black voter turnout fell in 2016, even as a record number of Americans cast ballots*. Pew Research. Accessed 2018. http://www.pewresearch.org/fact-tank/2017/05/12/black-voter-turnout-fell-in-2016-even-as-a-record-number-of-americans-cast-ballots/.

Kurtzleben, D. (2017, August). *Here's how many Bernie Sanders supporters ultimately voted for Trump*. NPR. https://www.npr.org/2017/08/24/545812242/1-in-10-sanders-primary-voters-ended-up-supporting-trump-survey-finds.

Larsen, S. (2017). *Do members of Congress enjoy free health care?* Snopes. Accessed 2018. https://www.snopes.com/fact-check/members-congress-health-care.

Luhby, T. (2017). *Repealing Obamacare affects everyone*. CNNMoney. Accessed 2018. http://money.cnn.com/2017/01/02/news/economy/repealing-obamacare-health-insurance/index.html.

Luibrand, S. (2015, August). *How a death in Ferguson sparked a movement in America*. CBS News. Accessed 2018. https://www.cbsnews.com/news/how-the-black-lives-matter-movement-changed-america-one-year-later/

Mahler, J., & Eder, S. (2016). 'No Vacancies' for Blacks: How Donald Trump got his start, and was first accused of bias. *The New York Times*. Accessed 2018. https://www.nytimes.com/2016/08/28/us/politics/donald-trump-housing-race.html

Miller, H. (2016, December 15). Ta-Nehisi Coates perfectly explains how racism helped Donald Trump win. 'Donald Trump had to be rich and white. That was it,' he said. *The Huffington Post*. Accessed 2018. https://www.huffingtonpost.com/entry/ta-nehisi-coates-trump-racism_us_5852a68fe4b0732b82ff04f8

Miller, Z. J. (2015). The GOP's first big 2016 test: Fitting candidates on the debate stage. *Time*. Accessed 2018. http://time.com/3846448/republican-debates-2016/

Murse, T. (2018, January). *Why Donald Trump's companies went bankrupt*. Thoughtco. Accessed 2018. https://www.thoughtco.com/donald-trump-business-bankruptcies-4152019

O'Connor, L., & Marans, D. (2016). Here are 13 examples of Donald Trump being racist. *The Huffington Post*. Accessed 2018. https://www.huffingtonpost.com/entry/donald-trump-racist-examples_us_56d47177e4b03260bf777e83

PBS. (2016). *Trump won't accept election results if he loses as Clinton expands campaign into red states*. PBS. Accessed 2018. https://www.pbs.org/weta/washingtonweek/episode/trump-wont-accept-election-results-if-he-loses-clinton-expands-campaign-red-states.

Pelissier, J.-P. (2016). *China repeatedly hacked US, stole data on nukes, FBI & war plans—security report*. R T America. Accessed 2018. https://www.rt.com/usa/364614-us-china-cyberattack-targets/.

Price, E. (2018). Trump allegedly lied about his wealth to get on the Forbes 400 list in the 1980's. *Fortune*. http://fortune.com/2018/04/20/trump-lied-wealth-forbes-400-list/

Reilly, K. (2016). Here are all the times Trump insulted Mexico. *Time Magazine*. http://time.com/author/katie-reilly/.

Revesz, R. (2016). How the 2016 presidential election was won: The timeline, controversies and seats that led to the White House. *Independent*. https://www.independent.co.uk/news/world/americas/us-elections/presidential-election-2016-results-timeline-controversies-quotes-seats-maps-polls-quotes-a7398606.html.

Rogan, T. (2015). Meet the candidates: 20 republicans who are vying to run for president in 2016. *The Telegraph*. Accessed 2018. https://www.telegraph.co.uk/news/worldnews/us-election/11357233/Meet-the-candidates-20-Republicans-who-are-vying-to-run-for-president-in-2016.html

Rosario, R. (2018). Bodycam footage exposes authorities' excessive force against Milwaukee Bucks' Sterling Brown. *The Vibe*. https://www.vibe.com/2018/05/%20sterling-brown-arrested-milwaukee-police-excessive-force.

Ruffini, P. (2017). *Black voters aren't turning out for the Post-Obama Democratic Party*. FiveThirtyEight. Accessed 2018. https://fivethirtyeight.com/features/black-voters-arent-turning-out-for-the-post-obama-democratic-party/.

Shane, S. (2017). These are the ads Russia bought on Facebook in 2016. *The New York Times*. Accessed 2018. https://www.nytimes.com/2017/11/01/us/politics/russia-2016-election-facebook.html.

Shanthi, R. (2016). *Every president who won the election but lost the popular vote*. Benzinga. Accessed 2018. https://www.benzinga.com/general/education/16/12/8776577/every-president-who-won-the-election-but-lost-the-popular-vote

Siddiqui, S. (2018). Mexico President hits back after Trump revives claim country will pay for wall. *The Guardian*. Accessed 2018. https://www.theguardian.com/us-news/2018/may/29/mexico-president-trump-border-wall-twitter

Sidner, S., & Simon, M. (2015). *The rise of Black Lives Matter: Trying to break the cycle of violence and silence*. CNN. Accessed 2018. https://www.cnn.com/2015/12/28/us/black-lives-matter-evolution/index.html

Silver, N. (2017). *The Comey letter probably cost Clinton the election: So why won't the media admit as much?* FiveThirtyEight. Accessed 2018. https://fivethirtyeight.com/features/the-comey-letter-probably-cost-clinton-the-election/

Sommerlad, J. (2018, October). Fred Trump: How the US president's father built the property empire that spawned his son's billions. *Independent*. Accessed 2018. https://www.independent.co.uk/news/world/americas/us-politics/fred-trump-tax-dodge-donald-inheritance-us-president-new-york-real-estate-queens-kkk-a8566421.html

Schwartz, T. (2017). I wrote 'The art of the deal' with Trump. His self-sabotage is rooted in his past. *The Washington Post*. Accessed 2018. https://www.washingtonpost.com/posteverything/wp/2017/05/16/i-wrote-the-art-of-the-deal-with-trump-his-self-sabotage-is-rooted-in-his-past/

Troy, G. (2016, March). Why Black voters don't feel the Bern. *Politico*. Accessed 2018. https://www.politico.com/magazine/story/2016/03/why-black-voters-dont-feel-the-bern-213707

Weigal, D. (2017). Sanders, Democrats rally thousands across the country to save Obamacare. *The Chicago Tribune*. Accessed 2018. http://www.chicagotribune.com/news/nationworld/politics/ct-bernie-sanders-michigan-healthcare-rally-20170115-story.html

Review

I. Checking What You Have Read

1. Identify the major issues that Americans faced at the time when Obama made his bid to become president.
2. What issues might a person born into a biracial family experience?
3. Explain the resistance to President Obama's efforts to lead the Congress.
4. Explain the reasons that the Republican Congress wanted to block the Affordable Care Act. Who are the people covered under it?
5. How did the issue of race and politics impact the Obama presidency?
6. Adults have an important influence on a child's social growth and intellectual development. What influences did Barack Obama's grandparents, mother, AND father have on his education pursuits and civic activism?
7. What were the reasons for the protests after the 2016 presidential election?
8. The experiences of young college students often define their social, education, psychological, and professional pathways throughout life. Compare and contrast Obama's experiences at Occidental, Columbia, and Harvard. What impact did each of these schools have on his later life?
9. What mistakes did both Clinton and Sanders make with regard to African American voters?
10. What do you think President Obama's legacy is as it relates to American politics and young voters? (Justify your position with research evidence.)
11. The election of President Obama (2008) has been described as a transformative political event. Besides being the first African American president, what two things were different about the 2008 presidential campaign that changed politics forever?
12. Explain what is meant by a progressive insurgent and what was the appeal of Bernie Sanders to younger college age voters?
13. Compare the Obama campaigns to the Trump campaigns. How could these two candidates appeal to some of the same voters?
14. The 2016 U.S. presidential race was marked by three vastly different candidates and political views. Discuss the three major candidates, and their appeal to voters.

15. Pick two issues from the 2016 campaigns and discuss how Trump and Clinton are different in either perspective and/or approach.
16. What issues related to race were relevant to African American voters in the 2016 U.S. presidential campaign?
17. Young and minority voters came out in record numbers to support Barack Obama in 2008 and 2012. What factors seem to influence these key democratic groups from being excited during the 2016 election?
18. Foreign powers may have played a role in cyber attacks that influenced voters and the election. Discuss two tactics used by foreign powers to sway the election results. How were African Americans targeted?
19. If the 2016 presidential election were held today, which of the three major candidates (Clinton, Sanders, or Trump) would be elected? Has the country become more polarized in support of opposition to any of these candidate? Explain your response.

II. On Your Own

1. Trace the route that Obama took for the presidential Inauguration. Compare it to the one that Lincoln took.
2. Which former presidents are Obama compared to and explain which you think he most resembled? Construct a timeline and place each president on it. Add to the timeline each American event or issue that was occurring at the time of each presidency on it.

The Browning of America and Its Implications

The New Demographics of a Changing Population

The United States' population is changing in big ways. Most noticeably, racial, cultural, and ethnic diversity is increasing. During the early years of the country, the nation's citizens were almost exclusively of Anglo-European ancestry. Peoples of color were not granted citizenship, either by blood or birth. Today, America's racial, ethnic, and cultural makeup is a mixture of different traditions, languages, faiths, and ancestries that represent the four corners of the globe. America now includes people from Central America, South America, Asia, the Middle East and Africa. The United States is a more diverse country than ever before.

Racial and ethnic diversity brings many benefits to all peoples. However, rapid changes brought on by racial diversity is unsettling to some. Fear and social-economic anxiety may be experienced by both members of minority and majority communities (Yetman, 1999). Rapid changes in ethnic demographics can potentially create tribalism based on racial identities.

According to the United States Census Bureau, people of color are becoming the new majority (Frey, 2018; U.S. Census Bureau, 2008). The U.S. Census Bureau (2008) has revised its racial population estimates. Since

2010 individuals can report their racial/ethnic identity in new ways. There is a new category for multi-racial individuals. The 2010 census report reflects the fact that the White population is growing older, but the birth rate is down among Whites.

New racial demographic changes have created a sense of hysteria for some who are part of the "fringes" of American politics according to Herbert Gans, a sociologist (2017). Fringe political activists exist on both the "left" and "right" of American politics and in other countries as well. The U.S. Census Bureau (2018) projects that by 2045 America will no longer be majority White. Further, it reports there are more children of color, age 10 and under, than White children. Reports from the U.S. Census Bureau (2018) predicted that by 2045, the population will be 49.9 percent White; 24.6 percent Hispanic; 13.1 percent Black; 7.8 percent Asian; and 3.8 percent multi-racial. Already the majority is the minority in California, Texas, New Mexico, Nevada, and Hawaii.

The country is changing and will look markedly different in just a generation. Extremists tend to either recklessly support open borders or exclusive immigration policies as a response to changing demographics. Their hysteria has been echoed in the news media and throughout individual social media venues. Some citizens have adopted the rhetoric of extremist pundits and echoed their sentiments in disparaging and antagonistic actions, as well as uncivilized behaviors.

The coming demographic changes will not be readily noticeable for the older age groups, like the baby boomers. The impact of this demographic change will not likely affect their group. Their lives have established routines within mostly homogenous institutional circles, such as church, work, communities, and social networks. Although not exclusive to one race, people tend to associate and feel most comfortable around folk who are like themselves. For baby boomers, diversity and cross-cultural interactions may be merely limited to business transactions or other quick encounters. Those are fleeting experiences and are not substantive enough to impact most baby boomers in any significant way.

The population change will become noticeable in the younger groups who are more cosmopolitan and have greater interaction with people of different races and ethnicities. Millennials have larger, more meaningful relationships with diverse social groups and experiences inclusive of people of other races. As a result of these social experiences, voting preferences will likely be more progressive. The wide appeal of Senator Bernie Sanders to young voters of all races is indicative of two things: first, younger folk have more inclusive ideas; and second, they are more likely to be more independent of the mainstream political ideas. Frey (2018) calls this younger group, generation "Z-Plus."

What does this mean for America's future? Herbert Gans (2017) says, it is panic, especially for older, more conservative Whites. Writers such as Frey (2018) are concerned that this new reality might be manipulated by public officials to suit their political agenda. The fact remains that, no matter the color, the Z-Plus generation will represent the near future. They will be contributing to the economy including to social security for years to come. They will also be voting based upon independent party affiliations.

The New Civil Rights Challenges

A tribal mentality, with its ensuing conversation, has emerged and is also present in the issues of race, economics, and class. From a historical view, Vance (2016) wrote that from the very founding of the country, America has never known how to approach race. He stated that of all the nations in the world, only the United States has attempted to construct a nation of tribes, not just a nation-state. Within this nation are included Blacks and Whites, Christians, Jews, and Muslims, and an ever-growing group of other minorities.

Additionally, Vance (2016) further divides these tribes into classes. In America's early history, eventually two social-economic classes with strong racial overtones developed. The first group was comprised of poor Blacks who were former slaves. The second group was comprised of poor Whites from Appalachia. Both of these groups belonged to the underclass. These groups predate the founding of America.

Vance (2016) describes the stages that both working classes of Whites and Blacks went through to build their lives, economically, socially, and politically. Economically, the industrialization of the North provided both Whites and Blacks new opportunities for employment. For Blacks this was essentially during the Great Migration (1915–1960) when many Blacks moved from the South to escape sharecropping and other issues such as political disenfranchisement (Christenson, 2007). Many people obtained employment in the factories in the North. African Americans and Whites made economic progress because of the work opportunities available.

Opportunities were marginally better for poor White Appalachian migrants to make economic gains. This was because they did not have to fight legalized and systemic discrimination against them. At one time the White working class was doing better than the working poor of other minority groups. However, they faced the scorn of urban and suburban Whites. Only a small percentage of Whites thought the next generation would fare better. The White working class was pessimistic about their economic future and generational class mobility.

The 1960s Civil Rights Movement was seen as an attempt to address the economic circumstances of Blacks. Although Blacks were hampered by legal discrimination, both groups, White and Black, were able to advance into the middle-class. The gains made by Whites, however, still outpaced the gains made by Blacks during this period.

Vance (2016) writes that the two groups focused on different political agendas. Working-class Whites focused on economic development and taught their children to not trust the White elites or richer Whites. Working-class Blacks focused on breaking down discriminatory barriers. During the 1950s and 1960s, not only was there a Black middle-class, they were mostly voting Republican. This trend continued until Barry Goldwater demonstrated that he was against civil rights legislation.

The financial crisis of 2007 in the United States was devastating for many Americans (Cappelli et al., 2018). The crisis had the effect of nullifying the economic gains that many Americans had made, from all groups. The Recession of 2007 was caused by stock values falling; and elaborate financial investment schemes that destroyed major parts of the housing market. Furthermore, complex relationships with banks and large financial institutions failed because of lax government regulations and oversight.

Not everyone has stocks, bonds, or an investment portfolio to secure their long-term financial well-being into retirement. However, for those people who work for companies that have retirement plans, the loss of investment funds could mean a delay in retirement. Others, who may have been ready to retire, might be forced to find second careers late in life. This could impact whether families could afford to send their children to college. Then there are those who are not at the points of retiring or attempting to attend college, but people who are just beginning their jobs and careers. All these groups have long-term financial security concerns.

An economic challenge facing American workers is securing long-term, living wage jobs which are becoming more divided by class and race. According to sociologist William Julius Wilson (1996), Americans are becoming more divided by class. One group will blame another for their economic woes, or they blame immigrants, who some feel, are taking the good jobs away from White middle-aged male workers. This is called scape-goating. The increase in automation in various industries and global competition is the real culprit for job losses. Unfortunately, there are few successful retraining programs to assist people in finding long-term living wage employment. Some writers, such as Packer (2011, 2013) state that income inequality and economic stratification threatens our democracy.

Packer (2011, 2013) also states that Americans are increasingly being separated along the lines of class. This means they are separated by the schools they attend, whom they marry, how long they live, and other socio-economic factors. Packer (2011, 2013) asks how are people able to meaningfully interact, in a constructive manner. This is because people live such different lives. Packer continues by stating that the once held idea that people can become anything no longer exists. The challenges are more difficult for African Americans and people of color to rise above their social-economic status from birth. The social-class divide and its impact also tends to be multi-generational.

The racial and socioeconomic divide in American society is growing. It is most evident in minority communities. Even questions as to certain rights guaranteed by the Constitution are challenged. Unlike communist governments, America is a country where people of different groups (e.g., ethnic, cultural, religious) have attempted to forge a democracy based on the promise of opportunities for education, work, religion, and individualism to improve their social position.

The challenge for America is making sure that all its citizens enjoy the same rights, protections, and liberties equally. Historically, African Americans and other minorities fought hard using law suits, economic boycotts, protests, marches, and voting to get fairer laws and equality of treatment. Modelling the examples of African Americans, other racial groups have used similar tactics to improve their opportunities in housing, schooling, employment, and access to health care. However, disparities based upon race and ethnicity remains. While it is doubtful that government can eliminate all the problems that come about because of race, public policy can be a useful tool to improve the conditions of the less fortunate.

In America, government policies, regulations and laws are supposed to be based on the will of the people. Politicians serve in public office to represent the people of their district, state, and county. Elected officials are accountable to the public and all the laws. That is not the case in Russia and other countries that have autocratic governments. In Russia, China, and other parts of the world, governments do not allow dissent or criticism of its leaders especially by the citizens or media/press.

In America dissent and criticism of various government policies takes place by the press and by citizens. It is a First Amendment right. Some American leaders attempt to paint the media as dishonest and dismiss citizen dissent as being un-American. Without robust public debates, access to a free press, the protections of "due process of law" and voting, democracy for all Americans is threatened. Even those without power, prestige, or high-status pedigree are supposed to be treated with the same rights.

In 2013, the Robert's Supreme Court significantly changed the provisions of the 1965 Voting Rights Act and how it would be applied. This Act was originally put in place to prevent states from instituting voting laws that would make it difficult for some citizens to vote. The Voting Rights Act of 1965 required that nine southern states and a number of other local counties and municipalities in other states get prior approval before changing their voting laws. The nine states were Alabama, Alaska, Arizona, Georgia, Louisiana, Mississippi, South Carolina, Texas, and Virginia. It also included Brooklyn and the Bronx in New York. In the Decision, *Shelby v. Holder*, the Supreme Court ruled that it no longer needed to keep all of the safeguards in place. The argument was made that racial minorities no longer faced as many voting barriers (*Shelby v. Holder*).

Immediately after the 2013 Supreme Court ruling, new state voting laws were passed that imposed stringent qualifications and restrictions on voter eligibility. For example, Texas announced that a previously blocked voter identification law would go into effect. North Carolina followed with their own law (Churchill et al., 2008). Former Supreme Court Justice Ruth Bader Ginsberg voted against the new guidelines in the Shelby case of 2013. She wrote in her dissent that the Voting Rights Act had challenged not only the barriers to first-generation but also second-generation voter access. The law prevented provisions that promoted racial gerrymandering and other tactics that denied the right to vote to Blacks. Ginsberg stated that the Court was making a grievous error with its decision to override key provisions of the previous rulings (Liptak, 2013).

Allegations of Black and Latino voter suppression were lodged during the 2016 and 2020 Presidential elections. Reports by the news outlets found significant barriers that prevented these two groups from voting. When Trump spoke about voter fraud, the only fraud that occurred were the tactics that the Republican Party uses to prevent people of color from voting. Numerous investigations into voter fraud have consistently found few instances of people illegally voting in U.S. elections at any level of government.

Government leaders tend to be from wealthy, powerful (elite) backgrounds. They have manipulated their way into powerful positions through political networks and financial support of causes or candidates (Covert, 2017; Knight, 2018). In many ways, the rule of law, protocols, and concern for the "general welfare" of all people is secondary to the interest of the powerful elite class. This political elite class guides American social institutions, educational systems, commercial regulations, and economic and international relations. It can be compared to a powerful political dynasty. With the exception of a few 20th-century presidents, most have come from money, power, prestige, or social privilege (Maranzani, 2017). This has had the effect of unduly influencing the American political processes. Left behind, with limited voices, are African Americans, Latinos, and other marginalized groups because they have no entry into the corridors of money, power, media, and influence.

Historically, African Americans, Latinos, Native Americans, and other racial minorities have seen their interests (waylaid) or ignored by politicians. The political elites have only two concerns. The first concern is about international business competition, or economic prosperity for the wealthy. The second concern is about domestic security. Domestic security includes foreign voter tampering, domestic terrorism, biological warfare, cyber infrastructure security, border defense, as well as law and order.

Since "9/11", these political elites have been preoccupied with domestic security, as it relates to terrorism. Protecting the United States against terrorists and cyber hacking is of course important. Neither one of these overarching agendas, however, focus on the needs of people of color, and their disenfranchisement. In other words, there is a lack of concern for the preservation and expansion of the American ideals of opportunity and freedom for all people. The new face of racism is the basic disinterest of the needs of minorities, who are not rich, powerful, or White.

Popular Vote vs. Electoral College

Considering all the negative media associated with the 2016 presidential campaign, one could ask how is it possible that a "fringe" candidate can become president despite losing the national vote count? The answer is easy: one only needs to win the Electoral College vote. In 2016, Trump lost the popular vote to Hillary Clinton. Donald Trump became president because he won the most Electoral College delegate count. When people vote, they are actually casting ballots for state delegates to vote on their behalf. In other words, the popular vote is used by each state's representative delegates to determine how to vote. The Electoral College vote is composed of 538 electors, of which 270 are needed to win. A similar situation, involving the popular and electoral vote, happened in the 2000 presidential race between Al Gore and George W. Bush. Gore won the popular vote; however, Bush became president because he obtained the most Electoral College delegate votes after winning Florida by 537 votes.

Two important lessons can be learned from the presidential elections of 2000, 2016, and 2020. First, democracy, civil liberties, rights, and the general welfare of all Americans requires citizen participation. Not voting equates to having "no voice" in governmental affairs, policies, and practices. Secondly, every individual vote is important in every state because of the Electoral College's use of "super delegates" which was key to Biden's 2020 presidential campaign victory. State elections are governed by popular vote count which is a better form of direct elections. They are as important as the national elections if not more so.

Post-Obama Neo-Conservative Policies and Practices

The New National Conservatism

The freedom of speech and press are how Americans learn what the government is doing. The freedom of press keeps the spotlight on important civic and civil issues. The freedom of speech allows citizens and politicians to vent their anger and disapproval towards opposition and members of the press. Some politicians, news sources, and activists do not value the First Amendment. There have been presidents who were skeptical of the free press. Some presidents have called the free press enemies of the people because of criticisms by journalists. However, they reluctantly tolerated journalists and the press. This type of behavior goes against the Constitution's guarantees of freedom of press and speech.

Freedom of the press and free speech have remained a vital part of African American's struggle for greater civil rights, women's rights, and opposition to political corruption. Minority news outlets provide a more comprehensive and in-depth coverage of issues from a different vantage than mainstream press outlets. In fact, the Black press was created largely because mainstream newspapers gave little or no coverage to issues related to civil rights, lynchings, school integration, and the freedom struggles of African Americans (Kelly & Greyno, 2021; Teresa, 2018; Crowder, 2010).

The oldest Black newspaper was *Freedom's Journal* that was started by John Russwurm and Samuel Cornish back in 1827. There were other Black newspapers such as the *North Star* by Frederick Douglass. More contemporary newspapers include the *Chicago Defender*, the *Pittsburgh Courier* and the *Criterion* in Buffalo, New York that started around 1925.

Voter Suppression Practices

Some politicians are correct when they say the "system is rigged." Partisan gerrymandering is a way to "rig" the voting system. Gerrymandering consists of drawing state and congressional district lines so that they benefit a particular party. As was stated, the Electoral College casts votes for the presidential candidates. If politicians draw the district voting lines of states in such a way that ensures a certain party wins, it defeats the purpose of each person having their vote count for the candidate of their choice (Gumbel, 2017). Both the Democratic and the Republican Parties have engaged in gerrymandering. However, neo-conservative Republican leaders have mastered the technique of using the rigged system to their advantage (Churchill et al., 2008; Tausanovitch & Root, 2020).

The Republicans gained a majority in the Congress during the term of President Obama. Even though the GOP suffers from high disapproval ratings, according to some polls, they still maintain power. As noted by some researchers, despite the Democrats winning vote tallies, they often lose elections because of gerrymandering. Both parties fear losing their power, influence, and political control of elections. Gerrymandering creates perpetual party victories for decades. These politicians have little fear of losing their office no matter how badly they govern (Newkirk, 2018; Tausanovitch & Root, 2020).

Gerrymandering has become so extensive that challenges have been brought to the Courts. Pennsylvania, for example, was ordered by the state's Supreme Court to redraw its congressional lines because it was so blatantly politically biased against Democrats and Black voters (Hananel, 2020; Tausanovitch & Root, 2020). In other cases, such as in Wisconsin and Maryland, the issue of gerrymandering has even made its way from the states' courts to the Supreme Court of the United States. Voter ID laws along with redistricting have the net effect of suppressing Black and minority voters (Churchhill et al., 2013; Tausanovitch & Root, 2020).

Traditionally, gerrymandering has better served Republican and Conservative candidates more than Democrats and Liberals during legislative elections. It did not provide an advantage for Donald Trump in the 2020 presidential election outcomes. He lost the 2020 popular vote and delegate count vote of the electoral college. Despite Trump's loss, the Republicans gained seats in the House of Representatives, the Senate, and control of more state legislatures (Montanaro, 2020; Skelley, 2020). This was primarily the function of "down-ballot" voting trends. The phenomena of "down-balloting" is where citizens vote for local and state candidates with greater loyalty than for national office seekers (Gabriel, 2020). Republicans have traditionally had stronger political networks with state and local governments. The result of "down-balloting" is the ability of the party to influence local legislative elections and ballot initiatives.

While over 70 million people voted for Trump in 2020, those votes were offset by the large number of Black and Brown voters (Deane & Gramlich, 2020). It should be noted that at the beginning of 2020, the United States and the world was experiencing a health pandemic. It was known as the coronavirus or Covid-19. Although the virus influenced how candidates campaigned, Americans voted in record numbers. Unlike the 2016 election, people of color and many other voters were willing to stand in long lines, despite the risk posed by the pandemic. Biden supporters used mail-in ballots, early voting, and absentee ballots more effectively than Republicans to capture the White House in 2020.

Trump vehemently disputed the election results and did not understand how he could have lost, since other Republican candidates won other offices. Early in the 2020 campaign season, Trump had expressed concerns about the efficacy of mail-in ballots. Trump fervently believed that there would be widespread fraud—especially if mail-in ballots were universally used. Mail-in, absentee, and early voting practices, however, were viewed by public health and state election officials as a safeguard for preventing Covid-19 transmissions and a way to make voting more accessible to constituents. Despite all his claims of potential voter fraud, and rigged machines, Trump, himself, voted by mail from Florida in 2020.

In the days following the 2020 presidential election, Trump attempted to disenfranchise voters by deploying lawyers to swing state in an effort invalidate the election results. They brought more than sixty legal challenges based on unfounded allegations of widespread fraud (Ngangura, 2020; Harriot, 2020; Rutenberg & Corasaniti, 2020). On December 8, 2020, the Supreme Court refused his lawyers an expedited appeal to weigh in on the mail-in and absentee ballot counting from Pennsylvania (Liptak, 2019.) A few days later, the Supreme Court refused to hear another case to overturn the election brought by Texas in conjunction with other states and Republican legislators (Totenberg & Sprunt, 2020).

Nationwide, Trump's lawyers focused on metropolitan areas and cities with large numbers of Blacks and Latino/as, such as Detroit, Philadelphia, Milwaukee, and others (Hill, 2020). It is noted that Trump's lawyers did not bring similar allegations of fraud against White communities where Trump lost ground compared with the 2016 vote count (Fahrenthold, 2020; Reuters et al., 2020). None of these legal challenges were successful in court. Even the Justice Department, Homeland Security Cyber Security Division, and FBI concluded that there was no evidence of system-wide fraud that would have impacted the 2020 presidential outcome (Lucas, 2020; Goldman & Kanno-Youngs, 2020; Johnson, 2020). Despite overwhelming evidence of no fraudulent voting, or biased state practices, Donald Trump maintained that he won the 2020 presidential election.

Voter suppression is a threat to democracy and individual rights. It is the new face of Jim Crow. It is about getting and holding power (DeRienzo, 2019). In 2020, with the coronavirus pandemic raging in America, instead of assisting voters, Republicans set up many roadblocks to limit voting. Some Republicans even stated that their goal was to make voting harder for some groups, not more fair (DeRienzo, 2019). After Georgia elected Raphael Warnock (African American) and Jon Ossoff (Jewish), Georgia implemented a slate of new voter protocols, procedures, and by-laws that would impact minority voter eligibility.

Post-Obama Political Era: Trump Versus Biden

It is documented that the Trump administration was characterized by divisive politics, a corrosion of the rule of law, and corruption to the extent that he was impeached (Fandos & Shear, 2019). This is in stark contrast to the Obama's presidency of inclusion and a philosophy of shared vision collectively achieved. According to some writers, Trump's presidency was flawed from the outset. Writers, such as Kaufman and Greenberg point to Trump's only asset of celebrity status, which turned out to be his fatal flaw (Harrison, 2020; Thomas, 2020). In addition to not having any experience, it was reported that Trump had no desire to learn nor read about complex policies and practices of government administration (Graham, 2018). Trump's only knowledge of executive level skills, organizational management, and leadership was based on a series of failed businesses. A prerequisite for serving in his administration seemed to have been loyalty to him. Government experience and an understanding of public policy were not a priority as was evidenced by his initial picks for secretary of state, Department of Education, Department of Housing and Urban Development, communications director, as well as other key high-level positions. Goldsmith (2017) stated that there has never been such an ill-informed president in modern history.

Trump's troubling behavior toward Blacks was well documented before he became president. It continued to be manifested throughout his term. With the exception of Dr. Ben Carson, and Omarosa Manigault Newman—for a brief moment, Trump had no persons of color in his cabinet or as close advisors. Trump's lack of empathy coupled with his limited world view—which some might call xenophobic—first led to the ban on immigrants from majority Muslim countries entering America. Later, Trump's policies led to the separation of children from their parents at the border with Mexico (Reuters et al., 2020). An integrated understanding of race, history, slavery, and families would have been a benefit when developing the migrant border policies.

Trump bragged about how much he had done for Blacks. While he signed the First Step Act, a bipartisan bill introduced by Senator Cory Booker, he took steps to undermine it (Rashawn & Gilbert, 2020; McCaskill, 2020; Frey, 2020). Trump signed a bill to renew funding for Historically Black Colleges and Universities, but that wasn't new. This is an on-going 10-year renewal bill. President Obama signed it during his two terms in office. Despite these behaviors, he claims to have done more for African Americans than any president since Abraham Lincoln (Glanton, 2020).

One of Trump's goals was to rollback all the legislative action and policies of the Obama administration. Trump did not act alone. He was assisted by the Republican senators. The Republican Party became the Trump party. The Republican Senate ushered in a slate of conservative of federal judges to the Supreme Court, Circuit Court, and Appeals Court. Not one Judge appointment was Black. The Trump Republican Party appointed 53 Appellate Judges and 3 Supreme Court Justices. These are long term appointments and, in the case of the Supreme Court, are life-long appointments (Ashbrook, 2020; Farivar, 2020). These judges and Justices will have a profound effect on women's rights, health care, education, voting rights, and civil rights for decades to come.

Conservative judges tend to issue legal opinions that negatively affect women, Blacks and people of color more profoundly than Whites (Sye, 2020). The impact of these conservative judicial opinions causes people of color to rely more on federal legislative measures to address social, political, economic, and legal disparities. Efforts to have legislatures make profound changes are extremely difficult, costly, and lengthy.

Another issue that the Trump administration championed that could adversely impact people of color was related to the 2020 Census count. The president attempted to exclude people from the U.S. Census who were considered illegal immigrants (Sherman, 2020; Schneider & Sherman, 2020). It was reported that there were already "irregularities" with the count that would result in an undercount of millions of people. The effect of such an undercount could lower the congressional seats for those states that have high numbers of illegal immigrants. Many of those state have Democratic governors. Moreover, federal monies to state and local government for schools, health services, roads, infrastructure projects, block grants, and discretionary and formulary spending on mandated projects would negatively be impacted. Poorer, older, and communities of color are harmed most by Census undercounts. Trump's assault on the Census may have far reaching consequences for years to come.

President Joseph Biden: Diversity Without Division

In contrast to Donald Trump, Joe Biden has a more expansive view on race and diversity. Although it is not comparable to President Obama's record and strategies to address race and diversity, it is more inclusive than Trump's. Joseph R. Biden's path to become president was riddled with political challenges. He served in the United States Senate for seven terms. Biden was first elected to serve as Delaware's senator in 1972, and he remained in that post until becoming vice president for Barack Obama in 2008. Biden's first presidential campaign was in 1984, then again in 1988, and 2008. Those bids to capture the Democratic Party nomination did not generate significant followers.

During Biden's time in the Senate, he fostered a political position as a centrist Democrat. Unfortunately, Biden's record on race issues, related to public policy, was tarnished. One was his opposition to forced busing. Another issue was partnering legislation with segregationist Jesse Helms to prevent the federal government from providing the racial composition data of school districts. Biden also sponsored legislation that would prevent the federal government from withholding monies from school districts that did not integrate (Levitz, 2019). The bills failed to gain the needed support to advance to through both chambers of Congress (Levitz, 2019). The net impact of these types of legislative moves would have made it easier for school districts to resist integration. During the 2020 presidential campaign, Biden clarified his earlier positions on school integration and busing by making the point that school integration was good, but busing was the wrong way to achieve it.

Another contradiction on Biden's record related to race relations and public policy was his sponsorship of the 1994 Biden "Crime Bill" (Levitz, 2019; Rashawn, 2020). The legislation called for harsher, longer jail sentences, and expanded the number and types of crimes eligible for capital punishment. It also limited prison education programs and increased prison populations exponentially according to the Brennan Center (Levitz, 2019).

Biden's 1994 "Crime Bill" essentially targeted Blacks, minority offenders, and poor defendants by reclassifying certain crimes to carry harsher offenses. While it is difficult to determine if Biden's senate legislative history was driven by race-based ideas, it definitely impacted people of color more profoundly. Senator Kamala Harris made this point during one of the 2020 Democratic candidate debates (Stevens, 2019).

The Biden 2020 presidential campaign was different than his past efforts. He had not done well in the first set of primaries. The endorsement by Senator James Clyburn, from South Carolina, uplifted his faltering campaign. Once Biden received that endorsement, he became the democratic nominee front runner.

Three things seem to have helped him win the presidency: (1) voter recognition and a practical understanding of national elections based on his experience as Barack Obama's running mate; (2) the selection of a female, vice president of color; and (3) a political theme that called for a healing of the "heart and soul of America" in lieu of the divisiveness that emerged during the Trump years. Biden pledged to build a cabinet and leadership team that mirrored the country's racial and ethnic composition. Creating an American society and fostering policies that are designed to recognize our nation's diversity, and use those differences of talents, traditions, and experiences to make America better for everyone is a throwback to President Obama's campaigns.

There are some new realities that American leaders and institutions will need to prepare for in the years to come. Among the new realities that confront the nation is a reckoning about issues of racial and ethnic inclusion, and respectful appreciation for diversity. America was built on the ideals of equality of opportunity. The ability of America to embrace diversity beyond food and culture will test the resilience of the nation. The nation is at a testing point as it grows into various hues of black, brown, red, yellow and white to find a way to become a more inclusive nation of the people, by the people, for the people that will not perish from the earth. The Road Ahead (Chapter 21) will present many challenges for leaders of business, government, religions, and other important American institutions.

The United States has endured for nearly three centuries because of its people's profound belief in the country's core values and ideas. There is a belief that leaders can meaningfully navigate the nation toward higher aspirations. Presidents Lincoln, Truman, Eisenhower, Johnson, and Obama were able to make significant strides towards racial inclusion despite overwhelming obstacles and odds. President Biden will have challenges that are no less formidable. The struggle to create a more perfect "Union" after the Trump era will ultimately be a test for all Americans to broaden their minds, hearts, and tribalistic tendencies.

Summary

Apart from Native peoples, America's ancestral roots lie outside its natural and geo-political borders. Be it Europe, Asia, South America, Africa, or some other distant land, the peoples of America and the United States are a mix of different cultures, customs, languages, traditions, beliefs, and have other distinct differences. It is those differences, coupled with laws and beliefs, that have made America's democracy possible since 1789. The U.S. Constitution starts with the words "We the people." Today that includes an array of peoples who were not originally envisioned but who are now an integral part of America's national historical narrative about inclusion and contribution to the country. The United States is changing. It is becoming much more racially diverse. While diversity may be a challenge to some, it can and does benefit the nation.

Historically, the nation has endured several episodes of extremist thinking. The country wavers between progressive liberalism and staunch conservatism. Social and political movements related to race are the most "polarizing" areas of American democracy. At the heart of America's debate about race and immigration is the issue of what the country stands for, what it is becoming as a people, and how it will respond to the needs of creating a more inclusive society.

The coming racial and ethnic changes will signal the end of an America of a bygone era. The mid-century notions of White suburbia are long since gone. The United States of America is growing and changing to reflect a global, multicultural society. It is evolving based on a natural evolution that is representative of the peoples of all 50 states and territories. The continued growth of American democracy will only be made possible through three things. First, there must be an informed public that understands more than sound bites and social media propaganda. Second, ordinary citizens' participation in the political process through a grassroots activism and voting is necessary. Third, constructive civil engagement and thoughtful, meaningful discourse with peoples unlike ourselves is needed. America's greatness lies in its ability to grow and change for the better for all its peoples—regardless of skin color (black, white, brown, yellow or red). America is supposed to be one nation that strives to be indivisible by race, based on the premise of equality and justice for all.

References

Ashbrook, C. C. (2020, March 1). *The Trump Legacy and Its Consequences*. The Belfer Center. https://www.belfercenter.org/publication/trump-legacy-and-its-consequences

Attiah, K. (2020, November 24). The health-care system has failed Black Americans. No wonder many are hesitant about a vaccine. *The Washington Post*. https://www.washingtonpost.com/opinions/2020/11/24/health-care-system-has-failed-black-americans-no-wonder-many-are-hesitant-about-vaccine/

Barrow, B. (2020, June). *Election chaos renews focus on Gutted Voting Rights Act*. AP News. https://apnews.com/article/f3beb94b851e2d413b2f5f3e18719606

Bennett, B. (2020, May). Trump's divisive instincts helped him win the White House. Where will they take America now? *Time*. https://time.com/5845714/trumps-divisive-racial-politics-floyd-protests/

Bobo, L. D. (2011). Somewhere between Jim Crow & post-racialism: Reflections on the racial divide in America today. *Daedalus, 140*(2), 11–36. JSTOR, www.jstor.org/stable/23047449

Borchers, C. (2016). On freedom of the press: Donald Trump wants to make America like England again. *The Washington Post*. https://www.washingtonpost.com/news/the-fix/wp/2016/10/24/on-freedom-of-the-press-donald-trump-wants-to-make-america-like-england-again/?utm_term=.ca088e0843ca

Boule, J. (2017, September). The wealth gap between Whites and Blacks is widening: The myth of racial equality is having real and devastating consequences. *Slate*. http://www.slate.com/articles/news_and_politics/politics/2017/09/the_wealth_gap_between_whites_and_blacks_is_widening.html

Brownstein, R. (2017, February). Federal anti-poverty programs primarily help the GOP's base: Republicans want to shrink government. But their core voters benefit from assistance, like the Supplemental Nutrition Assistance Program, the most. *The Atlantic*. https://www.theatlantic.com/politics/archive/2017/02/gop-base-poverty-snap-social-security/516861/

Callaway, D. (2018, May). Press freedom is under attack. Don't wait for a journalist to be murdered to protest. *USA Today*. https://www.usatoday.com/story/opinion/2018/05/03/press-freedom-donald-trump-journalists-column/572668002/

Cappelli, P., Barankay, I., & Lewin, D. (2018, September). *How the Great Recession changed American workers*. Wharton University. https://knowledge.wharton.upenn.edu/article/great-recession-american-dream/

Christensen, S. (2007, December 6). *The Great Migration (1915–1960)*. BlackPast, 11 May 2019, www.blackpast.org/african-american-history/great-migration-1915-1960/

Churchill, M., et al. (2008). Pennsylvania Redistricting Lawsuit. The Public Interest Law Center. www.pubintlaw.org/cases-and-projects/pennsylvania-redistricting-lawsuit/

Corasaniti, N. (2021, March 25). Georgia G.O.P. passes major law to limit voting amid nationwide push. *The New York Times*. https://www.nytimes.com/2021/03/25/us/politics/georgia-voting-law-republicans.html

Corasaniti, N., & Epstein, R. J. (2021, April 2). What Georgia's voting law really does. *The New York Times*. https://www.nytimes.com/2021/04/02/us/politics/georgia-voting-law-annotated.html

Covert, B. (2017, November). Our inordinately White, wealthy, male government. *The New Republic*. https://newrepublic.com/article/145839/inordinately-white-wealthy-male-government

Crowder, R. (2010, October). Black newspapers have long recorded our history. *Cleveland.com*. https://www.cleveland.com/call-and-post/index.2010/02/blacknewspapers have_long_rec.html

Deane, C., et al. (2020). *2020 election reveals two broad voting coalitions fundamentally at odds*. Pew Research Center. https://www.pewresearch.org/fact-tank/2020/11/06/2020-election-reveals-two-broad-voting-coalitions-fundamentally-at-odds/

DeRienzo, M. (2020, October 28). *Analysis: Voter suppression never went away. The tactics just changed*. Center for Public Integrity. https://publicintegrity.org/politics/elections/ballotboxbarriers/analysis-voter-suppression-never-went-away-tactics-changed/

Fahrenthold, D., Viebeck, E., Brown, E., & Helderman, R. S. (2020, December 8). Here are the GOP and Trump campaign's allegations of election irregularities. So far, none has been proved. *The Washington Post*. https://www.washingtonpost.com/politics/trump-election-irregularities-claims/2020/11/08/8f704e6c-2141-11eb-ba21-f2f001f0554b_story.html

Fandos, N., & Shear, M. D. (2019, December 18). Trump impeached for abuse of power and obstruction of Congress. *The New York Times*. https://www.nytimes.com/2019/12/18/us/politics/trump-impeached.html

Farivar, M. (2020, December). Trump-appointed judges balk at president's efforts to overturn election. *VOA News*. https://www.voanews.com/2020-usa-votes/trump-appointed-judges-balk-presidents-efforts-overturn-election

Fausset, R., et al. (2021, January 6). Democrats win Both Georgia Races to Gain Control of Senate." *The New York Times*. https://www.nytimes.com/2021/01/06/us/politics/warnock-loeffler-ossoff-perdue-georgia-senate.html

FindLaw. N.D. *First Amendment—U.S. Constitution*. Accessed 2018. https://www.pbs.org/newshour/politics/trumps-charity-admits-violating-irs-self-dealing-ban

Frej, W. (2018, September). Trump named the world's no. 1 oppressor of press freedom. *The Huffington Post*. https://www.huffingtonpost.com/entry/trump-oppressor-press-freedom_us_5a54bc75e4b003133ecc3439

Frey, W. H. (2018, June 22). *US White population declines and Generation 'Z-Plus' is minority White, census shows*. The Brookings Institute, June 22, 2018. https://www.brookings.edu/blog/the-avenue/2018/06/21/us-white-population-declines-and-generation-z-plus-is-minority-white-census-shows/

Frey, W. H. (2018, March). *The US will become 'minority White' in 2045, census projects*. The Brookings Institute, March 2018. https://www.brookings.edu/blog/the-avenue/2018/03/14/the-us-will-become-minority-white-in-2045-census-projects/

Frey, W. H. (2017, June 22). *Census shows nonmetropolitan America is whiter, getting older, and losing population*. The Brookings Institute. https://www.brookings.edu/blog/the-avenue/2017/06/27/census-shows-nonmetropolitan-america-is-whiter-getting-older-and-losing-population/

Frey, W. H. (2017, March). *Race, American identity and the census*. The Brookings Institute. https://www.brookings.edu/blog/the-avenue/2017/05/24/race-american-identity-and-the-census/

Frey, W. H. (2020, August 7). *Trump's New Plan to Hijack the Census Will Imperil America's Future*. The Brookings Institute. https://www.brookings.edu/blog/the-avenue/2020/08/07/trumps-new-plan-to-hijack-the-census-will-imperil-americas-future/

Gabriel, T. (2020, November 28). In statehouse races, suburban voters' disgust with President Trump failed to translate into a rebuke of other Republicans, ensuring the party's grip on partisan mapmaking. *The New York Times*. https://www.nytimes.com/2020/11/28/us/politics/democrats-republicans-state-legislatures.html?smid=em-share

Gandy, I., & Pieklo, J. M. (2019, April). The Republican takeover of the federal courts should terrify you. *Re-Wire*. https://rewire.news/article/2019/04/16/the-republican-takeover-of-the-federal-courts-should-terrify-you/

Gans, H. (2017, May 11). Opinion | The census and right-wing hysteria. *The New York Times*. Accessed 7 Jan. 2020. https://www.nytimes.com/2017/05/11/opinion/sunday/the-census-and-right-wing-hysteria.html

Gladu, A. (2016). The difference between the electoral vote & the popular vote shows why your vote matters. *Bustle*. https://www.bustle.com/articles/191141-the-difference-between-the-electoral-vote-the-popular-vote-shows-why-your-vote-matters

Glanton, D. (2020, October 28). Column: Trump's claim that he has done more for Black people than any president since Lincoln makes me sick. *The Chicago Times*. https://www.chicagotribune.com/columns/dahleen-glanton/ct-donald-trump-black-community-20201028-h6muhdj5ufarzimwhdbzqcxxfi-story.html

Goldman, A., & Kanno-Youngs, Z. (2020, September 24) F.B.I. director sees no evidence of national mail voting fraud effort: The comments undercut the president's claims about mail-in ballots. *The New York Times*. https://www.nytimes.com/2020/09/24/us/politics/fbi-director-voter-fraud.html

Goldsmith, J. (2017, October). "Will Donald Trump destroy the presidency: He disdains the rule of law. He's trampling norms of presidential behavior. And he's bringing vital institutions down with him. *The Atlantic.* https://www.theatlantic.com/magazine/archive/2017/10/will-donald-trump-destroy-the-presidency/537921/

Graham, D. A. (2018, January). The president who doesn't read Trump's allergy to the written word and his reliance on oral communication have proven liabilities in office. *The Atlantic.* https://www.theatlantic.com/politics/archive/2018/01/americas-first-post-text-president/549794/

Gumbel, A. (2017, September). America's shameful history of voter suppression. *The Guardian.* https://www.theguardian.com/us-news/2017/sep/13/americahistory-voter-suppression-donald-trump-election-fraud

Haidt, J., & Iyer, R. (2016, November). How to get beyond our tribal politics. https://www.wsj.com/articles/how-to-get-beyond-our-tribal-politics-1478271810.

Hananel, S. (2020, May). *RELEASE: CAP Report shows how partisan gerrymandering hurts kids in Michigan, North Carolina, Pennsylvania, and Wisconsin.* Center for American Progress. https://www.americanprogress.org/press/release/2020/05/28/485537/release-cap-report-shows-partisan-gerrymandering-hurts-kids-michigan-north-carolina-pennsylvania-wisconsin/

Harriot, M. (2020, December). Trump officially accuses Wisconsin's Black voters of cheating. *The Root.* Accessed 2020. https://www.theroot.com/trump-officially-accuses-wisconsins-black-voters-of-che-1845786731

Harrison, T. (2020, November 10). "Trump presidency was brief, but legacy will stretch further. *Missoula Current.* Accessed 11 Mar. 2021. missoulacurrent.com/government/2020/11/trump-presidency-legacy/

Hill, C. (2020, November). *Trump campaign sued for attempting to disenfranchise Black voters.* Yahoo News. https://news.yahoo.com/trump-campaign-sued-for-attempting-to-disenfranchise-black-voters-100000739.html

History.com Editors. *President Donald Trump Impeached.* History.com. Accessed 2020. https://www.history.com/this-day-in-history/president-trump-impeached-house-of-representatives

Holland, J. (2019, July 8) Ninth Cir Court close to having more Trump judges than any other. *Bloomberg Law.* https://news.bloomberglaw.com/us-law-week/ninth-circuit-close-to-having-more-trump-judges-than-any-other

Johnson, K. (2020, November 12). Election security officials: 'No evidence voting systems compromised. *USA Today.* https://www.usatoday.com/story/news/politics/2020/11/12/election-fraud-officials-say-no-evidence-voting-systems-compromised/6272326002/

Kelly, J., & Grenyo, M. (2021, February 11). How Black newspapers and magazines inspired social justice movements. *The Crimson White.* Accessed 24 Feb. 2021. cw.ua.edu/77395/culture/how-black-newspapers-and-magazines-inspired-social-justice-movements/

Knight, B. (2018, December 4). Why is the U.S. 'government by the rich and for the rich'? *Pekin Times.* https://www.pekintimes.com/obituaries/20181204/knight-why-is-us-government-by-rich-and-for-rich

Kochhar, R., & Cilluffo, A. (2018, July). *Key findings on the rise in income inequality within America's racial and ethnic groups.* Pew Research Center. http://www.pewresearch.org/fact-tank/2018/07/12/

key-findings-on-the-rise-in-income-inequality-within-americas-racial-and-ethnic-groups/

LeTourneau, N. (2018, February). The Nativist attempt to delay the browning of America. *The Washington Monthly.* https://washingtonmonthly.com/2018/02/07/the-nativist-attempt-to-delay-the-browning-of-america/

Levitz, E. (2019, March). Will Black voters still love Biden when they remember who he was? *Intelligencer.* https://nymag.com/intelligencer/2019/03/joe-biden-record-on-busing-incarceration-racial-justice-democratic-primary-2020-explained.html

Lewis, M. (2015, January). America's political parties are just tribes now. *The Daily Beast.* https://www.thedailybeast.com/americas-political-parties-are-just-tribes-now

Liptak, A. (2013, June 25). U.S. Supreme Court invalidates key part of Voting Rights Act. *The New York Times.* www.nytimes.com/2013/06/26/us/supreme-court-ruling.html

Liptak, A. (2019, June). Supreme Court bars challenges to partisan gerrymandering. *The New York Times.* https://www.nytimes.com/2019/06/27/us/politics/supreme-court-gerrymandering.html

Lucas, R. (2020, December 1). *Barr: DOJ has no evidence of fraud affecting 2020 election outcome.* https://www.npr.org/sections/biden-transition-updates/2020/12/01/940786321/barr-doj-has-no-evidence-of-fraud-affecting-2020-election-outcome

Maranzani, B. (2017, March 21). *America's richest (and poorest) presidents.* History.com. www.history.com/news/americas-richest-and-poorest-presidents.

McCaskill, N. D. (2020, November). Fact check: Trump's policies for Black Americans. Trump says he's the "bnest president" for African Americans. Is that really true?" *Politico.* https://www.politico.com/news/2020/11/01/trump-black-americans-policies-433744

Montanaro, D. (2020, November 11). Election was a good one for Republicans not named Trump." *NPR,* November 11, 2020. https://www.npr.org/2020/11/11/933435840/the-2020-election-was-a-good-one-for-republicans-not-named-trump

Moye, D. (2020, July). Trump mocked for claiming he's done more for Black Americans than Lincoln. *The HuffPost.* https://www.huffpost.com/entry/trump-black-voters-abe-lincoln_n_5f18c65bc5b6128e68205f88

Newkirk, V. R., II. (2018, July). Voter suppression is warping democracy. *The Atlantic.* https://https://www.theatlantic.com/politics/archive/2018/07/poll-prri-voter-suppression/565355/

Ngangura, T. (2020, November 11). Trump wants to steal the election by disenfranchising thousands of Black voters. *Vanity Fair.* https://www.vanityfair.com/news/2020/11/trump-wants-to-steal-the-election-by-disenfranchising-thousands-of-black-voters

Packer, G. (2013, May). Celebrating inequality. *The New York Times.* https://www.nytimes.com/2013/05/20/opinion/inequality-and-the-modern-culture-of-celebrity.html.

Packer, G. (2011). The broken contract: inequality and American decline. *Foreign Affairs, 90*(6), 20–31. *JSTOR.* Accessed December 16, 2020. www.jstor.org/stable/23039626

The Pew Research Center. (2016, June 27). *On views of race and inequality, Blacks and Whites are worlds apart*. Pew Research Center. http://www.pewsocialtrends.org/2016/06/27/on-views-of-race-and-inequality-blacks-and-whites-are-worlds-apart/

Pierce, O., & Rabinowitz, K. (2017, October). 'Partisan' gerrymandering is still about race. https://www.propublica.org/article/partisan-gerrymandering-is-still-about-race

Rashawn, R. (2020, November 24). *How Black Americans save Biden and American democracy*. The Brookings Institute. https://www.brookings.edu/blog/how-we-rise/2020/11/24/how-black-americans-saved-biden-and-american-democracy/

Rashawn, R., & Galston, W. (2020, August 28). *Did the 1994 crime bill cause mass incarceration?* The Brookings Institute. https://www.brookings.edu/blog/fixgov/2020/08/28/did-the-1994-crime-bill-cause-mass-incarceration/

Rashawn, Ray, & Gilbert, K. L. (2020, October 15). *How We Rise: Has Trump Failed Black Americans."* The Brookings Institute. https://www.brookings.edu/blog/how-we-rise/2020/10/15/has-trump-failed-black-americans/

Reich, R. (2014, March). The new tribalism and the decline of the nation state. March 2014. http://robertreich.org/post/80522686347.

Reuters Staff. (2020, October). Factbox: Donald Trump's legacy—six policy takeaways. Reuters. Accessed 2020. https://www.reuters.com/article/us-usa-trump-legacy-factbox/factbox-donald-trumps-legacy-six-policy-takeaways-idUSKBN27F1GK

Ropeik, D. (2012, May). *How tribalism overrules reason, and makes risky times more dangerous*. Big Think. https://bigthink.com/risk-reason-and-reality/how-tribalism-overrules-reason-and-makes-risky-times-more-dangerous

Rutenberg, J., & Corasaniti, N. (2020, November). Analysis: With election lawsuits, Republicans return to old playbook on disenfranchising Black Americans. *Chicago Tribune*. https://www.chicagotribune.com/election-2020/sns-nyt-republicans-disenfranchise-black-americans-20201127-kjvcuklyyjf6pd22nlgnvctnhi-story.html.

Schneider, Mike, & Sherman, M. (2020, November). *High court takes up census case, as other count issues loom*. APNews. https://apnews.com/article/donald-trump-coronavirus-pandemic-census-2020-us-supreme-court-courts-b1dd5b34583cb2d-276d939aa3edce2b7

Sherman, M. (2020, November). *Supreme Court seems skeptical Trump's census plan*. APNews, https://apnews.com/article/donald-trump-politics-census-2020-us-supreme-court-courts-646d4f2568ad89f5cc49e40c0006b767

Skelley, G. (2020, November). *Republicans are on track to take back the House in 2022*. FiveThirtyEight. https://fivethirtyeight.com/features/republicans-2020-gains-in-the-house-set-them-up-well-for-2022/.

Stevens, M. (2019, July 31). When Kamala Harris and Joe Biden clashed on busing and segregation. *The New York Times*. https://www.nytimes.com/2019/07/31/us/politics/kamala-harris-biden-busing.html

Sye, M. (2020, October). Charting the long-term Impact of Trump's Judicial Appointments. *Pro Pubica*. https://projects.propublica.org/trump-young-judges/.

Tausanovitch, A., & Root, D. (July 2020) How partisan gerrymandering limits voting rights. Center for American Rights. https://www.

americanprogress.org/issues/democracy/reports/2020/07/08/487426/partisan-gerrymandering-limits-voting-rights/.

Teresa, C. (2018). The Jim Crow-era Black press: Of and for its readership | the American Historian. Accessed 12 Mar. 2021. www.oah.org, www.oah.org/tah/issues/2018/august/the-jim-crow-era-black-press-of-and-for-its-readership/

Totenberg, N., & Sprunt, B. Supreme Court shuts door on Texas suit seeking to overturn election. *NPR,* December 2020. https://www.npr.org/2020/12/11/945617913/supreme-court-shuts-door-on-trump-election-prospects.

U.S. Census Bureau. (2018, July). https://www.census.gov/newsroom/press-releases/2018/acs1year.html.

U.S. Census Bureau. (2017, February). National African-American History Month: U.S. Census Bureau.

Vance, J. D. (2016, August). Why race relations got worse. *National Review.* www.nationalreview.com/2016/08/race-relations-getting-worse-america-why/.

Walsh, J. (2021, April 1) "Everything you need to know about Georgia's new anti-voting law. *The Nation.* www.thenation.com/article/politics/georgia-voting-restrictions/.

Wilson, W. J. (1996) *When work disappears. The world of the new urban poor.* Alfred A. Knopf.

Wolfson, S. (2018, May). After kneeling: The ways NFL players can protest despite the new rules." *The Guardian,* https://www.theguardian.com/sport/2018/may/29/nfl-protests-taking-a-knee-alternatives-new-rules-fines

Yetman, N. (1999). *Majority and minority: The dynamics of race and ethnicity in American life.* Allyn & Bacon.

The Road Ahead: Issues and Challenges

There have been significant achievements in the overall condition of peoples of color. Within the last twenty-five years, African Americans have risen to high political offices, corporate boards, and international business prominence. African Americans are now poised to make significant inroads into new areas of public life that were once unthinkable just fifty years ago. Although many African Americans and other peoples of color have made significant professional, social, and economic achievements, these gains are not reflective of most African Americans.

Social, economic, and professional benefits that have come with the 21st century have been enjoyed by a small segment of the African American population. As the nation moves forward in the post-Obama presidency years, African Americans are more anxious and vulnerable to a wide range of social, economic, and racial disparities. Those disparities are evident as it relates to a shrinking Black middle class; racial hostilities and antagonism; police bias and brutality as well as the disintegration of the Black family. Cumulatively, these challenges pose an imminent threat to the viability of long fought gains and the continued march towards full and unfettered participation in the larger society.

CHAPTER 21

Understanding the Interplay of Race, Culture, and History

To better understand the longer-term prospects of African Americans, a clearer understanding of race and ethnicity must be developed. There are several foundational, and historical facts that must be recognized, understood, and considered before one can genuinely assess the role of race in America in the coming years.

First, it is widely agreed and accepted that human beings originated on the continent of Africa. These earliest people migrated from Africa to different parts of the world. It was due to living in and adapting to different conditions in isolated communities in various parts of the world that the differences in physical features developed. Cultures also developed through the interaction of people in these various communities. Culture can be described as being comprised of customs, religious beliefs, knowledge, and ideas. It is the result of people living together as a community. Although cultures may be different, there is no such thing as different races. Whether one is African American, Native American, Asian American, or European American, all humans are part of one race: the human race. Although there may be differences in physical appearance and in culture, this does not alter the fact that all people belong to the human family. It would follow, then, that there should be mutual respect and appreciation of differences and similarities among all peoples.

Defense Secretary Lloyd J. Austin III poses for his official portrait in the Army portrait studio at the Pentagon, Arlington, VA, January 23, 2021. (*Photo by Spc. XaViera Masline, Public domain, via Wikimedia Commons*)

Secondly, any notions of racial superiority or inferiority are based on superficial physical differences. Racial genetics is "bad science" and has been widely disproven. There was once a strongly held belief in Europe and the United States about race and its relationship to genetics, and subsequently to the justification of superiority. The concept of race is invented as a means to show and justify bigotry and bias towards people of physical and cultural differences. Race is a social and economic construct not a biological one. Race bigotry permits one group to dominate another and justify this treatment based on superficial reasons.

Historically, during the European conquest and domination of the peoples of Africa, Asia, and America, many Europeans began to believe that it was the difference in appearance, or "race," which designated them as superior, with the right to dominate others. It should be noted that this idea had a much firmer foothold in northern Europe. The Spanish and Portuguese people knew better. The idea of race has now been discredited. Most scholars, especially anthropologists, among whom the idea of race first arose, have abandoned it. An outstanding anthropologist, Ashley Montagu, discussed this in his book called *Man's Most Dangerous Myth: The Fallacy of Race* (1997).

Third, one must also recognize the role that African peoples had in the development of Western Europe and in the Americas. Although people of African descent have lived in the Americas from very early times, they have not always been treated as equals by other groups of people. The accomplishments of African Americans and other minorities are often grudgingly admitted or denied altogether. There are also attempts to make the evidence of their accomplishments appear irrelevant or unimportant rather than approaching it with the careful study and debate that is given to other historical information. Common examples can be found in scholarship about these attempts are present in the discussions about the African identity of the ancient Egyptians, and the influence of the Moors in Spain and Portugal. These attempts are also present in the evidence relating to the early presence of Africans in America and the African influence on the Olmec civilization in Mexico.

Fourth, the stories of history are generated by the "powerful" at the expense of the "powerless." Whether it is contained in books, movies, oral histories, social media, or archival documents, these historical stories feature the dominant cultures. The experiences of minorities, women, and the disabled and other non-mainstream groups are either omitted or given little attention. The failure to recognize the achievements and the contributions of less dominate peoples to the development of the larger society creates misunderstanding, misinformation, and misperceptions.

Racism and stereotypes are based on incomplete information and propaganda that is used to justify discrimination. African Americans have been an integral part of the development of culture and history in the United States. Their unpaid labor established the economy, and their culture has influenced American culture. There has been such an extensive and profound influence of African American culture on the mainstream culture that it is difficult to know where African American culture ends and American culture begins. America, as a nation, was supposed to be a "melting pot" of different people. While it may have been true for Whites, people of color have not blended into the so-called American melting pot. America's culture, however, can be considered the true melting pot to which African Americans have greatly contributed.

Fifth, all too often history tends to avoid certain events in the American past. Perhaps the reason is an attempt to not offend the sensibilities of some readers, however, issues of racism and the brutality perpetrated against African Americans cannot be ignored. This information is a part of American history, albeit a very negative part. It cannot be erased, but it can provide a look at how America, as a nation, has developed. It can also provide insight into how and why racism started and why it still exists in society. The whole story must be told, or discussion and understanding will never occur. Neither will there be efforts to rid society of its evil. Unfortunately, we see that the seeds of White supremacist ideology, which is based in racism, have taken root. They have affected everyone from government officials to ordinary citizens. It has led law enforcement agencies to assist in the violation of civil rights and even the murder of African Americans.

Finally, it must be understood that the fate of America and its future is tied to African Americans and all the diverse peoples of this country. That has been evidenced in history, and will continue to be so in years to come. The United States has become a world leader, economic power, educational Mecca, and innovator because of its diversity of talents, ideas, peoples, backgrounds, and struggle to make America greater by inclusion—not exclusion.

Race and Inequality: Why the Disparities?

Numerous scholars have studied racial inequality and related attitudes in American society. A pioneering study on American values by Paul Sniderman and Michael Hagen (1985) researched this issue. This early work appears to remain relevant in the post-Obama era. Generally, the mixed racial group of participants in the study agreed that African Americans had less of the "good things in life" (housing, schools, jobs) than Whites. The question was why this racial inequality existed and what should be done about it?

There were several explanations that people gave as to why African Americans had less. While the study by Sniderman and Hagen was done in 1985, not much has changed in over 30 years. In this survey, one group of respondents believed God made different races. Another group said that African Americans were to blame for their problems. Their belief was that African Americans did not work hard enough. This group also felt that if African Americans and Whites were equally trained, that both had equal chances to be hired for jobs. Another group said that generations of enslavement and discrimination made it difficult for African Americans. Still another explanation given was that African Americans were inherently inferior, or that African Americans have different values. The last explanation given was that a small group of powerful Whites (elites) control various factors and work to keep African Americans down. Although the respondents, both White and Black, thought African Americans should have equal rights, they did not know what being in favor of equality meant. Equality was favored in general, but mostly in the abstract.

The explanations provided by the Sniderman and Hagen (1985) study of mixed group of participants shed important insights about perceptions on race and the resulting disparities. Some meaningful correlations can be drawn from these responses and how people view economic, class, and racial disparities. It is unfortunate, but some people think African Americans are inherently inferior despite all the scientific research done over the last century. One sees examples of this in hate groups such the Ku Klux Klan—although this group seems to hate nearly everyone. In the study cited, one could also say that God did make people different, but that goes for every one of us. Human beings are all individuals, and no one is exactly like anyone else. As for having different values, work ethics, and perceived inferior abilities, one can see that the history of African Americans demonstrates just the opposite of that. Other researchers (Flippen, 2001; Nackenoff, 1999) have also looked further in terms of the socio-economic issues and attitudes revealed in Sniderman's study.

Some people responded that the disparities in wealth, jobs, etc. were (and still are) rooted in genetic, social, and biological differences. The idea was that wealthy people are more prosperous because of racial genetics. There is no PEER reviewed evidence or facts to prove this. Wealth and poverty are not biologically based. Social, political, government, environment and other institutions perpetuate income and social class in America. Individuals may differ genetically based on parents, geography, and genetic mutations but those differences only apply to a specific individual. Those differences do not apply to a racial class of people in any meaningful way that can be universally applied.

The last explanation for disparities of wealth, etc. that participants gave to Sniderman was that a powerful group of Whites control things. This explanation has merit, not only for African Americans but also for the working class and the poor. It is a fact that there are far more poor Whites who are in the lower class, who are on public assistance, and need Medicaid than poor Blacks. The reason for this is simply because the majority of Americans are White, therefore the sheer population numbers makes this so. However, one might inquire as to whether the U.S. government is working to eliminate hunger or provide health care, especially for the working poor, who are mostly White? The answer is no.

In the Republican held Congress of the 2016 election, the primary goal of the Grand Old Party (GOP) party was to repeal the Affordable Care Act, also known as Obamacare. Most of the people who benefit from this law are rural Whites and the working poor, who are also White. Of course, it benefits Blacks, but as previously stated they are much fewer in numbers than Whites. African Americans may experience deeper poverty. The GOP, along with conservative Democrats, and Tea Party loyalists have attempted to reduce spending on Medicaid, during Trump's administration. This program provides medical assistance for low income people through appropriations to state governments.

The largest beneficiaries of the social welfare "safety net" programs that provide food stamps and public assistance are mostly Whites, the elderly, and some low-income, working-class people. The only reason that the Republicans have failed to repeal the health care law, also known as Obamacare, is that it has become popular with the American people. American citizens came out in great numbers to protest and lobby their Congressmen to not repeal it.

There are considerable economic and social differences between poor Blacks and poor Whites (Boule, 2017; Keyes et al., 2015; Neckerman &

Torche, 2007). This is especially true when one looks at the disparities in wealth accumulation and income, which is directly related to jobs, housing, health, and education issues. A study (Hanks et al., 2018) by the Center for American Progress (CAP) detailed how the Black-White wealth gap was created by America's structural racism. The wealth in America is unequally distributed and this is not due to laziness, or the unwillingness of Blacks to work. It is based on the conditions and laws that have prevented Blacks from being treated fairly. This includes the long history of employment discrimination and other practices that are discriminatory.

There is a difference between wealth and income which the CAP study describes. Wealth is considered someone's accumulated assets that yield financial benefits. This is what allows parents to purchase a house or send their child to college. Income can consist of earnings from a job, Social Security benefits, or pension benefits. In the case of a job, if that job is eliminated, then that income is gone, as well as any prospects of wealth accumulation. In the case of the fixed benefits just mentioned, they are just that, fixed. These funds (from income) provide only what is needed at that time. There isn't any extra money, assets, or wealth that can be used for emergencies or a rainy day, etc. The social and economic differences between poor Black and poor Whites may be fueling some racial tension.

The Great Recession of 2007 affected Blacks and Hispanics the most. People of color were already experiencing this gap in wealth and have not recovered. Even when middle class Black family wealth is compared to White middle class wealth, there is a large gap. A number of key factors are pointed out. One is that Blacks have less access to tax advantaged means of savings. Also, Blacks have fewer assets and carry larger credit card debt. In addition, African Americans are less likely to own their home or have a retirement account.

There are many factors that account for this wealth disparity, however, the main reasons for this situation are the policies that discriminate against African Americans. They include slavery, Jim Crow, redlining, school segregation, mass incarceration, and environmental racism. The system is rigged against Blacks, who are left to face these systemic challenges. Latinos and certain Asian Pacific Islanders are also in this situation. Hispanic families, however, have slightly more wealth than African Americans.

The Legacy of White Supremacy

The long and difficult struggle for equality continues partly because of bigoted mind sets and hearts. Even with changing laws, sometimes it is not enough. The struggle will continue as long as people do not recognize the fact that there is no superior or inferior race. Not enough progress in the struggle for human rights has been made in areas such as education, job opportunity, housing, and the protection of voting rights. Racism is one of the main reasons for the perpetuation of White supremacy. It is a troubling and evil matter that has resurfaced in full force and has been manifested with the election of Donald Trump, his administration, and many elements of his fringe supporters.

When one looks at the history of America and the rise of White supremacy, the effects on race relations to this day cannot be denied. In the "Old South" mindset, racism was the key to preventing poor Whites and poor Blacks from entering into any kind of beneficial alliance, according to O'Leary (2016). He also stated that an alliance would have threatened the continued power of the planter class, as well as White supremacy. There was, however, a short period of time when poor Whites and poor Blacks formed a coalition against the elite group, since both groups found themselves in the same financial situation.

It should also be noted that while the South was greatly implicit in the use of race to appeal to aggrieved Whites and pit them against Blacks, the North was not free of racism. O'Leary (2016) points out that what he calls old-style White supremacy had become increasingly virulent and strong in the South, in terms of the politics there. This strong, old-style White supremacy and its tactics did not have a plausible national leader until the 2016 election of Donald Trump. The GOP leaders seem to have returned to their previous strategies of promoting racial resentment and voter suppression.

The legacy of slavery is also one of the main factors in the poor socioeconomic status of African Americans. It contributes to a source of negative thoughts and behaviors of many White Americans. For example, when laws such as affirmative action are enacted, there is a backlash. Carter (2011) has a theory that he calls "interest convergence" which is applicable here. He states that unless the law or legislation being considered demonstrates that it will help the White population, there is little or no interest, but rather there are actual challenges to the law. Racism, which is fostered by the legacy of slavery and the rise of White supremacy has persisted to the present. Racism has been transmitted through generations of families and, in fact, has affected more Whites than is realized.

Keyes et al. (2015) discusses another form of racism, called White privilege. White privilege is described as a means to systematically empower one group over another. This is actually a concept that was studied by Peggy McIntosh (1990). White privilege, as described by McIntosh (1990), is a way of providing assets to Whites that are not available to people of color. McIntosh proposes that Whites can and do enjoy social and other benefits that they have not earned. In addition, Whites have become desensitized to discrimination of others because they don't have to consider how they have benefitted from being White (Keyes et al., 2015). Some Whites may consider the arguments that McIntosh puts forward as related to class, when they look at her work. However, even poor Whites cannot deny that they enjoy some of the privileges she cites in her work.

In terms of race relations, there is no doubt that in the era of Donald Trump they have grown worse. A Pew Research study conducted in 2017 showed that 60 percent of Americans say that Trump's election led to worse race relations. Another 8 percent said it led to better relations and 30 percent had no opinion. There were other polls conducted by Gallup and the Pew Research Center, among others that had the same or similar findings. Poor race relations were also blamed on President Obama.

One researcher, however, writes that President Obama was not to blame for poor race relations (Lamb, 2015). Race, politics, and opportunism are staples of political campaigns. Like former governors Orval Faubus, Ross Barnett, George Wallace, Richard Nixon, and Bush Sr., Trump tapped into White anxiety. Trump followed a similar strategy directed towards White Evangelicals and less-well off southerners. Trump, however, dramatically raised racial tensions with his words and deeds. The events in Charlottesville, Virginia, in 2017 was one example. Trump's tacit embrace of groups like the Ku Klux Klan through his acceptance of an endorsement by David Duke (the former grand wizard) demonstrated Trump's embrace of racism.

Another major issue in the Black community is the police shootings of Black men. When protests arise and develop into a movement, such as BlackLivesMatter, the protests and protesters are denounced. Even if a famous person, such as Colin Kaepernick, takes a stand or in this case, a knee against police brutality/shootings, he is considered unpatriotic and disrespectful. Kaepernick was instrumental in galvanizing NFL players in an organized protest against racial injustice. His example led to a fundamental awareness of the problem of police shootings and brutality that was aligned with the BlackLivesMatter Movement. Patriotism does not mean blindly following symbolic acts of nationalistic allegiance. Kaepernick was only exercising the right of free speech and the right to protest. The right of free speech and expression is a freedom guaranteed by the U.S. Constitution.

BlackLivesMatter: A Community Response to Injustice

Frequent incidents of racial profiling, police brutality, and White vigilantism has led to a heightened awareness of the dangers of being Black and/or a visible minority in America. Highly published incidents of police brutality have led to the BlackLivesMatter protests. Violence against African Americans is nothing new. What is new is the ability to capture and record events that are subsequently posted on social media for wide distribution and viewing. The result has been a pictorial catalogue fuelled by video evidence of rampant violence and brutality against people of color. In the era of the administration of the 45th president, violence against Blacks became "permissible" because of fears and bigotry directed at African Americans who do not conform to the common place, mainstream perceptions of non-threatening Black people.

During the Reagan, Bush Sr., and Bush Jr. presidencies, one of the outcomes of the government's "war on drugs" was racial profiling, which continues today. Racial profiling is the practice by which police and highway patrol stop and harass only people of color, principally young African American and Latino men. This practice of stopping or detaining people based on ethnicity was expanded. Since the attacks on the World Trade Center and the Pentagon on September 11, 2001, people of Arabic ancestry have also become targets. Racial profiling becomes a bigger problem when police brutality is added to the mix. Too often, African American men who are detained are also victims of police brutality.

Police brutality is an issue that has caused much outrage in the African American community. It came into focus with several incidents. So, the question must be asked, investigated and analyzed why so many African Americans are distrustful of the police and the judicial system? One of the first recorded incidents involved Rodney King in Los Angeles, California. In 1991, video recordings were made and later televised of his beating. Many people believed that the police used extreme violence to arrest him. An all-White jury found the officers who beat him innocent, which set off unrest in his community. Three years later, King was awarded over $3 million in damages.

Since the 1980s and 1990s, there have been more frequent incidences of racial profiling and police brutality throughout America. In response, communities have become incensed with these types of injustices, and some places have experienced rioting because of it. In 2014, riots erupted between African Americans and the police in Ferguson, Missouri. Tensions between the police and the minority community were already strained,

BlackLivesMatter Protest. Photo by Chris Henry on Unsplash

because these citizens felt that they were unfairly targeted. Racial profiling and the death of African American men at the hands of the police are the issues. Also, in 2014 there was the shooting of Laquan McDonald in Chicago, Illinois. Police officer, Jason Van Dyke, shot him 16 times as he was walking away. Another victim included Eric Garner who was held in a choke hold by New York City police who ended his life because he was selling lose cigarettes on the street. The death of George Floyd in Minneapolis by a police officer was a rallying cry against police brutality.

Often, when people feel disenfranchised or without hope, they will turn to leaders in their community. Reverend Dr. William Barber II is one of these people to whom some African Americans have turned in times of trouble. He is a minister but is known as a community leader, and civil rights activist. The responses to these types of injustices are not like the civil disobedience characteristic of the 1960s led by Martin Luther King, Jr. Resistance against oppression and the police occupation of African American communities during the new millennium is loud and recorded. When African Americans look at the police, the question becomes who they are serving and protecting. The police are often perceived as an occupying force by many in the Black community. It is said that the police officers don't come when you call them but come when you don't need them.

So, the question must be asked, investigated and analyzed why so many African Americans are distrustful of the police and the judicial system? The murder of Trayvon Martin in 2012 in Florida by a so-called neighbor vigilante calls into question Florida's "Stand Your Ground" law. There was civil unrest in Ferguson because of the killing of Michael Brown; the shooting of Tamir Rice in 2014 in Cleveland; and other questionable police killings have raised serious questions about law enforcement's perception of the value of Black lives.

Has police brutality increased or is it something else such as greater awareness of the problem via social media? Two events have happened in recent years that many believe provides the answer. The first is the documentation of such instances by cell phones, and the second is social media that broadcasts these incidences. The advent of these two major avenues of documentation corroborates what many members of Black communities already knew. These amateur digital media recordings serve to shed light on police accountability and what is occurring in Black communities. The use of cell phones with cameras and citizen journalism by social media have become important witnesses. The collective reactions to injustice and bias has been riots, rebellion, and resistance, and Ferguson in 2014 was one tipping point.

The death of George Floyd in 2019 was another. According to some writers, the cruelty exhibited in the death of George Floyd in Minneapolis by a police officer galvanized not just Blacks but many others against police brutality. One writer (Wortham, 2020) wrote that the BlackLivesMatter movement became "the biggest collective demonstrations of civil unrest" in the history of the United States. Wortham (2020) also points out that not only did protests occur in nearly every state but also in foreign countries such as New Zealand and in Europe (Wortham 2020; Buchanan, et al., 2020; Eligon, 2020).

BlackLivesMatter Movement Goes Global

The BlackLivesMatter movement in America has morphed into a global phenomenon.

The historical inequity faced by Blacks in America as well as in Europe has shaped it into a Pan-African movement. The movement is based upon the disproportionate number of people of African descent and their social, economic, and political disenfranchisement status in western society. The roots of historic inequalities can be found in the slave trade, the abolition movement, and the inability of Western nations to integrate the people of African descent.

Protests, rebellions, and awareness of the unequal treatment of people of color has been brought to the consciousness of mainstream media and public policy and has spurred institutional cries for change. The United States along with England, France, Italy, and other wealthy nations of Europe are confronted with the legacy and consequences of historical policies and practices that have fostered inequality throughout their countries. Although the BlackLivesMatter movement began in the United States with the death of George Floyd in Minneapolis, and has included Breonna Taylor, Rayshard Brooks, Eric Garner, and countless others, the similarities and symbols of police brutality and social isolation coupled with economic disparities were and still are common themes throughout America and Western Europe for many people of African descent.

The Trump administration responded to civil unrest and protesters by sending in federal troops to major cities to protect property (commercial and government) as well as to restore "law and order" in Portland, Oregon. While it is within the authority of the federal government to send in troops to help restore general order, their assistance is usually requested. In Portland, Oregon, however, federal intervention with law enforcement officers was done without the request of the governor or mayor. The Trump administration threatened to send troops into predominately democratic led cities and African American communities of the country. Trump identified Oakland, California, New York City, New York, and Chicago, Illinois, as examples of areas that had lost civil authority to protect government buildings and monuments.

Many people view this type of behavior as akin to autocratic leaders in third world countries that use their secret police to quell dissent. Dissent and peaceful protest is a vital and necessary component of democracy that makes leaders accountable to its citizens. Peaceful protests have called attention to issues that citizens expect government officials to address and fix. This is the central premise of a democratic county.

The BlackLivesMatter movement has gained allies across racial, political, gender, class, and national boundaries. This is nothing less than a sea of change of social and political consciousness globally. The BlackLivesMatter movement was important in the 2016 elections and was a hot-button issue in the 2020 presidential election.

A Future of Uncertainty Beyond 2020: What's Next?

The United States, and African Americans in particular, faced three crises during at the final stage of writing this book during the spring and summer 2020. Publishing deadlines and the fluidity of current events prevented me from doing more extensive research and writing about some relevant social and political events during the first half of 2020. However, at the time of this writing, several situations of crisis level warranted discussion.

The first major crisis was that of the Covid-19 pandemic and the resulting health disparities. This was magnified by the resulting economic impact on minorities. Second, the issue of police violence directed at African Americans was raised to a heightened level of national consciousness as a result of social media live posts showing how law enforcement officials treat Black "suspects." Third, symbols, monuments, and images of racial oppression came to the forefront of the national debate about racial stereotypes. The confederate flag and other icons of a bygone era were identified by communities, sports franchises, and corporations alike. The 2020 U.S. presidential race is overshadowed by these domestic controversies that will have a lasting impact on African Americans for years to come.

The Color of a Pandemic

In December of 2019, the World Health Organization (WHO) was alerted by Chinese authorities that a serious infection of unknown causes was erupting in a province in China. This virus was the novel coronavirus (Covid-19). The WHO eventually named the virus as a pandemic, meaning that it was an illness that would affect many countries. Since it was identified, it spread to over 200 countries. However, the country that has suffered the most infections and death has been the United States. The reason for this is that the Trump administration failed to take the outbreak seriously.

The novel coronavirus was known to have spread to the United States early in January 2020. It spread from China to Europe and eventually to the United States. Since the virus was new, there was no vaccine available, therefore other mitigation efforts were put in place. Those efforts were closing businesses, social distancing, and the wearing of masks in the effort to slow the spread. In the beginning, Trump made a half-hearted effort to adhere to the advice of the scientists leading the team that his administration convened. In March 2020 the coronavirus pandemic caused the NBA to postpone its season. Following that many other sporting events, tournaments, and major conferences were cancelled.

The closing of businesses as well as the cancellation of sporting events, tournaments, and major conferences seriously affected the economy. Early on the virus manifested itself in Washington State. Eventually the hospitalizations were reduced and the virus brought under control. It was after that when New York City became the epicenter of the outbreaks in the United States. Governor Andrew Cuomo enacted the strict mitigations recommended by the scientists and brought the number of cases down. He then proceeded to open various regions of the state in stages based on the infection rate. This greatly alleviated the high numbers of hospitalizations.

The effect of the closing of businesses as well as the effect on the New York Stock Exchange had serious consequences. Small businesses were severely affected. The pandemic's effect on the economy caused even greater concerns for Donald Trump's bid for a second term as president. As the summer months arrived and fearful for his election campaign for 2020, Trump abandoned the efforts at mitigation. He began to send mixed messages to Republican governors and the people of the United States to not wear masks and to encourage citizens of various states to rebel from the stay at home orders by the states.

Each governor is responsible for the operations of their state. As a result, while the pandemic was severely lessened in Washington State and New York State, there was an outbreak in the southern and western states. This has serious consequences for the elderly, those with pre-existing conditions and even young people. There are those people who are asymptomatic who can unknowingly infect others including parents and grandparents.

The short and long term impact of the Covid-19 pandemic are still being tallied. The loss of lives, housing, jobs, business, and impact on community institutions is not fully known. Even without a science-based impact study, African Americans and Latino communities faced greater social, economic, and health disparities than other groups—nationally and globally. Decades from now, the impact will still be felt.

The 2020 Presidential Election

The outbreak of hospitalizations and deaths due to the coronavirus has dire consequences for the 2020 elections. People who want to vote may be faced with the prospect of having to go out to polling places where few precautions have been put in place. In addition, many Republicans are against voting by mail as was seen in the primaries of 2020. The people in some state legislatures, who have the power over polling places, closed them particularly in minority neighborhoods. In some places the polling areas were changed at the last minute (for example, in Columbia, South Carolina). This forced people to wait in long lines just to exercise their right to vote. This is just one of the techniques that have been used by Republicans, mostly, to suppress the right to vote especially for people of color in the United States.

Summary

In the United States, the historic struggle has always been the inclusion and expansion of rights and privileges for all peoples. Vigilance, scholarship, and a sustained commitment to making the ideals of life, liberty, and the pursuit of happiness are no less important today than 300 years ago. African Americans have been an important force to make American values real in their principle and application. The history of the United States of America can be best understood through the struggle and triumphs of its peoples. African Americans have been an important element in creating a just and fair society for all peoples.

In the past ten years America has seen the growth and acceptance of a more diverse society. Some African Americans, women, and minorities have ascended to positions of power and prestige in contemporary American society. Although American society is making significant strides towards full racial inclusion, the struggle is far from over and complete. On the one hand, the United States has seen an African American become secretary of state and president of the United States. America has also elected the first Black woman as vice-president. Others are leaders of multi-national corporations, television and media icons, and innovators in STEM occupations. These achievements are significant but do not reflect the vast majority of African Americans in their quest towards social, economic, and political mobility. Issues of discrimination and bias remain in significant areas of African American and minority communities. These issues include police brutality, voter suppression, racial profiling, unemployment, lack of living wage jobs, health concerns, and poor schools.

Going forward in a multicultural racial society, the efforts of coalitions of multicultural politics will be needed. Tribal, identity, self-interest movements, only serve to hamper the American dream for everyone. What is needed is described as a third reconstruction, according to Rev. Dr. William Barber. "The Third Reconstruction" will be a movement of all races working together in tandem with government, business, schools, faith communities and civic groups to make America really great for everyone.

References

The African American odyssey: A quest for full citizenship free Blacks in the Antebellum period. Accessed 2018. https://www.loc.gov/exhibits/african-american-odyssey/free-blacks-in-the-antebellum-period.html

Agiesta, J. C. (2018). *Most say race relations worsened under Obama, poll finds.* CNN. Accessed January 9, 2018. http://www.cnn.com/2016/10/05/politics/obama-race-relations-poll/index.html

Anderson, B. (2020). *Timeline of Coronavirus, wildest two weeks in NBA, Utah Jazz history.* KSL Sports. Accessed 2020. https://kslsports.com/430806/timeline-of-the-coronavirus-and-the-wildest-two-weeks-in-nba-and-utah-jazz-history/

Austen, B. (2016, April). Chicago after Laquan McDonald. *The New York Times.* Accessed 2018. https://www.nytimes.com/2016/04/24/magazine/chicago-after-laquan-mcdonald.html

Badger, E. (2020). How Trump's use of federal forces in cities differs from past presidents. *The New York Times.* Accessed 2020. https://www.nytimes.com/2020/07/23/upshot/trump-portland.html?auth=login-google

Baker, P., Kanno-Youngs, Z., & Davey, M. (2020, July). Trump threatens to send federal law enforcement forces to more cities. *The New York Times.* Accessed 2020. https://www.nytimes.com/2020/07/20/us/politics/trump-chicago-portland-federal-agents.html

Barber, W. J., II. (2016). *The Third Reconstruction.* Beacon Press.

Berman, R. (2017). Republicans slap an expiration date on middle-class tax cuts. The new senate plan would have cuts for individuals go away in eight years but make them permanent for corporations. *The Atlantic.* Accessed 2018. https://www.theatlantic.com/politics/archive/2017/11/republicans-slap-an-expiration-date-on-middle-class-tax-cuts/545996/

Berson, S. (2018). "I'm not even fighting back!": Ex-NFL player thrown to ground during arrest, video shows. http://www.ledger-enquirer.com/news/state/georgia/article 209961214.html

Black Lives Matter. 2013. [Online]. Accessed 2018. https://blacklivesmatter.com/about/.

Blankenship, M., & Reeves, R. (2020, July). *From the George Floyd moment to a Black Lives Matter movement, in tweets.* Brookings. Accessed 2020. https://www.brookings.edu/blog/up-front/2020/07/10/from-the-george-floyd-moment-to-a-black-lives-matter-movement-in-tweets/

Blythe, A. (2017, May). Barber says NC NAACP and moral Mondays will be model for national poor people's campaign. *The News & Observer.* Accessed 2018. https://www.newsobserver.com/news/politics-government/article150663907.html

Borchers, C. (2016). On freedom of the press, Donald Trump wants to make America like England again. *The Washington Post.* https://www.washingtonpost.com/news/the-fix/wp/2016/10/24/on-freedom-of-the-press-donald-trump-wants-to-make-america-like-england-again/?utm_term=.e79d0276b523

Boule, J. (2017). The wealth gap between Whites and Blacks is widening: The myth of racial equality is having real and devastating consequences. *Slate.* Accessed 2018. http://www.slate.com/articles/news_and_politics/politics/2017/09/the_wealth_gap_between_whites_and_blacks_is_widening.html

Bridges, R. D. Betrayal of the Freedman: Rutherford B. Hayes and the end of Reconstruction. https://www.rbhayes.org/hayes/betrayal-of-the-freedman-rutherford-b.-hayes-and-the-end-of-reconstruction/

Brownstein, R. (2017). Federal anti-poverty programs primarily help the GOP's base: Republicans want to shrink government. But their core voters benefit from assistance, like the Supplemental Nutrition Assistance Program, the most. *The Atlantic.* Accessed 2018. https://www.theatlantic.com/politics/archive/2017/02/gop-base-poverty-snap-social-security/516861/

Buchanan, L., et al. (2020, July 3). Black Lives Matter may be the largest movement in U.S. history. *The New York Times.* www.nytimes.com/interactive/2020/07/03/us/george-floyd-protests-crowd-size.html

Callaway, D. (2018). Press freedom is under attack. Don't wait for a journalist to be murdered to protest. *USA Today.* Accessed 2018. https://www.usatoday.com/story/opinion/2018/05/03/press-freedom-donald-trump-journalists-column/572668002/

Carter, W. (2011). The Thirteenth Amendment, interest convergence, and the badges and incidents of slavery. *Maryland Law Review,* 71(1), 21–39. 19p.

Crowder, R. (2010). *Black newspapers have long recorded our history.* https://www.cleveland.com/call-and-post/index.ssf/2010/02/black_newspapers_have_long_rec.html

Curtis, J., & Andersen, R. (2015, January). How social class shapes attitudes on economic inequality: The competing forces of self-interest and legitimation. *International Review of Social Research* 5, 1, 4–19. ISSN: 20698267.

D'Antonio, M. (2016). Is Donald Trump racist? Here's what the record shows." *Fortune*. Accessed 2018. http://fortune.com/2016/06/07/donald-trump-racism-quotes/

Day, E. (2015). #BlackLivesMatter: The birth of a new civil rights movement. *The Guardian*. https://www.theguardian.com/world/2015/jul/19/blacklivesmatter-birth-civil-rights-movement

Eichenlaub, S., et al. (2010). Moving out but not up: Economic outcomes in the Great Migration. *American Sociological Review*, 75(1), 101–125.

Eligon, J. (2020, August 28). Black Lives Matter grows as movement while facing new challenges. *The New York Times*. www.nytimes.com/2020/08/28/us/black-lives-matter-protest.html

Findlaw. *U.S. citizenship through parents or by birth*. Retrieved July 2018, from https://immigration.findlaw.com/citizenship/u-s-citizenship-through-parents-or-by-birth.html

Flaherty, B. (2017). From Kaepernick sitting to Trump's fiery comments: NFL's anthem protests have spurred discussion. *The Washington Post*. Accessed 2018. https://www.washingtonpost.com/graphics/2017/sports/colin-kaepernick-national-anthem-protests-and-NFL-activism-in-quotes/?utm_term=.7c2941f01530

Flippen, C. A. (2001). Racial and ethnic inequality in homeownership and housing equity. *The Sociological Quarterly*, 42(2), 121–149. JSTOR, www.jstor.org/stable/4120744

Gramlich, J. (2018, January). *The gap between the number of Blacks and Whites in prison is shrinking*. Pew Research. Accessed 2018. http://www.pewresearch.org/fact-tank/2018/01/12/shrinking-gap-between-number-of-blacks-and-whites-in-prison/

Great migration. History.com. Accessed 2018. https://www.history.com/topics/black-history/great-migration

Gross, T. (2017, October). *"I Can't Breathe" examines modern policing and the life and death of Eric Garner*. NPR. Accessed 2018. https://www.npr.org/2017/10/23/559498678/i-can-t-breathe-explores-life-and-death-at-the-hands-of-police

Hanks, A., Solomon, D., & Weller, C. E. (2018). *Systematic inequality: How America's structural racism helped create the Black-White wealth gap*. Center for American Progress. https://www.americanprogress.org/issues/race/reports/2018/02/21/447051/systematicinequality/

Hughes, E. C. (1956). Review of A Black Middle Class by Franklin Frazier. *American Sociological Review*, 21(3), 383–384. JSTOR, www.jstor.org/stable/2089298.

Katz-Fishman, W., & Scott, J. (1994). Diversity and equality: race and class in America. *Sociological Forum*, 9(4), 569–581.

Keyes, A. W., Smyke, A. T., Middleton, M., & Black, C. E. (2015). Parenting children in the context of racism. *Zero In Three*. 35(4), 27–34.

Kochhar, Rakesh, & Cilluffo, A. (2018). *Key findings on the rise in income inequality within America's racial and ethnic Groups*. Pew Research, Accessed 2018. https://www.pewresearch.org/fact-tank/2018/07/12/key-findings-on-the-rise-in-income-inequality-within-americas-racial-and-ethnic-groups/.

Lamb, C. (2015). "Don't blame Obama if race relations are worse during his presidency. *The Huffington Post*, Accessed 2018. http://www.huffingtonpost.com/christopher-lamb/dont-blame-obama-if-race-relations-are-worse-during-his-presidency_b_6356746.html

Levey, N. N. (2018, June 19). Republicans outline their latest strategy to roll back Obamacare. *Los Angeles Times*. Accessed 2018. http://www.latimes.com/politics/la-na-pol-obamacare-repeal-revival-20180619-story.html

Levine, C., & Rebala, P. (2020). *I wanted my vote to be counted': In South Carolina, a peek at COVID-19's impact on elections*. Center for Public Integrity. https://publicintegrity.org/politics/elections/in-south-carolina-a-peek-at-covid-19s-impact-on-elections-polling-place/

Lopez, G. (2019). *Donald Trump's long history of racism, from the 1970s to 2019*. Vox. Accessed 2019. https://www.vox.com/2016/7/25/12270880/donald-trump-racist-racism-history

Madjani, A. (2018, October). Jury gets murder case against Chicago police officer Jason Van Dyke in shooting death of Laquan McDonald. *USA Today*. Accessed 2018. https://www.usatoday.com/story/news/2018/10/04/chicago-cop-jason-van-dyke-murder-trial-laquan-mcdonald/1518913002/.

Matthew, D. B., Rodrigue, E., & Reeves, R. V. (2016, October). *Time for Justice: Tackling Race Inequalities in Health and Housing*. The Brookings Institute. Accessed 2018. https://www.brookings.edu/research/time-for-justice-tackling-race-inequalities-in-health and-housing/

Matthews, C. (2018). *Rob Reiner: We're fighting the last battle of the Civil War*. MSNBC, 2018. Accessed 2018. http://www.msnbc.com/hardball/watch/rob-reiner-we-re-fighting-the-last-battle-of-the-civil-war-811874883961?cid=sm_fb_msnbc

McIntosh, P. (1990) White privilege: Unpacking the invisible knapsack. *Independent School*, 49(2), 31.

Montagu, A. (1997). *Man's most dangerous myth: The fallacy of race*. Sage Publications.

Moore, K. (2008, December). Class formations: Competing forms of Black middle-class identity. *Ethnicities*, 8(4), 492–517. Accessed 2018.

Muccari, R., Chow, D., & Murphy, J. (2020). *Coronavirus timeline: Tracking the critical moments of Covid-19*. NBC News. Accessed 2020. https://www.nbcnews.com/health/health-news/coronavirus-timeline-tracking-critical-moments-covid-19-n1154341

Nackenoff, C. (1999). Contested terrain: Understanding the persistence of racial inequality in America. *Polity*, 31(4), 683–691. JSTOR, www.jstor.org/stable/3235243

Neckerman, K. M., & Torche, F. (2007). Inequality: causes and consequences. *Annual Review of Sociology*, 33, 335–357. JSTOR, www.jstor.org/stable/29737766

O'Connell, HA. (2012 March). The impact of slavery on racial inequality in poverty in the contemporary U.S. South. *Social Forces*, 90(3), 713–734. Accessed 2018.

O'Leary, K. (2016, June 27). Trump and the racial politics of the South. *The American Prospect*. Accessed 11 Mar. 2021. https://prospect.org/power/trump-racial-politics-south/

Pickren, W. E. (2011, March). Psychologists, race, and housing in postwar America. *Journal of Social Issues*, 67(1), 27–41. EBSCOhost, doi:10.1111/j.1540-4560.2010.01681.x

Roberts, J. J. (2020, July 22). 'Trump troops' in U.S. cities: What the law says about their rights and yours. *Fortune*. Accessed 2020. https://fortune.com/2020/07/22/trump-federal-troops-portland-law-us-cities-chicago-nyc-baltimore-philadelphia-detroit/

Rosario, R. (2018, May 24). *Bodycam footage exposes authorities' excessive force against Milwaukee Bucks' Sterling Brown*. The Vibe. Accessed 2018. https://www.vibe.com/2018/05/sterling-brown-arrested-milwaukee-police-excessive-force/

Ravelo, J. L., & Jerving, S. *COVID-19—a timeline of the Coronavirus outbreak*. Devex. Accessed 2020. https://www.devex.com/news/covid-19-a-timeline-of-the-coronavirus-outbreak-96396

Sears, D., Van Laar, C., Carrillo, M., & Kosterman, R. (1997). Is it really racism? The origins of White Americans' opposition to race-targeted policies. *Public Opinion Quarterly*, 61(1), 16–53.

Sidner, S., & Simon, M. (2015, December 28). The rise of Black Lives Matter: trying to break the cycle of violence and silence. *CNN*. Accessed 2018. https://www.cnn.com/2015/12/28/us/black-lives-matter-evolution/index.html

Smith, D. (2017, October 31). *The backlash against Black Lives Matter is just more evidence*. The Conversation. https://theconversation.com/the-backlash-against-black-lives-matter-is-just-more-evidence-of-injustice-85587

Smith, J. S. (2018, November 14). *Hero security guard shot by police was expecting second child and now his girlfriend and family search for answers*. theGrio. https://thegrio.com/2018/11/14/hero-security-guard-shot-by-police-was-expecting-second-child-and-now-his-girlfriend-and-family-search-for-answers/

Sniderman, P. M., & Hagen, M. G. (1985). *Race and inequality: A study in American values*. Chatham House Publishers, Inc.

Spiller, J. (2009, December). African Americans after the Civil War: John Spiller surveys race relations in the United States during Reconstruction and constructs a balance sheet. *History Review*, (65), 38.

Squires, G. D. (2003). Racial profiling, insurance style: Insurance redlining and the uneven development of metropolitan areas. *Journal of Urban Affairs*, 25(4), 391–410.

Thernstrom, A., & Thernstrom, S. (1998, March 1). *Black progress: How far we've come, and how far we have to go*. The Brookings Institute. Accessed 2018. https://www.brookings.edu/articles/black-progress-how-far-weve-come-and-how-far-we-have-to-go/.

Vance, J. D. (2016, August 29). Why race relations got worse. *National Review*. Accessed January 9, 2018. http://www.nationalreview.com/article/439431/race-relations-getting-worse-america-why

Wolfson, S. (2018, May 29). After kneeling: The ways NFL players can protest despite the new rules. *The Guardian*. https://www.theguardian.com/sport/2018/may/29/nfl-protests-taking-a-knee-alternatives-new-rules-fines

Wootson, C. R, Jr. (2017, June 29). Rev. William Barber builds a moral movement. *The Washington Post*. Accessed 2018. https://www.washingtonpost.com/news/acts-of-faith/wp/2017/06/29/woe-unto-those-who-legislate-evil-rev-william-barber-builds-a-moral-movement/?utm_term=.096f1822dca0

Wortham, J. (2020, June 5). A 'Glorious Poetic Rage.' *The New York Times*. www.nytimes.com/2020/06/05/sunday-review/black-lives-matter-protests-floyd.html

Review

I. Checking What You Have Read

1. What challenges to democracy do you think America will need to overcome as the country grows more diverse?
2. How can immigration benefit the economy and programs like social security?
3. Explain how a candidate can win the popular vote, and still not win the presidential election?
4. Name two ways that are used by states to hamper people from voting?
5. The U.S. Census predicts minorities will surpass Whites in population size by 2045. How does younger people's attitudes contribute to racial diversity and related political changes?
6. Explain how your understanding of race and history may affect your relations with people of different backgrounds as a young professional.
7. Why is the free press important to government integrity?
8. How does Tribalism negatively affect democracy? What can be done to break down the barriers that "tribalism" creates?
9. Is Colin Kaepernick and the NFL players kneeling during the national anthem a statement of free speech or a form of disrespectful protest? Explain your answer in historical terms of political protest.
10. Is there a connection between the erosion of democratic ideals and virtues and the fate of African Americans? Why is it important to understand the link between democracy and social equality?
11. Explain some of the social and economic issues that some African Americans still face. Choose at least three and thoroughly explain. What recommendations do you have to overcome these challenges?
12. What is the relationship between White supremacy, bigotry, and BlackLivesMatter? Give at least two ways that they are connected.
13. How has the gutting of the Voting Rights Act affected Black and minority voters? Explain some of the tactics that have been put into place.
14. Social media plays a huge role in the lives of Americans. Explain the various roles of social media in the reporting of racial and other issues in American society.

15. How is the BlackLivesMatter movement and civil rights connected?
16. Explain at least three reasons people give for the wealth disparity between Whites and other minorities.
17. Race is a manmade concept. Are the biological differences between ethnic groups significant or superficial considering all peoples originate from Africa?
18. How would you explain White privilege and expectations in everyday society? Give at least three examples to support your answer.
19. The murder of George Floyd by police officers in Minneapolis sparked civil protests not only by BlackLivesMatter protesters, but also saw a multitude of supporters from other racial and ethnic groups. Give at least two reasons why people other than Blacks rose up in protests across the country? Across the world?
20. Monuments, statues, and flags symbolize events in American history. What significance do Civil War statues and the confederate flag symbolize to African Americans?
21. The pandemic of 2020 demonstrated how health and wellness affected different classes of people. What disparities were learned about in the pandemic and what effect does it have on education, employment, and childcare for African Americans and other minorities?
22. How does the BlackLivesMatter strengthen democratic principles of equality for all people?

II. On Your Own

1. Wealth disparities are deeply rooted in American society. Discuss one of the reason why you think some ethic groups and poor Whites have struggled to climb the social economic ladder. Are there institutional and social problems that make it harder for Blacks, Latinos, and other visible minorities?
2. The Rev. Dr. William Barber has suggested that fusion politics and a Third Reconstruction are needed in America. What does he mean by a "Third Reconstruction" and why does it represent the best pathway that democracy can offer to all peoples, of all races, cultures and backgrounds?

Epilogue

During the process of updating this book, events related to African Americans and other people of color rapidly developed. The cycle of events that impacted the economic, political, social, legal, and constitutional issues that came with the end of the Obama presidency were addressed in this book. In a topical, and thematic manner those issues were addressed. The realities of research and writing to meet publication deadlines, made it impractical to include all the "news that was fit to print." Greater attention and detail would have been devoted to the following subjects were there more time and space available to add greater depth and scope. More information related to the following issues need greater discussion:

- Immigration policies and detainment centers that resulted in family separations policies

- The relationships between the Robert's Supreme Court and Post-Reconstruction Era Civil Rights

- The Rehnquist/Roberts Court's retreat from issues relating to the American political process

- The rise of White supremacy pertaining to voting rights, ideology, conspiracy theories, hate group violence, and the January 2021 attack on the U.S. Capitol Building

- The similarities between current law enforcement, courts, local governments, and the sovereignty commissions of the civil rights era; and police lynching of African American suspects in custody

- The connections between the Mueller investigation, voter suppression, the influencing of the 2016/2020 elections via social media disinformation, trauma and its impact on minorities

- How the federal government has seemingly emboldened the states rights advocates as a means to retreat from enforcing national civil rights laws

Although some of those specific subject matters were briefly touched on, more emphasis to connect the substantive meaning and impact of those issues will need to be explored in depth in future editions. The focus of this book was to provide the reader with a survey of key facts, some contextual analysis of the impact of those events that have historical significance to African Americans, peoples of color, and the United States as a whole.

Finally, the history of African Americans provides a rich story about how a nation has grown and made strides toward inclusion. With the birth of the United States, there was an ambition to build a nation based on egalitarian principles of life, liberty, and the pursuit of happiness. Over the past three centuries, those principles have become truer to the original intent of the nation's founders. This book has attempted to catalogue and tell that story in a comprehensive but digestible manner as relates to African Americans.

Index

A

Aahmes I, 8
Aaron, Hank, 258
Abbott, Robert, 154
Abdul-Jabbar, Kareem, 258
Abernathy, Ralph, 197
abolitionist movement, 61–65, 73, 80
    Free African Society, 69–70, 104
    John Brown, 59–60, 61
Abraham, 5
Abubakari II, 22, 25
Abyssinian Baptist Church, 169
activists, 140–1, 203, 209–10, 219, 221, 242, 305, 338, 345
actors and entertainers, 156, 170, 257.
    See also specific people
Adams, Henry, 102
Adams, John Quincy, 61
Aeculapius. *See* Imhotep; Kemet
affirmative action, 220, 247–51, 368
Affordable Health Care, 306, 311, 327

Africa
    Americas and, 20–24
    ancient civilizations, 3–13, 275
    Europe and, xxviii, 18–20, 29, 39
    human origins and, 1–3
    map, xxxiv
    medieval civilizations, 24–30
    resistance to slavery, 55–61, 65–68, 72–73
    slavery and, 31–42
    women in, 8
African American churches, 104–05, 321
    Baptist, 104–105, 141, 169
    education and, 104
    Great Depression and, 136, 138–39, 149
    Methodist, 69–70, 80, 100, 104–105
    Presbyterian, 65
    See also King, Martin Luther, Jr.
African American culture movement, 216–18, 221, 257

African American history, 218, 274
  Black Studies, 218
  timeline, 33, 124, 168, 228
African American towns
  1700s, 69, 72
  1800s, 103, 118
  1900s, 127–28, 131, 185
African Dancer (Barthe), 159
African Methodist Episcopal (AME) Church, 58, 70, 80, 104, 105
African Methodist Episcopal Zion (AMEZ) Church, 70, 104, 105
African Presbyterian Church, 65
African Presence in Early America (Lawrence), 22
Ahmose II, 11
Ahmose Nefertari. *See* Nefertari
Air Corps, World War II, 175–77
Akan people, 40
Akhenaton, 6, 7, 8
Aldridge, Ira, 175
Alexander, John H., 117
Alexander the Great, 5
Ali, Muhammad, 231–32
"All Lives Matter," 328
Allen, Ethan, 76
Allen, Richard, 69–70, 72, 104
Almoravids, 25
Al Omari, 22
Amanirenas, 12
Amanishakhete, 12
Amasis. *See* Ahmose II
Amenhotep III, 7, 8
Amenhotep IV. *See* Akhenaton
American Bar Association, 260
American Catholic Tribune, 110
American Colonization Society, 72
American Federation of Labor (AFL), 133
American Red Cross, 179
American Woman Suffrage Association, 64–65

Americas
  Africa and, 20–24
  European exploration, 17, 21, 23–24
Amherst College, 179
Amistad revolt, 60
Anansi stories, 29
Anderson, J. D., 99–100, 144
Anderson, Marian, 160, 268
An Evening Thought (Hammon), 155
Angelou, Maya, 217
Angola, 38, 44
Anthony, Susan B., 63, 64
Antonio (of Jamestown), 32
apartheid, 71
Arabs, 19, 23, 28
Archer, Dennis, 260
Arizona, 176
The Arkansas State Press, 198
Armstrong, Louis, 159, 258
Armstrong, Samuel, 104, 144–45
army, 176, 199
  Civil War, 73, 75, 77, 83, 84, 85
  Iraq War, 233–35
  Korean War, 236
  late 1800s, 116–18
  Persian Gulf War, 232, 236
  Revolutionary War, 75, 76–77
  Spanish-American War, 87
  Vietnam War, 231, 236
  World War II, 175, 178–79
Asante, Molefi K., 126
Ashanti, 27, 38
Ashe, Arthur, 258
Ashmun Institute. *See* Lincoln University
asiento, 36
Askia Mohammed, 26, 29
Asklepios. *See* Imhotep
Association for the Study of Negro Life and History, 162–63
Assyrians, 11
Atlantic Monthly magazine, 126

Atlantic slave trade, xxviii, 20, 28, 30, 36-37, 39-42
    Africa and, 35, 38
Attucks, Crispus, 33, 76
Austin, Lloyd J., III, 362
Aviles, Pedro Menendez de, 23
Axum, 12–13

B

back-to-Africa movement. *See* resettlement movements
Baker, Ella Jo, 196, 197
Baker, Josephine, 160, 175, 178
Bakke v. Regents of the University of California, 249–50
Balboa, Vasco Nuñez de, 23
Baldwin, James, 175, 196, 258
Baldwin, Ruth Standish, 147
Banneker, Benjamin, 44, 45–46
    correspondence with Jefferson, 46–50
Baquet, Dean, 268
Baraka, Amiri, 216, 219
Barber, William, II, 371, 377
Barnard College, 158
Barnett, Ross, 369
Barthe, Richard, 159
Basie, Count, 159, 258
Bates, Daisy, 197, 198
Baumfree, Isabella. *See* Truth, Sojourner
Beckwourth, James, 114
Before the Mayflower (Bennett), 34
Bell, Alexander Graham, 109
Benedict College, 106
Benin, 27–28, 38, 40
Bennett College, 106
Bennett, Lerone
    colonial slavery, 32, 34, 35, 37, 40, 41
    1800s, 72, 84, 106, 126
    Great Depression, 169
    school desegregation, 199

Bennion, Mervyn, 176
Berry, Halle, 258, 268
Bethune, Mary McLeod, 170, 171
Bethune-Cookman College, 106, 170
Biden, Joseph, 213, 262, 284, 303, 205, 344, 346, 350–52
    1994 "Crime Bill," 350–51
Birth of a Nation, 125
Black Arts Movement, 216–17
"Black Cabinet." *See* Federal Council of Negro Affairs
Black Codes, 101, 108, 111, 183, 241
Black Entertainment Television (BET), 265
Black History Month, 162, 274
Black is Beautiful, 210
BlackLivesMatter movement, 213, 309, 328–29, 369, 370–74
Black Nationalism, 73. 147–48, 212, 231
Black Panther Party for Self Defense, xxxi, 168, 210–11, 221
    FBI and, 212–13, 231
Black power movement, 168, 205, 209–22
Black press. *See* periodicals
Blacks in Science (Van Sertima), 266
Black Star Line Shipping Company, 141, 265
Black Wall Street of the West. *See* Greenwood (Tulsa, Oklahoma)
The Black West (Katz), 116
Blair, Izell, Jr., 201
Bland, Sandra, 308
Bloody Sunday, 204, 205
"blue lives matter," 309, 328
Blues for Mister Charlie (Baldwin), 196
blues music, 156, 159, 161, 165
Boabdil, 35
Boley, Oklahoma, 103, 118
Bonaparte, Napoleon, 57
Booker, Cory, 349
Boone, Sarah, 265
Bornu, 27

Boston Guardian, 141, 154
Boston Massacre, 76
Boston University, 194
Bowdoin College, 65
boycotts, 195, 196, 205, 206, 341
Braddock, James, 182
Bradley, Michael, 21
Bradstreet, Anne, 45
Braun, Carol Moseley, 220, 268
Brazil, 55–56
Breedlove, Sarah. *See* Walker, Madam C. J.
"Brer" Rabbit stories, 29
Brewer, Rosalind, 269
Brooke, Edward, 218, 220
Brooks, Rayshard, 373
Brotherhood of Sleeping Car Porters, 133, 174
Brown, James, 217
Brown, Jim, 258
Brown, John, 59–60, 61
Brown, Linda, 192, 244
Brown, Michael, 308, 328, 372
Brown, Oliver, 244
Brown, Sterling, 329
Brown, William Wells, 155
"The Brown Bomber." *See* Louis, Joe
Brown v. Board of Education, xxxi, 193, 197, 199, 244–46, 252, 260, 276, 285
Brown II, 246, 276
Bruce, Blanche K., 107, 124, 218
Buffalo Soldiers (9th and 10th Cavalry), xxx, 87, 116–17, 118–19, 229, 236
Burke, Yvonne, 220
Burns, Ursula, 269
Burr, J. A., 266
Burridge, L. S., 265
Bush, George, 232–33, 369
Bush, George W., 233, 247, 260, 261, 263, 278, 280, 344

C

California, 63, 73, 79, 114, 117–118, 210, 220, 249–50, 338, 373
  gold rush, 117, 119
Cameroon, medieval, 40
Canada, resettlement in, 67, 68, 72, 73, 75, 77, 88
Candaces, 4, 5, 11, 12
Cann, Rebecca, 2
Cape Verde Islands, 22
carbon-14 dating, 21
Carmichael, Stokely, 201, 209, 210
Carnera, Primo, 181
Carruthers, George R., 266
Carson, Benjamin, 324, 348
Carson, Kit, 117
Carter, W., 368
Carver, George Washington, 110, 123
Center for American Progress (CAP), 367
Chaney, James, 200
charter schools, 278, 281, 283, 288
chattel slavery, xxviii–xxix, 30, 34, 35, 36, 38
Cheops, 5
Chesnutt, Charles, 155
Cheyney University, 106
Chicago Defender, 154, 185, 345
Chisholm, Shirley, 219, 221, 228, 320
Christianity
  abolitionism and, 47
  ancient civilizations and, 13
  early church, 18
  papal bull of 1493, 36
  slavery and, 39, 104–05
  See also African American churches
cimarrons, 55
Cinque, Joseph, 60
City College of New York, 262
civil disobedience, 195, 201–06
Civilian Conservation Corps (CCC), 170
Civil Rights Act
  of 1866, 242, 243

of 1870, 243
of 1871, 243
of 1875, 97, 111, 243
of 1957, 194, 246
of 1960, 246
of 1964, 203, 205, 206, 246, 250, 251
of 1968, 246, 247
of 1991, 246, 247
Civil Rights Commission, 194, 246, 247
civil rights movement, 108, 187, 193–197, 201, 206, 218, 220, 246, 260, 296, 321–23, 340. *See also* Black power movement
Civil War, 33, 78, 81–88
    Fort Sumter, 82
    Southern states' secession, 81–82
Clark, Kenny, 175
Clark, William, 113–14
Clay, Cassius. *See* Ali, Muhammad
Cleaver, Eldridge, 213
Cleopatra, 5
Clinton, Bill, 176, 312
Clinton, Hillary, xxxii, 287, 299, 302, 303, 313, 320–23, 325, 327, 330, 344
Clotel (Brown), 155
Clyburn, James, 351
Coates, Ta-Nehisi, 308
Cody, Buffalo Bill, 115, 116
COINTELPRO, 212–13
Cole, Nat "King," 268
colonial militias, 75
Colored Methodist Episcopal Church, 104
Columbia University, 157, 297
Columbus, Christopher, 17, 20, 21, 23, 28–29
Committee on Urban Conditions Among Negroes. *See* Urban League
Compromise of 1850, 79, 82
Congo, medieval, 27, 38
Congo River, 26
Congress for Industrial Organization (CIO), 133–134

Congressional Black Caucus, 219, 228, 235, 299, 321
Congress of Racial Equality (CORE), 200, 201, 205, 213, 221, 231
Conley, Elvira, 115–16
Connecticut colony, 34
Conyers, John, 234
Cookman Institute. See Bethune-Cookman College
Cornell University, 157, 184
Cornish, Samuel, 65, 345
Cortez, Hernando, 23
Cosby, Bill, 258
Cote d'Ivoire, 40
Cotton Club, 159
Cotton States and International Exposition, 125
Covid-19 pandemic, 346–47, 374–76
Cowings, Patricia, 266
criminal justice system
    civil rights activists and, 209
    discrimination, 148
    drug policy, 370
    ignoring crimes against African Americans, 364
    police brutality, 308, 328, 361, 369–72
    racial profiling, 148, 370–71, 377
The Crisis, 147, 154, 156–57
Criterion, 345
Crittenden, John, 81
Crittenden Compromise, 81
Croson v. Richmond, 249
Crow, Sheryl, 302
Crow Nation, 114
Cuba, 60, 61, 154
Cudjoe, 56
Cuffee, Paul, 33, 72
Cullen, Countee, 157, 175
Cuomo, Andrew, 375
Curry, Michael, 268
cyber security, 326, 329, 347
Czolgosz, Leon, 125

D

Daoud, 26
Dark Ages, 17–18
Daughters of the American Revolution, 160
Davis, Benjamin O., Jr., 168, 176, 177
Davis, Jefferson, 107
Davis, Ossie, 258
Daytona Normal and Industrial Institute for Women. *See* Bethune-Cookman College
"Deadwood Dick." *See* Love, Nat
Dearfield, Colorado, 103
Declaration of Independence, 45, 46, 68, 69, 74, 78, 87–88
    Banneker letter, 46–49
Dee, Ruby, 258
Deir el-Bahri, 8
Deferred Action for Childhood Arrivals (DACA), 304, 312
Delany, Martin, 72–73, 139, 140, 148
Democratic Party, xxx, 187, 261, 320–321, 323, 330, 350
    Democratic National Committee, 302, 329
    Democratic National Convention, 261, 299
desegregation, 197–200, 206, 245–46, 247, 276–78, 288
Democrat Select Committee, 219
Department of Justice, 246. *See also* Federal Bureau of Investigation (FBI)
Desert Storm. *See* Persian Gulf War
De Soto, Hernando, 24
Dessalines, Jean Jacques, 56
Developing Communities Project (DCP), 297
Dickerson, D. J., 299
Dinkens, David, 268
Diop, Cheik Anta, 24
District of Columbia, slavery in, 79
Djoser. *See* Zoser

DNA typing and earliest humans, 1, 2, 13
Dorantes, Stephen, 24, 114
Douglas, Aaron, 158
Douglass, Frederick, 61, 62–63, 64, 73, 124, 175, 345
down-balloting, 346
Dreamers. *See* Deferred Action for Childhood Arrivals (DACA)
Dreams from My Father (Obama), 298
Dred Scott decision, 81
Drew, Charles, 168, 179, 187
Du Bois, William Edward Burghardt, xxx, 154, 174, 175
    color line, 139, 148
    and the "Great Debate," 104, 142–44
    NAACP, 141, 146–47
    Niagara Movement, 124, 145
    Pan-Africanism, 148
    "Talented Tenth," 289
Duckett, Thasunda Brown, 269
Duke, David, 369
Dunbar, Paul Larence, 155
Dunham, Stanley Ann, 295–96
Dunmore, Lord, 76–77
du Sable, Jean Baptiste, 114

E

Easley, Annie, 266
Ebony magazine, 185
economics of freedom
    collective economics, 140–41, 216
    entrepreneurship, 264–65
    factory work, 130
    labor unions, 132–34
    New Deal, 169, 170, 174, 187
    poverty, problem of, 277, 279–280, 366
    sharecropping, 130–131, 339
    World War II, 167, 170, 174, 180, 187

Index

economics of Reconstruction
    homesteading, 102–03
    land redistribution plan, 101
    sharecropping, 101–02
economics of slavery, 31–39
    California gold rush, 117, 119
    plantation system, 42–44
    Triangle Trade, 39–42
Edison, Thomas, 109–10
education
    affirmative action and, 248
    African American history, 218, 274
    ancient world, 9–10, 13, 275
    Black Panthers and, 210
    Black Studies, 218
    charter schools, 281
    desegregation of schools, 197–99, 243–51, 276–78
    Every Student Succeeds Act, 288
    fraternities/sororities, 184
    Great Debate, 104, 142–44
    higher education, 284–86
    Historically Black Colleges and Universities, 106, 270, 284, 286, 289, 349
    importance of, 103–04, 273, 286
    independent schools, 280
    Moors and, 19–20, 275
    native schools, 100, 275–76
    No Child Left Behind Act, 279–80
    normal schools, 144–145
    and Prince Hall, 65
    public vs. private, 283–84
    school choice, 278–79, 283
    school vouchers, 281–82
    schooling vs., 103, 274
Egypt, ancient
    achievements, 6, 12
    Americas and, 21
    ancient Greece and, 13
    Kush and, 3–4, 24
    Late Period, 11–12
    modern historians and, 14
    New Kingdom, 7–10
    Old Kingdom, 6–7
    schools in, 9, 20
    slavery in, 34–35, 275
    timeline, 5
    women in, 8, 12
Eisenhower, Dwight D., 177, 351
    desegregation of schools, 197–98
elections
    end of Reconstruction, 101
    2008, 295, 302–03, 309
    2012, 304–09
    2016, xxxii, 182, 320–330, 343, 344, 366, 368, 374
    2020, 262, 284, 343, 344, 346–347, 351, 374–76
Elementary and Secondary Education Act (ESEA), 279
El Hajj Malik el-Shabazz. See Malcolm X
Ellington, Edward Kennedy "Duke," 159, 160
Ellison, Marvin, 269
Emancipation Proclamation (1863), 33, 85, 86, 96, 169, 174, 240, 241
England, resettlement in, 63, 73, 75, 77, 88
entrepreneurship, xxxi, 264–65
The Escape (Brown), 155
Estevanico. See Dorantes, Stephen
Ethiopia, 1, 3–4, 12, 13. See also Kush
ethnic pride. See Black Nationalism
Europe, 2–3, 6, 9, 17–20, 26–42
Executive Order 8802 (1941), 174
Executive Order 9981 (1948), 175, 229
Executive Order 10925 (1961), 247
exodusters, 103, 118
explorers, 17, 19, 21, 24, 39, 113–18
Ezana, 13

F

Fair Employment Practices Commission, 174

Fair Housing Act, 246
Fanti kingdom, 38
Fard, Wallace D., 214
Farmer, James, 200
Farrakhan, Louis, 215
Faubus, Orval, 197–98, 369
Fauset, Jessie, 156–57
Federal Bureau of Investigation (FBI), 141, 201, 211–213, 231–32, 329, 347
Federal Council of Negro Affairs, 170, 171
Feral Benga (Barthe), 159
Fields, Mary, 115
15th Amendment (1870), 33, 64, 97, 101, 106, 109, 242, 320
The Fire Next Time (Baldwin), 196
1st Amendment, 342, 345
First Step Act, 349
Fisher, Abigail, 250
Fisk Jubilee Singers, 161
Fisk University, 106, 158
Flemmings, R. F., Jr., 265
Flipper, Henry O., 117
Florida, 23, 44, 66, 126, 129, 171, 196, 282, 305, 344, 347, 372
Floyd, George, 371, 372, 373
FluteBoy (Barthe), 159
Forbes, 264, 269
Forest Kingdoms, 27
Forrest, Nathan Bedford, 109
Forten, James, 72
Fort Sumter, 82
Foster, Rube, 164
14th Amendment (1868), 33, 64, 97–98, 194, 242–43, 245, 250, 252
France, 229, 233, 373
    emigration to, 160, 161, 174, 196
    Louisiana Purchase, 57
    World War I, 134–35
    World War II, 174, 177
Franklin, Aretha, 217, 258
Franz Ferdinand, Archduke, 134
fraternal organizations, 70, 73

Frazier, Walt, 258
Free African Society, 69–70, 104
Freedmen's Bureau, xxix, 99–101, 102
freedom riders, 202–03, 205, 206, 212
Freedom's Journal, 65, 183, 345
Free Methodist Church, 80
French Revolution, 56
Frey, W. H., 339
Fugitive Slave Law (1850), 33, 67, 80
Fulani people, 40
Fuller, Meta Vaux Warrick, 175

G

Gandhi, Mohandas, 195
Gans, Herbert, 338, 339
Gao, 26, 27
Garner, Eric, 371, 373
Garnet, Henry Highland, 72
Garrison, William Lloyd, 65, 69, 141
Garvey, Marcus, 140–41, 265
    Black Nationalism and, 148, 210, 216
    Malcolm X and, 215
    resettlement and, 139, 148
Gaye, Marvin, 258
Geneva Peace Accord, 229
George Washington University, 262
gerrymandering, 342, 345–46
Ghana, 38, 40
    Kente cloth, 217
    medieval, 24–26, 29, 275
Gibbs, Joshua, 60
Gibson, Althea, 258–59
Gibson, Josh, 164
Ginsburg, Ruth Bader, 342
Giovanni, Nikki, 217
Glory, 83
Going to Meet the Man (Baldwin), 196
Goldsmith, J., 348
Goldwater, Barry, 340
Goodman, Andrew, 201
Gordy, Berry, Jr., 258

government/public service, 265, 267. *See also specific people*
Gratz v. Bollinger, 228, 250
Great Compromise, 68–69
Great Depression, xxx, 162, 165, 167–71, 303, 323
    Negro Baseball League and, 164
    New Deal, 170, 171, 174, 187
Greece, ancient
    Alexander the Great, 5
    slavery in, 35
Green Mountain Boys, 76
Greenwood (Tulsa, Oklahoma), 124, 126, 127–28, 136, 185
Gregory, Dick, 221
Gregory, Frederick D., 266
griots, 29
Grutter v. Bollinger, 250
Guinea, 23, 27, 40
Gullah/Geechee people, 44
Gullah Jack, 58
gun violence, 305, 326, 328

H

Hagen, Michael, 364–65
Haiti, xxix, 41, 56–57, 72, 96
Hall, Prince, 65, 70, 72, 276
Hamer, Fannie Lou, 247
Hammon, Jupiter, 155
Hampton University, 106, 285
Handy, W. C., 159
Harlem Renaissance, xxx, 124, 148, 153, 154, 156–162, 165
"Harlem Shadows" (McKay), 158
Harper's Ferry, 59, 61
Harper's magazine, 127
Harris, Kamala, 262, 267, 284, 351
Harvard Law Review, 298, 308
Harvard Law School, 264, 298, 301
Harvard University, 143, 157, 248, 296
Hastie, William, 179
Hatcher, Richard, 218

Hatshepsut, 8
Hausa Kingdom, 27
Hausa people, 40
Hayes, Cuff, 76
Hayes, Roland, 160–61
Haynes, George Edmund, 147
Hellfighters (369th Regiment), 135–36
Helms, Jesse, 350
Henry the Navigator, 28
Herodotus, 3–4, 13
Hickok, Wild Bill, 116, 117
Himes, Chester, 175
Hip Hop, 258
Hippocrates, 6
Hippocratic Oath, 6–7
Hispaniola, 56
Historically Black Colleges and Universities, 106, 270, 284, 286, 289, 349
Hitler, Adolf, 180
Holder, Eric, Jr., 267
Hollins v. State of Oklahoma, 173
Holly, James, 96
Homer, 3
Homestead Act (1865), 102
Hooker, John Lee, 159
Hoover, Herbert, 169
Hoover, J. Edgar, 213
horse racing, 117, 259
Houston, Charles Hamilton, 147, 173, 244, 259–60
Howard University, 106, 147, 158, 184, 259
Hughes, Langston, 157–58, 165, 258
humans, earliest, 3
Hurston, Zora Neale, 157, 158, 165, 258
Hussein, Saddam, 232–34, 263
Hyksos, 5, 8

I

Ickes, Harold, 160
"I Have a Dream" (King), 203, 220

Imhotep, 6–7
indentured servants, 20, 24, 31, 32, 34, 37, 39, 50, 57
indigo, 44
Inland Boatman Union, 134
interracial marriage, 295
inventors. *See* scientists and inventors
Iraq War, 233–34
Islam
    Almoravides, 25
    Axum, 12–13
    medieval Mali, 22, 25
    medieval Songhay, 24, 26–27
    Moors, 19
    Nation of Islam, 210, 214–15, 231–32
Israel, ancient, 12

J

Jackson, Jesse, 220–21, 228, 264
Jackson, John, 7
Jackson, Mahalia, 296
Jackson, Mary, 265
Jackson, Richard, 235
Jackson, Reggie, 258
Jairazbhoy, Rafique, 21
Jamaica, 56
James, Latitia, 268
James Meredith March, 205, 210
Jamestown, 32, 33
Jarrett, Valerie, 267
jazz music, 156, 159, 160, 161, 165, 170, 217, 258
Jefferson, Thomas
    Banneker letter, 46–50
    Declaration of Independence, 68
    Louisiana Purchase, 57
Jeffries, Jim, 153
Jemison, Mae, 228, 266
Jenne, 26
Jim Crow laws, 97, 108–09, 127, 130, 136, 143, 203, 218, 241, 243, 347, 367

Johanson, Donald, 2
"John Brown's Body," 60
Johnson, Andrew, 101
Johnson, Hazel, 268
Johnson, Isaac, 266
Johnson, Jack, 153–54, 181, 232
Johnson, James Weldon, 155, 156
Johnson, John H., 185
Johnson, Katherine, xxxi, 265, 266
Johnson, Lyndon Baines, xxxi, 204–05, 206, 230, 247, 251, 279, 351
Johnson, Robert, 159, 265
Johnson, W., 265
Johnson C. Smith University, 106
Jones, Absalom, 69–70, 104
Jones, Quincy, 258
Jones, Rene, 269
Jordan, Barbara, 220
Jordan, Michael, 258
Journal of Negro History, 162, 163
Joyner, Tom, 286
Joyner-Kersee, Jackie, 258
judicial decisions
    Bakke v. Regents of the University of California, 249–50
    Brown II, 246, 276
    Brown v. Board of Education, xxxi, 193, 197, 199, 244–46, 252, 260, 276, 285
    citizenship, 97, 109, 243
    Croson v. Richmond, 249
    Dred Scott decision, 81
    Gratz v. Bollinger, 228, 250
    Grutter v. Bollinger, 250
    Hollins v. State of Oklahoma, 173
    McLaurin v. Oklahoma, 244
    Murray v. Pearson, 243–44
    Plessy v. Ferguson, 194, 241–42
    reparation lawsuits, 128, 129
    school vouchers, 278, 281–83, 288
    Scottsboro case, 173
    Shelby v. Holder, 342
    slavery decisions, 61, 65, 81
    Sweatt v. Painter, 244, 285

Judson, Andrew T., 60
Juneteenth celebrations, 86
Just, Ernest, 163
justice. *See* criminal justice system

K

Kaepernick, Colin, 328, 369–70
Kamit. *See* Kemet
Kanem, 27
Kansas-Nebraska Act (1854), 80, 107
Kanuri people, 27
Karenga, Maulana, 211, 213, 216
Katz, William Loren, 116
Kellman, Gerald, 297
Kemet
    achievements, 6, 12
    Americas and, 21
    ancient Greece and, 13
    Kush and, 3–4, 24
    Late Period, 11–12
    modern historians and, 14
    New Kingdom, 7–10
    Old Kingdom, 6–7
    schools in, 9, 20
    slavery in, 34–35, 275
    timeline, 5
    women in, 8, 12
Kennedy, John F., 205, 206, 247, 262, 303
Kente cloth, 217
Keyes, A. W., 369
Kilwa, 28
King, Martin Luther, Jr., 168, 194–96, 285, 371
    FBI and, 213, 231
    Jesse Jackson and, 220
    Malcolm X and, 215
    marches, 203–05, 322
King, Rodney, 370–71
Knight, Gladys, 258
Knights of Labor, 133
Knights of Pythias fraternal organization, 70
Knights of the White Camellia, 109
Kolon, Ali. *See* Sunni Ali the Great
Kovalevski, S., 297–98
Korean War, 227, 236
Ku Klux Klan, 101, 107, 109, 128, 201, 203, 365, 369
Kush, 3–4, 11–13, 24
Kwame Ansa, 38
Kwanzaa, 211, 216

L

labor unions, 132, 133
Langston, Oklahoma, 103, 118
Latimer, Howard Lewis, 109–10, 123
Lawrence, Harold, 22
laws, post–Civil War
    affirmative action, 220, 247–51, 368
    Emancipation Proclamation (1863), 33, 85, 86, 96, 169, 174, 240, 241
    Executive Order 8802 (1941), 174
    Executive Order 9981 (1948), 175, 229
    Executive Order 10925 (1961), 247
    15th Amendment (1870), 33, 64, 97, 101, 106, 109, 242, 320
    Mann Act, 154
    No Child Left Behind Act, 279–80
    Reconstruction Acts, 95
    13th Amendment, 33, 96–97, 242
    timelines, 33, 240
    Tulsa Race Riot Commission (2001), 128
    24th Amendment, 205
    Voting Rights Act (1965), 205, 206, 209, 247, 251, 342
    See also Civil Rights Act; 14th Amendment; Jim Crow laws
laws, pre–Civil War
    Compromise of 1850, 79, 82
    Fugitive Slave Law, 67, 80

Great Compromise, 68–69
Kansas-Nebraska Act, 80, 107
Missouri Compromise, 79–81, 82
Northwest Ordinance, 79, 103
slave codes, 33, 42, 51, 82, 108, 239, 241
timeline, 33
See also judicial decisions
Leadbelly, 159
Leakey, Louis, 1
Leakey, Richard, 1
Leavitt, Joshua, 60
Lee, Carol, 274
Lee, Spike, 258, 285
Leidesdorff, William Alexander, 117
Leonard, Buck, 164
Lewis, John L., 133
Lewis, Oliver, 259
Lewis, Reginald, xxxi, 264, 265, 269
Lewis and Clark Expedition, 112
Liberator, 65, 141
Liberia, 72, 88, 141
Lies My Teacher Told Me (Loewen), 126
Lincoln, Abraham, 73, 81, 87, 323, 351
    Civil War, 83, 84, 95
    election of, 81
    Emancipation Proclamation, 85, 169
    and Barack Obama, 303
    resettlement views, 96
    slavery views, 82–83
    and Donald Trump, 349
Lincoln-Douglas Debate, 82
Lincoln University, 106, 284
Lindy Hop, 159, 165
literature and writers, 155–58, 258. *See also specific people*
Little, Malcolm. *See* Malcolm X
Livingston, Robert, 57
Locke, Alain, 156, 165
Loewen, James W., 126
Lomotey, Kofi, 274
Louis, Joe, 180, 181–82, 187
Louisiana Purchase, 57, 80
Love, J. L., 266

Love, Nat, 115
L'Ouverture, Toussaint, xxix, 33, 41, 56
lynchings, 109, 119, 126–27, 129–30, 171, 180, 193, 345, 386

M

magnet schools, 279
Maine, 86
Makeda, 12
Malcolm X, 210, 212, 214–15
Maleqereabar, 12
Mali, medieval, 22, 24–27, 29, 275
Malinke people, 25
Mandinka/Mandingo people, 22, 25, 40, 60
Manetho, 7
Manifest Destiny, 86
Manikongo, 27
Mann Act of 1910, 154
Mansa Musa I, 22, 25
Man's Most Dangerous Myth (Montagu), 363
manumission, 71, 183
Manumission Society, 71
Maraniss, D., 297
March Against Fear. *See* James Meredith March
March on Washington (1963), 203, 205, 206, 220, 322
Marines, World War II, 174
maroons, 55
Marrow, Desmond, 329
Marsalis, Wynton, 258
Marshall, Thurgood, 147, 173, 260
    Brown v. Board of Education, 193, 245
    Murray v. Pearson, 244
Martin, Trayvon, 308, 313, 328, 372
Maryland, 34, 45, 66, 83, 85, 99, 163, 199, 243, 264, 281, 346
Mason, Biddy, 64 117 118
Masonic Lodge, 70

Massachusetts, 32, 34, 45, 50, 61, 65, 72, 76, 83, 110, 143, 161, 218, 220
Matzeliger, Jan Ernst, 110
Mayer, John, 302, 303
McCain, Franklin, 201
McCain, John, 302, 314, 320
McConnell, Mitch, 309
McCoy, Elijah, 110, 123
McDonald, Laquan, 371
McGill University, 179
McGovern, George, 320
McIntosh, Peggy, 369
McKay, Claude, 157, 158, 175
McKinley, William, 125
McLaurin v. Oklahoma, 244
McNair, Denise, 260
McNeil, Joseph, 201
medicine, 4, 6, 12, 25, 26, 257, 269. *See also* scientists and inventors
medu neter, 7
melanin, 2, 3
Mende people, 60
Menelik, 12
Menes, 4, 5, 6
Menes, 4, 5, 6
Meredith, James, 199, 205, 210
Meroe, 4, 11, 12
Methodist Episcopal Church, 70, 80, 104
Mexico, 21, 41, 55, 67, 79, 326, 348
Michigan Baptist Church, 141
Middle Passage, 40, 41
migration north, 102, 124, 130–34
migration westward, 102–03, 113–19
Miles, A., 265
military
    Buffalo Soldiers, 87, 116–17, 118–19, 229, 236
    Civil War, 78, 81, 82–86, 88
    colonial militias, 75, 76
    draft, 134, 230–31, 234–35
    Iraq War, 233–35, 261, 263, 302
    Korean War, 227, 229, 236
    Persian Gulf War, 232–33
    Red Ball Express, 177
    Revolutionary War, 43, 75–77, 78, 83, 88
    Spanish-American War, 75, 86–87, 236
    Vietnam War, 221, 227, 229–32, 236
    volunteer, 83, 234
    War of 1812, 77–78, 83
    World War I, 131, 134–36, 140, 175, 227, 236
    World War II, 174–78, 227, 236
Miller, Dorie, 176,
Miller, Kelly, 147
Mills, Florence, 161
Mine, Mill, and Smelter Union, 134
Minor, Barbara, 282
Miracles, 258
The Mis-Education of the Negro (Woodson), 162, 163
Mississippi Freedom Summer Project, 200–01
Missouri, 79, 81, 83, 85, 371
Missouri Compromise (1820), 33, 79, 80, 81, 82
mitochondrial DNA, 2, 13
Mizraim. *See* Kemet
Mogadishu, 28
Mombassa, 28
The Monitor, 84
monotheism, 7
Monroe, James, 57
Montagu, Ashley, 3, 363
Montes, Pedro, 60
Montgomery bus boycott (1955), 195–96
Montgomery Improvement Association (MIA), 195
Montgomery March, 204–05
Moody Bible Institute, 171–72
Moors, 17–20, 28, 35, 275, 363
Morehouse College, 106, 194

Morgan State University, 163, 285
Morocco, 19–20, 27–28, 29–30, 114–15
Morrison, Toni, 217, 258, 285
Morton, Jelly Roll, 159–60
Moses, 5, 7, 9, 66
"Moses of her people." *See* Tubman, Harriet
Moskowitz, Henry, 146
Motown, 218, 258
Muhammad, Elijah, 214, 215
Muhammad, Fard, 214
Muhammad, Warif Deen, 215
Murray, Donald G., 243
Murray v. Pearson, 243
musicians, 156, 159–61, 165, 183, 221, 258. *See also specific people*
"mysteries" system, 9, 13, 275

N

Napata, 4–5, 11–12
Narmer. *See* Menes
National American Woman Suffrage Association, 65
National Association for the Advancement of Colored People (NAACP), 146–48, 154, 200, 206, 250
    Du Bois and, 144
    March Against Fear, 205
    Montgomery bus boycott, 195
    nonviolent protest, 221
    school desegregation, 197–99, 243–45, 252
    and Niagara movement, 141, 146
    and fight against social injustice, 172–74, 192
    Spingarn Medal, 171
    unions and, 134
National Education Association (NEA), 280
National Rifle Association (NRA), 305–06, 328

National Women Suffrage Association, 64
National Youth Administration (NYA), 170, 171
National Youth Movement, 211
Nation of Islam, 210, 214, 215, 231, 232
Native Americans, 36, 65–66, 113, 116, 118, 119, 221, 343
navy
    Civil War, 84–85, 109
    War of 1812, 77
    World War I, 134
    World War II, 174, 176
Nawidemak, 12
Nefertari, 8
Nefertiti, 8
Negro Baseball Leagues, 164, 184, 258
Negro History Week. *See* Black History Month
"The Negro Speaks of Rivers" (Hughes), 157
Negro Yearbook, 129
New Black Panthers, 211, 221
New Deal, 169–171, 174, 187, 310, 323
Newman, Omarosa Manigault, 348
Newton, Huey, 210, 212
New York, 44, 60, 63, 65, 67
New York University, 157
Niagara Movement, 124, 141, 144–46
Nicodemus, Kansas, 103
Nieto, Enrique Peña, 326
Nigeria, 28, 38
Niger River, 28
Nile River, 3, 11, 12
19th Amendment, 320
Nixon, Richard, 176, 248, 262, 304, 312, 369
No Child Left Behind Act (NCLB), 279, 280
nonviolence, 61–62, 195, 201–05
normal schools, 144, 275
North Carolina Agricultural and Technical College, 201

Index

northern migration. *See* migration north
North Star, 63, 345
Northwest Ordinance (1787), 79, 103
Nova Scotia, 67, 77, 88
Nubia. *See* Kush
Nzenga Maremba, 38
Nzingha, 38

O

Obadele, Imari, 212
Obama, Barack, 228, 235, 262, 287
    campaigns, 302–306
    challenges and successes, 304–06, 309–11
    community activism, 297–98
    comparison to predecessors, 303
    Dreamers, 304
    Dreams from My Father, 298
    early life, 295–96
    early political career, 298–99
    Every Student Succeeds Act (ESSA), 280, 288
    executive order, 304, 313
    health care, 306, 308, 311
    higher education, 296–97
    Nobel Peace Prize, 311
    personal struggles, 299–301
    political legacy, 311–13
    Harvard Law Review, 298
    Wright, Reverend Jeremiah, 300
Obama, Barack, Sr., 295–96
Obama, Michelle, 248, 298, 305
Obamacare. *See* Affordable Health Care
Occidental College, 296, 297
Odd Fellows fraternal organization, 70
Oklahoma State University, 128
O'Leary, K., 368
Olmec civilization, 21, 23, 363
Olympics, 180, 258
O'Neal, Shaquille, 258
Opportunity magazine, 154
Oprah Winfrey Foundation, 286

Oprah Winfrey Leadership Academy for Girls, 287
oral tradition, 9
Organization of African Unity, 215
Ossoff, Jon, 348
Otis, James, 68, 87
Ovington, Mary White, 146
Owens, Jesse, 180–81, 187, 258
Oyo Empire, 27

P

Packer, G., 341
Paine, Thomas, 45, 68
palenques, 55
paleoanthropology, 1
Palin, Sarah, 303
Palmares, 55, 56
Pan-Africanism. See Black Nationalism
Pan-American Exposition, 123–25
papal bull of 1493, 36
Parker, James "Big Ben," 125
Parks, Rosa, 168, 195, 202, 247
Payton, Walter, 258
Pennsylvania Abolition Society, 66
Pennsylvania Anti-Slavery Society, 68
People United to Save Humanity (PUSH), 220
periodicals
    The Arkansas State Press, 198
    Boston Guardian, 141
    Chicago Defender, 154, 185, 345
    The Crisis, 147, 154, 157, 340
    Criterion, 345
    Ebony magazine, 185
    Freedom's Journal, 65, 183, 345
    Journal of Negro History, 162, 163
    Liberator, 65, 141
    Negro Yearbook, 129
    North Star, 63, 345
    Opportunity magazine, 154
    Philadelphia Magazine, 45
    Pittsburgh Courier, 345

Perry, Matthew, 77
Persian Gulf War, 232–33
Peru, 21, 23, 49, 55
Petronius, 12
pharaohs, 6, 8
Philadelphia Magazine, 45
Philadelphia sound, 217
Philadelphia Vigilance Committee, 68
Phillips, Wendell, 65
Piankhy, 5, 11
Pickett, Bill, 115–16
Pieh, Sengbe. *See* Cinque, Joseph
Pittsburgh Courier, 345
Pizarro, Francisco, 23
The Planter, 84, 87, 368
Pleasant, Mary Ellen, 64
Plessy, Homer, 241, 242
Plessy v. Ferguson, 194, 241
Poems on Various Subjects, Religious and Moral (Wheatley), 45
Poitier, Sidney, 258, 268
political representation, 69, 76, 126, 241
Poor, Salem, 76, 183
popular culture, 217
Portugal, 18–20, 28, 35–36, 363
poverty, problem of, 277, 279, 366
Powell, Adam Clayton, Jr., 172, 187
Powell, Adam Clayton, Sr., 169, 172
Powell, Colin, xxxi, 228, 260–63
Poyas, Peter, 58
Price, Cecil, 201
Prosser, Gabriel, 33, 58-59
Protestantism, 42. *See also* African American churches
Ptolemy II, 7
Public Works Administration (PWA), 170
Punahou School, 296, 301
Purvis, Harriett Forten, 65
Pythagoras, 4, 9

Q

Quakers, 66, 70

Quarles, Benjamin, 104, 163
quilombos, 55

R

race
    and inequality, 364–67
    role in America, 362–64
    skin color, 2–3
    as social construction, 3, 363
racism
    basis of, 14, 364
    manifestations of, 125–30, 131, 148, 174, 178–79, 230, 328, 344, 367, 369
    perpetuation of White supremacy, 123, 364, 368
    responses to, 72, 109, 111, 118, 139–41, 154, 162, 165
ragtime, 159, 160
Rainbow Coalition, 220, 221
Randolph, A. Philip, 133, 174, 175
Rangel, Charles, 234
Rap, 258
Reagan, Ronald, 236, 249, 262, 304, 370
Reconstruction, 95–111
    constitutional amendments, 96–98, 99
    end of, 101
    backlash, 108
    Freedman's Bureau, 99–101, 104
Reconstruction Acts, 95
redlining, 367
Red Record (Wells-Barnett), 129
Red Summer (1919), 124, 127, 180
Reginald F. Lewis Foundation, 264
Reid, Harry, 308
Republican Party, 81, 107–08, 169, 261, 263, 288, 304, 310, 324, 343, 349
Republic of New Africa (RNA), 211, 212
resettlement movements, 73, 140. *See also* separatist movements

Revels, Hiram, 107, 218
Revolutionary Action Movement (RAM), 211, 212
Revolutionary War, 43, 75, 76–78, 83, 88, 239
Reyes, Francisco, 117
Rice, Condoleezza, 228, 260–61
Rice, Susan, 267
Rice, Tamir, 308, 372
Richmond, David, 201
riots, 119, 126–27, 136, 154, 180, 212, 371, 372
Ritchie, Lionel, 302
Robeson, Paul, 161
Robinson, Jackie, 164, 165, 258
Robinson, Max, 268
Rockefeller, John D., 142
Roman Catholic Church, 18
Roman Empire, 17–18
Roosevelt, Eleanor, 171, 174, 177
Roosevelt, Franklin Delano, 124, 169–71, 173–74, 180, 303, 323
Roosevelt, Teddy, 87, 117
Rosenwald, Julius, 147
Rosewood, Florida, 124, 126, 129, 136
Ruiz, Hosea, 60
Russell, Bill, 258
Russwurm, John, 65, 345
Rust College, 129

S

Sacajawea, 113, 114
Salem, Peter, 76, 183
Sanchez, Sonia, 217
Sanders, Bernie, 321–323, 325, 327, 330, 339
Sanders, Deion, 258
Sante Dominique, 56
Savoy Ballroom, 159
"Say It Loud, I'm Black and I'm Proud," 217
scape-goating, 341

Schmeling, Max, 182
Schomburg, Arthur, 163
Schomburg Center for Research in Black Culture, 164
school choice, 278–79, 283, 288
school vouchers, 281–83, 288
Schwerner, Michael, 201
scientists and inventors, 162–63, 265–66. *See also specific people*
Scotia Seminary, 171
Scott, Dred, 81
Scott, Janny, 296
Scott, Tim, 267
Scot, Walter, 308
Sea Islands, 44
Seale, Bobby, 210
Second Reconstruction, 203, 206
Secret Service, 125
Selassie, Haile, 12
Seminole people, 66
Senegal, 40
separatist movements, 211. *See also resettlement movements*
September 11, 2001, 233, 329, 370
Seward, William H., 80
Shabaka, 5, 11
Shabaka, 5, 11
sharecropping, 101, 102, 130, 131, 155, 180
Sharpton, Al, 268
Shaw University, 163, 197, 200
Sheba, Queen of, 12
Shelby v. Holder, 342
Shujaa, Mwalimu, 103, 274
Shurney, Robert E., 266
Sierra Leone, 44, 60, 72, 77, 88, 96
Simmons, Ruth, 268
Simone, Nina, 175
Simpson, Carole, 268
Singleton, Benjamin "Pap," 102
Singleton, John, 258
sit-ins, 197, 200, 201–02, 205, 206
Sixteenth Street Baptist Church, 260

slave codes, 33, 42, 51
slavery 183, 251, 273
    abolition of, 78
    in ancient times, 18
    Atlantic slave trade, xxviii, 20, 28, 30, 36–37, 39–42
    Christianity and, 39, 67, 104–05
    constitutional amendments, 96–99
    and Declaration of Independence, 68, 78, 87
    emigration and, 72–73
    Emancipation Proclamation, 33, 85, 86, 96, 169, 174, 240, 241
    indentured servitude, 31–31, 34
    Juneteenth, 86
    justification of, 68–69
    legacy of, 368–369
    plantation system, 42–44
    resistance to, 44–50, 59–67, 69–70, 73, 80, 104
    sharecropping, 101–02
    targeting of Africans, 34–39
    tensions between North and South, 78–82
Smalls, Robert, 84, 87
Smalls Paradise, 160
Smith, Bessie, 159
Sniderman, Paul, 364-366
Social Security Administration, 170
social welfare programs, 311, 322, 327, 366
Soeharto, Lolo, 296
Sofala, 28
Solomon, 12, 71
Solon, 4
Songhay, medieval, 24, 26, 27, 29, 275
Soninke people, 24, 25
The Souls of Black Folk (Du Bois), 139, 144
South Africa, 71, 287
South Carolina colony, 44, 57, 81, 84, 87

Southern Christian Leadership Conference (SCLC), 196–97, 212, 213, 231
Spain, 18–20, 23, 28, 35–36, 86, 114, 275, 363
Spanish-American War, 75, 86, 117, 236
Spelman College, 106
spirituals, 105, 159
sports, 164, 165, 258–59. *See also* individual sports figures
Spingarn, Arthur, 147
Spingarn, Joel, 147
Stanford, Max, 211, 212
Stanford University, 260
Stanton, Elizabeth Cady, 64
states' rights, 79, 82, 197, 241, 243
Staupers, Mabel K., 179
stereotypes, 125, 136, 374
Stevens, Thaddeus, 101
Still, Charity, 68
Still, Levin, 68
Still, William, 68
Stirling, Matthew W., 21
Stokes, Carl, 218
Stoneking, Mark, 2
Strabo, 12
Student Non-Violent Coordinating Committee (SNCC), 200–201, 203, 205, 210, 213, 214, 231
Students for a Democratic Society, 212
Sunni Ali the Great, 26
supply and demand, 25
Supreme Court
    affirmative action, 251
    Bakke v. Regents of the University of California, 249–50
    Brown II, 246, 276
    Brown v. Board of Education, 193–94, 199, 244–46, 276
    citizenship and, 97, 243
    Cruikshank Decision, 242
    gerrymandering, 347
    Gratz v. Bollinger, 228, 250
    Grutter v. Bollinger, 250

Index

Muhammad Ali, 232
Murray v. Pearson, 243
Plessy v. Ferguson, 194, 241–42
school desegregation, 147, 197–99, 276
school vouchers, 281
Scottsboro case, 173
Shelby v. Holder, 342
slavery decisions, 61, 81
Trump appointments, 349
See also Marshall, Thurgood
Swahili states, 27
Sweatt v. Painter, 244, 285

T

Taharka, 5, 6, 11
Talbert, Mary Burnette, 123, 140, 141, 145
Talbert, William H., 141
Tanner, Henry Ossawa, 175
Tappan, Lewis, 60
tax credits, 288
Taylor, Breonna, 373
Taylor, Fannie, 129
Taylor, Moddie D., 266
Tell Me How Long the Train's Been Gone (Baldwin), 196
Temptations, 258
Tennessee Real Estate and Homestead Association, 102, 103
Tennessee Valley Authority (TVA), 170
Terrell, Mary Church, 175
Texas, 250, 342, 347
Thacher, John Boyd, 23
Their Eyes Were Watching God (Hurston), 158
"The Third Reconstruction," 377
13th Amendment (1865), 33, 96–97, 101, 106, 109, 242
Thomas, Franklin, 269
Thomas-Greenfield, Linda, 267
Thompson, Frank P., 164

Thothmes I, 8
Thothmes III, 8
Three-Fifths Compromise, 69, 239
Till, Emmett, 194
Timbuktu, 26, 27, 275
Tiye, 7, 8
trade
  medieval, 23, 25–26, 28, 29
  slave, 17, 27, 28, 29, 35–37, 39–42
  See also Atlantic slave trade
Trail of Tears, 118
Travis, Dempsey, 265
Travis Realty Company, 265
Treaty of Ghent, 77
Treaty of Paris, 77
Triangle Trade. *See* Atlantic slave trade
tribalism, 337
Trotter, Joe William, 148
Trotter, Monroe, 141, 146, 148
Troy, G., 330
Truman, Harry S., 168, 175, 180, 229, 236, 351
Trump, Donald, xxxii, 154, 213, 283–84, 288, 313, 320, 322–30, 343–44, 346–51, 366, 368–69, 373, 375
Trump, Fred, 324
Truth, Sojourner, 63, 65, 84
Tubman, Harriet, 66, 67, 80, 83
Tulsa. See Greenwood (Tulsa, Oklahoma)
Tulsa Race Riot Commission (2001), 128
Turner, Nat, 59, 60
Tuskegee Institute, 106, 110, 125, 142, 168, 176
Tuskegee Airmen, 176, 177
Tutankhamen, 6, 7
24th Amendment, 205

U

Underground Railroad, 66, 67
The Underground Railroad (Still), 68
United Nations, 232, 233, 267

Universal Negro Improvement
 Association (UNIA), 140
University of California, 211, 249
University of Chicago Law School, 298
University of Denver, 260
University of Mississippi, 205
University of Sankore, 25, 26, 275
University of Texas, 199, 244, 250
Urban League, 134, 147, 148, 221
U.S. Census, 325, 337–38, 349–50
U.S. Constitution
  checks and balances, 319
  15th Amendment, 33, 64, 97, 101, 106, 109, 242, 320
  1st Amendment, 342, 3445
  14th Amendment, 33, 64, 97–98, 194, 242–43, 245, 250, 252
  Great Compromise, 68, 69
  13th Amendment, 33, 96–97, 101, 106, 109, 242
  24th Amendment, 205
US Movement, 211, 213

V

Vaca, Cabeza de, 23
Valdez, Maria Rita, 117
Van Buren, Martin, 61
Vance, J. D., 339, 340
Van Dyke, Jason, 371
Van Sertima, Ivan, 19–23
Vermont, 44, 76, 321, 322
Vesey, Denmark, 33, 58–59
Vietnam War, 221, 227, 229–32, 236
Vikings, 20, 29
Villard, Oswald Garrison, 146
violence
  during the early 1900s, 125–30, 153
  during the 1940s, 180
  during the 1960s, 203, 212, 218
  during the 2000s, 307–09, 326, 370–72, 374

  as form of protest, 57–61, 73, 210, 370
  and guns, 305, 326, 328
  in Latin America and the Caribbean, 55–56
  opposition to, 146–48, 328–29
  protection against, 101
  white terror, 109, 199, 201, 244, 305, 386
Virginia colony, 34, 50, 57, 81
Virginia State University, 264
Virginia Union University, 106, 285
voter registration movement, 218
  freedom rides, 200, 201, 210
  Mississippi Freedom Summer project, 200
voting rights, 205–06, 209, 247, 251, 342–43, 349, 368, 376. *See also* Jim Crow laws
Voting Rights Act (1965), 205, 206, 209, 247, 251, 342
voter suppression, 343, 345–48, 368, 376, 377, 386

W

Wallace, George, 369
Walker, Alice, 258, 285
Walker, Herschel, 258
Walker, Madam C. J., 110, 265
Walling, William English, 146
Walters, R., 299
War of 1812, 77, 83
Warnock, Raphael, 267, 348
Washington, Booker T., xxx, 106, 125, 140–41, 145, 148, 175, 177
  and Great Debate, 104, 142–44
  Niagara Movement and, 145
  Urban League, 147
Washington, Denzel, 258
Washington, George, 44, 77, 110, 123, 262
Washington, Harold, 298

Wasow, O., 302
Waters, Maxine, 267
Waters, Muddy, 159
Watkins, Frances Ellen, 64
Watts civil unrest, 209
Wayne State University, 212
The Weary Blues (Hughes), 158
Weil, Danny, 278
Wells-Barnett, Ida B., 129, 146
Wesleyan Methodist Church, 80
West, Cornell, 313
West, Mae, 159
West Indies, 32, 41, 77
westward migration. *See* migration westward
Wharton, Clifford R., Jr., 324
Wheatley, Phillis, 44–46, 155
Whig Party, 80
White, Walter, 171
White Brotherhood, 109
White supremacy, 95, 96, 109, 213, 260
    legacy of, 368–70
    See also Ku Klux Klan
Wilder, Douglas, 268
Wilkins, Roy, 193
Williams, Robert, 212
Williams, Serena, 228, 259
Williams, Venus, 259
Wilson, Allan, 2
Wilson, August, 258
Wilson, Joe, 307
Wilson, William Julius, 341
Wilson, Woodrow, 126
Winfrey, Oprah, 258, 265, 286–87
Wolof people, 40
Women Accepted for Volunteer Emergency Service (WAVES), 179
Women's Army Corps (WACS), 179
women's rights movement, 63–64, 141, 345, 349
Wonder, Stevie, 258
Woods, Granville T., 110
Woods, Tiger, 228, 259

Woodson, Carter G., 140, 162–63, 165
Works Progress Administration (WPA), 170
World War I, 124, 131, 134–36, 140, 175, 227, 236
World War II, 174–78, 227, 236
Wortham, J., 372
Wright, Jeremiah, 300
Wright, Richard, 175, 196

Y

Yale University, 321
Yes, We Can: Voices of a Grassroots Movement, 302
Yoruba people, 27, 40
Young, Charles, 117

Z

Zoser, 5, 6
Zimmerman, George, 308
Z-Plus generation, 339
Zumbi, 56

www.ingramcontent.com/pod-product-compliance
Lightning Source LLC
Chambersburg PA
CBHW052053300426
44117CB00013B/2112